Terrorism and Militancy in South Asia

Terrorism and Militancy in South Asia

by :
Niranjan Dass

MD Publications Pvt Ltd
New Delhi

ISBN 81-7533-098-8

Published by
MD Publications Pvt Ltd
B/231-E, Greater Kailash - I
New Delhi-110048.

Showroom :
"MD House"
11, Darya Ganj
New Delhi-110002

Printed by :
PRINTEXT
D2/149A, Jeewan Park,
Uttam Nagar, New Delhi-110059

Contents

Preface

1. Global Terrorism 1
2. Terrorism and Deadly Conflict 11
3. Political Terrorism 31
4. A Terrorism: UN Perspective 59
5. Fundamentalism of Terrorism in South Asia 71
6. Terrorism in South Asia 105
7. Support of International Terrorism 121
8. Terrorism in India 133
9. Terrorist Violence in India 153
10. Kashmir Question: Need for a Visionary Approach 173
11. Caste Conflict: Its Causes and Resolution 177
12. Impact of Terrorism on Indian Politics 183
13. Role of Media in Terrorism 195
14. Terrorism in South Asia: Bangladesh 207
15. Terrorism and Democracy: Pakistan's Perspective 215
16. Terrorism in South Asia: Pakistan's Perspective 225
17. Terrorism in South Asia: Sri Lanka's Perspective 247
18. Terrorism in South Asia: Nepal's Perspective 317
19. Cooperative Environment for Dealing with Terrorism 343
20. Working on Terrorism 371
21. Fight Against Terrorism 381
22. Human Violence Search for Peace 397

Bibliography 403

Index 407

PREFACE

Terrorism refers to a strategy of using violence, social threats, or coordinated attacks, in order to generate fear, cause disruption, and ultimately, bring about compliance with specified political, religious, or ideological demands. The targets of terrorist attacks typically are not the individuals who are killed, injured, or taken hostage, but rather the societies to which these individuals belong. Terrorism is designed to subvert existing political atmospheres, often with the aid of the mass media's influence.

In South Asia, states have consciously and persistently used force as an instrument of strategic and foreign policies towards other states. In doing so, terror as a method and a consequence of the use of force has been sought to be justified. The meaning and application of the concept of terrorism, as it is being employed in the emerging cotemporary context, particularly after the "11 September events", tend to get things presented in a simplistic form. Terrorism and its political consequences have directly and visibly affected interstate relations in South Asia, particularly so when force has been made an instrument of conscious state policy and the resulting terrorist violence has been rationalized. Such terrorism has vitiated interstate relations and brought about a drift and acrimony in neighbourhood interactions. In situations where terrorism has affected states negatively, in a similar manner, it has also brought the neighbours together, to cooperate in common interest.

This book reviews the terrorist environment in South Asia, concentrating on Afghanistan, Pakistan, and India, but also including Bangladesh, Sri Lanka, and Nepal. With U.S.-led counter terrorism efforts focused especially on Southwest Asia, the existence of international terrorist groups and their supporters in South Asia is identified as a threat to both regional stability and to the attainment of central U.S. policy goals. Al Qaeda forces that fled from Afghanistan with their Taliban supporters remain active on Pakistani territory, and Al Qaeda is believed to have links with indigenous Pakistani terrorist groups that have conducted anti-Western attacks and that support separatist militancy in Indian Kashmir.This book is an systematic, comprehensive and straightforward for analyzing and comparing insurgencies and terrorist movements in south Asia. Insurgency and Terrorism was first published in 1990 to broad acclaim. Observers, scholars, students, military personnel, journalists, and government analysts worldwide found it worthy of study.

1

Global Terrorism

Introduction

More and more religiously motivated terrorism has superseded other forms–or rather metiations–of terrorism. Compared with the 1980s and even 1990s, the so-called ideological terrorism, which aimed at the revolutionary change of social structures as well as the so-called ethno-national terrorism, striving for the liberation of a certain territory, seem to have been relegated somewhat to the backstage. However 11 September and more recent events like the bombing attacks in Bali and Al Ghriba, Tunisia, should not obscure the fact that ideological and ethnonational terrorism still exists in various parts of the world–not just South Asia–and that there are a number of groups (like Hamas and Hezbollah in the Middle East), which might fall into two or more categories. Yet, we have to take into account that religion is the motivation for terrorist acts more often dun ill the last few decades.

Globalization of Terrorism

Increasingly, terrorism goes global. Al Qaeda, as the most striking example, is a global network, which cooperates more or less closely with national or regional groups like the GIA in Algeria or the Jemaah Islamiyah in Indonesia. Furthermore, we have reports on ad hoc cooperation in various parts of the world with so-called non-aligned mujahedin, individual persons or small groups, which are not part of the Al Qaeda network, and do not belong to any other larger and somewhere hierarchically structured groups. Moreover, some groups which limit their terrorist activities to a certain country or region have established extensive networks for financing their activities around the globe, The more traditional forms of terrorism, as, for example, Sendero Luminoso in Peru or the Brigate Rosse in Italy, had only very limited international rebtions, even if they advocated the international solidarity of workers or similar aims. Paradoxically, Al Qaeda, with its rather anti-modern ideas and its opposition to open society, went global, whilst communist groups in the 1970s preaching international revolution had a rather parochial range of action. The use of all the achievements of globalization, like international telecommunication, unimpeded, real time easily transfers, easily accessible night schools and so on by terrorists striving for a rather medieval world has probably further deepened the shock of 11 September.

Modern Business-Like Leadership Structures

A major characteristic of modern terrorist organizations is the lack of central authorities, of clear hierarchies. Especially Al Qaeda, but also a number of other groups, are only loosely connected, with very flat hierarchical structures and no "military-style" leadership structure. This lack of hierarchy is possible because–unlike in the more traditional forms of ideological and ethnonational terrorism–only a loose political, ideological, or dogmatic framework exists. There are only very few leading principles, as, for example, the hate against America, against Israel, or against countries and governments supporting them. Furthermore, some rather vague ideas of revitalizing basic religious values, and, in the case of Al Qaeda (but also Hamas and Hezbollah), the establishment of an "Islamist Empire", a Taliban-style Caliphate–State as a response to the perceived dominance of the "Western World". Since there is no need for a detailed ideological or dogmatic dogmatic framework, there is also no need to gain the support of parts of the population of a certain country, or at least part of the politically active layers of society.

Assymetric Warfare: The Victim Not as Target, but as Part of a Communication Strategy

Eleven September has been a perfect example for asymmetric warfare. Only 19 suicide attackers and a financial input of probably US$500,000 killed more than 3,000 civilians and caused material damage of at least US$40 billion. But that is not all: the repercussions of 11 September resulted in a decrease of world economic growth of about 1 per cent, summing up to hundreds of billions of US dollars. Whilst no data is available on economic damage for Indonesia resulting from the Bali bombing attack, Tunisia has witnessed a decrease of income from tourism of 50 per cent after the (much less devastating) bombing of the Al Ghriba synagogue.

Most recent events, as in Tunisia, Karachi, offshore Yemen, and Bali, secm to indicate a new tendency (if not strategy) of international terrorism. Probably due to the hardening of targets, especially in the United States, terrorist attacks on the so-called "soft targets" like tourist or international trade facilities have increased. Since there are so many targets all over the world, it is absolutely impossible to protect them sufficiently. Even with more sophisticated intelligence, it will hardly be possible to predict the exact venue and time of a terrorist attack on, for example, a discotheque, a container ship or an oil storage facility. Furthermore, a successful attack on a soft target might well entail the same overall results as an attack against a hard target. It sends a shock wave proliferated by the international media all over the world, intimidating not only the local population or those being geo-graphically close to the scene of a terrorist attack, but also to people thousands of miles away, deterring them from visiting or investing in the country where the actual attack took place. In fact the victims themselves have no particular importance for the terrorist, except as part of a communication strategy, as conveyors of a triple message:

1. That the government isn't capable of guaranteeing security in the country;
2. That tourists, foreign communities, investors, should avoid the country; and
3. That the war against terrorism hasn't been and will not be successful, because the terrorists can select from a huge number of possible targets, all of them with major importance on local

and regional economics, and because they have enough human and financial resources to attack those targets at almost any time.

That is why terrorist attacks against so-called "soft targets" are probably not less dangerous than those against hard targets. The impact on the local and regional economics is certainly considerable, and the potential for economic destabilization of targeted countries and governments as well. Here, we find ourselves in a dilemma, which has been reflected in the ASEAN leaders' declaration adopted in Pnom Penh on 3 November 2002: "We call on the international community to avoid indiscriminately advising their citizens to refrain from visiting or otherwise dealing with our countries, in the absence of established evidence of possible terrorist attacks, as such measures could help achieve the objective of the terrorists." And indeed, we are between a stone and a hard place: on one side, some countries have a legal obligation to advise their citizens properly on possible risks of traveling abroad; on the other side, an over-reaction in terms of unnecessary warnings might (involuntarily) promote the objectives of terrorists desiring to destabilize national economies.

The Inseparability of Internal and External Security

Eleven September has taught us another terrible lesson. No country on our globe is immune against the scourge of modern terrorism. Even a mighty army, good relations with neighbours or vast oceans cannot protect our cities and citizens from major terrorist attacks. The security of our country isn't any more almost exclusively in the hands of our own and other government, in the hands of politicians, diplomats, generals, but increasingly of private actors. Terrorists, but also warlords and international organized crime, pose more and more a direct risk to the life, health and wealth of average citizens on our globe. Whilst state-sponsored terrorism still exists, albeit at a much lower level than in the 1960s and the 1970s, it is more and more the threat by non-state actors which characterizes modern terrorism. This double chellenge, the inseparability of internal and external security and non-state actors as a major threat for national and international security, has still not been tackled in a sufficient manner.

Preventing and Countering Terrorism

The International Coalition

Terrorism is an international, global challenge. Therefore, in most cases, a merely national or even regional counter-strategy will not suffice. With regard to Al Qaeda and the Taliban regime, the creation of a coalition against terrorism, including all five permanent members of the Security Council, the whole Western world, many states of the Arab world and of the G- 77, including India and Pakistan, is of tremendous importance for combating international terrorism. However, it is not an alliance based on common values, rather a coalition based on a limited convergence of interest for a given time. Therefore, the fact should not be overlooked the fact that the coalition is fragile, and that, for example, unresolved regional conflicts, the question of how to deal with the so-called states of concern or other political factors might overburden and thus imperil the coalition.

Looking to Asia, attention should be drawn to the recent declarations and action plans adopted by the second ministerial conference of the community of democracies in Seoul on 12 November 2002, the APEC leaders statement on fighting terrorism and promoting growth agreed in Los Cabos, Mexico, on 26 October 2002, and the chairman's statement made at the fourth Asia-Europe meeting in Copenhagen, Denmark, on 24 September 2002. These documents prove the increasing willingness of states and international organizations to cooperate globally in the struggle against international terrorism. It is also very encouraging that these declarations and action plans take into account economic factors. And underline the importance of respect for international law, including human rights.

Afghanistan

The success of "Enduring Freedom" and the destruction of the territorial basis of Al Qaeda has been an important success in the war against terrorism. Afghanistan is not any more the training ground and meeting point for poterntial terrorists. It is not any more a potential laboratory for the development of weapons of mass destruction. But it is still a country with very fragile structures, and far from being able to guarantee the safety of its won citizens. Much more needs to be done to build democratic structures, to firmly establish the protection of human rights and the rule of law, to extend the reach of the interim administration to all parts of the country, to have a functioning army and police force, to successfully combat drug cultivation and trafficking, etc. Recently, at a meeting of the Royal Institute for International Affairs, a high-ranking diplomat of a major power made a very pointed remark. He said: "...if we don't win the battle for rehabilitating Afghanistan we might lose the war against terrorism." I will not comment on this remark. But I do certainly agree that Afghanistan is an unfinished business, with tremendous repercussions on the war against terrorism.

Furthermore, the success of Enduring Freedom has not led to a complete destruction of Al Qaeda. To the contrary, and here a UN document, the so-called "Chandler Report" may be quoted: "Al Qaeda is fit and well and poised to strike again at its leisure." That is why we have to look beyond Enduring Freedom, beyond Afghanistan in our fight against Al Qaeda as probably the most angerours international terrorist organization of the early twenty-first century.

Important Counter-measures of the International Community

(a) United Nations (UN)

The shock of 11 September has sparked or sped up a numbers of countermeasures adopted by the international Community. The Security Council of the United Nations has unanimously and unequivocally condemned the terrorist attacks of 11 September and has qualified in its resolution 1386 of 12 September 200 1 any "act of international terrorism as a threat to international peace and security". The Security Council has, consequently, recognized the inherent right of individual or collective self-defence in accordance with the charter, if a state is the victim of a terrorist attack. The Security Council stressed also that those responsible for aiding, supporting or harboring the perpetrators, organizers and sponsors of terrorist acts will be held responsible. With resolution 1373 of 2R September 2001, a number of mandatory decisions were taken on terrorist financing, obliging states to refrain from providing support to terrorists and to take the necessary steps to prevent the commission of terrorist acts, including by early warning, denying safe haven, and by suppressing the financing of terrorist acts. With the same resolution, the so-called Counter Terrorism Committee has been established, to which all member states report on the steps they have taken to implement this resolution, The committee has, meanwhile, received more than 170 reports and has set up not only a directory of available help, but also identifies the need for assistance, mostly in developing countries. Ideally, it will match requests and otters fix assistance. Kofi Annan has qualified "the work of the counter-terrorism committee, and the cooperation it has received from member states,... as unprecedented and exemplary". Furthermore, the Security Council has reshaped the sanctions regime directed originally against Afghanistan, the Taliban regime, and Al Qaeda. Whilst Afghanistan an as a state has been removed from the target list, the sanctions regime under Security Council Resolution (SC-Res) 1267/1390 now focuses entirely on the Taliban and Al Qaeda, and particularly on the financing of those organizations. The sanctions committee established under Resolution 1267 has identified a considerable number of persons and organizations. Whose bank accounts are frozen, and who are prevented from entering or transiting the territory of UN member states.

Less encouraging is the situation in the UN General Assembly. Whilst the GA has been able to unite in the condemnation of the 11 September attacks and of terrorism in general, its legal committee has so far been unable to agree on the so-called draft comprehensive convention against terrorism. The reason for that is less a legal than a political one. A number of states represented by the Organisation of the Islamic Countries wish to add an exemption clause to the definition of a terrorist act, which would exclude "people's struggle including armed struggle against foreign occupation, aggression, colonialism and hegemony" from the scope of a terrorist crime. This far-reaching exemption is not only unacceptable to the Western world, but also to many G-77 members, who believe that liberation wars fall under international humanitarian law, and that an exemption clause in the terrorism convention would, at best, be superfluous; at worst, extremely dangerous. Unfortunately, it was not possible for the OIC to agree on a more flexible approach at the summit meeting in Kuala Lumpur last February despite the efforts of PM Mahathir. Let us hope that time will help to find a suitable compromise.

(b) European Union (EU)

The European Union has decided at the Sevilla summit last June that combating terrorism is a political priority which has to be mainstreamed in all EU policies. The EU action plan of September

2001, a living permanently-updated document, consists of up to 70 measures in the areas of justice and interior, foreign, traffic and financial policies. The most important achievements are an agreement on an EU-wide definition of a terrorist act, the harmonization of national penal codes in the area of international terrorism, the European arrest warrant which ensures automatic arrest in each EU member if one of the EU members has made an arrest warrant, increased exchange of information, and a number of measures with regard to freezing economic assets. In that contest, the EU member states created the so-called clearing house, which recommends to the EU ministers council the listing of certain persons or institutions involved in non-Al Qaeda related terrorist activities. The clearing house has been established in implementation of SC–Res 1373, and deals both with proposals by the EU member states, and with proposals made by third states.

(c) Asia

Some important political signals, but also more concrete steps, came from Asian organizations and forums, It may be highlighted here the declaration made by the ASEAN summit in November 2001, which condemned terrorism and underlined the multicultural and multi-religious character of ASEAN. In May 2002, Malaysia, the Philippines and Indonesia signed a framework agreement on combating terrorism. In September, the 4th Asia Europe Meeting (ASEM) took place in Copenhagen, attended by heads of governments of 10 Asian and 15 European states. They underlined their resolve to fight international terrorism, and adopted the Copenhagen Declaration on Cooperation against International Terrorism and the ASEM Copenhagen Cooperation Programme on Fighting International terrorism. Combating terrorism will be placed high on the agenda of an ASEM foreign ministers meeting inspiring 2003. Mention has been made already of the ASEAN declaration adopted in Pnom Penh on 3 November, which refers to a number of future activities, like a regional conference on combating money laundering and terrorist financing in Bali in December, an intercessional meeting on terrorism of the ASEAN Regional Forum in Malaysia in March 2003, and a number of other events. Also attention may be drawn to the activities of the Shanghai Cooperation Organisation which includes, besides China, countries like Russia, Kazakhstan, Kyrgyzstan, Uzbekistan, and Tajikistan. This is mentioned not only in order to commend these regional activities. But also because regional activities seem to be far more limited in western and southern Asia. Unfortunately SAARC has so far not been able to deal with issues like combating terrorism in a satisfactory manner.

The Legacy of 11 September

The legacy of 11 September is not simple. It is a multiple challenge. It is one about keeping the international coalition against terrorism alive, about rehabilitating Afghanistan, about taking all possible measures to counter terrorism, but even more it is the challenge to prevent terrorism. Obviously, it is much more efficient to prevent people from becoming terrorists than preventing terrorist acts from occurring. However, referring to a remark made by the UN Secretary General in autumn 2001, there will always be people who hate and kill, even if all injustice has been removed. So let us be clear that prevention of terrorism cannot simply replace combating terrorism cannot be successful if there is no meaningful of terrorism. And here, it is necessary to refer again to Kofi Annan, who said: "But if the world can prove, that she can continue, that she sustainably works to create a stronger, more just, more mereiful and more international community across all orders of religion and race, then terrorism, will fail to reach its targets." Prevention of terrorism and combating terrorism have to work hand in hand. Prevention of conflicts is always also prevention of terrorism. Even if the equation of poverty and injustice on the one and terrorism on the other side is far-fetched, even incorrect, it must be realized that prevention of goes well beyond police and judicial measures. Whilst 11 September has changed the world, it should be remembered, and here again Kofi Annan may to quoted, "that none of the issues that faced us on September 11 has become less urgent". In order to dry out breeding grounds for terrorism, and to lead potential followers on a path to peaceful solution of conflicts, a number of major political steps have to be taken.

1. Solution of the political and social conflicts, quite rightly emphasized in the Millennium declaration, as these form the breeding ground for the emergence of terrorism. A fair and peaceful solution for regional conflicts (and not only in the Middle East) is of utmost importance. It is a best of history that the best guarantee for successfully lighting terrorism is a viable strategy to deal with underlying root causes.

2. The people in all countries should be able to live in safety, freedom and without want. To achieve this, a system of global cooperative security is needed, which includes all levels of global policy relevant to security; the relations betweens great powers and their alliances, as well as the potential danger of regional crises, and the threat posed by asymmetreic conflicts. Since terrorism threatens world peace just as much as civil war and regional conflicts, such a system must not be toothless, but must function in all three fields through reliable verification systems and enforceable sanctions mechanisms.
3. A comprehensive global policy is needed which includes not only classic foreign and security policy, but also development and structural issues. International trade, financial systems, global environment, migration and debt management have to be seen in a cohesive manner, as part of an enlarged concept of human security.
4. A meaningful dialogue has to be strengthened between civilizations, among at peaceful solution of conflicts, and replacing prejudice by confidence.
5. Global security cannot work without respect for human rights. All efforts to secure peace will fail if human rights are not protected and duly implemented. A binding global set of values is needed to prevent and overcome conflicts that emerge due to inequality, injustice, and deprivation of freedom. Combating terrorism must not be a pretext to violate human rights. It is rather the other way around: only through respect of human rights, through good governance can the breeding grounds for potential terrorists be dried out.

2

Terrorism and Deadly Conflict

The US war on terrorism spills over on the foreign and domestic policies of many nations. Spillover effects from a pre-emptive war against Iraq, should it occur, will be even greater. But for residents of India, Pakistan, Rwanda, Colombia, Sudan, Bosnia, Sudan, Egypt, Palestine, Israel, and many other countries, deadly conflict has been a fact of life for years, or even decaues. "Terrorism" is only one manifestation of a deadly conflict syndrome that has been pervasive, protracted, and costly. Terrorist incidents cannot be understood, and will not be prevented, if they are viewed in isolation.

How can measuring the economic costs of deadly conflict and terrorism playa role in preventive strategies? Reading Kenneth Boulding's short volume, *A Primer on Social Dynamics: History as Dialectic and Development* 1970, first sensitized to the issues of the political and economic costs of deadly conflict's Boulding, a pacifist, argued that from the vantage point of a long-time horizon, use of violence as social change strategy could rarely, if ever, be justified, either politically or economically. Boulding argued that development tajectories in which the French Revolution, the Russian Revolution, and even the American Revolution, had not occurred might, over the long, term have produced more beneficial outcomes for almost all concerned, than the post-revolutionary trajectories that did, in fact, unfold. A touchstone of his argument explored only speculatively to be sure–was the devastating economic as well as political and social costs of these landmark events.

This facet of Boulding's work seems to have sparked little interest in either international relations or political science. Until recently measuring economic costs of deadly conflict and terrorism fell well below the radar screens of most scholars who were concerned with these subjects. Sri Lankan economist S. W. R. D. Samarasinghe discovered this in 1988, as we collaborated on an article that sought to measure the economic costs of Sri Lanka's two civil wars precisely (1991). An extensive search (this was before the days of the Internet, of course) turned up only a few general sources, and no readily adaptable frameworks that would serve our needs. Using a scheme that differentiated between the primary secondary and tertiary costs of violent conflict, we estimated the total costs of Sri Lanka's civil wars between 1983 and 1988 to be about 4.3 billion US dollars. This approximated the country's total capital expenditure during the period between 1986 and 1988. We noted that this massive expenditure had produced few if any beneficial results. Both civil wars were still going on at the time. The conflict between Sri Lanka's government and the Liberation Tigers of Tamil Eelam (LTTE) remains unresolved to this day, though a present round of peace negotiations–the fourth since 1987–seems to show some promise.

Interest in measuring economic costs of deadly conflict has grown in the ensuing years, and a broad-brush Internet scan, using the popular google search engine yielded a cornucopia of information. Review of a leading US Department of Delense Publication on "Principal Wars in Which the US Participated" (2002) reveals that the Revolutionary War had a "financial cost" of $1.2 billion (in 1990 US$), World War II cost $2,091 billion, the Korean war cost $264 billion, and the Viet Nam war $347 billion.

Mike Blakely's 1999 publication *The Cost of Conflict* provided information on recent insurgencies in which the US was involved, including El Salvador ($8.2 billion), Somalia ($7.3 billion), and Bosnia (a cost to "outside powers" of $53.7 billion). Blakely's estimate of Gulf war costs ($114 billion) more than doubled the DOD estimate, possibly because he included "direct economic losses" as well as "military costs".

Explicit costs-of-terrorism estimates are less common, but, not surprisingly, the World Trade Center and Pentagon bombings evoked such estimates. Two of the most authoritative are those provided by the International Monetary Fund's 2001 *World Economic Outlook* (2001), and a study conducted by tl1e University of Colorado's Natural Hazards Research and Applications Information Center, supported by the US National Science Foundation (2001). These two cost estimates diner so widely that a comparison of their principal tabulations is illustrative. The fund aggregated losses attributable to destruction of "structures, equipment and software" ($16.2 billion) plus "other insurance losses" ($5.2 billion), for a total of $21.4 billion. It also identified other possible categories of costs, including a number of possible "transaction costs", but did nor include dollar estimates. Overall, IMF analysts appeared to support "the most commonly held view.. .that there will be few consequences for the long-term outlook for the United States and elsewhere". By contrast, the NSF-supported study, completed roughly within the same time frame, reported a cost estimate of $111 billion, differing from the IMF estimate by more than *five orders of magnitude*. Components of this estimate included property losses ($34 billion), business interruption costs ($21 billion), "lost human productive value" ($11 billion), and airline bailout costs ($15 billion).

I could devote many additional paragraphs to compiling, tabulating, contrasting and evaluating deadly conflict cost estimates. But it is not clear that this exercise, which I will forego, would do more then reinforce two fairly obvious conclusions to which the analyses already cited point, so far. (1) Conflict and terrorism are economically costly, in addition to being politically and socially costly. (My own view, incidentally is that most published estimates are conservative. (2) Consensually accepted cost estimates do not presently exist, will be difficult to come by, and may be unattainable. Before proceeding down byways of academic research that might lead to more widely accepted cost estimates, we need to pose the question that comprises the second half of this paper's title.

Who Should Care and Why Should They Care?

The remainder of this paper provides lengthy answers to these two questions, supported by a fairly complex rationale. However, brief answers can easily be given.

Who Should Care?

Those who should care are politicians, business leaders, civilian and uniformed security force leaders (military and police) and development practitioners who exercise discretionary control over financial and human resources. These men are in the best position to initiate high-leverage actions that can prevent conflict and terrorism.

Why Should They Care?

Self-interest is the simplest and most persuasive reason. Often, leaders act as if their positions, power, and financial resources are invulnerable, but this is not the case. Political leaders arc driven from office, banished into exile, paraded before firing squads, or felled by assassin's bullets because of deadly conflict and terrorism. Businessmen see their assets, accumulated through years of effort, eroded in a matter of weeks or months. Development practitioners find themselves witnessing scenarios that are mirror images of those they planned and envisioned. "We had no choice", these once powerful actors often lament, but they did have choices. Deadly conflict and terrorism are predictable and preventable.

A third question follows logically: How can powerful men and women, whose concern about preventing deadly conflict and terrorism has been heightened, express that concern most effectively? The answer to this question cannot be given so easily, but will be provided in the remainder of this paper. It requires both a rigorous analytical foundation, and the recounting of a 30-year personal odyssey. The story begins in Iran.

"We Know Our People"?

My concern with preventing deadly conflict and terrorism linkages harks back to a memorable luncheon in the executive dining room of Iran's Plan and Budget organization, held in 1975. The late Prime Minister Amir' Abbas Hoveda presided. We were commemorating the completion of a long-term development planning model for the Shah's Government. In a quiet moment after the event, I asked the prime minister, privately, if he was not concerned with the potentially destabilizing social unrest that might be an unintended side effect of his government's aggressive development programmes. I could see the potential for this as I walked about Tehran in occasional free moments. "We know our people", was Dr Hoveda's confident reply. Four years later, a revolutionary tribunal sentenced Hoveda to be executed after several months of imprisonment and a brief hearing. He was immediately taken from the hearing room to a prison yard and shot to death, execution style.

The problem seemed to be this. "Development" was a goal that was mostly pursued by idealistic, good-hearted individuals like myself and colleagues who were typically members of the Society for International Development and like-minded organizations. We believed our work contributed to human well-being, specially to the well-being of individuals who seemed powerless to help themselves. But we were reluctant to ask explicitly whether some elements of international development practice were more likely to produce deadly conflict than enhanced well-being. We were reluctant to venture into a realm inhabited mostly by politicians, police, and military professionals. Nor were we, by and large, welcomed there, partly because we failed to make a convincing case that we had anything to offer these men and women (mostly men).

Political leaders and national security professionals faced a different set of problems. By the time terrorist incidents began to multiply or a full-blown insurgency broke out-often these were sustained by one or more well-organized, well-funded, resilient militant groups–they found their options severely limited. Often, they seemed to "have no choice", other than to implement draconian repressive measures, often with security forces that seemed unequal to the task. As US leaders discovered in Vietnam and Somalia, Russian leaders discovered in Afghanistan and Chechnya, Indian leaders discovered in Sri Lanka's northern province and in Kashmir, and leaders are discovering in the occupied territories of Palestine, even an overwhelming military force could be insufficient to defeat an adversary that skillfully used terrorism, guerrilla warfare and other militant tactics.

These experiences and many others motivated a search for early warning systems. The internationally riveting Rwandan genocide spurred creation of the Carnegie Commission on Preventing Deadly Conflict, charged with answering the question: "What might have been done at an early stage [of potential deadly conflicts] to avert mass violence and achieve a just outcome?"

The Commission's landmark report, "Preventing Deadly Conflict" (1997), was consistent with my own emerging ideas about the importance of development↔deadly-conflict linkages. It identified "structural prevention–or peace building" as a cost effective conflict prevention strategy. Important elements of structural prevention were the development, by individual states, of "mechanisms to ensure bedrock security, well being and justice for their citizens...[and] meeting people's basic economic, social, cultural and humanitarian needs... "The costs of prevention are miniscule," "Preventing Deadly Conflict" concluded, "when compared with the costs of deadly conflict and the rebuilding and psychological healing in its aftermath".

However, my own work, which by then had been going on for more than a decade, suggested that the early warnings envisioned by the Carnegie Commission would not come early enough. High-level leverage, cost-effective interventions needed, whenever possible, to come before what the report called "indicators of states and risk" became visible. My work on this problem continued for an additional five years, culminating in a book manuscript entitled "Development and Deadly Conflict: Lessons for Politicians and Practitioners from Sri Lanka's Civil Wars". The remainder of this paper responds to the questions posed earlier by summarizing some of the book's high points and recommendations.

System Dynamics Methodology, "Reference Modes", and the Questions They Raise

My approach has been strongly influenced by the computer simulation methodology I have used most in my professional practice as a systems analyst and modeler, called System dynamics. It was created by MIT computer engineer Jay W. Forrester. His work brought together ideas from three fields that were then relatively new: control engineering (the concepts of feedback and system self-regulation), cybernetics (the nature of information and its role in control systems), and organizational theory (the structure of human organizations and mechanisms of decision making). He supported software development, built path-breaking models, articulated guiding principles, and trained students. Flight simulators (another technology in which he pioncered) provided a metaphor for the project. Models, Forrester argued, could be used for experiments in the same way simulators are used to train pilots. Mistakes made on the model would not result in severe social costs or less of life.

Repeated experimentation would be helpful in solving difficult, complex problems.

System dynamic practitioners like to begin looking at a system by defining a reference mode, a graph of "problematic behaviour" over time. Many developing countries exhibit similar patterns. Monthly conflict intensities are based on a compilation of conflict incidents, politically significant occurrences that go beyond a country's norms and legalities, and often involve violence. For Sri Lanka, the duration, destructiveness, size and proximity to power-centres of more than six thousand incidents have been described and coded.

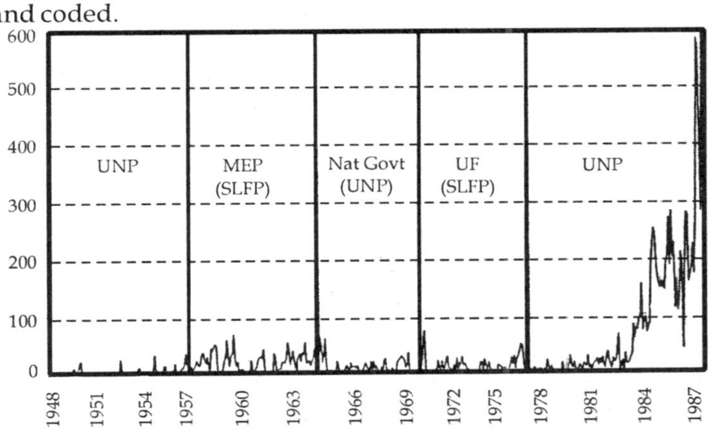

Fig. 2.1: Violent Conflict Intensity Reference Mode

For a system dynamics practitioner, this reference mode graph immediately highlights two questions. The first is the more obvious: What explains the patterns of escalation to protracted deadly conflict, beginning in about 1983? Answering a second question is equally important to understanding the system: What explains the period of relative equilibrium, during which deadly conflict did not escalate and become protracted, prior to 1983?

Viewing a second reference mode variable, which I call state-sanctioned violence, is also useful. Fig. 2.2 graphs both violent conflict intensity and state-sanctioned violence intensity in Sri Lanka's northern and eastern provinces during the period 1977 through 1988. This was the region of the country where fighting between government forces and militant Tamil Tiger guerrillas was most intense. State-sanctioned violence intensity is an index that takes press censorship, suspension of constitutional guarantees, arrests, exiles and executions, restrictions on political parties, and press censorship into account.

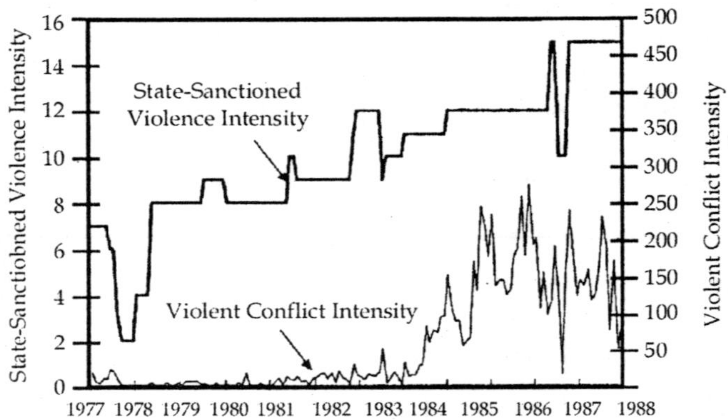

Fig. 2.2: State-Sanctioned Violence and Violent-conflict Intensity in Sri Lanka's North and East

Again, the pattern shown is a common one. Both deadly conflict and state-sanctioned violence escalate during the period examined. By the end, both are at very high levels. Since state-sanctioned violence is the principal remedy governments use to suppress deadly conflict, the question the graph raises is obvious. Why is state-sanctioned violence ineffective in attaining its goal? Two most recent examples of this ineffectiveness are, as noted above, Russia's attempts to suppress the insurrection in Chechnya, and Israel's attempts to suppress the insurrection in the occupied territories of Palestine.

System Dynamics Modelling

The next phase of project was to build a generic system dynamics model of development↔deadly conflict linkages. I mean by "generic", something analogous, though far less elegant than Jay Forrester's generic city model, described in *Urban Dynamics* (1969). The model was then applied to two countries with very different reference mode behaviours, Argentina and Mexico, over the period from 1900 to 1980. These results were summarized in a paper entitled "Violence and Repression: Unexamined Factors n Development Planning" that appeared in the journal *Futures* in 1987.

My intention was to continue the project by building a series of eight additional country-specific models focusing on different regions of the world. An important system dynamics principle, however is to "immerse yourself in the system", to become deeply familiar with your problem's context before or coincident with beginning model development. Thus, when an opportunity came to teach international relations in Sri Lanka, a country that was long touted as a development success story, but then over taken by not one, but two insurgencies, I volunteered. My wife and I lived in Sri Lanka for nearly a month in 1987, and then the entire year of 1988. These trips were the first of those that have become nearly annual visits ofto what was once known as the Isle of Serendip. I became so immersed in Sri Lanka that I have not yet built any of the eight models I contemplated. My long study of Sri Lanka's civil wars does draw heavily on my previous modeling work, however.

My goal has been to answer two fundamental questions that inhabitants of countries wracked by deadly conflict pose: First, "How could we have come to this, to our present state of physical destruction and social disintegration?" Second, "What can others learn from our experiences to avoid repeating them?"

In systems thinking terms, Sri Lankans' "experience" was represented by the exponential growth in conflict intensity (and state-sanctioned violence) pictured in the reference mode diagrams already described. More concretely; Sri Lanka was a country with one of the world's highest death rates from violent conflict, with bombings occurring in the capital city; with several top leaders assassinated, and with many civil liberties curtailed or suspended, specially in contested areas. For more than three years, the north eastern portion of the island was occupied by more than 50,000 Indian soldiers who, like Sri Lanka's military forces, were engaged in an unsuccessful attempt to defeat the militant LTTE".

"Bottom Line" Conclusions

First, most theories purporting to explain conflict escalation and protracted violent conflict do address linkages between conflict and development. These theories can be roughly grouped into seven contending schools of thought, to which I have given the following labels:

1. Primordial or Socially Constructed Ethnic Differences.
2. Unremedied Structural Weaknesses in Post-Colonial Economics.
3. Ruling-Class Exploitation.
4. Social Disruption Caused by Privatization, Deregulation, and Structural Adjustment.
5. Too Much Democracy, or Democratic-Governance Failures.
6. No Democracy, or Too Little Democracy (Repression).
7. Leadership Failures.

As with most academic debates, debates among proponents of these theories resemble the parable of the six blind men of whom each felt part of an elephant, and then disputed with his companions about the whole.

Second, while there are fundamental disagreements about root causes of conflict escalation, there is greater consensus about proximate causes. Disparate theories almost invariably point to widespread disillusionment with the established order of things, among major segments of a country's residents. This creates a climate of hopelessness that attracts youth to militant movements committed to violent means as the only way to remedy perceived injustices and effect radical change.

The Development↔Deadly-Conflict System Model

Third, contending theories can usefully he combined into a representation that I call the Development↔Deadly-Conflict System Model. This "model" is really just a diagram that is loosely based on my generic and two country-level simulation models. I use the term "model" as a convenient shorthand for non-technical readers. The model comprises sewn interlinked sectors, shown in Fig. 2.3. While a detailed description would exceed the length of this article, it is important fix readers to get a general idea of major sectors and linkages. Development↔deadly-conflict linkages are complex and do not lend themselves to simplistic representations.

This way of viewing social systems is powerful, system dynamics practitioners believe, because the way a system's variables are linked together in feedback loops determines the behaviour patterns that reference mode graphs exhibit. There are two basic types of feedback loops. *Reinforcing loops* produce exponential growth and collapse patterns that economists sometimes call virtuous or vicious cycles. *Balancing loops* produce equilibrating and goal-seeing patterns. The balancing of supply and demand, via prices (in an economist's "perfect market"), and the way the human body maintains its temperature at 98.6 degrees Fahrenheit in both cold and hot climates are two examples of behaviour produced by balancing loops.

The emphasis on how feedback loops generate reference mode behaviour patterns can be applied to the development↔deadly-conflict system model. Viewing the reference mode graphs and the model, the system dynamics practitioner will pose three questions. (1) When conflict intensity levels remain low in a nation for a period of time, what balancing feedback loops are dominating the system to produce that behaviour? (2) When conflict intensity levels escalate in a nation, what reinforcing loops are dominating the system to produce that behaviour? (3) What explains the transition from balancing to reinforcing loop dominance of the system's behaviour?

The answer to these questions is somewhat complex, but can be summarized briefly. Contemporary political systems that political scientists and philosophers describe are often grouped into three broad categories: democracies, one-party states, and dictatorships. All of these categories can be encompassed within the development deadly-conflict system. Fig. 2.4, "Stable Democracy and its Discontents", illustrates how this is done for one category.

A stable democracy manages conflict effectively by being open to political feedback about what is not working in the country and responding with remedial measures. It is a trial and error system. Possible remedial measures include changes in policies, or, if those are not sufficient, changes in leadership, or if those are not sufficient, even changes in constitutional "rules of the game".

Three linkages can destabilize democracies. First, political leaders may repress political feedback that is communicating dissent or "bad news", manipulate elections to remain in power even though they have lost support, or rewrite the constitution to perpetuate an unpopular regime. In each case, the fidelity of self-correcting mechanisms is distorted, making it more probable that overlong perpetuation of bad policies will perpetuate a crisis. Second, populist

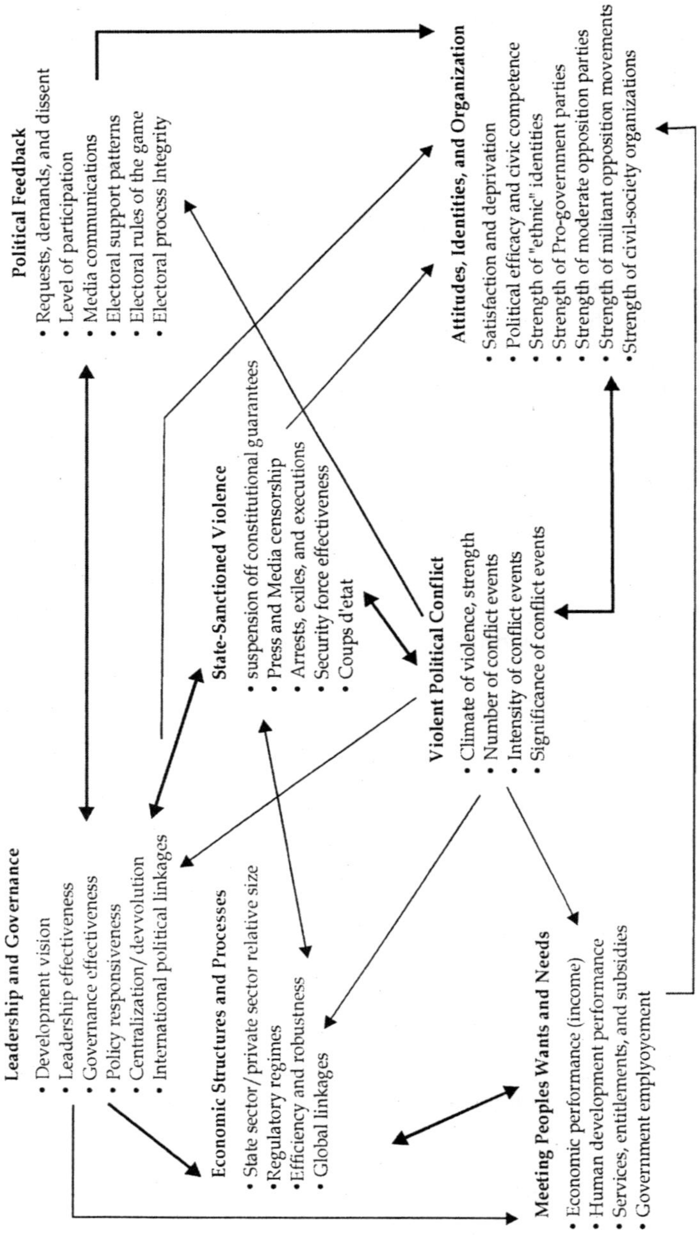

Fig. 2.3: The Development ↔Deadly-Conflict System Model

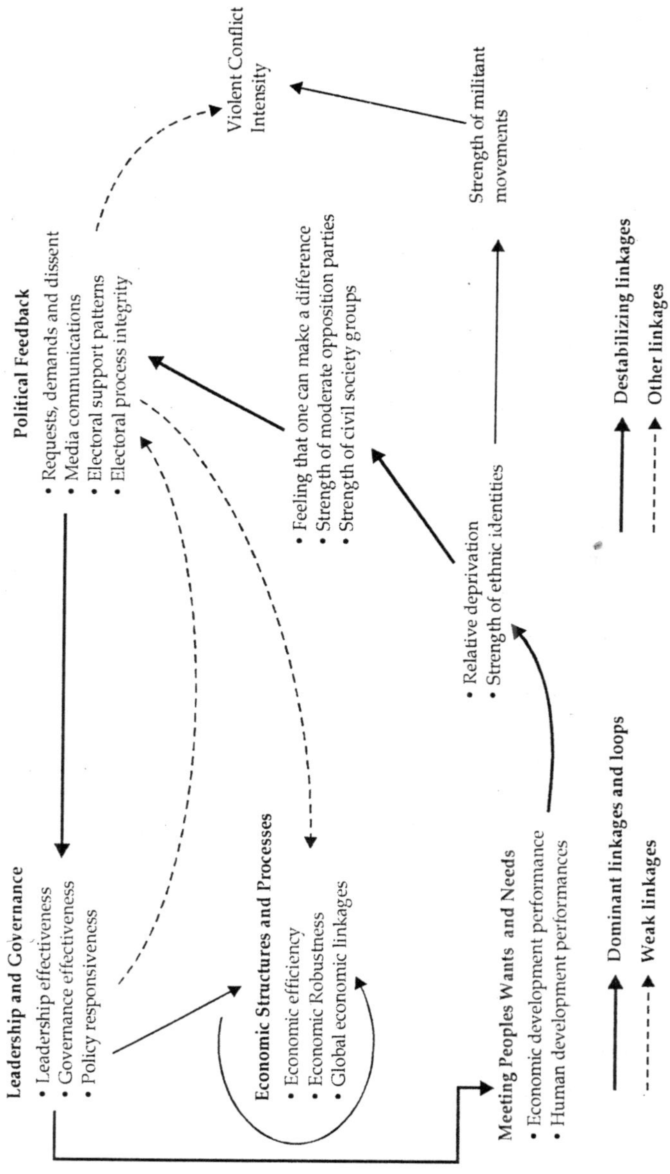

Fig. 2.4: Stable Democracy and its Discontents

or elitist movements may motivate leaders to pursue unsustainable economic policies. Most common arc ideologically driven dirigiste economic management schemes that are unresponsive to market forces, entitlement programmes that exceed a nation's resources, and autarchic regulatory policies that ignore both domestic and global economic realities.

One-party states (like China and Singapore, but also many failed regimes) and dictatorships (like North Korea, Burma, and Iraq) also exhibit stable and unstable states that can be represented within the context of the deadly-conflict system model. Space does not permit the exploration of each.

The Syndrome of Escalating Deadly-Conflict

A syndrome is defined as the "concurrence of several symptoms in a disease". Examination of instability dynamics in democracies, one-party states and dictatorships, as well as the contending theories of deadly-conflict escalation mentioned above, all point to common symptoms. There are five of these:

1. deteriorating economic performance;
2. an increasing number of development failures;
3. rising levels of relative deprivation, in ethnically diverse societies manifested as strengthened ethnic identities and groups mobilized around these identities;
4. declining effectiveness of state-sanctioned violence; and
5. growing strength of militant movements.

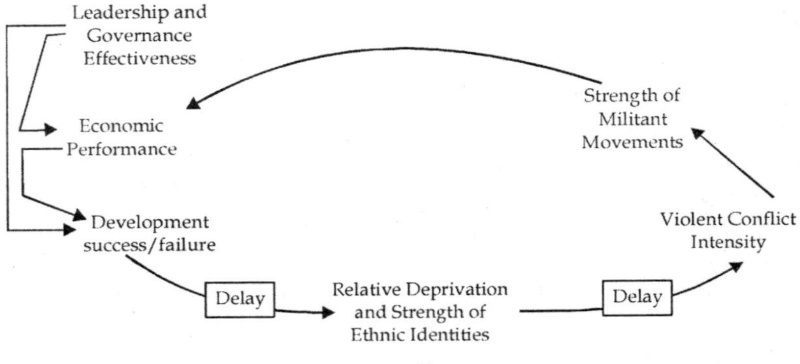

Fig. 2.5: Conflict Escalation from Development Failure

Returning to the development↔deadly-conflict system model, we find these symptoms are linked ill two reinforcing feedback loops, both characterized by significant delays between causes and effects.

I label the first, pictured in Fig. 2.5, "Conflict Escalation from Development Failure".

To fully understand the argument being elaborated here, definitions of "successful development" and "development failure" are needed. A country's development trajectory is defined as "successful" when it is widely perceived by a country's residents as constructively responding to their needs and aspirations. Thus, "successful development" is defined to be taking place in a country when most of its citizens generally feel good about their lives, the circumstances in which they live, and future prospects for themselves and their children. When a country's development trajectory is widely seen to be adversely affecting residents' needs and aspirations, this is defined as development failure.

A cycle of deadly conflict is likely to be eatalysed first by development failures, typically caused by some mix of bad policies, ineffective governance, and deteriorating economic circumstances. Development failures evoke heightened feelings of relative deprivation which, in ethnically diverse countries, are typically accompanied by heightened levels of ethnic consciousness.

Policies that reduce development failures are the high-leverage interventions that can reverse trends produced by this loop, but implementing such policies becomes increasingly difficult because of the adverse economic impacts that violent conflict produces.

The second reinforcing feedback loop is called "Conflict Escalation from State-Sanctioned Violence Ineffectiveness" (Fig. 2.6).

The agents of state-sanctioned violence–principally police forces and the army-win be ineffective to the degree that they are under-resourced, corrupt, undermanned, poorly trained, poorly led, and politicized. Bad policies and adverse economic conditions contribute to ineffectiveness. Corrupt and repressive security forces can provoke insurgency even in peaceful times. But violent conflict escalation due to development failures, evoking state-sanctioned violence that makes things even worse, is the more common scenario.

Policies that increase security force effectiveness, while maintaining high levels of state-sanctioned violence until violent conflict subsides, are the high-leverage interventions in this loop. Implementing these policies while a conflict is ongoing is difficult, however. Deteriorating economic performance complicates matters still further, specially since security force and development budget priorities win be competing.

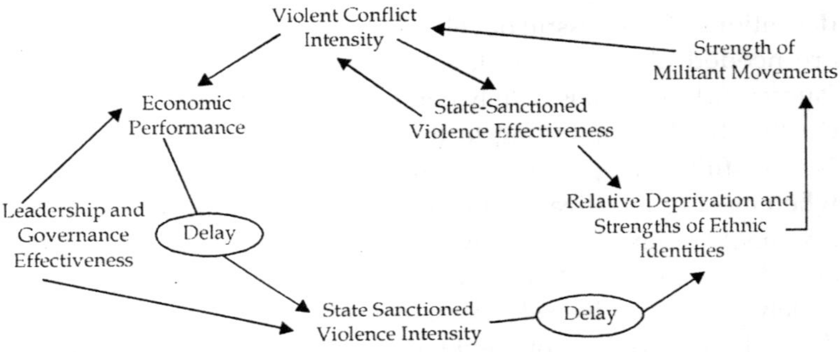

Fig. 2.6: Conflict Escalation from State-Sanctioned Violence Ineffectiveness

Politicians and Practitioners

Explanations of conflict escalation emerging from the Development↔Deadly-Conflict System Model point to my fourth "bottom line" conclusion: We know more than enough to choose policies that will help prevent protracted deadly conflict, and to not choose policies that win cause protracted deadly conflict. The situation is quite similar to our knowledge about the relationship between cigarette smoking and lung cancer. We know that smoking is the principal cause of lung cancer, though there are other causes. We know that refraining from smoking is the best way of avoiding lung cancer, though some non-smokers may still contract the disease.

My study of Sri Lanka's civil wars identified 10 development failures which, if avoided or corrected, could have prevented or mitigated protracted deadly-conflict. Among the most generally relevant are these seven: (1) unsustainable entitlement programmes; (2) polarizing political rhetoric and tactics that capitalized on ethnic differences; (3) failure to devolve power to local authorities (an "outstation" mentality in implementing development programmes); (4) perpetuation of statist economic management schemes long after their economic inefficacy had been demonstrated; (5) structural adjustment reform policies that were overambitious and over politicized; (6) politicization and ethnic homogenization of the police and military forces; and (7) attempting to subdue an ethnically motivated insurrection with police and military forces that were clearly incapable of attaining that goal.

These development failures correspond to "smoking" in my metaphor. The smoker's body corresponds to a country that the development↔deadly-conflict system model represents. Protracted deadly conflict is the cancer that consumes and may destroy it. But what is equivalent to the cancer avoidance strategy, "refrain from smoking"? A medical practitioner would not simply advocate abstinence. He or she might recommend regular exercise, a healthy diet, and a regimen of antioxidants. The prescriptions of an ayurvedic physician, taking the body as a whole system into account, would include much more. "Avoid development failures" is an insufficient prophylactic for protracted deadly conflict. Politicians, practitioners, and "the people" upon whose support they ultimately depend need more proactive remedies. The 10 "lessons from Sri Lanka's civil wars" that follow provide such remedies. They are more fully elaborated in my book. Many are little more than common sense, but that does not make them less useful:

1. Maintaining public order and preventing social turbulence from escalating into protracted deadly conflict are prerequisites to the success of all other development policies.
2. Polarizing political rhetoric and tactics should be foregone, however tempting their short-term benefits may seem. Like mustard gas, which had to be abandoned as a weapon in World War I, this strategy "has an erratic tendency to blow back upon the user".
3. Meeting the needs and aspirations of fighting-age young men should be the first priority of national development polices and of programmes funded by international donors.
4. Developing countries should have internal security forces (police and paramilitary) that are generously funded, professional, apolitical, and trained to meet the complex challenges of maintaining public order in a changing society.
5. Development policies that meet human beings' common aspirations-to feel good about their lives, the circumstances in which they live, and future prospects for themselves and

their children-will contribute most effectively to keeping violent conflict within acceptable bounds.

6. Those who frame development policies should seek a middle path between capitalism's efficient but Darwinian, precepts and socialism's egalitarian but stultifying precepts.
7. Good governance and democratization should be part of the "successful development" mix. Most important are governance institutions that are open to "bad news" and self-correcting.
8. Multinational corporations, businesses and businessmen's organizations should play a more active role in supporting successful development policies, good government, and democratization.
9. Successful development requires a long-term view. Giving sufficient weight to the long term requires institutional mechanisms and discourses that extend beyond the next election and term in office of political leaders presently in power.
10. If policy makers are realistic about opportunity costs (the "what might have been") , then there are few circumstances where they (have no choice", other than precipitating or escalating deadly conflict.

A Development Vision that would Facilitate More Proactive Collaboration

Their respective goals of political stability, economic prosperity, people-centred development, and security need not change, but must be situated in a broader context so that the dynamics of development deadly conflict linkages are more fully taken into account. Years of leading workshops with diverse audiences and educating international development practitioners has convinced me that there is a more common vision of what this mean than we may think. A powerful statement is found in the following imperatives, quoted in *Beyond the Limits; Confronting Global Collapse–Envisioning a Sustainable Future.*

1. Sustainability, efficiency, sufficiency, justice, equity, and community as high social values.
2. Leaders who are honest, respectful, and more interested in doing their jobs rather than in keeping their jobs.

3. Material sufficiency and security for all. Therefore, by spontancous choice as well as by communal norms, low death rates, and stable populations.
4. Work that dignifies people instead of demeaning them. Some way of providing incentives for people to give of their best to society and be rewarded for doing so, while still ensuring that all people will be provided for sufficiently under any circumstances.
5. An economy that is a means, not an end, one that serves the welfare of the human community and the environment, rather than demanding that the community and the environment serve it.
6. Political structure that permit a balance between short-term and long-term considerations; some way of exerting political pressure on behalf of the grand–children.

Protracted deadly conflict is predictable and preventable. Political leaders, business leaders, development practitioners and security professionals should be functioning as colleagues, not inhabitants of distinct cultures that rarely communicate with one another. They share a common goal, to shape more politically stable, economically productive, humane and peaceable development scenarios. Such scenarios could make it unnecessary for future generations to contemplate protracted deadly conflict's legacies. Devastation, suffering and hopelssness.

3

Political Terrorism

First, the present complex technological society is highly vulnerable to unsuspected, ruthless, random acts of small groups of dedicated and determined terrorists, because transportation centres, communication facilities, oil fields and factories cannot be always protected against terroristic acts. Second, highly sophisticated weapons which can be fired from light shoulder launches are easy to obtain, And in future, terrorists are likely to have access to biological, chemical and nuclear instruments of death and destruction. Third, the availability of modern warfare capabilities to terrorist groups challenges the very stability of society. The newly found power by sub national groups does not let them remain "powerless" but gives them formidable strength. Fourth, the advances in science and technology are slowly turning modern society into a potential victim of terrorism with no immunity for the noncombatant segment of the population or of nations and peoples with no direct connection to grievances motivating terroristic acts. Fifth, communication and transportation networks have enabled an international network of terrorism to develop with a certain degree of centralised organizational structure, comparable to that of a multinational business organisation. Sixth, as the world is shrinking through the growth of communication technology, terrorists are assured of wide publicity for their wanton acts and enunciated causes. Terrorism is a low-tech, logy-cost, high-result route to a world-wide audience.

In addition to the factors inherent in modern civilization, several other circumstances contribute to terrorism: e.g. confrontation from East and West, ideologies of Right and Left, rise in ethnic, linguistic, racial and religious and national consciousness of groups throughout the World. Moreover some state systems actually support political and ideological violence; Iraq, Libya, Somalia, Uganda and South Yemen supply weapons to terrorists. Further, liberal democracies are prevented from taking effective action against terrorism because of their concern for civil liberties or state policy.

Concept of Terrorism

Even though we seem to have entered the "age of terrorism" there is no precise or widely accepted definition of `terrorism'. For like many other political terms, it is pejorative. One man's 'terrorist' is another man's 'freedom-fighter' or patriot. In fact it is contended by some political sociologists that no definition of 'terrorism' is in principle possible, for the very process of definition is a part of the wider contestation of ideologies or political objectives.

The "Encyclopedia of Terrorism and Political Violence" by John Richard Thackra (London, Routledge, Kegan Paul, 1987) lists 67 definitions of terrorism, beginning from 1936 and ending upto 1982, with only 9 definitions upto 1968 and the rest between 1970 to 1982. The selection is limited to definitions of terrorism in terms of its ultimate objectives, rather than in terms of ideology or manner of action. It is concluded that it is easier to identify that which is not terror than label exactly what that which is terror.

Stephen Segaller in his "Invisible Armies: Terrorism into the 1990s" (London. Michael Joseph 1986) however argues that by enumerating the features and consequences of a terrorist act, it is possible to give an objective definition of terrorism and lists these as follows:

- Terrorist acts on campaigns have two objectives: the tactical goal of publicity and recognition of a claim: and the strategic goal of absolute change, freedom, independence or revolution.
- Terrorism always involves a criminal act: the use or thrust of use of violence against persons in the form of murder, kidnapping or hostage taking; the use of violence against

property and assets in the fore of vandalism, arson and bombings.

- Terrorism displays a readiness to kill at random, not in anger or hatred, but in cold blood to produce a political shockwave with the intent of bringing about change.
- Terrorism is not war in which by convention (Napoleon code) many classes of persons are given immunity. Terrorists ignore the conventions defining neutral territory, noncombatants, and forbidding the taking of hostages and ill-treatment of prisoners. In fact, terrorists attack "soft" targets for reasons of convenience.
- Terrorism involves surprise and therefore needs to be planned in advance, though specific targets may be selected for reasons of opportunity.
- Terrorism plays no part in riots, for riots lack any calculating element of blackmail.
- Terrorism presents demands for immediate action and guarantees escalation if demands are not met.
- Terrorist is almost never a lone individual.
- The Left has no monopoly over terrorism; there is Right terrorism as well. But, Left terrorism has more incidents, damage and victims than Right terrorism. Right terrorism acts less systematically but in a more shocking way.
- Terrorists will never fail to claim responsibility for their violence, for without that the act is pointless. Without political motivation, mere criminal violence would have no impact or repercussion.
- Terrorism is the antithesis of assassination, for assassination involves selective killing in the hope that the victim's policies will die with him.
- The physical target of a terrorist act, the individual victim, may be unimportant, even random or indiscriminate. The most important target is the larger audience.

Political Terrorism

If a terrorist act or campaign has a political objective, the terrorism is "political". Segaller (*op.cit.*) in giving his objective definition of terrorism has equated it with "political terrorism". But terrorism can also be "religious". The Assassins of Arbia,900 years ago, committed assassination at the command of their leader in the belief that killing the unrighteous guaranteed their salvation and assisted in overthrowing a corrupt ruler. Their terrorism was both religious and political.

The strategies and tactics of political terrorism are directed at three groups generally: the populace, the regime and the terrorist organization itself The over-all objectives of these are to gain popular support, to destroy and disrupt military and psychological strength of the regime, and to achieve internal stability and growth. If it is conceded that political terrorism is primarily aimed at the psyche rather than "military hardware" per se, the killing of a carefully selected important and unpopular public official may boost the terrorists' morale, create sympathy among the populace, and provoke the regime to adopt repressive measures that further alienate the populace.

There are five short-term basic objectives of political terrorism: morale building within the ranks; advertising the movement; disorientation and psychological isolation of the populace; elimination of opposing forces; and provocation of Government. These objectives are inter-related and mutually reinforcing. Political terrorism is essentially "propaganda by deed"; hence advertising is basic to its purposes. The most important objective is to provoke the Government to adopt repressive measures. These measures induce a breakdown in social norms and help create conditions for public dissatisfaction and alienation. If such an atmosphere can be-sustained over time ,it can be exploited to terrorists advantage.

State Terrorism

Terrorism and state terrorism are often looked upon as two sides of the same coin, but the latter is a separate subject. Its characteristics are (Segaller *op. cit.*):

- State terrorism is the abuse of legitimate power for the legitimate purpose of national defense. domestic order and state security.
- The methods and apparatus of state terrorism - false imprisonment. torture, disappearance, death squads - are different from those of terrorism. The state acts against known opponents; the immediate targets are the problem;

not the wider audience. But terrorism is fought by an invisible army.

- State terrorism is the breeding group for terrorism or its military cousin - guerrilla warfare. The equivalent of guerrilla warfare is not terrorism but insurgency. Insurgency is recognised by military men, but not by domestic police and security forces. Guerrilla warfare is a prelude to civil war.
- Guerrilla groups usually operate in semi-developed states or in the less urban areas; terrorism almost always has an urban setting.
- Guerrillas almost always hold territory within the state which they plan to overthrow, or have secure cross-border base; they usually have the direct support of a state hostile and probably adjacent to the one they are opposing.
- Guerrillas generally attack the state's infrastructure; terrorists attack the political figureheads and symbols.
- Guerrillas often abduct or coerce civilians to join them and to fight against the government; terrorists are extremely careful to screen their recruits.
- Guerrillas operate relatively openly and have a form of military common structure, as they are engaged in semi-conventional warfare; while governments often respond to terrorist compaigns with enhanced police activity and legislation, guerrilla warfare brings in a military response.

International Terrorism

State or domestic terrorism is also distinguished from international terrorism. The Foreign Intelligence Surveillance Act of USA defines international terrorism as that which occurs totally outside the United State or transcends national boundaries in terms of means by which terrorist activities are accomplished, the person the activities are intended to coerce or intimidate or the location which the perpetrators operate or seek asylum. The Central Intelligence Agency of USA makes a distinction between international and trans national terrorism. The latter is carried out basically by autonomous, non-state actors - with or without support from sympathetic states; the former is carried out by individuals or groups controlled by a sovereign state. International terrorism can be distinguished from domestic terrorism by the presence of an international jurisdictional element.

Approaches to Terrorism

There is no rigorous theory of political terrorism. But there are three main approaches toward such theory. First is the political approach. It concentrates on the political pre-conditions, on structures of power and mobilization processes, and their inter-relationships. The key premise of this approach is that revolutionary violence stems from conflicts within and between a country's political institutions. Revolutionary violence is the result of conflict about legitimacy, political rights and access to power. It often is a product of the incapacity or refusal of a government to meet certain demands upon it by a powerful group or a Boalition of groups. Feliks Gross (1957, 1969) has advanced two models of terrorism: one for the causation of tactical terror against domestic autocracy or against foreign rule, and the other for the causation of individual violence as a tactic against democratic institutions. He defines three seminal elements for the first model : (a) a widely perceived condition of oppressive rule. This element is sociological because it arises out of ethnic or class subordination or stratification as well as foreign rule. It does not constitute a sufficient condition of terrorism. (b) The sociological element must co-exist with an organized group with terroristic tactics; and (c) with activist individuals willing to make political choice and to respond with direct action and violence to conditions of oppression. He defines the antecedent conditions for the second model as follows: (a) an erosion of democratic values, a state of anomie or a crisis of democratic institutions; (b) a terroristic organisation: (c) and a pre-assassination phase directed at subverting and defaming democratic leaders and institutions', (d) activistic individuals prepared to initiate terror.

A variation of the political approach is provided by Hannab Arendt (1973). Arendt suggests that acts of extreme revolutionary violence may be a form of revolt against "rule by nobody" i.e. of the anonymous bureaucratic state. Simone Well (1958) has castigated the bureaucratic machine in Communist Russia for excluding all judgement and all genius; and for concentrating all power in itself. The alienating and atomising effect of the modern bureaucratic social system cannot be denied. Orvick suggests that the all-pervasive nature of government in post-industrial society has rendered the insurrection and coup d'etat obsolete, tempting small extremist groups to try assassination as an alternative weapon of social change. He observes that in an age of bureaucratic, tyrannicide is plainly less useful than terror.

The second approach is psychological. It is concerned with the study of terrorists themselves, their recruitment and induction into terrorism, their personalities, beliefs, attitudes and careers (= their new profession of terrorism). A most thorough going exploration of the terrorist in modern literature is provided by Malraux in his novel, "La Condition Humaine" in which the professional terrorist is shown to try to escape from his private anguish, his extreme loneliness, and his need to serve a cause while lacking faith in everything except his own power to destroy, making terrorism an end in itself. Camus in his "Les Justes" however distinguishes the opportunist terrorist from the idealist revolutionary, suggesting that terroristic acts of the latter alone are justifiable.

The third approach is military. This approach has been Puite influential, although it is fruitless. The French have notably contributed to this approach, which has also been cultivated to some extent in USA. The most notable exponent of this approach is Thornton. His model of insurgency is presented below:

Phase	Insurgents		Incumbents		
	Agitational	Enforcement	Enforcement	Agitational	Totals
Preparatory	0	0	Low	0	Low
Initial violence	High	Low	High	0	High
Expansion	Medium	Medium	Low	Low	High
Victorious	Low	High	0	Low	Medium
Consolidation	0	0	0	0	0

The deficiencies of the model are obvious. It is clearly applicable to only certain archetypal internal war situtaions, and does not fit cases of struggles waged almost entirely by means of terrorsim. Many of these cases do not conform to the phasing of the model. Thornton does not offer any account of terrorist motivations or of conditions conducive to the adoption of revolutionary behaviour. Another lacuna in the approach is the role of weapon availability and supply, and of development of new weaponry in terrorism. One of the significant development is the ability of the terrorist to kill at greater distance than in the past. This makes for the prevention of aggressive acts from the constraints of face-to-face fighting, and also enables a person to kill a large number of individuals single handedly. Assassins sometimes fail in their first attempt because of the look of goodness and serenity they see in the victim's eyes.

The Terrorist: Demographic Profile

Charles A. Russell and Bowman H. Miller (Profile of terrorist, in Freedman, L.Z. & Alexander, Y. "Perspectives on Terrorism" Delhi. Hindustan Pub. Crop. 1985, pp. 45-60) have presented a demographic profile of the terrorist based on published data related to 350 individual terrorist caders and leaders belonging to 18 terrorist groups in Palestine, Japan, Germany, Italy, Ireland, Turkey, Spain, Iran, Argentina, Brazil and Uruguay, and active during 1966-76. Even though the data are out dated. they are being presented here for want of better information. It is a pity that parallel data about terrorist in Punjab are not available (at least to the author).

Age: Within the 18 groups studied, the age of the active terrorist cader members was between 22 and 25 except for members affiliated with German. Palestinian and Japanese organisations. In Japan, the average age was 28, in Palestine the terrorists were in the late twenties, and in Germany the average age was 31.3 years. One possible reason for the higher age in German and Palestine is that members there are university graduates engaged as junior doctors, lawyers, and so forth. While age trends have been stable over the last decade, them are indications that the 22-25 age level may be dropping in Spanish, Latin American, Irish, Iranian, and Turkish groups. The anarchist-revolutionary philosophy seems to have permeated into the secondary level, i.e. cadre members are in their teens. Leaders of terrorist groups belong to a higher age level. In Brazil the top leaders were in their late 40s or early 50s.

Sex: Despite minor variations, urban terrorism is predominantly a male phenomenon. Well over 80% of all significant terrorist operations in the period under review were directed, led and executed by males. Within Latin American terrorist groups, female membership was less than 16 percent. Among these groups, the Tupamaros made maximum use of females, but in supportive roles (intelligence collection, couriers, nurses, maintenance of safe houses, storage of weapons, propaganda, false documentation, funds, and other supplies). There are notable exceptions to the supportive role of female terrorists. Laila Khalid and Fusako Shingrobu were highly active leaders in Palestine and Japan respectively. The supportive role of females is not due to male chauvinism, but pragmatism. Women are simply more effective in these roles than men. Women by virtue to their sex arouse less suspicion and thereby succeed in operations where males are a risk. Women however occupy a very important position in Germany, where they are one-third operational, and where there appears. to be no real division of labour based on sex.

Marital Status: Unmarried terrorist is the rule. The requirements of mobility, flexibility, security and dedication preclude family responsibility for all operational caders. Over 75-80 percent of arrested terrorists are single. Some of the married terrorists in Germany severed connection with the family and children in order to pursue terrorism. Only in the case of the Tupamaros, who make the greatest use of women, less than 30 percent of terrorists are married. The problem with married terrorist is that when the wives are arrested and subjected to interrogation, morale considerations almost compel the group to seek their release and operations have to be launched for that purpose. Therefore, the decision to utilise unmarried personnel seems to be sound from an operational point of view.

Rural urban origin: Since the terrorist must be intimately familiar with the territory in which he operates, it is not surprising that most urban terrorists are natives or long-time residents of metropolitan areas, especially cities in w hick they operate. In Spain, while members of Communist FRAP are from large cities, members of ETA-V are from smaller centers. In addition to urban background, several European terrorist groups have tended to operate in a specific region or city of origin.

Social and Economic background: In conjunction with their urban origin and longtime residence in metropolitan areas, many terrorist cadres and leaders possess a predominantly middle class or even upper class background. In the sample studied, over two-thirds came from middle or upper class in their respective nations or areas. III most instances, the parents were professional people, government employees, diplomats, clergymen, military officers, even police officials. The parents were generally liberal in outlook and advocates of significant social and political change. These parental views, reinforced by radical socio-economic thought prevalent in the universities, added to the general distrust of democratic institutions as effective agents of implementing social change and induced young men to use terrorism or guerrilla warfare for achieving the desired change, or for obtaining power to implement such change. Members of IRA Provisional Wing are an exception. This may be due to what has been pointed out in several studies, that Catholic families in Northern Ireland have been relegated by political means, to the lower economic and social levels. It is not surprising therefore to find that many members including leaders of IRA-P are not drawn from the middle or upper classes.

Education Occupation: The vast majority of those involved in terrorism as cadre members or leaders are quite well educated. About two-thirds of those identified as terrorists possess university training (graduate and postgraduate). In Latin American countries, the figure goes upto 75 percent. In Germany the percentage goes upto 80 to 100. Geor9c Habbash, Chief of PFLP is medical doctor; Yasser Arafaat is graduate engineer. The formal training of both cadre members and leaders in most terrorist groups studied tended to be in the humanities, especially law, history. economics, education. sociology, philosophy. and Iranian and Turkish terrorists (encrusts (glided to be educated in the enact sciences, particularly iii technical fields like engineering. An exception to this is the IRA-P and even in its leadership has practically no intellectuals. The reasons has been mentioned earlier in connection with remarks about their social background.

Method and place of recruitment: In view of the fact terrorists are largely students and university graduates (or dropouts), it is natural that the universities should be the primary recruiting ground for operational terrorist cadres. The Universities are hospitable to Anarchist-Marxist doctrines that appeal to young men. For those few terrorist groups that include both intellectual and criminal elements, the place of initial recruitment is the prison; such is the case Italian Armed Proletarian Nuclei.

Political philosophy: Political philosophy are hard to classify. However three basic ideologies arc at play in most terrorist organisations. viz. Anarchism, Marxism-Leninism, and Nationalism. Nationalism is significant in ETA-V, IRA and PFLP (Popular Front for Liberation of Palestine); even in these it is blended with Marxism.

Structure of Terrorist Organisation

It is claimed by J.K. Zawodny that the infrastructure of a terrorist organization affects the behaviour and activities of its members. By "infrastructure" he means the internal organisation structure including formal and informal networks within that structure. The data for the claim from unclassified, open sources in five languages dealing with active terrorist movements in USA during and as of 1980.

The relatively small size of terrorist groups is the primary characteristic that affects their infrastructure. By contrast, the European underground movements during World War II were huge organisations, patterned on military models. The 16 groups in USA noted by the author did not have a membership each of more than 40 to 50. The Red Bridge in Italy is estimated to have 400-1000 members. The Baader-Meinhof Gang in Germany was composed of 100 members. The Japanese Red Army fluctuates in membership between 30-40. El Ansar in Palestine has less than 200 and Action Organization for Liberation less than 300 members. In view of the small size of the terrorist group, its infrastructure is centri-fugal. The structure resembles the solar system. The leader is the Sun, and the members the surrounding planets, usually within the range of direct contact. While in the hierarchical system, the leader is at the top, in the centrifugal system he is at the centre. The terrorist group's centrifugal infra-structure spells important consequences for the behaviour of members.

There are eleven ways in which the infrastructure affects the behaviour of members.

1. The leader not only acts as a direct catalyst of operations by planning and giving orders, but also by participating in the operations. The leader has a high degree of visibility. He suffers equally with the members. He shares psychological stress before action, and decompression after action. The sharedness builds more personalised loyalties than those characteristic in hierarchical organisations.
2. The centrifugal system secures more direct and rapid communication that increase flexibility of action and success in combat operations, by allowing the leader to personally assess the feasibility of new action. Moreover, it saves the low-ranking leaders from the dilemma of deciding whether to

execute an action that has been rendered unfeasible, due to changed circumstances, or to disobey orders and face ostracism by peers.

3. Direct responsibility to leader enables him to tap and react immediately to schemes conceived and the location of targets reported by rank and file. This further enhances tactical flexibility and permits operations against targets of opportunity.
4. A hierarchical system cannot exist without extensive social support. And it takes one to two years to build it up. A centrifugal system can exist independently and can be re-located quickly. An organisation independent of social support suffers from no constraints. This is a dangerous situation. In a hierarchical organisation, public opinion can obstruct recruitment eventuating in its collapse. In a centrifugal system, a gradual elimination of the immediate environment does not affect the physical integrity of the unit - it moves to another area.
5. Direct access to the leader by rank and file allows the latter to vest the leader with charismic qualities and to participate in his charisma. Moreover leaders have the opportunity to give direct moral dispensation for deeds which might otherwise be repudiated by certain standards of society or early upbringing of the members. All these factors are helpful in freeing the members of internal dilemmas and in giving them self-confidence as heroes with a unity of purpose.
6. The leader in a centrifugal system is directly involved in the selection and recruitment of new members. This involvement is so gratifying to the incoming members that they do not bother about the success of the organisation.
7. Centrifugal groups tend to seek cooperation not with groups stronger to them but those whom they can easily manipulate. Hence, they coalesce on peer level and avoid groups that may impose demands on them and curtail their freedom because of their superior strength. The major world powers have seized upon this tendency and have assisted terrorists through the smaller states indirectly. The tendency to coalesce on peer groups has led to the development of informal networks and has influenced both the training and operations of terrorists.

8. The less anonymity a member has in a terrorist group, the less he feels personally responsible for actions of the group to outsiders. In view of the fact that in a centrifugal system, members have direct access to the leader, it is difficult to say whether there is less identity in such a group as against a hierarchical group.
9. In all types of human organisations, there is a tendency for a working group (bureaucracy) to emerge. A comparative study of clandestine hierarchical organisations in France, Italy, Poland, USSR and Vietnam has shown that overtime, the presence in their structures of two bureaucratic phenomena: an increase in the number of bureaucrats in excess of actual need, and the Peter Principle or movement upward on the administrative ladder to the point where one reaches one's maximum level of incompetence. But there is no bloating of bureaucrats in a centrifugal organisation for two reasons: such bloating would hamper the leader's direct exercise of power and the small size of the group militates against it. The combined effect is enhanced efficiency.
10. The leader's direct control over membership is tremendously enhanced in a centrifugal organisation. Members are within the direct range of the leader's vision. Control is exercised speedily and mercilessly. The consequence is that it is much easier to join a terrorist organisation than to withdraw from it.
11. Despite the differences between hierarchical and centrifugal organisations, their is one point of similarity between them. When either type is threatened from within the leaders of both the types use external violence to keep members together. Internal problems of the organisation often serve as catalysts of external violence. Many operations ordered by leaders are not dictated by tactical, strategic or political reasons, but to fulfil the need of the internal problem to restore cohesion or for reasons known to him alone. These operations are always carried in the name of Great Cause.

Beliefs and Attitudes

A "belief system" is composed of dominant images, symbols and myths, and contributes to perceptions (or misperceptions) that determine actions and expectations. The perceptions of terrorists are at variance with those of Government and society. One of the aims of terrorists is to convince their audiences to see the world as they see it. An important aspect of this discrepancy in perception is the definition of the conflict between them and the adversaries. The content and origin of belief systems of terrorists affect the why and how of their strategies, their reactions to government policies and the outcome of terrorist challenges.

A significant element in the belief system is the image of oneself, (or self-perception), of another actor and of the world. Images are frequently stereotypical and simplify reality. Dehumanisation and deification of the enemy dominate thinking. The enemy is perceived in impersonal and abstract terms like `bourgeoisie capitalism' communism or capitalism. He is seen as monolithic. Right-wing terrorists are less likely to see the Government as enemy, but are prone to ethnic or class attributions. Most leftist terrorists do not see themselves as aggressors but as victims. Their self-perception is that they are representatives of workers or peasants. The latter are helpless and ignorant. The terrorists being enlightened in relation to the masses; see themselves obliged to come to the rescue of the helpless masses. They often think of themselves as morally superior, more sensitive, and more noble. The term `terrorist' is in their mind given by the enemy; actually they are freedom fighters' or national liberators. Many terrorists look upon themselves as 'sacrificial victims', because the Government is much more powerful than them, with many alternatives at its disposal, while they have only one alternative against Government - terrorism.

There are two intriguing aspects of the terrorist's belief about the nature of conflict. First is the tendency to define conflict in legalistic terms. Terrorists do not see themselves as murdering or killing victims but as executing victims after due trial. Victims are called traitors and they are executed for their treachery. Kidnapped persons are kept in 'people's prisons'. Second, is their military image and symbolism of struggle. Though terrorists appeal for popular support; the role of popular support is not clearly defined. Rather the availability of support is assumed.

These tendencies reflect fantasies of omnipotence corresponding to the individual's own violence may also be an outcome of identification with the violent acts of father-figures (a violence that several terrorists had actually experienced); that is, an identification with the aggressor. Jager (1981) however found no common pattern in attitudes of West German toward violence; rather some individuals reported a strange prior aversion to violence. He concludes that these attitudes depend on individual socialisation and are not particularly significant.

It is rather possible that instead of being attracted to the inherent, violence of terrorism, some individuals are seduced to terrorism by the lures of omnipotence and grandeur to compensate for feelings of inferiority and impotence. Kaplan (1981) maintains that the self-righteousness of terrorism conceals the terrorist's insecurities and that terrorism is a response to a lack of self-esteem. . Sullwold (1981) suggests that West German terrorists are persons who have high levels of aspiration but are internally conflicted and prone to failure because of unrealistic demands on themselves. Instead of adopting a level suited to their capability, they raise the level in the face of failure. Such neurotic response involves clinging to irrational goals regardless of outcomes and refusing to engage in activities that might test one's abilities.

Motives and Traits

Stress-seeking: Terrorism differs from other counter culture activity not only in its violence, but in its stress-producing nature. The glamour and excitement Of terrorism lie partly in the physical danger that it comports. Terrorists may be "stress-seekers" attracted to behaviour designed to increase the intensity_ of emotion or level of activation of the organism. Stress seekers carefully plan their behaviour; they respond more to internal than to external imperatives and they return repeatedly to stressful situations. Repetition of stressful activity becomes not only obsessive but also escalatory (as is the case with drug addicts). Stress-seeking in itself does not lead to antisocial behaviour; in fact adventurism in Western society is admired. It is in conjunction with other predispositions that stress-seekers turn to violent defiance of government and society.

Stress-seekers seem to be of two types: individual stress-seeker and group stress-seeker. The former is being narcissistic. He seeks self-affirmation in the face of danger. The latter, on the other hand, seeks to abandon the self in the group. He identifies himself with the group and merges himself completely in the collective personality. The distinction has implications for terrorist ròles between leaders and followers. Whereas leaders may possess latent dispositions and traits that make violent, stressful, oppositional behaviour attractive, followers may be attracted more to the group than to its activities. Followers exhibit strong affiliative needs.

Sullwold (1981) believes that a notable distinction exists between leaders and followers in terrorist groups. Leaders are more likely to be people who combine a lack. of scruples with extreme self-assurance; the, often lead by frightening or pressurising their followers. She notes two types of personality traits among leaders. The first is extremely extroverted type whose behaviour is unstable, uninhibited, inconsiderate, self-interested and unemotional. (These attributes characterise a narcissistic personality). Emotional deficiencies blind them to the- negative consequences of their actions. They possess a high tolerance for stress. He is a stress-seeker for whom the excitement of danger compensates for the absence of feeling. Such persons do not accept responsibility for their actions and dislike boredom. The second type is neurotically hostile. Suspicious, aggressive, defensive and intolerant, he rejects criticism and is extremely sensitive to external hostility.

Need to belong: For the majority of terrorists who are followers the dominant motive for joining terrorism is the need to belong. While the assassin acts alone, the terrorist acts in a group. The path to joining a terrorist group is often through other groups. such as West German residential cooperatives. communes or prisoner's help groups. The recruitment process of ETA is a slow and gradual moving from legal to illegal assistance rather than an instances conversion. As individuals joined groups that became more and more radical, then were drawn closer to the inner circles that espoused violence. The decision to use violence came only after association with them, the choice was between participating in violence or leaving the group

Jerrold Post notes that there is a particularly striking similarity of behaviour among terrorists despite their widely differing individual circumstances. He attributes this similarity to the fact that the recruit to terrorism finds himself/herself feeling as if he/she fully *belonged* for the first time. Recruitment is due to this need belong, ideological reasons are rationalisations. Recruits experience relief at joining. The need to belong is always an attraction to marginalised persons, and to this category the terrorist belongs. For the member who has found a home in the terrorist group, the primary goal is to feel that he belongs and fighting the good fight; the goals of publicity and ultimate victory for the cause are secondary and tertiary. For tire group there is an equivalent primary goal– to insure that it survives as a group. According to Post, for alienated individual (and the terrorist is such an individual in his eyes) joining a terrorist group represents the first real sense of belonging after a lifetime of rejection and the terrorist group becomes the family he never had. Upon joining a terrorist group, the individual breaks off all previous affiliations and becomes dependent on the group for emotional support.

Students of terrorism in West Germany have noted the importance–of personal connections and relatives in the process of joining a group. It w as found that a large number of couples and brothers and sisters participated in terrorism. This finding reinforces the argument that the terrorist group is a family substitute. It was noted that in some cases the relationships with other influential persons were so significant that without them the terrorist's personal development would have taken a different direction. Leaders of terrorist groups often fulfil the role of mentor, by becoming substitute parents.

Personality or Mind-set

Research in terrorism has been marked by contradictory assumptions about the terrorist. He is regarded on the one hand as psychotic or fanatic and on the other as highly rational governed by good planning and armed with an ideology, sound information about objectives and weapons. Also, he is taken to be a dedicated person on the one hand and on the other a mercenary whose rewards may not be financial but psychological or ideological. There may be some truth in the assumptions, but what is indubitable is that he is a human being, subject to the laws of behaviour. This is the case for a study of the terrorist's personality or mind-set which is the over-all determiner of behaviour.

Unfortunately the psychological approach to terrorist's personality has been dominated by the psychopathological orientation. It is argued that any one who is different is not normal; the terrorist is different in opting for extra-normal use of violence for gaining his ends; hence lie is pathological. This approach is counterproductive, because the belief that he is crazy is likely to increase the general public's perceived threat and the consequent effectiveness of the terrorist act. People have a prevailing fear of the irrational and negotiations with the irrational are difficult, if not impossible. All the available evidence, however, suggests that terrorists are not crazy. In fact there is no "personality" distinctive of terrorists.

Franco Ferracuti of Rome University and Adviser to Italian Secret Service during 1970s has analysed the career and personalities of arrested terrorists in two ways: by collecting information on demographic variables and by applying psychological tests to build a typology of terrorists. He however makes a useful distination for diagnosing the "terrorist condition" between radical political dissent which is ubiquitous and the specific use of violence which is not. Upon basis of his analysis, Ferracuti's answer to the question, "Are terrorists crazy?" is an emphatic No. His answer is based on a study of revolutionaries, not separatists. Robert P. Clark on the basis of his study of ETA activists concludes that terrorists are not alienated and psychologically distressed, rather they are 'psychologically' healthy persons for the most part strongly supported by their families and ethnic community.

Rasch (1979) a psychiatrist who analyzed several members of the West German terrorist organisations finds no conclusive evidence for the assumption that a significant number of terrorists are disturbed or abnormal. In his opinion, the argument that terrorism is pathological behaviour is an attempt to avoid discussion of the political and social issues raised by terrorism. His position is reinforced by a study of 227 leftist terrorists in West Germany (Jager, Schidtchexn and Sillwold (1981) and of IRA members (Heskin 1980), who are not psychopaths, predisposed to violence or mentally abnormal. Corrado (1981) has examined theories that regard terrorism in Western societies as rooted in sociopathy, narcissism, death wish or physiological impairment (e.g. neurological disorders leading to antisocial behaviour).

A possible reason for the small number of pathologically ill persons in the ranks of terrorist is that most terrorist organisations are careful about whom they recruit and screen out those potentially dangerous to group survival. The practical rule of organisational security and maintenance excludes persons of unpredictable or uncontrolled behaviour. In a less hierarchical model with a loose structure, where there is less control over membership, there is less obstacle to the mentally ill being inducted into the group.

There is some evidence found by Ferracuti and Bruno (1'981) that left-wing terrorists rarely suffered from serious personality disorders in contrast to right-wing terrorists who showed a much higher incidence of borderline or even psychotic personalities and of drug addiction. Right-wing terrorists are more frequently examined by psychiatrists because insanity defense is employed more frequently in their case. The glorification of violence in right-wing ideologies of terrorism may explain their attraction for mentally disturbed individuals. The West German study however does not bear out Ferracuti and Bruno's conclusion. There were 23 rightwing terrorists in the study, but they were not more disturbed than left-wing terrorists, although they did possess several distinctive personality traits (Sullwold 1981).

Typology : Jerrold Post analysed anything written or spoken by a terrorist for its linguistic clues about aggression, conciliation, violence or instability likely to be encountered during a crisis and administered the Adjective Check List (due to Gough). He compared the results obtained from terrorists with those from control groups matched in age and back-ground and arrived at a sketch of dependence, aggressiveness, masculinity, femininity, instability and deviance of the subjects. He tested four groups of people: left-wing terrorists, right-wing terrorists drug addicts of comparable age and left-wing `politically involved non-terrorist'. He found that on the adjective Check List, the four groups were quite distinct. Of the 300 adjectives in the List, there were only four adjectives common to all the four groups : of these two were 'adventuresome' and 'aggressive'. No common 'terrorist personality' emerged. The right-wing terrorists were most psychopathic and the least deviant were the leftwing politically involved nonterrorists. But the difference did not amount to psychopathology. The implication is that a teenager who begins to behave antisocially on Adjective Check List might have a tendency to move towards terrorism of extreme right. His finding about there being no terrorist personality agrees with that of Ferracuti 's about there being no terrorist 'mind-set' .

Frustration-aggression Theory

It has been argued that since the psychopathological orientation to terrorism is counterproductive, it is better to study the objectives, goats, relationships. styles of thinking and decision-making of the terrorist the approach of general or normal psychology. From this angle, the frustration-aggression hypothesis of the Yale psychologists come readily to mind. Much terrorist behaviour is a response to frustration of various political. economic and personal needs or objectives. A terrorist act is often intended to elicit a response that will demonstrate that Government will continue to frustrate the terrorists legitimate aspirations. This response explains and normalises terrorist activity. Terrorism becomes 'self-fulfilling'. The belief that the terrorist act is lawful scientifically (for frustration produces aggression) provides the terrorist with responsibility without guilt. The terrorist's motivation is strengthened because of his political objectives mesh with his personal and psychological needs. The moral of these points is that we find a weakness in a terrorist situation and thereby attempt to disrupt it.

According to the frustration-aggression hypothesis, the nearer one approaches a desired goal. the stronger is ones need for satisfaction. The attempt to escape at a time when release of a prisoner is near is illogical, but lawful according to this hypothesis. When the curve of intensity of need increases sharply as an individual approaches a positive goal, the curve of avoidance feeling increases even more sharply as one approaches a negative goal or a situation that is feared or dislike. One can experiment with the possibilities of such curves to find-out ways in which tension. motivation even direction of activity of the terrorist can be altered by controlling the psychological distance from the positive and negative goals.

The approach of experimental psychology to terrorism can be fruitful in other ways as well. For example a study of the full development of the Zeigarnik effect would suggest a wide range of applications in negotiation settings and in other crisis situations. Further, research findings on the conditions of decision under uncertainty can be used to deal with uncertainty about task or the objective, information received, the characteristics of the information source or the competence of the decision-maker. Again, the Office of Naval Research of USA has funded some research associated with cognitive style (field-dependence and independence) that can be usefully transferred to work in terrorism. Moreover, research on stimulus deprivation can be useful in studying terrorists. Stimulus deprivation leads to loss of confidence, uncertainty, and some disorientation. Deprivation theory can best be used with marginal individuals or groups who are uncertain of their place :n the terrorist movement and generally lack the approval of the larger terrorist apparatus. This stratagem probably explains the decision of hijackers of KLM plane to surrender to the Christian President of Cyprus.

Narcissistic Rage Theory

John Crayton terrorism in terms of the psychology of self developed in the works of Kohut, Kernberg, Freud, Hartmann and others. In doing so, he does not rule out biological, intrapsychic, group, social or cultural factors in terrorism. He also takes care to define terrorism as an attempt to acquire or maintain power or control by intimidation, by instilling fear of destruction or helplessness in the objects of terrorism. He also points out that terrorists operate in groups under the banner of a cause. The group or the cause is highly idealised and an air of absolute conviction is held about the truth or righteousness of the group's aims. The terrorist group grows out of a situation of deprivation. All of these characteristics of terrorism are typical of an exaggerated group narcissism. Moreover, terrorists feel that they lack access to a responsive social system. Terrorist groups are led by charismatic figures who personify the plight of the group. Terrorists crave publicity which serves to enhance the self-image of the group and self-esteem of individual members.

According to Heinz Kohut lines of psychological development that begins at birth and continues into adulthood. First the individual develops a repertory of interactions with objects outside oneself–parents, friends. environment. He has instinctual aims towards objects, such as to love and be loved, to be competent, to succeed. The second line of development that occurs along with the first is concerned with the individual's relationship with himself, how he views himself.

The first phase of the latter line of development is that of primary narcissism. The infant is involved with himself. with no differentiation of "I" or "Thou". This phase gaves way as the infant confronts the painful realities of environment, to two alternative psychological forms: the "grandiose self' and the "idealised parental ago". These two narcissistic reactions have both positive and negative aspects, depending on individual circumstances. The grandiose self when attenuated adequately by reality testing is an essential ingredient of healthy ambition, self-confidence, and development of mutual loving human relationships. If not neutralised by reality, testing, the grandiose self produces individuals who are sociopaths. arrogant, and lacking in regard for others. Similarly, the idealised parental imago contributes to a healthy regard for others and maintenance of societal ideals and customs. But when the reaction is excessive, it can produce a condition of helpless defeatism, overly high expectations of an idealised other, and a vulnerability to disappointment when expected responses are not forthcoming.

The lines of development outlined above are normal. Each one of us goes through these successive stage. Each one of us is however vulnerable to one or the other of those phases when placed in a situation that rearouses the threatened sense of self.

When an individual is frustrated in attempts to maintain healthy self-esteem and cohesion, he may react with responses that may be more or less useful. Shame and anger, if not overwhelming can be the basis for constructive efforts to establish self-respect and healthy regard for others. But narcissistic defeat can lead to reactions of race and a wish to destroy the source of narcissistic injury. There is, according to Kohut, a biological basis for narcissistic rage. The injured individual responds either with shame-faced withdrawl or with narcissistic rage, analogous to the flight-fight pattern. Narcissistic rage is a persistent and frequently chaotic pattern of aggress ion designed to re-establish self-esteem following humiliation.

Kohut believes that narcissistic rage can be understood in terms of the frustrated expectations of absolute power or omnipotence by the grandiose self. Hence, the psychological mechanism of regulating aggression are mobilised in the service of achieving absolute control and master over self-object; e.g. feared and hated foreigners. A cute narcissistic rage can give way to chronic narcissistic rage when the ego further relinquishes its reasoning capacity and even more persistently demands the limitlessness of the power of the grandiose self. Through the defense mechanism of splitting, the self renounces any suggestion of inherent limitations and attributes all failures and weaknesses to others.

Negative/Confused Identity Theory

Erickson is well known for his theory of identity formation. He bases his concept of personality on the child's development through a series of cumulative development stages, each of which is a "crisis" (in the sense of turning point, not catastrophe), and a test of the individual's ability to resolve the crisis. Details of the stages are given below:

Life stage	Psycho-socialcrisis	Significant relations
1. Infancy	Trust v. mistrust v. to give in return	Maternal persons to get
2. Early childhood	Autonomy v. shame & doubt, to hold (on) v. to let (go)	Parental persons
3. Play stage	Initiative v. guilt to make v. to make like (play)	Basic family
4. School age	Industry v. inferiority to make y. to make things together	Neighbourhood/ School
5. Adolescence	Identity v. identity diffusion to be one self (or not to be) being, oneself	Peer groups; out groups; models of leadership to share
6. Young adult	Intimacy v. self-absorption to lose & find oneself in another	Partners in friendship sex, competition, cooperation.
7. Adulthood	Generosity v. self-absorption; to make v. to make care of	Divided labour, & shared household
8. Mature age	Integrity v. despair to be through having been: to face not being	"Mankind" "My kind"

If the crisis is resolved, the result is matured integration; unresolved crises torment the individual throughout later life. The successful development of personal identity is essential to the integrity and continuity of the personality. Identity enables the individual to experience the self as something that has continuity and sameness, to act accordingly, and to be confident that one's sense of self is matched by one's meaning for others. Erickson considers the development of basic trust in the infact as the cornerstone of a vital personality. Early mistrust, accompanied by rage and fantasies of domination or destruction of the sources that give pleasure or provide sustenance, is revived when society fails to provide needed assurances. These conflicts of infancy and early childhood re-surface in later extreme circumstances, especially in adolescence, when the crisis facing the individual in finding a stable identity. Earlier failures to establish trust, autonomy initiative or Individual handicap the adolescents search for positive identity, leading in some cases to extreme identity confusion and in others to the formation of a negative identity. Identity is something not found alone, but in a collectivity and is rooted in one's ethnic, national or family past "fidelity, a need to have faith in something or someone outside ones and trustworthy in its service. Ideologies are thus guardians of identity. Erikson further suggests that political undergrounds utilize youth's need for fidelity as well as the store of wrath held by those deprived of something in which they have faith. An identity crisis (when the individual who finds self definition difficult is suffering from ambiguity, fragmentation and contradiction) makes some adolescents susceptible to "totalism" or to totalistic collective identities that promise certainty. In such collectivities, the troubled young person finds not only an identity but an explanation for his difficulties and promise for the future.

Bollinger (1981) has found support for Erikson's theories, in his psychoanalytical study of eight indicated or convicted members of West German terrorist group. His subjects showed serious traumas during critical stage of development, especially in failures to establish trust, autonomy and initiative. The over controlling and unaffectionate parents of the subjects had turned all relations with the child into a struggle for power, leading the child to clash repeatedly with outside authorities. Upon reaching the formative identity period, these individuals found an ideology based on conflict between oppressed and oppressor highly attractive. Acquisition of weapons made the "child" feel less weak and helpless before powerful authority. Thus for the subjects studied by Bollinger, layer on layer of development and experience did not smoothen scars but reopened old wounds. Such individuals reached puberty with the crisis of identity formation seriously impoired and unfavourable to a positive identity formation. For them joining a terrorist organisation was the last act of a series of attempts at identity formation.

Knutson (1991) uses Erikson's theories, specially his concept of negative identity to account for terrorism. Negative identity is defined as an identity perversely based on all those identifications and roles which at critical stages of development, had been presented as most undesirable or dangerous and yet also as most real. It involves a vindictive rejection of the role considered as desirable and proper by the individual's family and community. It probably results from excessive normative ideals demanded by ambitious parents or actualised by superiors. In support of this theory, Schmidtchen found that many terrorists came from homes where there as a strong pressure for achievement. If a positive identity is not possible, the individual prefers to being a "bad' person to being nobody or partially somebody If steps toward acquisition of negative identity are interpreted as final, individuals may be pushed into conformity with the worst that people expect of' them. Knutson emphasizes, in this connection, the role of government actions in narrowing individual choices and pushing the individual into the assumption of a negative identity. She cites the example of Croatian terrorist Zvaonko Busic, a member of an oppressed minority, who disappointed by the failure of his goal of university education that blocked the path toward a positive identity, assumed negative identity.

In the case of nationalist or separatist terrorism, negative identity has a subtler meaning. Such terrorism has social approval within the minority community. Joining a nationalist terrorist group does not represent an absolute 'negative identity. Rather, the negative identity reflects values instilled early in life, and may reflect ethnic roots and traditions. One should therefore he careful in attributing all terrorist activity to the individual's rejection of, or inability to pursue, a positive identity. Moreover, not all acquisition of negative identity is politicized; many young persons rebel socially - in clothes and manners–without political purpose. Such individuals may neither have the inner needs nor the opportunity to join violent undergrounds.

Kohut's psychology of the self relates narcissistic rage to group psychology, since most terrorist activities are carried out by groups and group dynamics plays a central role in fostering terrorism. Some groups are held together by shared grandiose self rather than shared ideals. The shared grandiose self is personified in the leader for two reasons : idealisation in the form of meaningful ideals that protects members from experiencing shame; and idealisation prevents members from inter group feelings like jealousy, envy or rage. Group cohesion and individual cohesion are facilitated by uniting to destroy a common foe. The foe, being all bad, reinforces the group's sense of being right and just.

Kohut describes certain features suited for becoming charismatic leaders. These are an unshakable confidence in themselves and voicing opinions with an air of absolute certainty. The leader's self esteem is high, even though the maintenance of self-esteem may call for the use of manipulative techniques like continually judging others, establishing himself as guide and god of those who are in need in guidance, leadership and a target for reverence. He has identified himself fullly either with his grandiose self or his idealised superego. 'The result is a serious inclaslicity of personality for elasticity comes from reliance on different sources of self-esteem. He has no dynamically effective guilt feelings and never suffers from pangs of conscience about what he is doing. He is sensitive to injustice done to him, quick to accuse others and thus evoke guilt feelings in others. Kohut believes, unlike Freud, that these leaders have a stunted empathetic capacity; they don't understand the wishes and frustrations of other people. The terror is act is intended to hurt the selfesteem of victims. The Stockholm syndrome (of a captive hostage coming to like the captor) is explained in terms of identification with the terrorist out of a sense of guilt.

The consequences of strong cohesiveness of terrorist groups are several. The formation of strong effective ties between members in a Cohesive group means that approval of other group membersbecomes more important than achievement of group goals. Under these circumstances, the goal of the organisation may become selfmaintenance rather than transformation of society. Another consequence is the tendency to encourage the pursuit of violence. As isolation deepens, information about the out side world is filtered through the group. Growing misperceptions reinforce group beliefs and value. It becomes easy to depersonalise victims. The need to deflect internal conflict leads to extreme aggressiveness to outside enemies. Because terrorism takes place in a group setting, a "risky shift" may occur. Individuals in a group are more likely to take risks than they would when acting alone. The increase in risk-taking propensity may encourage escalation, as terrorists become less inhibited by the prospect of negative consequences.

Membership in a primary group also may help in coping with guilt. The degree of guilt varies with individual personality and the strength of group influence over member. We are not sure whether terrorists experience guilt over their violent acts, but if it does occur then it creates more stress for the individual and dependence on group, with the result that the member conlnuts more guilt-inducing acts. It then becomes difficult to leave the group, for the deserter would confront not only social opprobrium and legal sanctions but also remorse. A component of terrorist's belief system that he is "sacrificial animal" acts as a form of atonement for guilt and thus enables coping with it. Further the image that terrorists hold of themselves as soldiers acting in the name of duty and a higher call nlav also he an outlet for denying personal responsibility for acts of violence.

The likelihood that a conflict will take a constructive or destructive course depends on the nature of tile issue: its size, its rigidity, its centrality, its relationship to other issues and the level of consciousness oftltc issue. The constructive and destructive processes of conflict resolution are equatable with cooperative and competitive processes respectively. Psychologists have well-established knowledge of the typical effects of cooperative and competitive process and thus knowledge can be applied to conflict resolution in either direction. Thus, if one wants to create conditions for destructive process of conflict resolution, one would introduce into the conflict the typical characteristics and effects of a competitive process: poor communication, coercive tactics, suspicion, the perception of basic differences, challenges to the legitimacy of the parties and so on. On the contrary, if one wants to create conditions for a constructive process of conflict resolution, one would introduce into the conflict the typical effects of a cooperative process: good communication, the perception of similarity in beliefs and values, problem-centred negotiations, mutual trust and confidence, informal friendly contacts, information sharing and so forth. The role of mediators and conciliators or similar third parties is to produce constrictive conflict resolution by creating conditions that characterise an effective, cooperative, problem-solving process.

Most of the important work on the question of the circumstances, strategies and tactics that lead one party to do better than another in a conflict situation has been done by economists and political scientists rather than by psychologists. Psychologists have succeeded in providing some support and some qualification of preexisting ideas about bargaining strategy and tactics. Their research relates to the strategies of being tough, being ignorant, threats and promises and bargaining power. It has lent some support to the tactic of "being ignorant"nd raised some doubt about the advantages of "being tough", "coercievetactice" and "supeior bargaining power" strategies. However, the research has not eventuated in a systematic theories od seduction, coercion, blackmail, bluffing. There has not been enough knowledge of these black arts to provide a "curriculum for a school of scoundrels."

Accord: Research on the question of that determines tile nature of agreement between two conflicting parties, if they are able to reach an agreement, is the latest addition to the social psychology of conflict resolution. The determiners appear to be "perceptual prominence" and "distributive justice".

Schelling has proposed that perceptually prominent alternatives permit bargainers to come to an agreement. The saliency of alternatives depends on perceptual uniqueness, simplicity or "good form". Most bargaining situations, he point out, ultimately involve some range of possible outcomes within which each party would rather make a concession than fail to reach an agreement at all. The final outcome must be a point from which neither party expects the other to retreat. The main ingredient of this expectation is what one thinks the other expects the first to expect ad infinintin. These infinitely reflexive expectations must somehow converge on a single point, at which each party expects the other not to expect to be expected to retreat. A perceptually prominent agreement, say "equal concessions" or 50-50 split is an obvious place to converge and stop making or expecting further concessions. There is empirical support for Schelling's idea.

4

A Terrorism: UN Perspective

Terrorism is as old as human history—may be it is prehistoric for in pre-history terrorism was the only means of survival. Ordinarily terrorism should have declined with every advance in civilisation because civilisation itself signifies peace and development.

Unfortunately it did not so happen; on the contrary, new means and methods of terror were raised and developed to subdue and conquer others. Terrorism today has assumed new forms and shapes which sometimes defy imagination. The wide network of terrorism is now global, and no individual sate on its own, is capable of fighting, much less eliminating terrorism. The fight against terrorism has to be global, hence the involvement of the United Nations in the fight against terrorism for terrorism anywhere is a danger to peace and security everywhere.

In his address at the outset of the General Assembly's annual high-level debate, Secretary-General Kofi Annan on 10 Nov. 2001 outlined his priorities for the coming years while reviewing the guiding principles for the United Nations.

The Secretary-General said, "no words could adequately convey his 'revulsion and sorrow' at the 11 September attacks, adding that, like the United States, the UN was determined to overcome the forces that inflicted this ordeal upon us."

"One is tempted to say t hat we must now focus all our energies on the struggle against terrorism, and on directly related issues, yet if we did so we should give the terrorists a kind of victory," he said. "Let us remember that none of the issues that faced us on September 11th become less urgent."

At the current juncture, he said, the world clearly understood the need to resist the looming danger of division within the human family. "We face two possible futures: a mutually destructive clash between so-called 'civilizations' based on exaggeration of religious and cultural differences; or a global community, respecting diversity and rooted in universal values," he said. "The latter must he our choice — but we can achieve it only if we bring real hope to the billions now trapped in poverty, conflict and disease."

Outlining fundamental guiding principles for the UN, the Secretary-General pointed out that the Organization must always stand for the rule of law "in international and domestic affairs". In addition, it must make full use of its multilateral institutions and procedures while placing people at the centre of everything it did, enabling them to meet their needs and realize their full potential. "That can only be achieved in a world of effective, accountable States, which use sovereignty as a means to ensure the security of their peoples, and to uphold-not violate-their human rights," he said.

Security Council's Call

Declaring terrorists acts to be one of the most serious threats to international peace and security in the 21st century, the United Nations Security Council on 12 November 2001 called on all countries to intensify their efforts to eliminate the scourge of terrorism.

The call came in a resolution adopted unanimously during a meeting at the level of Foreign Ministers, which was convened on the initiative of Ukraine and chaired by Foreign Minister K.D. Knight of Jamaica, the Council's then President.

In the next, the Council called for countries to take 'urgent steps' to put into action its resolution 1373 adopted on 28 September 2001, which spelled out wide-ranging strategies to combat international terrorism and which also set up a committee to monitor its implementation. The Council underscored that under resolution 1373, Member States had obligation "to deny financial and, all other forms of support and safe haven to terrorists and those supporting terrorism".

The resolution also welcomed the commitment expressed by States "to fight the scourge of international terrorism," and called on them to become parties as soon s possible to the relevant international conventions and protocols relating to international terrorism.

General Assembly Debate

As world leaders converged on New York for the opening of the General Assembly' high-level debate, most Head of State and Government used their 15 minutes at the podium to pledge support to the fight against terrorism, but often disagreed on where to look for its root causes.

Nearly all speakers reiterated their Government's condemnation of the violent attacks on the United States on 11 September 2001 but differed as to appropriate response to that aggression, and to terrorism as a whole.

The leaders of predominantly Muslim nations warned against the tendency–particularly in Western countries–to associate terrorism with Islam, defending their faith as peaceful and compassionate. They spoke of the danger of creating an 'us' versus 'them' dynamic, which they said would only fuel divisions. Instead, the world should look at what motivates such horrific acts, and take steps to heal the desperation, isolation and abandonment felt by many of the world's people due to gross inequalities in the distribution of wealth, and lack of respect for basic human rights, they said.

Many countries also spoke of the need to differentiate between criminal terrorism and legitimate struggles against oppression, and stressed the need for the international community to define what it means by the term 'terrorism'. Some of the European countries stressed the importance of enforcing existing legal instruments in the struggle against terrorism.

The plight of the Afghan people also surfaced in many speeches. Although many voiced support for the anti-terrorism efforts of the United States and other countries, they also expressed concern about Afghan human rights.

For several Latin American delegations, the fight against terrorism was akin to–if not intertwined with-the fight against the illicit trade in narcotics and therefore required the same approach of shared responsibility by the international community. The continent's leaders also said help from the international community to fund alternative development programmes would go far in reducing the continent's production of crops used for drugs.

The link between social development and peace were high on the agenda for the African delegations, many of which attributed the continent's conflicts to the persistent and extreme poverty faced by many Africans. Noting that they were not looking for charity, the African leaders said they wanted more accessible conditions for their countries' row materials, and products at fair prices. Debt relief was also crucial, they said, to prevent conflicts and terrorism.

Some Asian leaders warned of the need to strengthen the globalization and sustainable development processes, so that they could generate finances for poverty alleviation, and prevent terrorism.

The 56th session of the United Nations General Assembly on 10 November 2001 began its annual high-level. The week-long meeting drew more than 40 Presidents and Prime Ministers and well over 100 Foreign Ministers. In opening the 'general debate', Assembly President Han Seungsoo of the Republic of Korea noted that it was postponed from its traditional September schedule after the terror attacks against the United States. The actions of the United Nations in the past two months "give proof of our united response to the challenge (of terrorism)," resolution by the General Assembly on 12 September and the two important resolutions of the Security Council, we have moved quickly and decisively to address the overriding issue of terrorism."

In his statement to the Assembly, Secretary-General Kofi Annan outlined his priorities for the coming years and reviewed fundamental guiding principles for the United Nations.

Leading off the session, President Fernando Henrique Caruoso of Brazil said that while it was only natural that issue of international security be given high priority after the events of 11 September, terrorism should not stifle the debate on cooperation and other issues of global interest.

Calling on the world community to focus on the 'fundamental imperative' of promoting development, President Cardoso said that the process of globalization was tainted by an undeniable sense of unease. "There is a governance deficit in the international sphere, and it results from a democratic deficit," he said. "Globalization will only be sustainable if enriched by a sense of justice. Our motto should be 'globalization in solidarity' rather than the symmetrical globalization of today."

The President of the United States, George W. Bush, said that every nation had a stake in the fight against terrorism and that the leaders of every country must carefully consider their responsibilities in that respect. "It is our task-the task of this generation-to provide the response to aggression and terror," he said. "We have no other choice, because there is no other peace." The President said the time for action had arrived. "These obligations are urgent, and they are binding on every nation with a place in this chamber," he said, underscoring the UN Security Council resolution adopted in September that required all countries to cooperate on terrorist financing and sharing intelligence, among other measures.

Terrorism has shown in a very graphic, tragic and painful manner, as it did also in Kenya and Tanzania, "that our very humanity renders all of us, without exception, into potential targets of cold-blooded murder," he said.

The Emir of Qatar, said the word 'terrorism' must be defined in order to distinguish it from legitimate struggles to end illegitimate occupation and subjugation. "Terrrorism has taken root not only because of our inability to tackle world tension hot-spots but also because we have tolerated for too long those who pursue politics of repression," Hamad bin Khalifa Al-Thani said.

Vicente Fox, President of Mexico, told the Assembly that in the search for lasting solutions to the new threats faced by the international system, "we should not overlook the situations that have contributed to their emergence, such as the lack of economic development in many nations."

President Fox called on the international community to make the fight against poverty and social exclusion a priority and reaffirmed his country's interest in promoting the agenda for development, providing it with a renewed impetus and more effective approach to tackle terrorism.

Mohammed Khatami, President of the Islamic Republic of Iran, said the beginning of the new millennium had been marred by blood and gloom, referring to the attacks on the US and other violence that persisted throughout the year. In response, the leader of the Islamic Revolution in Iran had spoken of "Jihad against the evil phenomenon" in order to highlight the genuine view of Islam and the Islamic Revolution vis-a-vis terrorism, he said.

"The disaster in the United States is so tragic and grave that it implores all thinkers to engage in deep reflection and dialogue on its real cause," he said, stressing however that a definition of terrorism was needed, in order to differentiate between "blind criminal terrorism and the legitimate defence" against violence and occupation. The Iranian leader recommended that a global summit be convened to articulate practical and serious policies to eradicate the menace of terrorism. He also highlighted the importance of such endeavors as the 'Dialogue among Civilizations', which he said offered a new paradigm of interaction among nations and cultures.

Atal Bihari Vajpayee, Prime Minister of India, said his country supported the current campaign against the terrorist networks in Afghanistan and hoped for its early and successful conclusion. He urged the international community to work towards establishing a broad-based, representative and neutral government in the country so that a political vacuum could be avoided at the end of the military campaign and terrorism could be effectively dealt with.

Louis Michel, the President of the Council of Europe and Vice Prime Minister of Belgium, said a new global dynamic must be fostered, with the UN playing a central role in creating a coordinated strategy. He welcomed the UN Security Council's adoption of resolution 1373 following the World Trade Center attacks, and said the European Union and its Member States had already begun implementing its recommendations. Other issues addressed in his speech included human rights, the establishment of International Criminal Court, which he saw as particularly essential now to enforce international law, human rights etc.

General Pervez Musharraf, the President of Pakistan, said his country has condemned the vicious attack against the US on 11 September, but that now was the time for introspection. "The religion of Islam, and Muslims in various parts of the world, are being held responsible for the trials the world is facing," he said, warning that this point of view was 'totally misplaced'. For the Pakistani leader, the root causes for terrorism were the unresolved political disputes such as in Bosnia, Kosovo, Palestine, Kashmir and other places

The Foreign Minister of China, Tang Jiaxuan, said the United Nations had an 'irreplaceable role' in international cooperation in response to globalization and that it should increase its input in development and work more effectively to fulfill the development objectives set forth in last year's Millennium Declaration.

Erkki Tuomioja, the Foreign Affairs Minister of Finland, said the 11 September attacks required a changed thinking within international organizations. "We must respond quickly and efficiently to the challenges of the real world," he said. "We cannot be buried in old rhetoric and positions when people outside require concrete action and help," The UN's efforts–from conflict prevention through crisis management to post-conflicts peace–building needed a fresh approach, he said.

The Minister of Foreign Affairs of Italy, Renata Ruggiero, said no peacekeeping action could achieve lasting results unless it was coupled with measures to strengthen government institutions, safe guard human rights and rebuild the economic and social fiber of affected areas.

In his address to the Assembly, Yasser Arafat, Chairman of the Executive Committee of the Palestine Liberation Organization and President of the Palestinian Authority, claimed that the Palestinian Intifada was in response to Israel's 'non-compliance' with the peace process.

As the General Assembly began the third day of its high-level debate, speakers addressed a broad range of issue–from international terrorism to the situation in the Middle East and Africa, peacekeeping operations, climate change, as well as fishery management and marine ecology.

Kenyan President Daniel T. Arap Moi emphasized the need to tackle the crippling poverty afflicting millions of people across the world. "Poverty is a fertile breeding ground for conflict and instability and even terrorism," he pointed out.

Foreign Minister John Manley of Canada told tile Assembly that the pledges d the Millennium Summit in September 2000 must not be overshadowed by the urgency of the events one year latter. "Indeed, their fulfillment can and must form an integral component of how we create a strong, equitable global environment-one that can be neither attacked nor exploited by terrorists," he said. In order to achieve those goals, Mr. Manlcy said, national governments must take responsibility, and be held accountable, for their actions and decisions–for fighting terrorism, for undertaking political and legal reforms, for resolving disputes, and for establishing the conditions in which democracy flourishes and development is sustained.

Much of the debate also centered on the efforts needed to combat the root causes of the kind of discontent that might lead to such extreme actions, such as poverty, hunger, underdevelopment and neglect of human rights. For his part, Sheikh Sabah Al-Ahmad Al-Jaber Al-Sabah, the Acting Prime Minister and Minister for Foreign Affairs of Kuwait, called for an international conference on terrorism in order to agree on a definition of the scourge, one that would distinguish it from the right of peoples to struggle against occupation. He stressed that an effective fight against terrorism required maximum international cooperation and coordination and also demanded a 'soul searching' review of the world's current political, economic and social policies and practices in dealing with current global challenges. The goal was to minimize, if not eliminate, the ills that might be exploited by evildoers to carry out their terror schemes in a bid to advance their own agendas.

Kitchi Miyazawa, a Member of Parliament of Japan, said his Government was ready to cooperate with developing countries in controlling the financing of terrorism, and on a wide range of issues, including immigration control, aviation and maritime security, and biological and chemical weapons.

Abdelaziz Belkhadem, Minister of Foreign Affairs of Algeria, said anti-terrorism efforts should focus on the dismantling of terrorist bases and the freezing of finances linked to such acts, as well as on international cooperation in information sharing and the provision of assistance to countries that fall victim to terrorism, which create the conditions favourable to extremism and intolerance.

President Stipe Mesic of Croatia said the threat of terrorism was not due to a clash of cultures or religions, but was a confrontation of civilization and non-civilization. There is no such thing as 'our' and 'their', or 'justified' and 'unjustified' terrorism, he pointed out. The nature of such acts-whether masked by an ideology, religion or a liberation war is to kill innocent people, and that is terrorism. For the problem to be solved, two types of changes must take place in the way the world functions, he said. First, we should move beyond the dichotomy of choosing between terror imposed anarchy on one side and autocracy as a response to the threat on the other. Fighting back through democracy and the rule of law is the only best tactic. The second change involves rethinking the way countries interact and tackling the reasons why people turn to terrorism, President Mesic said.

For his part, the Minister of Foreign Affairs of Jordan, Abdel-Elah Khatib, warned that terrorism would political, economic and social imbalances and the absence of justice to advance its goals. Therefore, addressing the main causes of despair, frustration and sense of injustice in a serious manner was perhaps the most effective way to confront terrorism and pre-empt its potential appeal and support.

Recalling last week's regional anti-terrorism conference hosted by his country, Poland's Foreign Minister, Wlodzimierz Cimeszewicz, said that the forum's declaration indicated strong political commitment to fight against that menace. "The adopted plan of action spells out concrete measures," he said. At the same time, he called for increased vigilance about weapons of mass destruction. "The spreading anthrax scare, representing but a tip of an iceberg of potential danger of bio-terrorism, spreading of fissile materials and chemical weapons are a powerful argument for the urgent need to strengthen and strictly enforce the Biological Weapons Convention of 1972, and some other legal instruments in this sphere," he said.

Abdurrahman Mohammed Shalghem, Secretary of the General People's Committee for Foreign Liaison and International Cooperation of Libya, stressed t he need for international agreement on a definition of terrorism. We cannot condemn terrorism and fight it when it hits one's country and turn a blind eye when it hits other countries and peoples," he said, calling for the General Assembly to convene a special session on terrorism to examine the issue in all of its dimensions.

The Foreign Minister of New Zealand, Phil Goff, said the events of 11 September had made it even more imperative that countries minimize the threat that chemical, biological or nuclear weapons could fall into the hands of extremist groups. He called for all countries to ratify treaties against biological and chemical weapons, as well as the Comprehensive Nuclear-Test-Ban Treaty. In addition, he said the terrorist attacks against the US "should encourage all countries and organizations, but most particularly those directly involved, to renew their efforts to find a just and peaceful solution to the Middle East crisis."

Ireland's Foreign Minister, Brian Cowen, said those responsible for the 11 September terrorist attacks could and must be stopped. At the same time, he expressed hope that the military campaign now under way would achieve its objectives in as short a time frame as possible.

Joseph Pique, Minister for Foreign Affairs of Spain, called for efforts to finalize the comprehensive convention against terrorism. "The goal must be to draw up an operative and executive instrument that cannot be paralysed by discussions of a political and not legal nature," he said. At the same time, he urged attention to the situation in the Middle East in order to "stop the blind cycle of violence and return to the negotiating table." Talks should lead, ultimately to a point where "the State of Israel and the Palestinian State will coexist peacefully within secure borders."

Pointing to the "avalanche of drugs, drug money, weapons, and warlords spilling out of Afghanistan," Jozias Van Aartsen, Minister of Foreign Affairs of the Netherlands, said there was every reason to focus attention on terrorist groups in different parts of the world. "Look at the blood diamonds streaming out of Africa," he said. "Think how failing States attract parasites, how they turn into breeding grounds for terrorism, havens for international crime."

For his part, Felipe Pervez Roque, the Minister for Foreign Affairs of Cuba, said only under the leadership of the UN can the world defeat terrorism, noting that Cuba supported the adoption of a general convention on international terrorism that would allow the international community to define terrorism with accuracy. "This has been an old aspiration of the Non-Aligned Movement," the Cuban Minister said.

The need for a closer look at the phenomenon of terrorism, including its causes, was also underscored by Lakshman Kadirgamar, the Minister of Foreign Affairs of Sri Lanka. He said that such an endeavour did not mean the international community was 'giving in' to terrorists, because it was "axiomatic that a contented people do not rise up to destroy the society in which they live." Noting that the world had indeed changed since 11 September, Mr. Kadirgamar said "Sri Lanka had been a victim of terrorism for two decades, but received little more than expressions of condolences from the international community. When half of the national airline's fleet was wiped out by terrorists on 24 July, the Government was advised by other nations to negotiate. We were reminded that 'violence begets violence'," he said. That approach has changed dramatically, or so it seems, in recent times because terrorism has assailed the national interests of many countries. Terrorism is no longer the curse of the poor.

Naji Sabri, Minister of Foreign Affairs of Iraq, said his country was suffering from aggression and terrorism. Its officials and nationals had been subjected to numerous terrorist attempts on their lives, while Iraqi towns have been targeted by terrorists infiltrators coming from across the border who were sponsored, trained, financed and armed within the framework of State terrorism. Both the aggression and the comprehensive sanctions constituted State terrorism directed against an entire people. "Terrorism' as a designation is also true of the use by the United States and Britain of more than 300 tonnes of depleted uranium ammunitions against the people of Iraq in 1991," he said, stressing that such acts violated the principles of international law.

The Minister for Foreign Affairs of Syria, Farouk Al-Shara' said the Middle East has never known terrorism until after the 1948 creation of Israel, which had sown the seeds of terrorism and fear in Palestine and outside it. Israel invented new types of terrorist practices in order to continue occupation of Arab territories.

Also speaking about the injustices that lead to frustration in developing countries, N. Hassan Wirajuda, Minister for Foreign Affairs of Indonesia said the global economic environment was becoming less hospitable to the aspirations for growth in poor States. This is encouraging terrorism.

For Eduard Kukan, Minister of Foreign Affairs of the Slovak Republic, the legal instruments devised in the UN were a good basis for increasing the effectiveness of the fight against terrorism. "The only thing that remains to be done is to implement all the good principles which are already laid down," he said.

The Minister for Foreign Affairs of Uzbekistan, Abdulaziz Kamilov, told the Assembly that in rallying the international coalition against terrorism, the world community should not neglect another equally dangerous threat, drug trafficking, which was the main financial support for terrorist and extremist activities.

Sule Lamide Minister for Foreign Affairs of Nigeria, said it was regrettable that conflicts and wars continued to be waged and that

Africa had a disproportionate share of those conflicts. Yet the experience in Liberia and Sierra Leone had shown that the United Nations, in close partnership with regional and sub-regional organizations, could facilitate the return to peace and security.

Concerning the need for sustained international cooperation, the struggle against terrorism must be waged on as broad a basis as possible. The UN is committed to working with international partners in the fight against terrorism, and to achieving unity of purpose and action.

The United Nations Counter-Terrorism Committee (CTC) has played a significant and worldwide role in combating the scourge since its creation last year.

A growing number of States have ratified the 12 international conventions and protocols related to terrorism. A year ago, only Botswana and the UK had ratified all 12 instruments; and have, 24 states have done so.

Recognizing that no nation is safe from terrorism if its neighbor is not, states are working together to combat the threat. Nearly 180 countries have reported to the CTC adding that the committee responded to almost all of these first reports and had begun to review the 86 follow-up reports which States have provided. To date, the total number of reports received by the CTC stands at 265.

Hailing the progress achieved by the Counter-Terrorism Committee set up in the wake of the 11 September attacks against the United States, the United Nations Security Council on 8 October called for those States that have failed to report to the panel to meet their obligations promptly.

In addition, the Council has invited international, regional and sub-regional organizations to continue to find ways of improving their collective action against terrorism, and where appropriate, the work with donor countries to establish suitable programmes.

Thus, it is amply evident that the United Nations is fully seized of the problems which threaten world peace and terrorism. It is doing what it can to tackle the menace of terrorism, as best as it can, along with the ever present danger posed by weapons of mass destruction which the terrorists are so desperate to acquire and use for their selfish nefarious ends. What the UN now needs and hopes for is greater public cooperation in combating terrorism.

5

Fundamentalism of Terrorism in South Asia

In historical terms, the phenomeno-logical manifestations of extreme revivalism and fundamentalism have always been closely linked. So inextricably have they intermingled that one cannot consider one without the other. Historical understanding of the close relationship between revivalism and fundamentalism, as conceptualizations of social phenomena, prompts a closer examination ot' the origins of these terms as such. This is important because the terms are so widely applied to movements all over the world. Indeed, Buddhist revivalism and fundamentalism, Hindu revivalism and fundamentalism, Muslim revivalism and fundamentalism, Sikh revivalism and fundamentalism, and other forms of revivalism and fundamentalism in South Asia cannot be fully or properly understood, without reference to the historical context out of which such movements have come. Moreover, many scholars using such conceptualizations do not know that both terms have their roots in the crises which have beset evangelical Protestants in North America since the middle of the nineteenth century and especially in conflicts which arose among such Christians during the years from 1870 to 1925.

By 1925, a profound change in social climate had occurred. America's evangelicals, once among the most respectable of the country's citizens–once among those who had set many of the intellectual, moral, and social standards for American culture as a whole–no longer mattered. They had become despised and, worse, ridiculed. William Jennings Bryan's behaviour at the Scopes trial in Tennessee, in 1925, served to symbolize that change. Those events made evangelicals a laughing stock across the country and the epithet "fundamentalist" came to characterize an especially militant and obscurantist brand of anti-modernism, anti-liberalism, and anti-secularism. Evangelicals had virtually become strangers in their own land.

How and why this came about has been brought to light through the penetrating and thorough scholarship of such historians as Ernest Sandeen (1970) and George Marsden (1980). In a comprehensive study entitled *Fundamentalism and American Culture: The Shaping of Twentieth Century Evangelicalism: 1870-1925*, Marsden (1980) explored the earliest use of this term among revivalist evangelicals and carefully traced the growth of the fundamentalist movement in North America. He followed its tortured path, from its sunlit heyday in the time of Dwight L. Moody, through crises engendered by the First World War, and found that the terms "fundamentalist" and "fundamentalism" came from the name for a series of books which were published in defense of "*the* faith." These works constituted an attack upon what were considered to be the excesses and foibles of higher criticism (upon Scripture), of modern science (in evolutionism and scientism), and of "liberal" or anti-theistic theology. The books condemned any public practice or preaching which might he seen as a hidden danger or an overt threat to that popular American culture which was by then so often described as "the faith once delivered to the saints, "a phrase lifted out of the Epistle ofjude (1:3), the context of which (*c.* AD 68) was a warning for believers to beware of apostasy, an exhortation for them to "earnestly contend for the faith which was once delivered to the saints."

The Fundamentals, in short, were a series of twelve paperback books' published between 1910 and.1915, which came out of the imaginative inspiration of a California oil magnate. They were edited by popular evangelists and teachers whose intentions were to mark down those basics of "*the* Truth," chose essential and irreducible absolutes which constituted *the* foundations of the faith. An attempt was made to distribute free copies of these books–"some three million individual volumes in all"-to every Protestant, religious worker in the English-speaking world. While this distribution failed to bring the great public response which had been hoped for or even to arouse more than passing notice in either serious journals or popular periodicals, the books did produce one important long-term consequence. *The Fundamentals* not only became a symbolic point of reference for identifying a "fundamentalist" movement as such; but, perhaps more significantly, they and the movement they represented also unwittingly served to spawn a new concept.

This concept has served ever since as a neat, although somewhat simplistic instrument of social analysis. Indeed, in the course of time, the term has come into common (and even popular) usage. It has been applied more generally to other social phenomena and to ideological, political, religious, or social movements in every corner of the world. As such, the term itself has become widely if inexactly used for assessing, naming, and measuring all sorts of movements.

Just as fascinating is the. relationship of this term to that of revivalism, a concept which also has roots in radical conversion movements and in their periodic millenarian rcawakenings. More specifically, the origin of the term and its use in modern times can be traced back into the evangelical "revivals" of the seventeenth and eighteenth centuries (Stoeffler 1965, 1971, 1973). From these came the Great Awakening in America, the Evangelical Awakening in Britain, and the Methodist revivals which periodically thereafter have swept various parts of the English-speaking (and European) world-and which still continue so to do. So profound were the impacts of these revivals that, even today in the colloquial language of the American South (and also occasionally in the so-called "Bible Belt"), regular or periodic "revivals" are held. As a form of populistic religious rally or evangelistic campaign (or what was once called a "tent meeting"), these are no longer merely forms of spontaneous social combustion, but are planned and scheduled, if not staged (Ahlstrom 1972: 263-329; McLoughlin 1959; Sweet 1944). It is out of such traditions as these that, during this century, the great nationwide campaigns of Billy Sunday and the greater world-wide campaigns of Billy Graham have come. It is also out of these traditions that many of the current weekly appeals and programs ot radio and televisions preachers-composing the so-called "electronic church"---have arisen. Commencing a half century ago with the wide-ranging network radio programs of Charles E. Fuller, this phenomenon is now most manifest in regular weekly programs of such fundamentalist (and populist) television preachers as Jerry Falwell, Pat Robertson, Jimmy Swaggart, Oral Roberts, Robert Schuller, or Herbert Armstrong.

Thus, there are strong historical grounds for linking revivalism and evangelicalism. There is both an intimate and a legitimate connection between these two concepts. Revivalisms, especially those which are most extremely radical, have almost invariably been, and in some particular and predominant way continue to be, fundamentalistic.

Several semantic classifications are essential in order to differentiate concepts more exactly and use them more finely since everyday language often confuses the usage of some of our most common concepts (Higgs and Dahlberg 1982). In much of our common language, and in the language of the public media, ideological kinds of concepts are often confused with institutional kinds of concepts. There is no conceptual reason, for example, why "conservative" and "liberal" should necessarily or always be antithetical. Such concepts as "conservative" and "radical" and "reactionary" are, in fact, essentially institutional. In their intrinsic character, these concepts are ideologically contentless or neutral. But, like receptacles, institutions to which they refer can be ideologically loaded. The only ideologies inherent within such concepts pertain to whether what exists in institutional form should be kept (status quo) or eradicated.

That what actually exists, institutionally, may indeed possess– in fact, almost invariably does possess within it-the quality or ideology of being liberal or authoritarian is not relevant to the concept. That institutions which do exist– and which their upholders may which to conserve-may actually happen to have ideological content should not cause confusion. On the other hand, such concepts as "liberal" and "authoritarian" are intrinsically ideological or value-laden. As such they are without any inherent or intrinsic "institutionality." Purely metaphysical, nothing but abstractions of world-views and values concerning ethical or moral or religious or issues, such ideals could conceivably remain without institutional embodiment, always and ever aspiring and never becoming embodied or institutionalized.

Nevertheless, within the common conceptual nomenclature of our culture these two kinds of concepts are constantly being confused. Without defining precisely the grounds on which they differ, "conservatives" and "liberals" constantly and perennially talk past each other. They are commonly seen to be inherently at odds. But, unless clarifications are made about what it is conservatives actually wish to conserve and what exactly liberals wish to keep or make "free" (or "liberated"), confusions multiply and Babel is rebuilt. One occasionally finds that conservatives are actually more liberal than those who, in the name of liberalism, wish to exchange what actually exists for something more authoritarian and autocratic. Of course, liberals will often piously claim that they do this "for greater equality between men" or "for the good of the common man"–who is helpless and cannot do for himself what he needs. On the other hand, conservatives are often heedless of how much so-called "liberty for all" becomes unrestrained liberty for a few to the detriment of the liberty of many and how much such liberty under law may undermine that "equality" between people within a society which is so necessary to their liberty.

Therefore, when we say that revivalist movements have been radical in a particular way, we often mean that such movements have not only been '"anti-conservative" but that they have also been radical in a special direction. That is, they have been "radical-in-reverse" or "reactionary." They have sought to "recreate" something which once was thought to be but which, in actuality, never existed. Moreover, if "*romantic*" (as distinct from but very similar to "*utopian*"), they have actually sought for something which can never be, something chimeric from a golden age. To be reactionary, in other words, is to be radical backwards. Such radicalism is sometimes also confused with conservatism. Any attempt to alter profoundly the *status quo* is inherently anti-conservative. Going backwards to" *the* roots;" backwards to the rediscovery of what once was; backwards to the recapturing or to the trying to recapture past glory; backwards to preserve the sense of what was there before what looks dangerous appeared; backwards to the time before some present sense of danger or threats to security came into existence: that is fundamentalism. That is what "Going back to Fundamentals!!" means. It can be, and usually is, extremely radical (or reactionary, as the case may be).

Curiously and paradoxically, fundamentalists are invariably doctrinaire and, as such, altogether uncompromising. Fundamentals of doctrine will admit no contradiction, no qualification of "*the Truth*," no betrayal of the essentials, and no compromise with "*the enemy*." This characteristic, in one way or another, can make fundamentalists "anti-intellectual -and- even anti-political, often to the point of self-destruction.

A typology of conversion movements suggests that, although there are many kinds of fundamentalist and revivalist movements, all such movements are, at least in some measure, connected to some sort of "reconversion" or to some sense of "radical reconversion." In other words, fundamentalist movements are almost invariably revivalistic. Many such movements, moreover, seem to have been highly contagious. They have been of such a nature that, regardless of the actual content or internal quality of any given movement, they have always tended to ignite or provoke further movements either proliferating or reticulating out of the original movement or reacting to it.

Following this logic, it is further suggested that many such movements of radical conversion, revivalist reconversion, and fundamentalism have produced phenomena and have drawn upon concepts which, by and large, might be traced to some common historical root. Many of them, indeed, can be seen to have been affected, in one way or another, by a contagiously "prophetic" tradition of radical conversion movements, the roots of which go all the way back into the ancient Middle East-back to what, for want of better metaphor, might be called "the seed of Abraham." By this line of argument, connections by means of some sort of cultural contact can be traced among sub-sub-branches and sub-branches and branches and so forth, which can be seen to stem from this one root. In modern times, such prophetic movements could be divided into .two categories—those which have been theistic and those which have been non-theistic (even anti-theistic). If one goes back far enough, they all hark back to prior Judaistic, Christian, and Islamic kinds of theistic models, together with all of their manifold offshoots, both orthodox and heterodox. These offshoots, in more modern times, then developed non-theistic counterparts–most notably, different kinds of nationalisms, socialisms, and Marxisms (not to mention certain kinds of "scientisms"). From the Law (Truth) of Moses down to the Law of Marx, one might suggest, there have been movements which, in one way or another, are connected to each other by contagious chains of causal reaction. Each of these variant forms has been capable in turn of generating its own intrinsically unique kinds of revivalism and fundamentalism.

Given the preceding epistemological framework, more specific observations can be made about the four studies of fundamentalism and revivalism in South Asia which follow:

First, there may be some overlap or confusion between what are essentially reformist movements and what are revivalist. While one may not wish to quibble, there is a difference between completely and radically re-creating something anew and merely reasserting, recapturing, re-defining, rediscovering, or even revivifying something from out of a forgotten past. What, for example, was the "Hinduism" which emerged into self-consciousness and generated an All-India identity during the nineteenth century? Was it the awakening of something old? Or, was it perhaps the creation of something altogether new, albeit out of ancient materials? If the latter, was it radically new in reaction to other radical movements which had become so powerful during the Victorian Age? Was it a reaction to an aggressive Christian evangelicalism and to mass conversion movements generated therefrom? It might be useful, on such questions, to separate out those elements which have been, in fact, wholly new–new ideas and techniques taken out of (or used as backfires to counter) radical conversion movements–from those which were, in fact, reformist attempts to Recapture vital elements taken out of an older, long forgotten (or lost) past. Not as extreme as "revive, "the term "reform" denotes a mending process or a restoring to previous form elements which were once a part thereof. A reformation need not be revlvalistic; it need only be restorative and melliorative.

Occasionally both reformist and revivalist features might be found in a socio-religious movement. More often, the two become one and the same when that which is being "recreated" from the past (and thus reactionary) is just as radical as that which is being made entirely from scratch and hence truly and entirely "new. Revivalists will often say that they are bringing back what once existed; but in fact they too may be creating something which is as altogether new as what Utopian radicals claim they are trying to create.

In other words, there are plenty of grounds for considering that what emerged in India during the late eigheenth to the twentieth centuries under the label of "Hinduism" was, in fact, the emergence of an almost entirely new religious system within the context of indigenous cultures, a religion the likes of which India had never before seen. Moreover, it was this new and "syndicated" kind of religion, this phenomenon now so loosely and vaguely lumped together and called "Hinduism" which, by borrowing much from the prophetic and radical conversionist traditions, became radical, revivalist, and eventually, even fundamentalistic in ways hitherto unknown. Perhaps the earliest glimmerings of what may be called "Hindu fundamentalism" are those which were stimulated by fundamentalistic missionaries at Serempore It is this kind of phenomena, as epitomized in such terms as "Arya Dharma" and "Sanatana Dharma" and as organized by such fundamentalist movements and parties as the Vibuti Sangama, the Arya Samaja, the Nagari Pracharini Sabha, the Hindu Mahasabha, and the Rashtriya Swayamsevak Sangh (RSS), and the Jana Sangh, which Kenneth Jones has so brilliantly brought to light. In similar fashion, the explosive new forms of Buddhism, Sikhism, and Islam which have arisen in South Asia–as characterized respectively by de Silva, Wallace, and Ahmed and as epitomized in such revitalized agencies as the *Buddha Sasana* for some Sinhalese, the *Singh Sabha* for some Sikhs, and the *Jama'at-i-Islami* for certain Muslims of Pakistan--have all had varying shades of extremist fundamentalism within them.

Second, there is the issue of that hoary and now rather shopworn historiography on the denigration of "Hinduism" which is charged against Europeans. Tins kind of caricature, as found at the beginning of Jones' essay (and often parroted in much of the literature), may not only be less than fully accurate or complete but, indeed, may also be all too simplistic. It is important to note, in this connection, that during the eighteenth century few of the gentry among "Hindus" or "Native Indians" or "Indians" (or "East Indians") were uniformly looked down upon by the British, certainly not in the same way as would later occur more generally by the middle of the nineteenth century. Indeed, the term "Hindu" often meant "Indian" and, for a while (as sometimes even now), the terms were virtually synonymous. Nathaniel Halhed and William Jones, not to mention their mentor (Warren Hastings who was Governor-General), were frank and open admirers of cultures which they found in India.

Fascinated by the complexities of this ancient and high civilization and anxious to learn more, these servants o the Company were the founders of Oriental studies, Orientalism, and the whole ethos of the Asiatic Society of Bengal. The climate of discovery, excitement, and wide-eyed wonder at what they found never disappeared–nor, for some, has it yet. Thereafter, there have always remained a coterie of admiring, even wonderstruck Europeans (and Americans) who, to this day, have devoted themselves to learning more about "Hindu" India. Rarely if ever defined with precision, the concept "Hindu" is applied vaguely to cultures, peoples, and religions of India which are neither Muslim, Christian, nor Judaic–yet, even this consistency breaks down because references to "Hindu" Christians, "Hindu" Muslims, and such abound in early writings. Many of the early nationalist leaders, indeed, first gained their knowledge of the cultural heritage of their own civilization from these fascinated Europeans. Gandhi, Nehru, and many others read their Hindu classics in the English translations of such scholars as Max Mueller and Edwin Arnold. The ironies of this circumstance did not escape the notice of many among the more perceptive nationalists.

Thus, to dwell too exclusively upon the position that Europeans had a denigrating view of Hindu culture-seeing India as hopelessly if not totally degenerate and depraved–without indicating that there was also a strong opposite tendency among Europeans, is to miss the whole picture. There is a danger, in consequence, of grossly oversimplifying and even distorting that picture. How representative of European views these different kinds of expression and influence were is a subject which scholars have yet to address adequately. Indeed, the very idea that the "Hindu degeneracy" view was really a reaction to Hindu India by only two forces, however accurate this idea may be, *as far as it goes*, is also too simple. Utilitarianism and Evangelicalism certainly were two streams of influence which were flowing out to India from Britain during the nineteenth century. But by the time this reaction took place among Europeans, some sort of a Company raj–first a micro-raj and then a macro-raj of imperial dimensions–had already been in place for over a century. Moreover, by the third decade of the nineteenth century, the Company's larger imperium had itself been established for several generations.

Inherent contradictions in justifications for the existence of the Raj were certainly manifold. For example, some of those who were later to use the "civilizing" ("Hindu" degradation and European moral-superiority) argument were among those pamphleteers of the Anti-Idolatry Connexion League (c.1833-1845 A.D.) who attacked the Indian Empire precisely because of the excessively "Hindu" and "Heathen" (and hence, by implication also "corrupted") character of the British Raj. These pamphleteers saw the Company's Raj itself as a "Heathen" empire. In this, they were merely responding to their own belated discovery of such things, as Madras Regulation VII of 1817, which put the care of all religious institutions under Government What business did the British Nation have, they asked, in helping the Company to construct and maintain an empire which was so completely pagan and idolatrous and, hence, so diabolically evil? Why should those of the Company's civil and military officers who were Christians (even if only a minority) be obliged, against their own private consciences, to attend and serve temple ceremonies, rituals, and festivals (pujas, abhlishekams, melas, tirnals, and such)? During the 1830s and early 1840s, the Anti-Idolatry Connnexion League sent petition after petition and lobbied members of the British Government. Their purpose was to force the Company into disassociating itself, its Raj, and its local governments in India from having any connection with "Heathen" worship and into ending all maintenance of Hindu temples by the Company's officials. They demanded a complete separation of the Company's ruler-ship from indigenous religion. Yet, these same pamphlets never advocated complete removal of Western missionaries, any prohibition of their proselytizing activities, nor any cessation of other forms of interference and meddling with indigenous religious institutions in India.

The Company's Raj had, in fact, always been deeply involved and could never have extricated itself from such involvement (Frykcnberg 1979). Indeed, recent research indicates that there may have been a pro-Hindu Raj or a Hindu-exalting phase long before there was an anti-Hindu campaign or a Hindu-denigrating historiography. The issue certainly requires much more investigation, more sophisticated questions, and a thorough revision.

The same kinds of questions also need to be addressed to the interactions of religion and state in Sri Lanka. Admittedly complex in ways entirely different from conditions in the subcontinent itself, there are nevertheless some factors relating to the very logic of power on the island which might have required certain kinds of responses from any regime, whether Sinhalese, Tamil, Portuguese. Dutch, or

British. Furthermore, the very fact that, at least initially, it was the Company rather than the Colonial Office which succeeded to rulerships over Sri Lanka prompts us to enquire whether initial policies with respect to indigenous religious institutions may not have been similar to those of the Madras Presidency. If so, then what are called "Buddhist temporalities" would have enjoyed much more state support than now supposed and what identity there may have been between Christianity and the state would have been minimal, if not initially hostile. The East India Company itself, it should be recalled, remained implacably opposed and profoundly suspicious of all alien missionary activities within its domains, even after admission of such agencies was imposed upon its Raj by Parliament as a price for the Charter renewal of 1813.

Likewise, therefore, our assessments of European missionary activities and attitudes must be no less exacting and free from reductionistic or simplistic elements. One must look carefully at the programs and styles of both Catholic and Protestant misionaries who had" been working in India long-before" the-ar rival of the British"(and American) evangelicals. Those groups which had been active in India long *before* the arrival of European evangelicals and reformers of the early nineteenth century and long *before* the Indian reformers who worked with these late arriving Europeans (e.g. Raja "Ram Mohan Roy and others) were still in India". Danish-German pietists, for example, seem to have been rather more irenic and intellectual in their missionary enterprises, more sensitive to existing social sensibilities. Their work emphasized a more contextuahzing and indigenizing approach to local institutions. In their day, such concepts as "Hinduism" or "Indian" had not yet been coined; and, even after the words emerged, the concepts were as yet far from clear in value, meaning or content.

Again, the older the Christian communities in various parts of South Asia were and the longer different kinds of missionary agencies had been active in one region or another, whether they were indigenous or alien {European and American) and whether Nestoriau, Syrian ("Mar Thoma"), Catholic, or Protestant, the more complex and compounded were the different kinds of local relationships which developed. While it is certainly true that some peoples of Sri Lanka experienced over four centuries of "colonial" rule and almost as long a period of sometimes aggressive intrusion and expansion by various Christian communities, it is no less true that extreme differences of approach, method, and style between and among some of these Christian communities can be found. In struggles between the Padroado of Goa and the Propaganda Fides of Rome, as now revealed in recent research (Boudens 1978), there were far greater resonances of Sinhalese and Tamil cultures with the Catholicism of South India than with that of Europe. And the brilliant and cogent analysis of the place of one Christian caste, the Paravas, on both sides of the Palk Straits as well as in the Gulf of Mannar shows us something altogether new and far more complex. Instead of the simplistic old story of conquest and imposition by an alien civilization, fresh elements were introduced into an already intricate mosaic of reciprocities, with participants rather than conquerors rendering services and receiving benefits. In short, in neither India nor Sri Lanka can elements of "Christian" culture be studied either exclusively or merely as "alien" imports.

Third, studies of fundamentalism and revivalism in this volume suggest something which Rothermund (1965) has labelled the "differential impacts" of the Raj. Impacts upon India by elements from various European movements cannot be lumped together but must be chronologically and geographically differentiated. Different movements coming out of Europe, coining at different times, or taking root or growing up within different parts of South Asia, either simultaneously or at different times, not unnaturally produced very different consequences. All movements were not equally radical, either in their origins or in their impacts. Movements which began in the seventeenth or early eighteenth centuries and which germinated slowly and developed gradually did not have effects which were as radical or disruptive as movements which arrived much later and which struck much more suddenly and much more disturbingly. Older movements may even, in fact, have generated strongly conservative and indigenous features.

In short, we must ask to what degree we are talking about parallel or synchronic processes, to what degree we are dealing with non-synchronic or sequential processes. We must discover in what measure we arc concerned with processes the impact of which can be seen to have been, both in qualitative or quantitative terms, "differential." To what degree are we talking about the impact of events which were prior in Europe or prior in India? To what degree were processes and their impacts almost being felt both in India and in the West simultaneously? How synchronized or dissynchronized were impacts of the same movement in India and other parts of the world?

For example, the Great Awakening in America, the Evangelical Awakening in England, and the Tranquebar Mission in Tanjore and Tinnevelly were closely parallel and simultaneous events, with all three having origins which can be traced back to Herrenhut, Halle University, and influences of the Moravian diaspora. Likewise, what happened in Punjab was very different in its impact from what had happened earlier in the original "down country" presidencies. The late arrival of the Raj in Punjab, from 1846 onwards, was very sudden. It came all at once, all in a rush, and all in its most radical forms. Moreover, it was accompanied by the entire panoply of the Company's huge Imperial system, with its extensive entourage. As such, it was a Bengali-British phenomenon, a cumulative system which had taken two centuries to develop before it struck Punjab. This system included, in addition to the tiny elite of British mandarins, hosts of Bengali bureaucrats and civil servants, along with hosts of sepoys from various parts of India; the latest and most recent technologies of the West; and the latest and the most radical manifestations of British (Anglo-Saxon or European) culture. Such an arrival– with roads, bridges, canals, postal and telegraph services, railways, schools, and much more–was bound to be profoundly disruptive to local institutions and disturbing to local elites. More disturbing still was the policy victory of John Lawrence over his brother, Henry. Henceforth, measures aimed at social "levelling" would prevail over more cautious attempts to work with the old aristocracies of Punjab, thereby removing that buffering of cultural and social cement between the different communities by a modicum of domestic tranquillity which had been secured under previous dynasties. In such circumstances, one can begin to imagine how severe and sudden the impacts of changes upon the entire social fabric of Punjab have been. Perhaps in no other part of South Asia were impacts of sudden change so drastic. And, once the aristocratic culture was removed, or at least weakened, certainly no other region in South Asia possessed such an explosive combination of fundamentalist communities and movements.

Thus, when we look at what Kneneth Jones has learned about the radical impacts of Western culture upon "Hundu" (Non- Muslims and Non-Sikhs of high caste) in the Punjab or when we look at what Mumtaz Ahmad and Paul Wallace tell us about those same impacts upon Muslims and Sikhs, it is not difficult to understand how each scholar has come to his position. To repeat, in the Punjab, the Raj and Western influences came all at once and all in a rush, and all in their most radical and sometimes most rank forms. Some of these ingredients were often not just imperialistic but blatantly "colonialistic" in a classic sense. In Punjab were what in the Bible Belt of America would be considered "redneck" preachers railing against degenerate "heathen" and "native" customs, arousing antagonism and controversy by the very confrontational manner in which they assailed their adversaries.

By that time, meanwhile, the influences of Western culture in Bengal were nearly two centuries old and had been pervading the countryside slowly and steadily for much of that time. Bengal had already been the very heart of the Raj for a century; and Bengalis had long collaborated with Britons in the cumulative building of a common Indo-British civilization. If this were the case for Bengal, it was even more so for the upper caste gentry of Madras where mutual collaboration had been profound from the very beginning. Even for Bombay Island, where its previous history as a Portuguese enclave and overwhelming Maratha power had produced a kind of defensive isolation, there had been a long and slow incubation before the Company's Raj gained its final paramountcy in 1818. Thus, the original growth of the Company's first city-states had been cautious and slow: the micro-raj at Madras which began in 1639; that of Bombay which began in 1661; and that of Calcutta which began in 1692. And slow also had been the early impact of the Danish-Halle-SPCK missionary enterprises at Tranquebar and Thanjavuru (Tanjore) which began in 1706. The impacts of ventures which grew gradually and which drew substantially upon indigenous manpower and partnerships for their successes, were not as disruptive as the impacts of what happened in Punjab. It is no wonder, under the circumstances, that Punjab became and has remained such a seething caldron.

Buddhist Revivalism in Sri Lanka, while it parallels what happened elsewhere in South Asia, is in many ways quite obviously different and unique. Yet many ot the observations made about the clashes of antagonistic fundamentalisms in the Punjab (Christian, Hindu, Muslim, and Sikh) can be applied with equal validity to what K. M. de Silva has described as clashing fundamentalisms in Sri Lanka. The successive phases of Buddhist-Christian confrontation have been revealed in rich detail. Yet, as, in the case of India, we cannot too easily jump to hasty conclusions about the nature of the connections between British rule and religious institutions. Special relationships there may have been with each religious community, but whether these were nearly as monolithic as one might first assume seems far from clear.

If anything, one is forced by what we have learned to ask whether the rulers of Sri Lanka did not face some of the same kinds of dilemmas or experience some of the same kinds of inner contradictions which one finds within the subcontinent. The long-established linkage between state and religion which had existed before the arrival of European power and the continuance of this linkage by the Portuguese, the Dutch, and the early British (Company) finds its parallels in India.

The explosive blending of Buddhist revivalism with Sinhalese nationalism has produced a religious nationalism which is clearly fundainentahstic. In some sense, when people undergo radical reconversion to "*The Truth*" insomuch that they see themselves ' *The Select*" whose destiny it is to achieve "*The New (or Perfect) Order on Earth,*" when people perceive that there is threat to what they hold most dear and most basic, and when people are prepared to die before they give up "fundamentals," essentials from which they will not budge, then a situation occurs in which violent struggle and martyrdom arc not only acceptable but mandatory and sacred. Incarnate evil may then be identified as consisting of all alien elements, whether Colonial rulers, Non-Buddhist (Burgher, Christian, Muslim, or Hindu) communities, or secessionist Tamil (Eelam) Tigers, together with the cultures which they represent. Attainment of an ideal "Pure Land" may then require a drastic cleansing and scrubbing away of all impure remnants, at whatever cost. Such feelings explain how monks, feeling betrayed by Bandaranayake, could resort to assassination and how military forces can turn upon the entire population of Jaffna Tamils.

The necessary logic of power in India is not like that of Pakistan or Sri Lanka. For any larger state, but especially for an All-India political system, whether imperial or national, no single religion, certainly no religion with a fundamentalist ideology, can be afforded. The ancient symbol for state power, the Mahachakra or Great Wheel, was no accident. *Mahachatra* ("Great Parasol" or "Great Umbrella") for State Authority, *Chatrapati* ["Lord of the Parasol (of Authority)"] and *Chakavartin* ("World-Conqueror"), are symbolic variants of this basic logic Without giving balanced and equal tension or–treatment to each of the many (thousand) spokes of social diversity, how could the peripheral rim of many peoples and religions he bonded to the hub of central power? If one were to favor any one revivalist movement to the exclusion of others, whether Hindu or Sikh, Christian or Muslim, the state itself would find itself in dire trouble. The very notion that there can be a Khalistan, or a Pakistan, or even a "Hindustan," lor that matter, becomes, by this logic, altogether intolerable. Yielding to such a notion opens a Pandora's Box of "fissiparous tendencies." By this logic, there never could be any such thing as a "majority community." The very nursing of such a notion is profoundly dangerous.

Yet, within India itself, Sikhism has generated all of those ingredients which are so essential in a revivalistic fundamentalist movement. Elements of radical reconversion to a fundamentalist ideology–namely, *the* Truth, *the* Prophet(s) or Messengers (who are Instruments) for carrying this Truth, *the* (Chosen, or Select) People, the (Promised, or Sacred) Land, the Locus of (Sacred and Central) Authority (within the Akal Takht of the Golden Temple in Amritsar), and *the* (Utopian) Ideal Solution of Khalistan (as a completely independent Sikh State)-arc all present. Thus, when one looks at the struggle which developed between the Akali Dal under Longowaland the militantly extremist forces of the Damdani Taksal led by Bhindranwale, it becomes clear that all of the established lines of external (state) authority were perceived as having failed. Having endangered the Sikh *panth* by falling away from *the Truth* as defined by the fundamentalists and having betrayed the Sikh community, all established Sikhs institutions-such as the Akali Dal and its dissident branches, the SGPC (Shiromam Gurdwara Prabandhak Committee), and the High Priests–became stigmatized as the enemy within. For fundamentalists there has got to be both *the enemy within and the enemy without* which together are hindering fulfillment of that destiny, that ultimate arrival in "the promised land" which alone can usher in the expected millennial Utopia. All apostates, like dirt, must be scrubbed away if the true faith is to be purified and made worthy of its destiny.

Thus, as *all* authority systems in Punjab began to break down after 1978, one might well ask for greater specificity. What authority systems were breaking? Did the commitment of many peoples from many religious to a larger Common Wheel with many spokes leading to its hub begin to crumble? Was such a commitment replaced by commitment to smaller wheels which might be defined in narrower and more fundamtntalistic terms, whether Hindu or Sikh? Had the great Humpty Dumpty now and forever fallen, never to be put together again? Notwithstanding Operation liluestar, communal riots, and the assassinations of Indira Gandhi, Sant Longowal and others, attempts to repair and restore the balanced .spokes of the *Mahachakra* in Punjab have not ceased. The fires of extreme fundamentalism, both Hindu and Sikh, have yet to be quenched, or even (as of this writing) brought under control. This crisis, requiring astute management and extreme restraint at o the Centre, through the assuaging of fears and the granting of concessions, is still far from over. Neither Barnala nor Rajiv's ministers have found ways to gain control.

As for the position of Islam in South Asia, there remains a continuous if not chronic tension between the Islam of India and the Islam of Pakistan. The more successfully that India can manage to assuage the fears of various Muslim communities within its borders, the more it can find ways to provide security and satisfaction for its Muslims, the more India remains as a standing threat to Pakistan and all that Pakistan stands for. On the other hand, the more successfully that Pakistan, with its prophetic religion and its military rulership, can combine fundamentalism with economic security and social tranquillity, the more its continuance and strength can pose a threat to India. This is both the dilemma and the irony. The stability and strength of either serves, by that very fact, to threaten the other. India with its ideal of secularistic anti-fundamentalism and Pakistan with its ideal of religious fundamentalism are, by their very natures, at war with each other. Yet, further compounding this irony, is the fact that India itself, quite apart from Bangladesh, holds more Muslims than Pakistan. Moreover, India's Muslims not only have grounds to consider that they possess the strongest Islamic institutions of South Asia (i.e. Deoband as well as Aligarh) but also grounds to feel that Pakistan was founded by modernistic and apostate "winebibbers and porkeaters" who were anything but devout. ("When we Muslims first came into India a thousand years ago,"-goes the argument, "we were but few. Look how God has increased our numbers! Is God still not Great?")

Finally, there is the vexing and mischievous issue which keeps rising to the surface in almost every confrontation and in almost every debate: the issue of *majority* as against *minority*. Perhaps no single concept during the past century has done as much damage to political stability in South Asia as the concept of "majority." Surjit Mansingh, while far from the first to emphasize the essentials of the central fact which underlies this crucially important point, puts it aptly. In her words, "It is clear from recorded history that *no single group became all-engulfing in number, or unformly dominant in power, either throughout South Asia, or in constituent elements of it*" (emphasis added; sec chapter below). In other words, no country nor region of South Asia has ever had a "majority" as such. Neither in terms of caste, community, ethnicity, or religious identity, has there been such a thing as a "majority."

The cogency of this crucial factor can be argued and demonstrated in a number of ways. One can look at the sense of being a beleaguered "minority" which, according to Kenneth Jones afflicted the high caste leaders of the "Hindu" revivalists of North India during the 19th century. Nor were such feelings confined merely to the Punjab. There is hardly any region in the subcontinent in which "Hindus," as they defined themselves before Gandhi attempted to co-opt or incorporate all Untouchable communities into the "Hindu" fold, represented a cohesive or clearly identifiable "majority" community. Perhaps no study has done more to show the sinister implications of this notion than that produced by Saraswati (1974); *Minorities in Madras State* effectively destroyed the historical validity of "majority" as anything but a mischievous, if inadvertent, invention of modern times. It demonstrates that, within a highly complex socio-political mosaic of "minorities"-where there had never ever been anything but minorities but where some elite minorities had always succeeded in dominating the rest, albeit under circumstances which minimized polluting contact (whether in streets, temples, or anywhere else) and where devices for control had necessarily had to be more discontinuous than direct–the conjuring up of this concept can be seen as nothing more than another attempt by one elite minority or coalitions of elite minorities to dominate all others. In this connection, the profound *"discontinuities"* between castes and communities of the incredibly fractured and pluralistic and segmented populations of each region had, until modern times, prevented both the formation and the mobilization of "majorities" among them.

Socio-Religious Movements of Hindus of British India

Central to these efforts to reconstruct society was a series of changes in the social position and role of women. Movement after movement pointed to the inferior status of women and called for a dramatic transformation in their condition. "The crusade for emancipation of Indian women became the first tenet of the social reform movement everywhere in India". In the past, historians have Accepted the central role of women's "emancipation" as an obvious and dramatic example of nineteenth century progress. It has been pointed to with pride and satisfaction by Hindu leaders as clear evidence of the regeneration of society and of its march toward "modernity." It is the intention of this study to re-examine social change in the nineteenth century as it related to the role of Hindu women. It will focus on two aspects of this process of change: first, the degree of actual change achieved; and, second, the motivations behind such changes. More questions will be raised than answered, but it is hoped that a new understanding will result along with a different and more sophisticated dialogue on the nature of social change during this century.

Religious ferment among Bengali Hindus started with Ram Mohan Roy in the nineteenth century. As did later religious leaders, he considered contemporary Hinduism to be degenerate, filled with superstition and errors. He used this critical stance to justify the rejection of a wide range of Hindu beliefs: idolatry. Brahmin priests, elaborate rituals, polytheism, numerous established customs, and female deities. Roy maintained that the worship of Kali and Tantric Hinduism encouraged immorality and debauchery through "human sacrifice, the use of wine, criminal intercourse, and licentious songs....". Roy's message was a strongly puritanical one that asked for a purging of social sin and a restructuring of social behaviour.

Many of the elements Roy condemned directly affected the treatment of Hindu women. The custom against which Roy fought the hardest with dramatic personal conviction was sati, the immolation of widows on their husbands1 funeral pyres. In 1829, after years of agitation, Roy and his Hindu and resident English allies succeeded in persuading the government to outlaw sati which became a criminal offense and was treated as a form of murder. Roy also spoke against polygamy and child-marriage. He favored education for women, but did not define its extent, and little was done prior to his death in 1833.

Roy described the source of the secondary status of women as arising from their physical characteristics. "Women are in general inferior to men in bodily strength and energy; consequently the male part of the community, taking advantage of their corporeal weakness, have denied to them those excellent merits that they are entitled to by nature, and afterwards they are apt to say that women are naturally incapable of acquiring those merits". The writings and work of Ram Mohan Roy became the . basis for later Brahmo Samaj attempts to restructure the social role of women. He instigated a wide ranging debate over the value of education for women, women's status, child marriage, and widow remarriage among the upper castes. This debate, however, was conducted by men and the prime subjects of this controversy remained largely excluded. Actual change was slow to take place. Rhetoric rather than action dominated during the first half of the nineteenth century.

By the 1850s and 1860s, a more radical activism entered the Brahmo Samaj as a new generation of young, educated Bengalis began to aspire to leadership in the Brahmo Samaj. The rise of a social radicalism was centered on the figure of Keshab Chandra Sen, who joined the Samaj in 1857. Sen was a Vaidya, a member of the doctor caste, and thus lower in status than the Brahmins who had provided leadership in the movement until then. He demonstrated a willingness to attack social beliefs and to strive openly for greater women's equality. In 1860, Sen founded the Sangat Sabha, a subdivision within the Samaj, composed of individuals who pledged to put their religious ideology into action. One of their concerns was the encouragement of women's education. In 1863, a group of Sen's disciples organized the Bamabodhini Sabha and it in turn published the *Bamabodhini Patrika*, a women's journal with a greater circulation than any other. In 1865, another organization was established, one dedicated to "female improvement," the Brahmika Samaj (Brahmo Ladies Prayer Meeting), a society intended only for Brahmo women. This was a radical step and produced immediate opposition from orthodox Hindus even to the extent that Brahmo supporters found themselves excommunicated by their orthodox relatives. In 1862, K. C. Sen had faced similar reactions in his attempt to break the tradition of seclusion by taking his wife with him to the home of Debendranath Tagore.

The issues of "female emancipation" and "improvement" covered a variety of social practices. Emancipation meant an end to *purdah*, the exclusion of women from public life and their seclusion in a section of the family home. Improvement included a wide variety of efforts to educate women, change marriage customs, and expand the sphere of acceptable activity for women. In 1864, Sen and fellow radicals dared to celebrate an inter-caste marriage that was also a widow remarriage. This action shocked orthodox Hindus and older members of the Samaj (*ibidem*: 151-152). By the 1870s, issues of female emancipation divided many of the Brahmos into radical and moderate members, as one issue after another arose, was debated, and then transformed into organizational policy. In 1872, Durga Mohun Das, one of the younger Brahmos, demanded that women be allowed to sit with their families in the weekly services. Previously all women had remained behind a screen so that *purdah* was maintained. After considerable heated debate Sen allowed women of the "advanced" families to sit with their relatives Similar issues flared up and on occasion died down with little aftereffect. In 1856, champions of change led by Pandit Vidyasagar had won a victory with the passage of the Widow Remarriage Bill, but enthusiasm for this cause then waned and few such marriages were actually performed. The education of women, however, remained a concern for Brahmos throughout the latter half of the nineteenth century.

Although Ram Mohun Roy had advocated educating girls, little was done by the Brahmos prior to the 1860s. Christian missionaries and a few Hindu proponents of education attempted to establish schools for women. They were frustrated by shortages of trained teachers, appropriate texts, apathy, and hostility. There was considerable confusion about what such education might entail and whether it should mirror the schooling of boys. England provided a ready model for women's education in the nineteenth century. A textbook for girls published in 1849 included needlework, popular in England, but not part of women's culture in India. Brahmo interest in women's education was strengthened after K. C. Sen returned from a trip to England. In February 1870, he founded a Native Ladies' Normal School to train teachers and then added a girls primary school later that same year.

This concern for women s education was also demonstrated by the Sadharan Brahmo Samaj after its formation in 1878. They strongly supported the equality of women and proudly opened a

Brahmo Girls School complete with a boarding house as a concrete expression of their ideals. The Victoria Girls School, founded by Keshab Chandra Sen, did not seek equality, but taught a domestic arts curriculum described in a statement by the school administrators:

> *With a view to avoid masculine training and meet the special requirements and develop the softer susceptibilities of the female mind, special subjects were included in the curriculum besides the ordinary course of studies, such as domestic economy; drawing, music, cookery, needlework, and laws of health.*

The Adi Samaj, the conservative wing of the Brahmo movement, carefully advocated an "education for intelligent wifely companionship and motherhood" By the last decade of the century, women's education had gained sufficient acceptance that the orthodox leaders of HIindu society established their own school, the Mahakali Pathsala, opened in 1893. Debates then turned to whether women should be educated at the collegiate level or whether this was inappropriate for them and would lessen their effectiveness as wives and mothers. By the end of the century, literate Hindus had accepted primary education for women. A small group of women were educated to an advanced standard and a few had even achieved a degree of economic independence.

As the first of the nineteenth century Hindu social reform movements, the Brahmo Samaj articulated an ideology of social change in female gender roles as a major part of its vision of a purified and rationalized Hinduism. These "reforms" included a number of issues: sati, widow remarriage, education of women, the custom of child marriage, inter-caste marriages, and the removal of immoral religious and social customs. These issues were not limited to either Bengal or the Brahmo Samaj, but concerned a variety of movements and individuals throughout the subcontinent. An examination of other struggles to change social behavior will provide a clearer understanding of the "motivation behind these attempts to restructure the role of women in Hindu society. The two customs that received the earliest and most vigorous attention were sati and female infanticide. They were the first to be outlawed and thus transformed into criminal acts rather than questions of social custom.

After conquering a new territory British officials and missionaries attempted to end the practice of female infanticide. In these campaigns they sought and generally received the active support of religious and secular leaders. In Gujarat during the early

1800s, Sahajanand Swami, founder of the Swami Naryana Sampradaya, rejected decadent Hinduism, including religious rituals that contained elements of sexual practices, superstition, magic, self-torture, and elaborate rituals. His was a puritanical ideology that also attacked all forms of immoral and improper behaviour. Sahajanand Swami condemned adultery, the use of bawdy songs at marriage celebrations, and the lewd customs of Holi. He banned the use of alcohol and drugs instructing his disciples to follow a life of discipline and purity. To Sahajanand, the Hindu worshippers of the Shakti cults and the mother goddesses represented the worst elements of Hinduism, elements which should be purged. He attacked the worship of tribal deities and condemned infanticide and sati, which he considered to be errors within Hinduism.

The initial concern over sati and infanticide did not lead to the advocacy of further changes in the social position of women. Instead, Sahajanand Swami articulated a return to the traditional role of women as subservient to their husbands and subject to the rules of purdah. He stressed the necessity of separating women during all rituals and created temples solely for his female followers. He warned his male ascetics to refrain from seeing or even thinking of a woman. Should they touch one, they were required to fast on the day of their transgression. Within this socio-religious movement then there were two distinct trends in regard to women's role in society: first, a concern for sati, female infanticide, and the plight of widows; and, secondly, a reinforcement of the traditional role of women including the institution of purdah. There–were no further "reforms" in regards to women. The reasons for this pattern may well result from Sahajanand's contacts with English officials and missionaries who opposed sati and female infanticide.

A similar pattern of interaction between the English and local leaders was manifest in the Punjab where, in 1853, a large gathering was assembled in Amritsar at the instigation of British officials. This gathering included local chieftains, landlords, merchants, and representatives of the ruling Punjabi families. It was dedicated to the eradication of female infanticide and to limiting both the cost of dowries and general marriage expense. Other meetings took place throughout the province and resulted in tracts and pamphlets on the custom of infanticide and the need to limit dowries.

In Gujarat and Punjab the British publicly condemned sati and infanticide. In the Punjab this was done as part of government policy with the result that these customs became an acute embarrassment to Hindu leaders. A willingness to attack these customs publicly offered an opportunity to gain approval from the English. Other "reform" issues also won similar positive reactions from the new rulers of South Asia; however, this was only one of several possible reasons for advocating change in the role of women. The question of education stemmed from a wider variety of motivations, as was to be demonstrated by leaders of the Arya Samaj, a reform and revival movement centered in Punjab.

Founded in 1875, the Arya Samaj championed women's education. As with many of the socio-religious movements of the nineteenth century, its followers were expected to find the proper forms of belief and behaviour from scriptural sources. If unable to read the scriptures themselves, they should turn to the literature written by leaders of the movement. Thus, literacy was a necessity and a religious virtue. All Aryas should be literate, but in practice Aryas focused on the education of males through the creation of the Dayananda Anglo-Vedic (D.A.V.) College and its associated schools. The earliest and for some years the only girls school was located in Ferozepore as an adjunct of the Arya Samaj orphange founded in 1877. The drive for expanded education of girls began in December 1890 with the establishment of the Arya Kanya Pathshala of Jullundur. This was an elementary school that taught basic literacy and some general knowledge along with "sewing,, stitching, drawing, doing of Havan and singing of Bhajans" Leadership in the field of women's education rested with two Aryas: Lala Dev Raj, for whom this became a personal crusade; and Lala Munshi Ram, a dynamic exponent of radical Aryanism who later became President of the Jullundur Arya Samaj.

Munshi Ram moved quickly to gather support and won other Aryas to his cause with the result' that they founded the Pathshala. This school in turn evolved into the Kanya Mahavidyalaya, a girls high school, opened in 1896. The attempt to provide more advanced education for women met with stiff resistance from the Hindu community in general and from the Aryas who were involved in the D.A.-V. schools. They claimed that such education was unnecessary and feared competition for the limited resources available within the Hindu community. The Aryas who advocated women's education did so on the grounds that "a country can never rise high without giving high education to its women. No reform can be brought in any field without bringing reforms in your women." The arguments that swirled around this new education discussed what was, in fact, a rather limited form of schooling. "In addition to basic literacy, the girls learned sewing, embroidery, drawing, cooking, some music, poetry, games, arithmetic, hygiene, and the religious literature of the Samaj. The Kanya Mahavidyalaya was at most a parochial finishing school designed to provide wives with a minimum academic education and a set of social and homemaking skills.

Education was not intended to prepare girls for careers outside the home or to an independent existence except in one area, namely, teaching. All efforts to open girls schools collided with an almost total lack of teachers. Since women were uneducated, they could not teach; and given the social taboos of Hindu society, men could not teach young girls. The Kanya Mahavidyalaya became a source for new teachers who began their own schools. Thus a respectable profession for women, perhaps the sole such profession in the Punjab of the nineteenth century, grew out of the movement for women's education. A majority of those studying to be teachers were widows, women who remained longer in school and who were free to accept a career Girls of tenleft school at young ages, usually when they were called upon to fulfill the role of wife and mother.

By the end of the nineteenth century, the education of young women was just beginning to affect the literate classes of Punjabi Hindus and had also established a new female role, that of teacher. A teaching career provided a few widows with dignified positions in Hindu society. The Arya Samaj then demonstrated the importance of communal defense against Christian missionaries as an initial driving force behind efforts to educate girls. There was, however, another set of motivational forces that stimulated efforts at social reconstruction. These are most tlearly demonstrated through the records of the Amritsar Dharm Sabha.

Under the leadership of Uai Bahadur Bihari Lai, a group of the leading citizens, both Hindus and Sikhs, founded the Amritsar Dharm Sabha and held their first meeting on 30 September 1872. The Sabha was dedicated to "the betterment and cultural uplift of the whole of the Hindu community. . . ." Its purpose was to remove all "evil practices. . . which are opposed to the Shastras and to intelligence, which are in vogue among the Hindus. ..." Although general in its stated aims, the Sabha concentrated on the customs and behavior of women as major problem areas within Hindu society. Munshi Kanhayalal Alakdhari summed up this situation. The women becoming free of all proper and necessary restraints, gave up all their duties, and all initiative was lost. Whoever threatened or flattered them, they became his followers, and they fell at the feet of anybody who was stronger, while they became lions for the weak. Nobody was born with good intentions, and bad ways led to worldliness and license.

One of the first customs attacked by the Sabha was the use of dowries. Alakdhari condemned it, stating that "marriages of girls are performed in exchange of money, which other people call the sale of girls." He claimed that dowries were against the teachings of the *Dharma Shastras* and also a humiliation for the girls involved. His remarks led to a decision by the Sabha to ban all acceptance of money at the tune of marriage and to threaten excommunication of anyone who defied this ban. The Sabha moved on to consider other customs, primarily among women. Extended periods of mourning by women were rejected because they produced a "hellish life" for all the male members of a family. One Brahmin attending this meeting complained that he was 41 years of age and "this mourning was not lifted for a single day and he had not known one day of happiness and had passed all his life in sorrow. ..." The Sabha quickly moved to limit mourning to 17 days; after which women were expected to attend to "all worldly affairs without restraint of any kind." From its concern with marriage and death rites the Sabha moved on to examine questions of social morality.

As did many moral crusades, the Dharm Sabha condemned prostitution, an institution already under attack from the Amritsar Municipal Government. Houses of ill fame had been closed and, in discussing this achievement, the Dharm Sabha demonstrated the reasons for its opposition to prostitution. With a sense of relief, they declared "that during the last four months or so, no respectable woman became a public woman, although formerly about four or five women from respectable families used to become prostitutes in the past every month." Not morality as such, but concern over the status and honor of middle and upperclass families lay behind this campaign against prostitution. A similar motivation led to attempts to end various forms of public nakedness such as the occasions when women bathed at ponds, wells, and along the river banks, and in the process exposed parts of their bodies much as they did in various rituals of public mourning. Also condemned were certain customary festivals at which women sang bawdy and obscene songs.

Firstly, no woman belonging to the Hindu community would bathe naked at any ponds, wells, rivers or canals, but she would take her bath in her own home behind a curtain, and if no such bathroom with curtain be available, then she would take her bath with a chadar or dhoti on her body; secondly, no love songs or obscene words would be uttered by any women at the time of marriages, etc., in marketplaces or streets and lanes, openly or from behind a curtain; thirdly, no women would carry out mourning in market places and tourist resorts etc., with naked heads or breasts; fourthly, the mourning period of three years, practiced at present would now be reduced to seventeen days only, and after that one Jay every six months and one day on the death anniversary of a dead person would be permitted for the performance of religious rites connected with the dead . . ., fifthly, women would not put on shameless dresses, and their dress in the future shall be: first, a ghagra with a wide girth; second, a pyjama under it; third, a kurta; fourth, a dopatta; fifth, a chadar made of long-cloth.

Attempts to control the female members of society led to criticism of the institution of the guru, the initiation of women by a holy man, a rite conducted when one finds a religious preceptor, is given a mantra or sacred verse, and accepts his authority over their life. Clearly the person of a guruprovided a rival and threat to the authority ot a husband over his wife:". . . for a married woman, who has her husband living, her husband is like her guru, according to the Shastras. When any man gets tor his wife a guru mantra from some other person, such a woman becomes a most debauched person." The acceptance of a mantra and the authority of a guru threatened not only to degrade a woman, but to harm her husband. "Any woman who takes a Mantra by herself in the lifetime of her husband reduces the life span of her husband, and ultimately goes to hell." This institution struck partly at family honor but more directly at the power and privileges of the Hindu husband.

More directly related to respectability were three women's festivals, *Katiagats*, *Moh Main*, and *Sada Talla*, which degraded male society and were, as a result, condemned by the Dharm Sabiia. The orthodox leader, Pandit Shraddha Ram Phillouri, described this custom with disgust and sonic degree of apprehension"... during the period of *Kanagats*, the women of one Mohalla, or locality, after putting on their best clothes and jewelry, according to their position and status, collect together as a group and take their stand at any road crossing or other place of importance and start hurling insults and abuses on the women of another Mohalla or area near by and start quarrelling. "The women did not abuse each other, but taunted each other's husbands, parents, or relatives. According to the Pandit this form of public abuse expanded and "now, the situation has become such that nobody of any consequence in the city, i.e. nobody of position and status and respect in the city or town, is spared, even though women of these families might be present there...." This form of public ridicule dishonored "the wives and daughters of such a family, and it by chance any woman of one mohalla or locality happens to pass another mohalla... within fifteen says of *Kanagats*, her clothes are torn and she is badly belabored. ..." *Kanagats* often degenerated into "hand fights and even wrestling," much to the amusement of the hundreds of men who collected to watch.

Kanagats exemplified the "bad and evil", customs that plagued Hindu society. It was also a ritual occasion on which women could vent their accumulated frustrations and strike back at the male members of their world; so too was *Moh Mahi*.

The festival of *Moh Mahi* was celebrated during mid-winter. On this day little girls and even grown-up adults and young women, both rich and poor, put on costly dresses and ornaments, as they move about the various localities and market places in group. As soon as they conic across any miserly person or stranger, they tease and harass him to such an extent that they even tear ott his clothes. Until and unless lie pays pice or two. he cannot secure his release, and tlm uncultured way of begging is called *Moll Mahi* by name.

The Dharm Sabha also rejected the festival of *Sada Talla*, a fertility rite performed by the Hindu women of Amritsar.

Hundreds or women, both from rich families as well as from poor families, put on their best dresses and jewelry and go to the Tek Chand Garden and the Guru Bagh, ami gather together, while there are in front of them thousands of men ot all classes, collected together to see this entertainment or drama, and these women bare their bodies up to their breasts and then start rolling on the ground with great zest and enthusiasm, shouting with their mouths in loud voices: 'I have laid down on a wheat field, may my womb become fertile.' During this action of theirs almost the whole of their bodies become naked. The women believe that by this action of theirs, they become pregnant immediately thereafter.

As with the other women's festivals, this was proclaimed as "shameless" and "evil" and the Sabha declared it would bring it to a swift end, as they asserted control over their female relatives.

The Sabha passed resolutions, organized committees to stipervise their neighbors, threatened social boycotts to enforce its decisions, and took steps to draw up new "proper' rituals and rites to replace those considered decadent, hi addition to the standard ideological explanations of irrationality, uselessness, or actions that are contrary to religious texts, the Sabha expressed its concern for respectability, especially in relation to the English ruling class: ". . . you can get honor only when you have modesty first. Our rulers, who are Englishmen, also feel happy on seeing good characters and respectable persons. What I mean to say is that this great shamelessncss and immodesty has spread among the women folk of this city, on seeing which other people ridicule us. Let us adopt measures, by means of which this blot giving us a bad name might disappear." The motivation that undergirded the Amritsar Dharm Sabha centered on the desire of a male-dominated society to protect its sense of worth in general and the honor of each family in particular, and to do that through a restructuring of women's customary behavior. In order to accomplish this, male authority was extended in areas previously beyond its jurisdiction, as men sought to extinguish festivals conducted by and for women.

Attempts to curtail "bad customs" were not limited to the Punjab, but had been articulated by numerous religious leaders from Ram Mohan Roy in Bengal to Swami Narayana Guru in Kerala. As with other Hindu "reformers," a number of the "bad customs" that Swami Narayana condemned were part of female culture. He called for his followers to cease celebrating *Thalikettu*, an expensive festival held at the time of a girl's marriage; *Thirandukuli*, a bathing ritual conducted on the occasion of a daughter's first menses; and, Pulikudy, a ritual celebrated when a woman became pregnant for the first time, all festivals held by women for woman.

A century of progress and social change witnessed the end of sati and female infanticide, since these customs were defined as criminal acts and outlawed by the British Indian Government. The only other legal step taken was raising the age of cohabitation from ten years to twelve years of age. All other changes derived from social pressure by individuals and socio-religious movements or by a general change of attitudes on the part of Hindu society. The age of marriage gradually rose throughout this century as least among the educated classes. Accompanying this was a demand for education for both men and women, but for different purposes, Inns were educated as preparation for a career and girls were educated to increase their value within the system of arranged marriages. For members of the literate Hindu classes an educated girl was considered prepared tor marriage and motherhood. Widow remarriage made some limited gains, but only for a virgin widow. On the question of elaborate marriage rites and expensive dowries, there seems to have been very little progress, although many movements struggled against the use of dowries. Little evidence exists on the fate of women's rituals and festivals, but it is likely that their popularity was restricted among women of the educated classes. The nineteenth century then was a period of conflicting trends and limited results, a period that cannot be understood by simple, one-dimensional explanations.

The evidence presented here points to a variety of aims among those who advocated modifications in the social behaviour of women and in the institutions that gave form to that behavior. This search for motivation, however, must be conducted within half of society, the male half. 'Die debates over the proper role of women were between men, and only rarely did a woman participate. In northern India the literature or discussion was written in languages unknown to most women so that even in theory tracts were written by men, for men. This was especially so prior to the last two decades of the nineteenth century. Organizations were created by men with a male membership and consequently the programs they created served male interests and responded to male sensitivities.

Most movements of social change had within them a strong desire for approval from the English community. Meredith Borthwick has noted that the educated elite of Bengal was extremely sensitive to English criticism of the status of Bengali women and had absorbed the idea that the position of women was a gauge of a civilized society. They also had uncritically accepted an idealized vision of the English woman. The Amritsar Dharm Sabha openly stated its desire for general social respectability and specifically for English approval.

The attempts by male organizations to remove "bad customs" and replace them with "proper" social behavior must be examined with more than one dimension in mind. First, many of the "evil" practices that were attacked were general in nature and were not associated with either sex. Lying, cheating, stealing, adultery, and the use of intoxicants had been rejected by socio-religious movements for many centuries. Other "bad customs," however, were rituals and festivals that were part of women's society. The Amritsar Dharm Sabha and similar "reformist" organizations spent much of their efforts to end such ceremonies. Women's society was, within its limits, more openly erotic and contained behavior that both embarrassed men and also attacked their sense of superiority.

The removal of "bad customs" then meant that men were extending their control over women by entering areas of social life that previously had been beyond their authority. This expansion of male control over women ran in two directions. First, it meant diminishing and, perhaps, removing completely all traditional practices that were disapproved of by men, and that caused inconvenience to them or that threatened the status and authority of the Hindu husband. Secondly, male control was extended by "reformers" who defined the new areas of women's activity and their phice in the changing world. Where she could go outside of the house, what she was allowed to do, her role as a "modern" mother and wife, the type of education she was given, and even the nature of her clothing were all debated and specified by men. Women remained subservient to their husbands and to males in general.

Women's education illustrates the variety of motivation that lay behind such questions. Lala Munshi Ram and his fellow Arya Samajis reacted to fear of Christian missionary influence and of conversion. For them education had to be Hinduized as a means of communal defense. Similar dynamics existed among those Muslims who advocated the education of girls For members of the English educated elite, and especially for those who worked directly under the British, a wife who could socialize and who possessed a degree of education was a distinct advantage. They needed women who could travel with them, as they were posted from town to town. Such a wife was an asset to an official's career. Initially women's education was structured to serve the interests of men and their social needs as they perceived. them. In time, however, education created a class of women who could and did begin to articulate their own priorities and programs for social change.

The social changes in the role of women within Hindu society were legitimized by appeals to reason or logic and to various torms of religious authority. The former, however, could not be the only basis for advocating new social or religious practice. The authority of a reinterpreted religious text, the teachings of a new religious leader, or a combination of the two were needed to gain the acceptance of new ideas. Ram Mohan Roy spoke of reason and used rationality to judge numerous Hindu customs, but then he turned to a reintcrpretation of scriptural texts for the final authority needed to legitimize his arguments. Tins appeal to religion was framed in terms of a return to proper practice and to the "fundamentals" of Hinduism. Within Hinduism and other religions of South Asia movements of return constituted "the fundamentalism" of the nineteenth century. At this time, there- was no other type of ideology that could provide legitimization for social and cultural change. By the end of the century and into the next, new secular ideologies began to appear with the emergence of nationalism, then socialism and, after World War I, the arrival of Marxism.

The degree to which this was, a period of "progress," of "liberalism" and positive change for Hindu women remains an open question, one that depends as much on the attitudes and suppositions of those who provide answers as on the data now available. Two things stand out, however. First, our knowledge of social change in this century is still fragmentary and somewhat superficial, largely through the limited use of non-English language sources and the tendency to accept the statements of various movements at face value. Secondly, if Hindu men actually extended their power over Hindu women during the nineteenth century, then what does this tell us of the relationship between technological and cultural change, on the one hand, and on the other, the goals of political and social development? Perhaps "progress" should be understood as change that is advantageous to a particular group rather than some all encompassing step toward an undefined and undefinable "modernization." A similar rethinking may be needed for such favorite terms as "liberalism" and "rationalism." There is no immediate answer to this question, but it is evident that e must re-examine, if not simply reject, many of the suppositions that lie beneath the standard historical interpretations applied by numerous scholars.

6

Terrorism in South Asia

Terrorism is a question of methods, not of motives, in a given context of conflict. As a method, it gets manifested in almost every conflict, be it an insurgency, an ethnic conflict, state-led law and order or security operations, or even an interstate proxy war. Both state and non-state actors are prone to employing extreme intensity of violence, often bordering on terror or actually being terror, either as a means of conveying political messages, or as an instrument in securing tactical or even strategic military and political advantages. In South Asia, states have consciously and persistently used force as an instrument of strategic and foreign policies towards other states. In doing so, terror as a method and a consequence of the use of force has been sought to be justified. The meaning and application of the concept of terrorism, as it is being employed in the emerging cotemporary context, particularly after the "11 September events", tend to get things presented in a simplistic form. So much so that almost every manifestation of anti-state violence is being described as terrorism. The conceptual parameters of the terms in vogue hitherto, like proxy wars, insurgencies, wars of national liberation, people's wars, asymmetric and unequal conflicts, other ideological and political conflicts, even social crimes, etc., arc all wrapped up in the term "terrorism". There is no doubt that there could be (and are) elements of terrorism in all these conflicts, but all these diverse manifestations of political conflicts and violence cannot and cannot and must not be indiscriminately condemned as terrorism. A new lexicon of international politics is emerging which, though simple on the face of it, is highly misleading and confusing as a tool of understanding and analysis of complex developments and problems.

A number of Western policy analysts, observers and scholars have tried to define terrorism through a sophisticated terminology that highlights the elements of "premeditated", "political violence" against "non-combatants". Now all these terms arc vulnerable to subjective and contextual meanings and interpretations. For instannce, in an ethnic conflict, anyone holding extremist ethnic views against another community would be perceived as an adversary by the latter. If violence is on in the conflict, then such individuals would not be treated as non-combatants. Similarly, in a situation of a people's war, or even a war of liberation, a small district or village officer is the tail-end representative of the so-called oppressive/exploitative/colonial, etc. "State". The "rebels" or the "freedom fighters" would not treat him as an innocent non-combatant, and killing him, from their point of view, would be hailed as a part of their struggle, and not an act of terrorism. This is how subjective meaning of the term "non-combatant" would depend also upon the context of a given conflict. It is such subjective interpretation of a particular act of terrorism or otherwise that is underlined in the assertion that one man's terrorist can be another's freedom fighter. There are any number of definitions of terrorism available, but the problem about their conceptual clarity continues to haunt even the United Nations. The definitional and conceptual riddle must be seriously and dispassionately addressed, because in the South Asian situation, between India and Pakistan, its significance is critical and decisive in conditioning interstate relations. The other day, Pakistani President Gen. Musharraf also publicly suggested that terrorism should not be defined by the individuals or affected states, but by collective bodies like the UN.

Terrorism and its political consequences have directly and visibly affected interstate relations in South Asia, particularly so when force has been made an instrument of conscious state policy and the resulting terrorist violence has been rationalized. Such terrorism has vitiated interstate relations and brought about a drift and acrimony in neighbourhood interactions. In situations where terrorism has affected states negatively, in a similar manner, it has also brought the neighbours together, to cooperate in common interest.

US as a Regional South Asian Player

After the intensive bombing of Al Qaeda and Taliban establishments in Afghanistan for nearly three months in retaliation to the "September 11 events", the US-led "global war against terrorism" was extended to other pans of Asia. South Asia has since become a principal focus of anti-Al Qaeda operations. To sustain and carry out this global war, the US has not only established bases and access rights in Central Asia, but India and Pakistan have also offered such access rights, with the Pakistani security forces even coordinating and collaborating to conduct operations jointly with the US forces in the region, comprising south and south-western Afghanistan, and the Baluchistan and north-western provinces of Pakistan. Not only this, the US has also got actively involved in other South Asian countries in pursuance of anti-terrorist objectives. In Nepal, the US is extending all possible support to the government's efforts in containing and fighting the Maoist's rebellion through military and economic assistance. In Sri Lanka, the US is supporting the Norwegian mediated peace process between the Sri Lankan government and the Liberation Tigers of Tamil Eelam (LTTE), to find a final and lasting solution of the ethnic conflict. Secretary Colin Powell, during his visit to Sri Lanka in support of the peace process, said that the US commitment to this process was next only to that of the Sri Lankan government. Fear has been expressed in some quarters that the growing rift between the LTTE and the Muslims in the east may drive the latter towards extremist and terrorist activities, even through link-up with the Al Qaeda, if not contained in time. And in Bangladesh, the US is nudging and encouraging the government with necessary incentives to keep an eye on the Islamic extremist groups, including the Rohingya refugees coming from Myanmar, and their possible linkages with the Al Qaeda network.

Two sets of objectives underline the US "counter-terrorism activism in South Asia. One is obvious and openly stated. It is to hunt down the Al Qaeda fugitives, particularly in the Afghan-Pakistan border areas, and to eliminate their possible linkages with local/South Asian regional terrorists. In this context, the removal of terrorists' challenge in South Asia, through peace processes as well as counter-terrorism is also necessary to ensure that the global terrorist networks do not find a fertile ground in South Asia to reinforce or re-establish their roots. The thrust of this stated objective may sound valid in the cases of Pakistan, India, Bangladesh and also Sri Lanka, but it does not carry strong credibility in the case of Nepal, where the Maoists have no foreseeable prospects of getting linked to the Al Qaeda.

The second set of objectives relate to the overall thrust of US foreign policy in the "post-9/11" context. A careful look at the 11 September events would suggest that the events were not acts of mere wanton terrorism. If at all, terrorism was a necessary and inherent consequence, and not the principal goal of the Al Qaeda strikes. It was an extreme but most perfect example of unequal or asymmetric conflict, where the vehicles of civil aviation were turned into weapons of mass destruction, resulting in terrorism. The 11 September attacks on the US were a challenge to its hegemony and unquestioned status of sole superpower. The targets chosen were the icons of the US economic, political and military power, namely; the World Trade Center, the Pentagon, and the missed target of the White House.

Even in the World Trade Center, the attack could have been carried out a little later when all the office-goers could be in their offices. It was this attack on the US hegemony that rattled the Bush administration and called for the massive retaliation that followed in the form of relentless bombing of the Afghan mountain ranges. There were attacks on US military and diplomatic establishments prior to 11 September as well, but the retaliation was neither as massive nor was that followed by a "global war against terrorism". This global war, in an unguarded and spontaneous response, was described as a "crusade", and expected to last long, as long as the Cold War. In its own way; the Cold War was also a campaign to establish and sustain the US and Western hegemony in the post-World War II world.

The global power structure dimension of the "war against terrorism" is reflected in any reference that compares it with the shaping of the Cold War and the situation prevailing during the late 1940s. Condoleezza Rice, President Bush's National Security Advisor, clearly underlined the broader picture of the post-9/11 strategic drive in the US foreign policy when she said:

I really think this period is analogous to 1945 to 1947 in that the events...started shifting the tectonic plates in international politics. And it's important to try to seize on that and position American interests and institutions before they harden again.

Elaborating this point, Joseph Gerson wrote:

Since September 11, the Bush Administration has acted not only out of political expediency, but to push through its staggering pre-9/11 military and foreign policy agenda. The goal, as our national CEO Dick Cheney described last spring, is to create "the arrangement (for) the twenty first century" in order to assure that "the United States will continue to be the dominant political, economic and military power in the world". Stephen Hadley; one of Condoleezza Rice's senior deputies reports that, not unlike the elder Bush's New World Order, this Bush Administration seeks "a whole new world", US global domination based ultimately on its nuclear and high-tech arsenals.

Accordingly the "global war against terrorism" needs to be viewed at least in parts, as an instrument, of the overall US strategic approach to the world order. In this approach, the US has preferred to take allies and partners whenever possible, but is committed to unilateralism wherever needed. The US role in South Asia should be understood in this perspective. The US activism in South Asia, in this respect, ret1ccts both the aspects of the overall US strategy identified above, i.e. (l) to eliminate the threat to its hegemony and dominance arising from the Al Qaeda network and its possible future protegees, and (2), to harness the capabilities and potentialities of the South Asian states in its drive to restructure the world order, particularly the Asian order, so as to ensure and reinforce US dominance.

There are a number of layers of the operative aspects of this strategy in South Asia. At one level, the US operations are being carried out in collaboration with Pakistani security forces in the Baluchistan and North West Frontier Provinces. There are serious internal political implications of these operations within Pakistan, which Gen. Musharraf has to face. The strong performance of the Islamic religious parties Muttahida Majlis-e-Amar (MMA) in the recently held general elections in Pakistan and the difficulties in formation of a new government that can also accept Gen. Musharraf as the unquestioned president and the Army Chief are part of such implications. There are regular media reports of deep American concern and influence in the internal process of government formation in Pakistan towards damage control to its overall objectives. The Urdu Daily *Nawa-e-Waqt* wrote recently:

> *Now again, Pakistan faces a multi-dimensional crisis. The perception has grown that the country has been mortgaged to the U.S. The presence and free movement and operations by U.S. troops and FBI, apart from the arrest of prominent citizens, strengthen the view that the U.S. treats Islam and jehad at par with terrorism. So much so that these expressions have begun to be used by us, too. It is now an open secret, that the MMA is sought to be blocked from assuming office because of its religious identity. One of the two parties is sought to he discouraged from allying with it lest the U.S. should be incensed.*

The latest in this respect is a direct allegation by the MMA leaders that the US ambassador in Islamabad had frustrated the possibility of MMA and PPP (parliamentarian) forging an anti-Musharraf coalition to rule Pakistan.

Similarly, the US involvement in containing terrorism and militancy in Jammu and Kashmir, as well as in Nepal, Sri Lanka, and Bangladesh, is a pan of its efforts to contain terrorism. In the context of terrorism in Jammu and Kashmir, the US did not get much disturbed during the initial phase of its "war against terrorism". More so because Gen. Musharraf of Pakistan had put forward two conditions for its cooperation with the US in this war, namely, that Pakistan's strategic assets (i.e. nuclear arsenals) should not be compromised and its Kashmir policy, of supporting the alleged "freedom struggle" should not be changed, This initial US casual attitude towards terrorism in Jammu and Kashmir could not be sustained in the take of increased terrorist activities marked by attack on the Indian Parliament on 13 December 2001, followed by unprecedented full mobilization of Indian military forces, including the strike brigades, against Pakistan for a possible punitive action. There were also reports that some of the Al Qaeda fugitives were shifting their bases, with the connivance of Pakistan's Inter-Services Intelligence (ISI) agene); to Pakistan-Occupied Kashmir (POK). The US could not afford the possibility of war between India and Pakistan, as that could jeopardize anti-Al Qaeda operations in full swing in Pakistan.

Under these conditions, the US was forced to pressurize Pakistan's Gen. Musharraf to come out, on 12 January 2002, with a statement indicating stoppage of cross-border terrorism. But in due course of time, this position has been diluted, where the US does not hold Pakistan alone responsible for infiltration into Kashmir. It seems that the US has accepted only (what a Pakistani scholar describes as) "basically a tactical, operational shift in Pakistan's Kashmir policy", which did not mean that "Pakistan was washing its hands off the legitimate Kashmiri struggle for self-determination have always been signs that the US was looking for some sort of a trade-off between India and Pakistan, where complete stoppage of infiltration from the Pakistani side must be matched by India by opening up Kashmir as a subject not only for debate and discussion, but also suitable compromises, understandably to accommodate the Pakistani point of view, preferably made through US mediation or facilitation. There is no doubt in the minds of many well-placed Indians that the US interests are well served by keeping the Kashmir question simmering, if not exploding. In any case, the US has succeeded, as never before, in positioning itself as an influential factor on the Kashmir question between India and Pakistan. The repeated US claims to remain closely and permanently engaged on the Kashmir issue gives it a unique advantage to be in a position to influence both the claimants of Kashmir.

At another level, the US has tried to enlist both India and Pakistan as allies in its overall strategy. This has been a long-standing objective of US policy even during the Cold War years. In the post-9/11 context, access rights, growing military cooperation and intelligence sharing, softening of non-proliferation constraints (including lifting of post-1998 sanctions), casing of debt burden on Pakistan and saving the state from failing and falling have been geared to building this dual alliance. In the case of India, the stated objectives or the' us collaboration are: (1) to promote peace and freedom in Asia (2) to combat international terrorism; and (3) to slow down the spread or weapons of mass destruction.

The US sees this dual alliance as an asset in its diverse objectives, like securing the energy resources of Central Asia, containing China, and maintaining a "desirable" balance in South Asia. This dual alliance, along with the US presence in Bangladesh and Sri Lanka, can also be profitable in controlling commercial and military activities in the Indian Ocean. The US agreeing to use Indian naval escorts for the ships sailing through the Malacca Straits has significance in this respect. The US presence in Nepal may be of potential advantage if China has to be contained on its vulnerable western flanks, particularly the Tibet region. The fact that the CIA carried out a subversive war until 1974 against China in the Mustang region, an area presently affected by the Maoist insurgency is not without significance in this respect. The strong US presence on India's South Asian periphery is also convenient in facilitating India's compliance with the overall US global strategic objectives. The US, along with other donors, is fabricating a structure of their presence in South Asia through various apparently multilateral committees to deal with the problems of economic and military support that work within the overall direction set by the US. India is being asked to join such committees in Nepal dealing with political and security matters, along with development and economic reconstruction. India is naturally reluctant to do so, because that would curtail the strategic space enjoyed by India in its neighbouring countries like Nepal, and qualitatively change India's relations with these countries to its disadvantage.

Of course, both India and Pakistan have been more than forthcoming in seeking alliance with the US in outwitting each other and enhancing their respective political and strategic leverage vis-a-vis each other. But herein lies the inherent contradiction in the US approach towards Indo-Pak issue. While it has got deeply involved in their bilateral affairs, neither feels happy and fully satisfied with the US, or even treats it as a dependable ally. The Indian leadership, which was expecting the US to declare Pakistan a terrorist state, has started confessing the limits of the US desire and efforts in forcing Pakistan to stop cross-border terrorism against India. It is indeed a dilemma of the US policy to retain and possibly strengthen this dual alliance with Pakistan and India in the face of irreconciliable antagonism between the two countries.

A broader political consequence of sustained counter-terrorism operations under the US leadership in South Asia will be the strengthening of autocratic regimes be they military rulers or traditional monarchs. Even where such autocracies are not in power, or are not likely to be in power, the states will get more oriented towards national security norms, with more military and law and order operations against every possible dissent in the society, evolution of harsher domestic legal regimes with increasing curbs on basis freedom, greater indifference to human rights violations, and restrictions on democratic functioning, In the Sri Lankan case, it remains to be seen if the externally backed peace process would prove to be a stronger and lasting incentive for an organization like the LTTE to learn democratic conduct and discipline. Tensions are already mounting on account of simmering conflict between the Muslims of eastern Sri Lanka and the LTTE. There have also been reports of Tamil activists belonging to other political parties being abducted and killed by the LTTE, and also of the LTTE continuing to procure arms and military equipment.

Terrorism and Bilateral Relations

Terrorism and Acrimony

Terrorism, as broadly understood in the present context, has been playing a critical role in influencing the thrust of bilateral relations in South Asia. There have been dear examples in the region where an attitude of acquiescence or even encouragement has been adopted by one state towards terrorist violence in or on another state. Such situations have naturally resulted in added acrimony and tensions between two neighbouring states. One can recall the case of Indo-Sri Lanka relations during the early years of Tamil insurgency, before 1987. The operations of Tamil militants in Sri Lanka from safe sanctuaries and bases in India gave rise to serious strains in Indo-Sri Lanka relations. Just prior to the signing of the Indo-Sri Lanka Agreement of July 1987 on the ethnic conflict, the Government of India had directly intervened (in early June 1987), under the pretext of dropping food supplies to the beleaguered Tamil militant groups. Perhaps India had its own reasons for this intervention, but this period (from the late 1970s till July 1987) witnessed tremendous acrimony in Indo-Sri Lanka relations.

Tensions have also been generated between India and other neighbours, like Bangladesh, Nepal, and Bhutan on account of the latters' connivance or cavalier attitude towards the threat of terrorism posed to the former. In the case of Bangladesh, India's complaints of continuing ISI activities and shelter and support provided to the North-East insurgents constitute an area of tension, because some of the North-East insurgent leaders move freely, have bank accounts, and run profitable businesses in Bangladesh, possibly with the connivance of the government and the security agencies. In the case of Nepal, the hijacking of IC 814 in December 1999 brought the bilateral relations between the two neighbours to their lowest ebb in the past few decades. Indian media reports have extensively covered India's disappointment with Nepal on accounts of ISI activities aimed against India through Nepal. Some of the prominent Nepali political leaders and their relations were suspected to be on the payroll of the ISI. An undercurrent of tension has also been witnessed in India-Bhutan relations since the late 1970s on account of intelligence and media reports of Bhutan's soft attitude towards Bodo and ULFA insurgents seeking sanctuaries and bases in the Bhutan Duars.

Indo- Pak relations present the worst case of terrorism spoiling bilateral relations. Pakistan's terrorism against India in the name of a "freedom movement" in Kashmir is, in reality, Pakistan's proxy war against India. This war may not really end even with the resolution of the Kashmir problem, which in any case looks remote. President Gen. Musharraf had, in fact, said so soon after assuming power in 1999. Pakistan has always used force in disturbing the bilateral status quo, and the grand objective behind sponsoring terrorism seems to be a manifestation of the ISI's resolve to weaken India internally. India's insistence on ending cross-border terrorism as a condition for having normal communications and relations with Pakistan seems to be a desperate policy posture. India was on the verge of going to war with Pakistan to force an end to this terrorism. It may still come to that dangerous point quickly; even after the demobilization of Indian forces ordered in early November 2002. There are strategic analysts in India who plead for organizing counter-terrorist attacks on Pakistan. No one in South Asia, or for that matter in the world, doubts today that terrorism can lead to interstate war between the two adversarial neighbours.

The degree of acrimony generated by terrorism between or more states in South Asia, has been conditioned by two factors, namely: the degree and nature of involvement or the state in sponsoring terrorism against the other one, and the approach to terrorism in the victim state. Some examples may illustrate the point better. Let us take tensions and acrimony generated by terrorism between India and Pakistan, India and Nepal, and India and Bhutan on account of cross-border terrorism. Between India and Pakistan, the Pakistani-sponsored terrorism is a part of the conscious and sustained policy approach as noted above. This involvement is total, deep, and long-lasting. The result is a very high degree of acrimony and conflict, leading to intense diplomatic rivalry and a distinct possibility of war. In the case of Nepal, even if the allegations of connivance with ISI activities in some sections of the Nepali establishment are accepted on face value, no one in India believes that allowing itself to become a transit route of Pakistani terrorism against India is a conscious and sustained policy of the Himalayan kingdom. Whatever support and encouragement is obtained by the ISI in Nepal is largely a part of administrative inefficiency and a casual political approach on a rather limited level. So also is the case of Bhutan, where the ULFA and Bodo insurgents arc using Bhutanese territory for shelter and sanctuaries on their own. Even if there is some sympathy or support for these insurgents in some quarters in Bhutan, for the large part, the Bhutanese security forces arc not well-equipped and confident enough to deal firmly with cross-border activities of the insurgents. Accordingly, in both the cases of Nepal and Bhutan, terrorism has had only a limited effect on generating acrimony. The broad range of bilateral issues has continued to be dealt with in the normal course, without affecting overall cooperative relations in an adversarial manner in the long run.

The second factor is that of the approach of the victim state to the menace of terrorism. The example of a comparison of India's approach to terrorism during the Congress rule of Mrs. Gandhi and Rajiv Gandhi with the present NDA regime under Atal Behari Vajpayee may be looked at. Mrs. Gandhi dealt with the Sikh revolt and demand for a separatist state (1980-84), as well as the insurgency in the North-East (period of 1966-74), both having cross border dimensions, involving Pakistan and China respectively. There were tensions ill India's relations with these two neighbours arising out of cross-border terrorism, but these tensions were seen as still manageable within diplomatic rules of engagement. Mrs. Gandhi did not make them a major foreign-policy issue, and tried to deal with the manifestations of terrorism within India through counter-terrorism operations, and also political negotiations. The Punjab issue, which lingered on even during Rajiv Gandhi's period, was also dealt with in the same framework. Rajiv Gandhi also succeeded in persuading his Pakistani counterpart Benazir Bhutto to distance the Pakistani establishment from the Sikh insurgency. That she could not do so even after a positive assurance to India is a different matter. She had been snubbed by Pakistan's military regime on the count that the military was the dominant player in Pakistan's India policy. In the perceptions of the regimes of Mrs. Gandhi and Rajiv Gandhi, terrorism and insurgency's domestic causes were more decisive and important, and, therefore, firm and imaginative domestic action was needed to deal with this problem. The results were Operation Blue Star, and the Rajiv-Longewal Agreement. For this reason also, the North-East insurgency and the Naxalite challenge were also tackled largely on the internal front, rather than by precipitating a major bilateral issue with China, which had provided support and encouragement to the groups involved.

The question of cross-border terrorism and the role of the sponsoring state have emerged as major factors in the NDA Government's approach to terrorism. In this approach, the domestic causes of insurgency and revolt, like political alienation and socio-economic problems, have been accorded lesser priority. The principal factor behind terrorism is its sponsorship by Pakistan through cross-border infiltration. There is no doubt that the nature of Pakistani support to the Kashmir militancy and present-day cross-border terrorism is radically different both in extent and quality from similar Pakistani support to the Sikh insurgency earlier, but an imaginative and efficient Kashmir policy could always blunt Pakistan's efforts to keep Kashmir burning and the rest of India bleeding. In the context of North Indian politics, a series of internal developments from the Babri Masjid, to the Ram Temple, to the Mumbai (Bombay) riots, to Godhra and Ahmedabad have led to a perceptive degree of alienation of the Muslim minority in India. Some sections of the alienated youths and poorer households of this minority community may have, accordingly, become vulnerable and easily pliable to ISI operatives for local recruitment. If the basic political agenda of even the extremist fringe within the BJP's "Sangh Parivar" is to cultivate Hindu votes, then Gen. Musharraf and his Pakistan have done every thing possible to become an ideal adversarial target. Maybe Gen. Musharraf has his own compulsions within Pakistan, or even within the military establishment, to be unable to change his policy of bleeding India internally. The imperatives of internal political dynamics are in full force in both countries. In India, this is loud and clear in Gujarat in the statements of Deputy Prime Minister Advani, Chief Minister Modi, and VHP General Secretary Praveen - togadia. Such political dynamics certainly pose difficulties in the way of any attempt to reopen normal diplomatic relations between India and Pakistan. One wonders if greater stability and confidence in Jammu & Kashmir under the newly elected regime will create conditions for moderating, if not eliminating, acrimony in Indo- Pak relations.

Terrorism and Cooperation

Terrorism has also led to cooperation in interstate bilateral relations in South Asia. This has happened in the situations when one state, in contrast to support, encouragement, or acquiescence (as a part of its conscious policy) to terrorism in another state, treats terrorism as a common threat, and decides to cooperate in eliminating such a threat. India's cooperation with Nepal during the early 1950s in helping Nepal deal with internal political revolts and disruption was extended within the framework of expanding and consolidating close bilateral relations. India's cooperation with Sri Lanka first in 1971 during the threat posed by the JVP insurgency, and again after 1987, under the Indo-Sri Lanka Agreement of July 1987, may also be recalled in this respect. The prospects of internal political instability in Nepal, and the rise of violent and aggressive Tamil nationalism, at different points of time, were seen as common security challenges by India with its respective neighbours. In the case of Sri Lanka, India went to the extent of sending a peacekeeping force (IPKF) to get the July 1987 Agreement implemented, and when difficulties were raised in this implementation by the LTTE, this force committed itself to fighting the Tamil guerrillas. The cooperative relationship between India and Nepal on the question of combating terrorism has also significantly improved in recent months

South Asia has also witnessed a shift in the terrorism-based acrimonious to accommodative and cooperative bilateral relations between states. In Indo-Sri Lanka relations, the shift from acrimony (during the period from the late I 970s to July 1987) to cooperation (post- July 1987) has been mentioned earlier. The exception in this respect was the period 1989-90, when a new president in Sri Lanka, Premadasa, demanded the withdrawal of the I PKF even before the task of taming the Tamil Tigers (LTTE) had been achieved. The main reason behind this demand of Premadasa was related to internal political dynamics. He had decided to develop a political equation with the LTTE to ensure unit votes in the process of consolidating his political position. He went to the extent of supplying arms to the LTTE in their war against the IPKF, without realizing that its long-term consequences were to be hazardous for Sri Lanka's peace and stability. However, India, under a new political dispensation, conceded Premadasa's demand, and, since then, India has adopted an extremely cautious approach to Sri Lanka'ss concerns arising out of the Tamil insurgency.

Such a shift also look place in case of Indo-Nepal and Indo-Bangladesh relations. In Indo-Nepal relations, while India complained of indifference and connivance on the part of Nepal about ISI-supported terrorist activities, Nepal has also complained to India about its indifference and tacit support to the Maoist rebels in their use of Indian territory for shelter and sanctuaries. In the changed regional context of post-9/11 developments, and under the overall influence of enhanced US counter-terrorism presence in South Asia, there is now much greater cooperation between India and Nepal to deal with the common concerns arising out of the Maoists' activities. The Maoists have effectively networked with similar extremist ideological groups like the Naxalites, Maoists Communist Centre, People's War Group, and even some of the North-East insurgents like the Kamtapur Liberation Organisation (KLO). India has provided military and economic support to Nepal to deal with the Maoist challenge. Without adequate assessment of the domestic consequences of the Maoists' challenge in Nepal, India declared them as a terrorist group even before Nepalese government could do so. The Nepalese side now also promises to be more alert and committed in dealing with India-targetted ISI activities in and through Nepal. Both India and Nepal have developed better mechanisms for border management and intelligence sharing. In the context of meeting the Maoist challenge, Nepal may also be able to get a greater margin of freedom in procuring arms from countries other than India, notwithstanding the treaty provisions of the 1950 Indo-Nepal Treaty.

In Indo-Bangladesh relations, there was almost a situation of support and counter-support for each others' terrorist groups, leading to serious bilateral tensions. The Indian North-East insurgents not only enjoyed support, shelter and sanctuaries in Bangladesh, but Prime Minister Khalcda Zia at some stage even described them as freedom fighters. This was countered by the support and sanctuaries enjoyed by Bangladesh's Shanti Bahini, the Chakma Buddhist Tribal insurgent group in Indian territory. A change in this situation was initiated with the government of Sheikh Hasina that succeeded Begum Zia's BNP regime in 1996. Sheikh

Hasina looked at the domestic roots of the Chakma insurgency and reached an agreement with them. This resulted in the end of the insurgency and the return of some 40,000 Chakma refugees from India. Bangladesh then also started curbing the activities of the Indian North-East insurgents operating from their sate havens in Bangladesh. This led to an improvement in bilateral relations. Unfortunately, the Indian insurgents still enjoy Support in some sections of the Bangladeshi security forces due to the ISI influence in Bangladesh's Armed Forces and security, establishments. In 2001, the BNP led by Begum Khaleda Zia came back to power, and there are fears in India's official circles that the leads provided to the Bangladesh government regarding the cross-border activities of the Indian insurgents are not being followed pursued sincerely. The North-East insurgents are enjoying freedom and support in Bangladesh. The post-9/11 developments do not seem to have made a decisive impact in alleviating India's concerns, but perhaps it will, in due course of time, as the US counter-terrorist activity gathers momentum in this respect. It is also hoped that Bangladesh realizes that playing with terrorism in pursuance of short-term foreign-policy goals may prove to be disastrous in the long run.

Terrorism and Regional Cooperation

It must be said to the credit of the SAARC founding fathers that they were sensitive to the menace of terrorism from their very first meeting. This led to the adoption of the SAARC Convention on Suppression of terrorism at the 3rd summit held in Kathmandu in November 1987. The convention was based on UN resolutions and various other international conventions adopted on related aspects. Accordingly, it was:

> *required that each state should refrain from organizaing, instigating, assisting or participating in acts of civil strife or terrorist act in another state or acquiescing in organized activities within its territory directed towards the commission of such acts.*

The problem of this convention was that it had to be ratified by each of the signatories separately. This took years. In addition, each country had to enact enabling legislation domestically so as to facilitate the implementation of its critical provisions, including extraditing those involved in terrorist activities. In view of Indo-Pakistani difficulties that gathered momentum with the launching of cross-border terrorism by Pakistan by 1989-90, not much seriousness was shown in pursuing the provisions of the convention. Bilateral difficulties in other interstate relations among the SAARC members further added to lack of sincerity and commitment on the regional goal of suppression of terrorism.

In the context of the 11 September developments, which were also preceded by a spurt in cross-border terrorism against India, particularly the hijacking of Indian Airlines flight IC 814 from Kathmandu to Kandahar, the question of terrorism has resurfaced in the SAARC forum. In the Kathmandu SAARC summit in 2001, terrorism dominated the proceedings, and it was decided to reinforce the 1987 Convention so is to make it meaningful and effective. The summit decided to set up a committee of legal experts to go into it and suggest possible changes in the existing convention. This may, in fact, turn out to be a device to avoid serious action, particularly in view of the sharp acrimony between India and Pakistan on the question of cross-border terrorism. There is little hope of concerted regional action to fight the menace of terrorism in South Asia, though bilaterally, except in the case of India-Pakistan, the coming years may see greater consensus on coordinated, if not united, response to the challenge of terrorism.

It would not be an exaggeration to say that while "suppression of terrorism" as a goal has not been pursued seriously at the regional level in South Asia, in turn, terrorism related issues have inflicted greatest damage to the SAARC process. Such issues have eroded the credibility of SAARC as a regional forum. And this is not only because of the Indo-Pakistan hiatus. Terrorism-inflicted bilateral relations did not allow SAARC summits to take place in 1989 (India-Sri Lanka), 1992 (India-Bangladesh, and Nepal Bhutan), and 1999-2000 (India-Pakistan). Even the prospects of the next' summit hang in uncertainty due to the Indo-Pakistani conflict on the question of cross-border terrorism, though it has been combined with possible signs on a sincere approach on the pan of Pakistan on the process of economic cooperation in South Asia.

7

Support of International Terrorism

Terrorism is a means and not an end unless, like anarchism, it becomes an end itself. Thus, if terrorism is a means of coercion, then it should be seen as one end, may be an extreme end, of a broad spectrum of coercion, ranging from political protest, extremism, guerrilla warfare, insurgency to rebellion, etc.

Political protest is an open form of dissent movement which functions largely within the available political framework of the state. Insurgency or guerrilla warfare often challenge that political framework. They also involve a substantial percentage of the population without whose support the movement cannot be sustain-ed. While insurgency or guerrilla warfare might include some acts of terrorism, terrorism *per se* is the act of a few persons and is the last resort in 'protest'. The ITTE today is resorting to terrorism because of heavy pressure mounted by the IPKF. Thus, there is a dividing line, though a thin one, between insurgency or guerrilla warfare and terrorism.

While other terms of violent political protest like insurgency, guerrilla war, etc. have been clearly defined, attempts to evolve a definition of terrorism acceptable to all, has evaded scholars so far. It is a highly sensitive and a value-loaded terms. However, there is broad acceptance on several common characteristics of terrorism.

All agree that the psychological aspect connected with terrorism differentiates it from other forms of violent protest. In this case 'terrorism' itself is used as a political instrument. Terrorism, there fore, is the use of violence for effect. The real damage may not be in proportion to the 'dramatic' impact upon the mind not only of the target group but also upon the public at large.

There are other factors that also help in understanding terrorism. One is the sense of absolutism felt by the terrorist. The other is the reaffirmation of the self' esteem whether it be the case of the Palestinians or the Sikhs. The third is the desire for self-sacrifice or the concept of *Shahadat*. There are also other factors like fanatical loyalty bordering upon group narcissism, role of a charismatic personality, conviction in the purity of the 'cause' behalf, rightly or wrongly, that they cannot achieve their goal by legal means, etc.

Despite these commonly accepted characteristics, the term terrorism still evades an acceptable definition. Even the resolutions of the UN and the SAARC serve more to define and condemn acts of terrorism rather than to define the term per se. However, the following can be a working definition of terrorism. Terrorism arises out of the use of threat of use of violence by a well identifiable group whether acting for or in opposition to the established authority when its action is designed to create extreme anxiety and to induce fear in a target group that is larger than the direct and immediate victims, with the purpose of coercing it into acceding to the demands.

Of late, the term 'international terrorism' has gained currency. But even that terns defies an adequate definition. It is true that terrorists in many cases get support from abroad. That support can come from individuals or groups sympathetic to their cause, like the support to the IRA or the Armenian groups hostile to Turkey from the people of the Irish or Armenian origin in the USA. It can also come from states like the support given by some Arab states to the Palestinian groups or the support given by President Qadafi to organizations ranging from the IRA to the Moro group in the Philippines.

The West in general and the USA in particular has, as a policy, condemned international terrorism, especially when Arab states are involved but have been almost silent in several cases of international terrorism where the West and its support base in the developing world has been directly and indirectly involved. The killing of innocent civilians in indiscriminate gun and rocket attacks and bomb explosions, etc. by the Pol Pot-led group in Kampuchea from adjoining bases in Thailand, in Afghanistan from bases in Pakistan and by the Contras in Nicaragua are only a few of such examples. One also feels the hidden hand of international terrorism behind the terrorists activities not only in the Punjab but also in Jammu and Kashmir and in the North-East in India.

Another factor that has been highlighted and dramatized by the scholars dealing with terrorism is the fear of nuclear terrorism. Several scholars have argued that terrorists can get hold of either enriched uranium or plutonium of weapon-grade quality and fashion a crude nuclear explosive device so as to terrorize the community. While theoretically all things are possible, one doubts if small terrorists groups, with their limited resources, can get not only the weapon-grade material but also other sophisticated component that go to make a nuclear bomb. Even states find it difficult to acquire such bombs. President Qadafi has been reportedly trying to acquire one for years.

However, one has to be very cautious. Though the possibility of terrorists making a nuclear bomb are remote, their capability to attack and destroy the civilian nuclear reactors and associate parts should not be underestimated. There have been several reports not only of sabotage but also attacks on nuclear installations. Reportedly, members of the Pacifist and Ecologist Committee blew up parts of a French nuclear plant in 1979, causing $ 20 mn damage.

Such attacks s point to the need for extra security of nuclear installations lest some misplaced 'pacifist' blows up the place and creates another Chernobyl. While the threat of nuclear terrorism is highlighted, similar danger exists in the field of use of chemical and biological weapons. They are equally dangerous and more easily available. Some of them are even available commercially or can be produced in small laboratories.

Acts of terrorism and the media publicity often lead to panic response among the public which gets reflected in the highhanded official response. Terrorist may well believe that, by their action, they can provoke the government, especially in a democratic country, to take actions that would curb democratic liberties, thereby creating a rift between the people and the government and thus eroding legitimacy of the government. But, it is also possible that the publicity of terrorist acts may create public opinion that might indirectly help the government to take strong measures that other wise would have been termed as anti-democratic. A heightened sense of risk and insecurity is more likely to increase acquiescence to and dependence upon established authority, and to legitimize its use of force.

Question of legitimacy is of great importance not only to a terrorists but also to those who have to confront the threat posed by them. This question has also so far defied all attempts at reaching a consensus acceptable to all the parties. Especially, the developing countries have insisted upon treating the struggle against colonialism and racism separately and their point of view has been incorporated in the UN Resolution. Even the crucial UN General Assembly resolution (A/Res/40(61) of 9 December 1985, while condemning terrorism as a criminal act, reaffirmed the inalienable right to self-determination and independence of all peoples under colonial and racist regimes and other forms of alien domination, and upholding the legitimacy of their struggle, in particular, the struggle of national liberation movements, in accordance with the purposes and principles of the Charter and the Declaration on Principles of International law concerning friendly relations and cooperation among states in accordance with the Charter of the United Nations.

Legitimacy of terrorism depends upon several socio-economic and political factors. But one factor merits special consideration. Since terrorism is considered as the last resort in political struggle its legitimacy can be strengthened if it can be proved beyond doubt that all other available means of struggle were tried and had failed. On the other hand terrorism will lose its legitimacy if it can be proved that available political or legal means have been bypassed before resorting to the use of terrorism. . Thus, while PLO, SWAPO and ANC retain their legitimacy, other groups like the IRA in Ireland, Quebecois in Canada, Basque in Spain, Croatians in Yugoslavia,. Kurds in Iraq, Khalistanis in India, Moros in the Philippines, the Red Brigade of Italy, the Baader-Meinhof gang of West Germany, etc. have not acquired that legitimacy.

Responses to terrorism are manifold. Often, states treat terrorism not as political but as criminal acts. That enables the state to press for extradition if necessary. Also, since the state machinery is geared to look after law breakers, those entrusted with antiterrorist role are inclined to meet force or threat of force with superior counter-force. Just as the acts of the terrorists need to be seen from the perspective of psychology, so also the actions of the state officials need to be seen from that angle. They do not fear the criminals, but they do fear any appearance of importance or inefficiency in dealing with the criminals. They may even regard the hesitation in the use of counter-violence or search for an alternative as signs of weakness on their part. Because they have been trained to act tough, they are inclined to regard toughness as an end in itself. Naturally, while counter-force is essential when dealing with terrorist, force in itself is not an answer to a complex socioeconomic, political and psychological problem.

Besides state's unilateral response to terrorism, efforts are also being made to coordirate counter-terrorist measures at international levels both within and outside the UN. International community was concerned of the growing threat arising from hijacking and often the blowing up of commercial aircraft, violation of diplomatic immunities and the taking of hostages by the terrorists. Hence, series of conventions dealing with these specific issues were negotiated. Three conventions were signed concerning offences on board aircraft.

Other important conventions dealing with terrorism are the convention on the violation of diplomatic immunity, signed in New York on 14 December 1973. Another one dealt with the question of taking of hostages and was signed in New York on 17 December 1974. Even the UN definition of "aggression", in its article 3(9), teeth includes sending of armed ganga, groups, irregulars or mercenaries to another country. It, therefore, 'does cover international terrorism to a great extent.

The UN General Assembly also passed a major and a comprehensive resolution (40/61) on 9 December 1985, without vote, on measures to prevent international terrorism. Among other things, it unequivocally condemned, as criminal, all acts, methods and practices of terrorism wherever and by whomever committed. It appealed to all states, that has not yet done so, to become parties to international conventions relating to various aspects of international terrorism. It also called upon all states to refrain from organizing, instigating, assisting or participating in terrorist acts in other states, or acquiescing in activities within their territories directed towards the commission of such acts. It also urged all states to cooperate with one another through exchange of relevant information and by prosecution or extradition of the perpetrators of such acts and to enter into treaty obligation to that effect.

Success of terrorism, whether national or international, depends to a large extent upon its support base. This support includes not only social and political help but also more crucial inputs dealing with funding of the movement, weapons and training.

No organization or movement can function without financial support. Terrorists get money through different ways like 'donations' and 'taxes' from people, through bank robberies, collection of ransom for hostages and hijacked planes, etc. Weapons were often looted from civilians or snatched from the police, paramilitary and even military personnel or purchased from abroad. Sometimes international organizations or even states become sources of weapons and training. The PLO, for example, acquired weapons not only from the Arab states but also from China and the USSR.

Yet, despite the social, political, economic and military support, many of these organizations were often starved of funds and weapons. They were also more dependent upon others for their operations. That had to some extent retarded their operations. Unfortunately, now the tide has turned in their favour, especially in the developing world. Today, terrorism is developing an independent power base thanks to its growing linkage with smuggling of drugs and weapons.

This new development has not only blunted the earlier difference between political and criminal terrorist but has given the terrorists a world-wide-underground network, access to billions of dollars worth of illegal drug trade and also the lucrative clandestine trade in modern sophisticated arms, ammunition and explosive devices. The developing countries are the most affected by this new phenomenon. Of them, India is the worst affected.

India is boxed from three sides with insurgency and terroristprone areas. To compound the matter further, these areas are also directly or indirectly linked with drugs and arms trafficing. They are the 'Golden Triangle' in the East, the Golden Crescent' in the West and the destabilized situation in Sri Lanka in the South. Drugs, arms and terrorism in these three corners of India not only do not destabilize each of these three flanks of India but are also spilling over into India and have tile potential of causing substantial destabilization at least in the adjoining parts of India itself. A 35-page UN report released by the International Narcotics Control Board, Vienna, in January 1987, linked illegal drug production and trafficing to illegal arms trade and international terrorism.

This linkage has been very well brought out in several other studies including the article by Mark S. Steinitz, who was working for the US drug enforcement organization. He says that, in Afghanistan, opium production increased from an estimated 200 metric tons in 1980 to about 400-475 tons in 1983. This increased production was in the areas of Eastern Afghanistan where the Mujahedeen,s were waging guerrilla struggle. The production increased further by 1986 when it was reported that enough opium was grown in Afghanistan to produce mountains of heroin.

The increased production of Afghan opium compensated for the loss of opium cultivation in Pakistan. Pakistan was producing about 800 tons of opium in 1978. In 1979, under the US official pressure, Pakistan was forced to ban poppy cultivation and the production dropped to about 45-50 tons of opium in the early 1980's. It, however, reportedly shot up to about 100-200 tons in the years coinciding with accelerated US arms deliveries to the Afghan guerrillas!

Today, drugs produced in Pakistan and in the guerrilla-controlled areas of Afghanistan reportedly supply about one-third of the drugs consumed in the USA. *Washington Post*, quoting the US drugs enforcement agents, said that the USA had tolerated poppy cultivation and the setting up of laboratories by the tribes is NWFP and also in the areas of Afghanistan controlled by the guerrillas but, now that the Geneva Accord on withdrawal of Soviet troops has been signed, it would not tolerate it. In fact, the USA had threatened to cut aid to Pakistan by half unless the latter cracked down on the frontier opium production and the refining laboratories.

These statements clearly identify not only the areas of opium and other drugs cultivation and refining but also point to the linkage not only between the drug and insurgency but also towards. the direct and indirect involvement of the Pakistani and the US. administration in this. It had two-fold impact upon South Asia. Firstly, the area of transit, whether Pakistan or India, also became an area of consumption. Secondly drug trade, which bad links - with guerrillas, also promoted trafficing in arms in South Asia and increased terrorist activities.

In Pakistan, reportedly there is a 50% increase in the number of heroin addicts. The increase is from 3.5 lakhs to 4.5 lakhs between 1984 to 1986 alone. Assuming consumption of even one gram a day per addict, the total consumption in Pakistan amounts to about 150 kg per day or about 45 metric tons per year. Since Pakistan does not produce that much opium, the drug is flowing,. according to the Pakistani daily *Muslim*, from Afghanistan and India. The trade in narcotics and also arms has seriously affected the socio-economic and even political fabrics of Pakistani society. The ethnic riots in Karachi between the *Pathans* and *Mohajirs* are reportedly connected with that.

India too is directly affected by the situation in Afghanistan, that had led to increased drug production coupled with flow of sophisticated small arms, missiles and explosives into the hands of irresponsible people. Drugs and arms link the Punjab terrorists to the Mujahedeen of Afghanistan and their link-men in Pakistan. In this drugs-for-arms deal they reportedly convey drugs in return for arms! It is reported that several well-known Punjab terrorists. were smugglers previously. S.S. Virk, former Senior Superintendent of Police, told *India Today* correspondent, Raminder Singh, that both Jinda and Bakshish Singh were earlier very active as smugglers. It was reported that Jinda (or Harjinder Singh) had higb-grade heroin on him when he was caught by the Delhi Police in August 1987P The former Home Minister, Buta Singh, while inaugurating the Interpol Conference in New Delhi, painted a grim picture of the threat posed by terrorism in Punjab and said that if the nexus between terrorism and drug was not broken it would erode the democratic foundations of the country!

The eastern sector of India poses different sets of problems. India's boundaries turn and twist among those of the neighbouring states and often cut across tribal and ethnic groups like the Mizo, Naga, Chakma, Burman, etc. Though India's boundaries, with the exception of China, have been delimited, the area is not easily approachable to outsiders. Hence, trans-border movement goes on. Sometimes it is legalized, but often the passport and customs formalities are largely ignored by the local population. That would not have mattered much but for the fact that the North-East also has its problems of insurgency and drug trafflcing. Fortunately, both are on a low-key at the moment.

Insurgency and its off-shoot terrorism were posing a serious problem in that area in the sixties and the seventies when they were being supported extensively by China and Pakistan. However, today the democratization process has replaced the use of violence as a political weapon. The latest example is the return of the Tripura

National Volunteers from their camps in Bangladesh. The drug trafficing is also on a much lesser scale in this sector though it is next door to the so-called Golden Triangle in South-East Asia.

Burma is a major producer of opium. An estimated 630 metric tons of opium was produced in 1984. That trade is controlled by the Kachin and the Shan tribes and by the Burmese Communist Party. They all operate in the northern and the eastern regions of Burma. Bulk of the drug trade of the Golden Triangle moves through Thailand and only a small portion moves through Burma. According to statistics, hardly 1-2% of the total seizure of drugs in India is accounted for by the drug trafficing through the North–East. That might mean either that the area is very porus or that the drug trade is getting diverted from Burma to Bangladesh either directly through the Arakan region or through some areas in the North lust like the Mizoram. It is possible that with the recent collapse of law and order in Burma the North-East sector may become more active. The Burmese Armed Forces were keeping pressure on the Kachins across India. Now the Kachin Independence Army, about 5000 men, would have a relatively free hand.

The southern sector of India was a relatively quiet sector but has become an active one since the major destabilization in Sri Lanka following the 1983 riots. The ethnic linkage of the Tamils provides local sympathy for the Sri Lankan Tamils in India. However, some Tamil militants have also been indulging in drug trafficing and gun-running through India. Reportedly, drugs from Afghanistan and Pakistan are routed through India to the Sri Lankars who take them to destinations in the West. A large number of Sri Lankans have been caught in Europe while smuggling drugs. Money thus acquired is reportedly used to buy arms in black market. Some of these arms are also directed against the IPKF in Sri Lanka.

The question of terrorism is closely linked to the procurement of weapons and the facilities for training in their use. Earlier, Indian insurgents were being trained in camps in China or in East Pakistan. Also weapons were provided largely by the Chinese or were snatched from the Indian police and the para-military forces. But the supply of weapons was restricted. The Afghanistan question has totally altered the situation. Today, large quantities of automatic weapons, sophisticated missiles and explosives are available against payment or for services rendered.

According to one estimate, in 1982 the CIA provided Afghan guerrillas with bazookas, mortars, mines, etc. worth about $ 30-50 mn a year. Covert arms aid subsequently increased to $ 600-$1000 mn a year. Thus, by a conservative estimate, Afghan guerrillas would have received light arms worth more than $ 2 bn. Since the types of weapons they received are not expensive, as compared to the weapons used in conventional wars like aircraft, tank, heavy artillery, warships, etc. quantity of arms given to Afghan rebels must have been very large; in fact much more than they could have effectively used.

Large number of these weapons have been acquired by the Punjab terrorists also either against payment of cash or in return for transit of drugs through India. Reportedly, $ 250,000 worth of arms were also purchased for the Punjab terrorists by the Canada-based International Sikh Youth Federation. The weapons used by Punjab terrorists are not very expensive. According to newspaper reports, the AK-47 Chinese assault rifle costs about Rs. 25,000 each. A rocket launcher costs Rs. 45,000 and a pistol only Rs. 15,000. The cost of explosive charge is Rs. 500 per unit. Thus, sufficient weapons and ammunition can be acquired in return for even modest sum in the international underground arms bazar. According to K.E. Rustamji about 1000 AK-47 assault rifles, a few rockets launchers and explosives have been smuggled into India from Pakistan. Of those, more than 150 AK-47s have been captured.

Conclusion

Response to terrorism has to be very guarded and well thought out. There has to be a close nexus between public opinion and official policy. Media has a major role to play in that lest it helps to create a public opinion that forces the government to take steps that might prove counter-productive. While the government has a major role in curbing the terrorist activities, public too has a role in winning over the terrorists through several positive actions like greater communal harmony, an effective rapport between public and the officials, etc. Thus, the public opinion helps in building up a climate which can lead to a political dialogue through which alone the question can be fruitfully resolved.

Two new factors have further complicated the question of terrorism. They are narco-terrorism and underground market for sophisticated men-portable weapons that are most suitable for acts of terrorism. Thus, drug control is directly linked to control of terrorism.

Terrorism and inslrrgency are major factors for destabilizing the developing world. Though the North may well shout about terrorism it is still a stable society that cannot be destabilized by terrorism. Afro-Asian societies are very fragile and are still in the process of nation building. Hence, they are much more vulnerable to the destabilizing effects of terrorism than the Western society. Thus, fight against terrorism should be seriously taken up at all levels, especially in the developing world.

South Asia is one of the worse affected areas in this context. Drugs, guns and forces of destabilization have already weakened the societal structures in Pakistan, India and Sri Lanka. Hence, it needs a regional solution. Fortunately the SAARC is deeply concerned with the question of terrorism. The question was first raised at the Dhaka Summit in June 1986 and a study group has met and recommended concrete suggestions which are based to a large extent upon the UN General Assembly resolution of December 1985. India has ratified the SAARC convention on terrorism. There are still a few differences on points of interpretation but the fact that the SAARC is prepared to discuss the question itself is a very healthy attitude.

8

Terrorism in India

Violence, however, is an essential part of terrorism. It is not at all easy to evolve a universal definition of terrorism. As a political activist with limited knowledge of history, I may make some observations. Terrorism represents an attempt to attain some political objective by creating terror by violence. Objective can be just and good as well as unjust and wrong. It can be really in the interests of people in whose name terror is used. It can also be very much against the interests of those very people. Violence used to create terror can be targeted as well as indiscriminate, senseless and unpredictable. This often depends upon the nature of objective and on the nature of motivation of those using terrorism.

Terrorism cannot succeed even if objective is noble and just. The justness of the objective can help in the method of terrorism being given up. To the extent it does not happen, terrorism results in degeneration of even well-motivated persons.

There is plenty of material in our own history to support and substantiate the above propositions.

Some terrorists of today try to exploit the name of our great martyr Bhagat Singh. But this is what Bhagat Singh himself said on February 1931 in his message to his revolutionary comrades, just a few weeks before he was hanged:

"Apparently I have acted like a terrorist but I am not a terrorist. Let me announce with all the strength at my command that I am not a terrorist and I never was except perhaps in the beginning of my revolutionary career. I am convinced that we cannot gain anything through these methods."

It is not necessary to add anything. There were also the Babber Akalis who too had the purest of motives and a noble objective. Their targets were agents of imperialism. They would announce their targets beforehand and also the names of persons who would kill them so that it would be almost impossible for the British rulers and their police to harass any innocent persons. Their targets never included women and children of even informers. Experience made them give up the method of terrorism.

Naxalites too are motiviated by an objective which is noble. They want a classless society in which there is no exploitation of man by man. What has been the experience of use of terrorism by Naxalites ? Many have given up terrorism and have joined the mainstream of the Left movement in India. Many have left not only terrorism but have also given up politics. They have splintered into a large number of groups. Some are moving in the direction of giving up terrorism while those doggedly refusing to do so are degenerating into groups indulging in casteist wars.

Some may argue that terrorism has succeeded in Nagaland, Mizoram, Darjeeling, Tripura, etc. The argument has no weight whatsoever. Those using the method of terrorism in these parts of India had to give up their original secessionist objectives. They had even to give up terrorism or agree to give it up. What they have achieved is at best equal to linguistic reorganization in the rest of India. Let it be remembered that this was achieved much earlier as a result of mass movements which were in the main and predominantly non-violent.

Let us now come to terrorism in Punjab. We intend to deal with its various aspects though not at great length for reasons of space.

Objective of Punjab Terrorists

The objective or Punjab terrorists is "Khalistan", i.e. an independent, sovereign theocratic Sikh state. It is not only against the interests or Indian people as a whole. It is against the interests of Sikhs themselves. Nowhere in the world a theoratic state has done any good even to the people–the common people professing the state religion. 'The Islamic State of Pakistan has not brought any happiness to the cowman Muslims of that country–workers, agricultural labourers, poor peasants and middle class people. Almost throughout the existence of this theoratic State, people stood deprived of even the most elementary human rights and, of course, of democracy. Unemployment for Muslim youths has not disappeared. Women have been sought to be reduced to the status of second class citizens in every aspect of life. Instead of Hindu-Muslim riots, Pakistan now has Shia-Sunni riots, riots between Muhajrins and the locals.

If India were to say that Muslims who migrated from post-1947 India to Pakistan can return to and settle in India, I am sure a very large number would do so with a big sigh of relief. Even though there is much misery, wrong and injustice in secular India, the reality of situation in theoratic Pakistan surely has a lesson for those who may feel attracted by the slogan of Khalistan. Nepal is a Hindu State. We in Punjab know how poor are the poor Hindus of Bihar which is the poorest state of India. We know because lacs of them come to Punjab for work. They work in industries of Punjab and also in the agricultural fields owned mostly by Sikh landowners. But in Bihar itself you can find poor Nepali Hindus trying to find work to be able to survive. The poor of "Hindu" Nepal are poorer than even the poor of our poorest state. This should provide some food for thought for those who want Hindu Rashtra in India and also for those who want "Khalistan" in Punjab. We had once the princely State of Patiala. It used to be described as a Sikh State by -the topmost Akali leaders because it was ruled by a Sikh Maharaja. The Sikh tenants and other common Sikhs suffered most–perhaps more than anyone else in India–at the hands of the Sikh Maharaja, their police and other minions.

There never was a Hindu rule or Muslim rule or Sikh rule in India. These terms were coined by our British rulers. Actually only Icings were Hindus or Muslims or Sikhs. There were good kings and bad kings. But even under the rule of good kings, even common people professing the same religion as the king were far from being happy. This is true of Akbar's rule as well as of Maharaja Ranjit Singh's, it is also true of the "Golden age" of Guptas.

A theoratic State in today's society can only mean greater miseries for the common people. It can at best only be a State of the vested interests belonging to a particular religious community but never a state of the common people of that very religious community.

There is much in our archives to prove that in fact the thesis "Sikhs-are- a-nation" and the slogan of Khalistan were first inspired and encouraged by the theoreticians of British imperialism to weaken freedom movement and our country-in the same way as were the theses of "Muslims are-a-separate nation" and the slogan of Pakistan.

In brief, the demand for Khalistan is as much anti-Sikh as it is anti-India.

Terrorism in Punjab

In the earlier stages of terrorism in Punjab, the left had to argue hard in support of its contention that behind the terrorists was the hand of imperialism operating from our own soil but mainly through the rulers of Pakistan which has a long border with Punjab as well as some neighbouring states. Today this external factor is recognized by one and all except those who deliberately do not want to see this or are interested in denying it. Evidence which has come to light already is indeed overwhelming and is too well known by now.

Imperialism does not like India's anti-imperialist role in the. international arena and her refusal to go neo-colonial, notwithstanding all the concessions which are given to the multinationals by our government. Imperialism therefore wants to weaken, destabilize and even disintegrate and balkanize India. Towards that end it encourages, aids and abets such slogans as "Khalistan", and "Azad Kashmir" and also Hindu Raj in India. Not very long ago, a world conference of the Hindu Vishwa Parishad which was held in the USA and which demanded Hindu Raj in India was patronized and attended by some from the ruling classes of that country.

Towards that end, US imperialism has been helping the Khalistani terrorists, mainly but not only through Pakistani rulers. Besides the fact that Zia was a US stooge, Pakistani ruler; have their own axe to grind too. Their calculations are not difficult to see. If at a time of crisis, say another Indo-Pak war they can occupy parts of Amritsar and Gurdaspur districts bordering Pakistan, Kashmir gets virtually cut off from India. This is their real practical ojbective, even when they encourage the slogan of Khalistan while carrying on an anti-Sikh campaign in their our country through publications in Urdu. This is one reason why the terrorists from the very start have concentrated on these two districts, while developing the capacity to strike in any part of Punjab and even outside Punjab.

Internal Forces and Factors

The capitalist landlord class and upper sections of rich peasants have been the biggest beneficiaries of the Green Revolution in Punjab. They are the dominant group in Punjab's economy. They want to become politically dominant too. They have their interests, ambitions as well as problems. Like the big industrialists, they too want to make bigger and bigger profits. Actually the rate of return from agriculture has started decling. Also, their interests conflict with the industrial capitalists who want cheap raw materials. They also want more avenues of investments. The need of developing industries in Punjab was not given adequate attention at the proper time. The scope for developing agro-industries was not paid for long the attention it deserved. To the extent the representatives of the rural bourgeoisie of Punjab were to demand growth of industries in Punjab and more powers for states, progressive forces would readily support the same. Actually they go much beyond that. While they talk of remunerative prices for agricultural produce to rally behind them the middle and poor peasants who are denied the same, they actually want profitereing prices for themselves. They actually want the right to sell their produce anywhere in the international market, howsoever adverse effect it may have for the common people of India including of Punjab and for the Indian economy. In fact they deny the very need for a common Indian economy. They mouth the just slogan of more powers for states but in fact want to make centre nothing more than a myth. They want to rule Punjab. It so happens that the overwhelming majority of the landlords and kulaks in Punjab are Sikh by religion and same is the position of the toiling peasantry. To have a strong mass base. and power, the class demands they put forward are described as- , "Sikh demands." They misuse religion and resort to religiosity and religious fundamentalism.

These vested interests are represented by the Akali leadership. The Anandpur Sahib resolution of the Akali party mirrors their demands and ambitions. It does contain some vote catching populist slogans but its essence is obvious and is two-fold.

One, it demands that Punjab should be a Sikh theocratic state, i.e. a state ruled by Sikh vested interests. Second, it demands that this Sikh theocratic State should have all powers except four departments, e.g. foreign affairs, defence, means of communication and currency. In other words, there should be no common Indian economy. The centre will not have the powers even to raise funds for the four departments. Punjab will contribute its share in proportion to its representation in the parliament. The ruling class at the centre has reduced states to the status of Municipalities. The Akali leaders including moderates want the centre to become a myth. They want a virtual Khalistan–in India–with a very weak centre.

If conceded, Khalistan will be a stepping stone to another partition of India. Even otherwise it would prove disastrous for the country. It would strengthon the demands for theocratic states in other parts of India and also all those who want India to become a Hindu fascist state. The Anandpur Resolution of the the Akali party, the Akali resoultion of "Sikhs-a-separate nation," its false propaganda about Sikhs being second-class citizens, etc. have been a source of big help to the terrorists. In the concrete situation of Punjab, it is not surprising that sections of landlords have gone a step further and become supporters of Khalistan as well as of terrorism. Some of the Akali leaders too have followed the same road. There are others who have developed all India economic interests, who are moderates and who really stand for India's unity. Any positive role they play must be welcome. Their tragedy lies in their communal outlook, their commitment to the Anandpur resolution and in the fact that they are willing to fight separatist-terrorists only on their own ground and by appeasing them which can prove counter-productive.

Another internal factor which helped the terrorists in Punjab is of Hindu communalism and its line of falsely holding the entire Sikh community as responsible for the crimes of the terrorists and its slogan of revenge and retaliation against innocent Sikhs. The Hindu communal organizations have links with Hindu vested interests like big traders, which feel threatened by the Sikh vested interests. The RSS slogan of "Hindu Rashtra" and its line that only Hindus can safeguard unity of India brings grist to the mill' of the terrorists. Sikhs are not a homogeneous economic community. Sikh landlords and Sikh tenants and agricultural labourers have sharply conflicting interests despite common religion. So also Sikh workers and Sikh capitalists. At the same time Sikh workers, Sikh agricultural labourers, Sikh poor and middle peasants, etc. have common interests with their counterparts professing other religions. In other words, Sikhs today have no separate and independent political and economic identity. But they do have a separate religious identity. Sikhism no doubt arose on Indian soil. All religions have something in common but Hindu and Sikh religions have much more in common than any other two religions. All this does not mean that Sikhism is not an independent religion. It has definitely since-long grown into one and is so recognized by the Indian constitution.

Bhajan Lal's (the then Chief Minister of Haryana) approach to teach Sikhs a lesson by humiliating and harassing a large number of Sikh passengers travelling to Delhi by buses, cars, etc. in the name of ensuring failure of the threat of disrupting the Asian games, rendered immense help to Bhindranwala.

Economically Sikhs are perhaps the most well-off community of India. They have a share in services (defence as well as civil) far in excess of their proportion in the population. There are many more gurudwaras in India per 1 lac of Sikhs now than in 1947. Allegations of discrimination therefore are false. However, a Hindu bias is there in the leadership of the country. For instance, just when the Akali demand for declaring Amritsar as a holy city was refused, Kurukshetra was declared one. This bias helps anti-national forces and must so.

The internal factor which ha. perhaps helped the terrorists most is opportunism of the bourgeois parties and not only the ruling one-indulged in for short term electoral or other political considerations. Many examples can be given but only a few will suffice.

As is universally known by now, Jarnail Singh Bhindranwala, a religious personality, was brought into politics by Congress with the aim of weakening the Akali party, its rival in the matter of power in the state of Punjab. The Akalis thought that they could play the Bhindranwala card better than the Congress. They first allowed him to stay in the Guru Nanak Niwas. Then they allowed him to stay in the holy Akal Takht, where even no Guru had ever stayed, and to convert the Golden Temple complex proper including the Akal Takht itself into an armed fortress and a big training camp for terrorists.

A very prominent General Secretary of the Congress(I) certified that Bindranwala was only a religious personality even when he had already become the leader of the terrorist killers and when he had already been calling for killings. Almost at the same time not one but three much respected opposition stalwarts visited the Golden Temple and issued certificates to the effect that they did not find any arms inside the Golden Temple complex when one even from outside could see many installed inside the complex and even on its outer walls.

Assassination of Prime Minister Indira Gandhi was the most despicable act master-minded by the terrorists and their patrons, imperialists. Those who celebrated the assassination deserved to be strongly criticized. Notwithstanding all this. the anti-Sikh riots resulting in killings of about 3000 innocent Sikhs in the Capital alone were totally unjustifiable A They constitute one of the blackest spots on India's fair name. They were not altogether spontaneous. Some VIPs played a big part in organizing these even though in not a few places old Congressmen too like the communists and others helped save many Sikhs, even at the risk of their own lives. For narrow party considerations, there has been a persistent refusal to prosecute the guilty. This grave injustice has been fully exploited by the extremists in Punjab and has done them very great service indeed. 'Again and again there have been attempts on the part of the Congress(I) high 'command to make a deal with a section of the terrorists sometimes with the help of Sunil Muni Jain and Darshan Singh Ragi, sometimes with the help of Badal (even though a novice in Punjab politics could tell that Badal would not oblige) and sometimes through Jasbir Singh Rode. Every such effort has proved counter-productive. It has only demoralized the security forces and has strengthened the terrorists. And yet this is not being given up for the sake of electoral considerations.' Not more than fifty in the Jodhpur Jail are terrorist killers or their organizers.

Yet many more are still there to be used as a bargaining counter. Non Left opposition parties too do not seem averse to making an unprincipled deal. Some top opposition leaders have been maintaining a strange silence regarding Punjab. Some have been saying that the Punjab problem would get resolved only when opposition comes to power in New Delhi. Some have started providing alibis for the terrorists by saying that all the killings are being done by the government agents.

The ordinance which the government issued to prevent places of worship from being used for storing weapons and from being used for political purposes was half-hearted. The Akalis opposed it.

Other bourgeois opposition parties instead of demanding it being made more effective, at best expressed only lukewarm support for it.

The terrorists are not concerned with the territorial disputes and the dispute regarding surplus river waters. They have often said so. But they have not failed to exploit the fact that these disputes (given communal colourings by the Akalis) remain unresolved. One of the main reasons for the disputes not getting resolved is the opportunism of the bourgeois parties. While communists take one and the same stand and put forward the same in the concerned states, every bourgeois party takes one stand in the parliament while giving full freedom to its state units to take different and mutually contradictory stands. It is not necessary to give more examples. The fact that the type of employment avenues desired by the youth are not there, and coupled with lure of weapons and money, it has played a part in spread of terrorism, though this is only a secondary factor.

Strategy, Methods, Tactics and Targets

As in the case of all terrorist movements, a key element in the strategy of the Khalistan terrorists is to create terror, to undermine the authority of the administration and to demonstrate their own strength. The strategy of the Khalistani terrorist however contains other key elements also specific to them. One is to appear as defender of Sikhs and Sikh religion, to widen the gulf between Hindus and Sikhs, to create a situation in which large scale Hindu Sikh riots break out, to force Hindus of Punjab to migrate to other states and to create a situation in which Sikhs from other states arc also forced to migrate and are also encouraged to do so. Anyone who was not with Bhindranwala during his life time remains an enemy.

They started by killing Nirankaris including Nirankari Sikhs because orthodox Sikhs have strong prejudice against them. Then it was the turn of Hindus in general and such individual personalities whose killings would provoke Hindus in and outside Punjab into senseless violent acts against innocent Sikhs. Of course, those who opposed them were bound to become their targets. Thus came also the turn of Sikhs who dared oppose them. They, were most vindictive against such Sikh families as were sympathetic to and helped them in various ways in the beginning but refused to do so later or turned against them. They would also kill those who would refuse them shelter, meals, etc. Later on they began killing those Sikhs who did not or could not meet their demands for huge amounts of money.

Of course policemen and men of the security forces have been killed in quite a large number. Most of men of the Punjab Police are Sikhs.

Thus very large number of Sikhs have been killed-not only policemen but also ordinary Sikhs, political activists and leaders belonging to different political parties. At the same time, Sikhs have as yet not been killed indiscriminately. For mass killings such places and bazaars are chosen where the victims would be mostly Hindus. Of course, in such killings not only some Sikhs but also Christians and Muslims too get killed or injured. When buses are hijacked to kill passengers, the practice has been to first ask the Sikh passengers to get away.

In the initial stages, such methods as placing cow heads before Hindus temples, breaking of idols of Hindu gods, etc. were also adopteds with the object of bringing about Hindu-Sikh riots. Hindu communalists, including–some Hindu Congressmen, would retaliate by attacking gurudwaras, by throwing cigarettes into Sikh temples and by damaging model of the Golden Temple.

An interesting but significant fact in connection with targets., needs to be noted. Mass killing of migrant (Hindu) labourers working in Punjab–especially in agriculture–has generally been avoided. The reason is that this would hit the economy of landlords and kulaks. Migrant labourers were attacked in a big way for the first time immediately after the Black Thunder operation of May 1988 which had given them a big set back. To show that they were still strong and to provoke anti-Sikh sentiments in states other than Punjab, they killed a large number of migrant labourers. Significantly the main targets were the labourers working on Sutlej-Yamuna link canal which would provide to Haryana its share of surplus waters. A number of agricultural labourers were killed also at least in one village of Amritsar district. This however was not repeated because of negative reaction even from their supporters. Only in the first week of November 1989, the terrorists again attacked the migrant labourers in a big way.

To increase their mass support, the terrorists adopted a social reform movement. Most of the items were aimed not at social reform but to encourage religious fundamentalism. For instance, barbers, those trimming their beards and such heads of schools, and teachers who would not make their pupils wear uniforms prescribed by extremists were threatened and made targets. The only items relating to social reform were regarding dowry, strength of marriage parties and liquor. Interestincly, many of those who killed liquor vendors were heavy drinkers themselves. Exemption in all the item's of social reform was given liberally in return for big sums of money. No wonder the movement petered out and ultimately has not helped the terrorists.

Degeneration of Terrorists

From the very beginning, a nexus between terrorists and smugglers was developed. One of the top acid most notorious smugglers of Amritsar was killed inside the Golden Temple at the time of the Bluestar operation. Anti-social elements were recruited from the very 'beginning. In course of time, many of those who were originally motiviated by religiousity or some such other factors too have degenerated. This degeneration and utter lack of humane feeling are reflected in killings of even women and children. Killings have been done for sex too. Many have become professional killers. 'Most of the normal killings too are now being done by terrorists for money. There are mutual rivalries amongest terrorist groups and also mutual killings.

The ugly face of the terrorists was fully exposed by the Black Thunder operation of May 1988-which was carried out with the entire press watching it and which was also televised. It became widely known that the Golden Temple had been turned into a torture house; how those who refused to pay up as per demand were subjected to horrible torture and then killed ; how even Amritshari 'Sikhs were not spared ; how even women were raped, tortured and killed.

About 50 dead bodies were discovered from below the debris of the Akal Takht. Only a few could be identified. To their great horror and shock, people learnt how a number of militants had remained all the time within Harminder Sahib proper for two days. 'While this exposed their claims of being true Sikhs, the way they surrendered instead of living up to their boasts that if necessary they would embrace death while fighting and thus achieve martyrdom showed them up as cowards. Their isolation became complete, which was also reflected in the fact that there was no response to the call to march to the Golden Temple to protest against the alleged invasion though the same was given by almost all the Akali leaders, the Panthic Committee as well as by rival sects of Head priests.

It was the most opportune time for the government to continue the offensive into the Mand area (another important centre of operation of the terrorists) and simultaneously to take correct political initiatives for a political solution. Opportunist considerations prevented this, enabling the terrorists to regroup themselves.

All that we have said above does not imply that there are no misguided youths amongst the terrorists. There are and all efforts need to be made to bring them back into the mainstream. However, such efforts are likely to bear fruit only when the backbone of the terrorist organizations has been broken.

One thing more needs to be made clear. We are not against. talks with extremists, but these should not be held when that wilt only help the terrorist killers and demoralize the security forces. Right time would be only after they have been forced to give up the demand for Khalistan as well as for a theocratic state and after the killings have stopped.

Methods of Collecting Funds and Recruitment

Main sources of fund collections by the Punjab terrorists have been as under:

(i) Huge amounts have come from abroad from those who are sympathetic to the `cause' including from millionaire non-Indian Sikhs. Collections in such gurudwaras in foreign countries as are controlled by extremists have also been utilized for the purpose.

(ii) Big amounts have also come from cities like Bombay and Calcutta contributed and collected by supporters of the 'cause'.

(iii) Collections of gurudwaras in Punjab when controlled by terrorists or their friends have also been used.

(iv) Banks dacoties, robberies, etc. In some cases of robberies, the victims happened to be Sikhs. They pleaded for being spared. They were told that they might fulfil the demand out of sympathy or at the point of gun-the choice was theirs.

(v) Extortion through threats. First, Hindu businessmen and professionals were the targets. Then the operation was extended to Sikh businessmen and professionals and thereafter also to comparatively well-off landowners.

An interesting aspect of this operation has been bargaining indulged in to decide the exact amount to be given with the help of mediators. In some cases terrorists known to be the targets have also helped to lower the demands. Of course at the time of the negotiations, AK-47 Chinese Assault Rifles and other sophisticated weapons would be on display.

Groups like teachers of a particular school have been made to pay fixed monthly contributions.

(vi) Ransom on the basis of kidnappings. This method has been adopted in a big, way only recently in the sub-division Patti in Amritsar district. Main targets are shellac and brick kiln owners and their children, well off shopkeepers, etc. Amounts demanded are quite big. In some cases the mediators would get the demand lowered. In some other cases hostages have been shot dead too. Targets are Hindus as well as Sikhs. On a smaller scale this has been happening since long and also in the districts of Gurdaspur and Ferozpur.

(vii) Another method adopted from the days of Bhindracwala and which continues till today though exact procedure has been varying at different times. On the basis of some complaint of someone, the complainant and the opposite party would be summoned. Decision would then be given and its implementation would be demanded under threat of liquidation. The beneficiary party or both would also be ordered to make handsome contributions.

(viii) In the days of the so-called social reform movement, liquor vendors and others would be spared for considerations.

The above may not be an exhaustive list of the methods used.

It may be mentioned that not all the money goes to the 'cause' — for purchasing weapons, for paying to the recruits, etc. A number of terrorists, though not all, have used a part of the collections for themselves–for acquirlng luxury items as well as for immovable properties.

A few words about the methods of recruitment.

There is the appeal of the religiosity. Also the promise of a 'Khalistan in which will flow rivers of milk and honey, in which nobody would be unemployed, there is also the pull of weapons and of money. Youths whose fathers do not have big landholdings get attracted easily. There are also many anti-social elements turned terrorists because that makes their job easier and also 'respectable'.

Despite all this, there is the significant fact that the number of terrorists from families of Sikh agricultural labourers who are the poorest in the Sikh community has been negligible. Their reactions even to events like Bluestar operation and killing of Bhindranwala were quite different from those of the landowning peasantry.

There is also the fact that quite a number of terrorists have come from families of the rich and quite a few had even good decent- jobs. The financiers and willing providers of shelter and stores for weapons and the members of the brain trust include big landlords and even some IAS, IPS, and other top officers coming from landlord families. Generally these officers are retired but the possibility of some serving ones being their comrades-in-arms cannot be ruled out. Some caught too badly had to be dismissed.

When the terrorists are at the receiving end, recruitment goes down. When they are an top or when the security forces get orders to stay their hands, recruitment goes up. Such has been the experience at least in Amritsar district.

Some Other Connected Points

1. It is rightly said by some that one of the causes for the trouble in Punjab is the fact that at one time big majority of Punjabi Hindus lying in the face of truth denied that Punjabi was their mother tongue and instead recorded Hindi as such. This was the result of bad advice given by the then Jana Sangh as well as the Hindu Congess leaders. All this however is a part of the truth. The other part, equally wrong and imaging, is the fact that the Akali Party championed the cause of Punjabi language as if it was a part of Sikh religion and as if its development was linked with their original demand for a Sikh state and then for a Punjabi-speaking state in which Sikhs would be at least sixty per cent.

Communalists of both hues have contributed a lot towards disruption of development of common Punjabi consciousness, of the Punjabi nationality within the great Indian nation. To reverse the process is a hard and long term job. It requires a prolonged fight not only for separation of religion and politics, or religion and state but also of religion and language, i.e. Punjabi language. Some intellectuals including a few who claim to be Left refuse to see the need of this fight or are not ready for it. They are putting forward the dangerous thesis that today Sikhs alone are true Punjabis, that Sikhs are fighting the battle of Punjabi nationality, etc. I am afraid such intellectuals are only providing grist to the mill of the extremists and even of the terrorists killers, even though unconsciously. There is a view point that a really big economic package by providing employment will lead to a solution of the problem. To the extent the past mistake is rectified and proper attention is given to the development of such industries in Punjab as are needed and for which there is the necessary potential, that will be a welcome thing. In the long run, it will increase the weight of the working class in the political life of Punjab and that will be a set back for divisive forces. It is however an illusion that any economic package can do the trick and lead to an instant solution. After all an economic package including a Railway Coach Factory was given to Punjab by the Prime Minister some years ago. And that coach factory has already started production. Has it led to a solution of terrorism. There is also another important aspect of the problem.

Development possibilities within the capitalist system are much less than the needs and even the actual potential. The available cake of development must be shared equitably between all states, keeping in view the special needs of backward regions. All progressive forces must fight for bigger development of the country as a whole and also for going forward to anti-capitalist path. As things stand today, no government in India can go on depriving other states of their share of development projects to give some really big economic packages to some other state. It can be done only to a limited extent. Let me recall what happened when the Railway Coach Factory which had originally been allotted to Kerala was instead given to Punjab. One Minister of the then Congress (I) led government of Kerala threatened to create Punjab like situation in Kerala. Even the Left Parties in that state did not find it easy to swallow the decision to take away the coach factory from Kerala.

Negative Aspects Of Government Policies

Even apart from what has been referred to above, some other negative aspects of the government policies need to be noted.

1. There are quite a few elements even today within the administration including police which are pro-extremists and who help them in one way or another. There was a time when the decisions taken even in the Governer-in-council would reach the terrorist leadership in less than an hour while government intelligence amongst the terrorists organizations was non-existent. Situation is not very satisfactory even today. Steps are necessary to improve the situation.
2. There is lot of corruption in the police. There have also been excesses on the part of the police and the-- security forces for reasons other than corruption. For instance, error of judgement, overreaction, officers/officials getting mixed up with local feuds and committing excesses upon one party at the instance of the other, etc. There have been lot of extortions and minting of money by the corrupt in the police. Victims do not belong exclusively to one community.

   It is necessary to expose and fight all excesses–not only for the sake of justice but also because some of the excesses bring grist to the mill of the extremists. While the extremists have sought to exploit the excesses even by exaggerating them, the left has been exposing the same and has been fighting concerty for justice. I do not however subscribe to the theory of state terrorism in Punjab. Excesses are one thing and state terrorism is quite another thing. The theory of state terrorism was put forward to provide an alibi for killings by the terrorists. It is argued even today that individual terrorism is the result of state terrorism in Punjab. This is a case of turning facts upside down.
3. As far as anti-terrorist fight on the administrative front is concerned, the government has been acting as if that means only by the police and the security forces.

The terrorists have been acting on many fronts.

In the field of education, they have killed a large number of teachers. School education has come to a virtual end in many parts of Amritsar and Gurdaspur districts. Some institutions of higher education have become preserves and even centres of operation of the terrorists or of anti-social elements passing for terrorists. Mass of students in these feel helpless and disgusted.

A large number of employees of the Punjab State Electricity Board, of the Banks, of the Health Department too have been killed. In certain areas, their branches/ units have virtually closed.

The terrorists have succeeded in paralysing the judiciary. Even killers of dozens would get bailed out. A father would not be willing to give evidence even if his real son had been killed by terrorists before his very eyes. Recently a spokesman of the government made a significant admission that it had not been able to obtain even one conviction so far.

The terrorists walk through fields and *pagdandis*. The security forces often are unable to use even link roads effectively because they are so damaged that their vehicles cannot move on them even at the speed at which a man normally walks. It has not struck the departments concerned to repair such damaged link roads in the terrorist stronghold areas on a priority basis.

In short, there has been failure to evolve a comprehensive policy to fight terrorism covering all departments. No wonder many secretaries of key and sensitive departments have been enjoying long foreign trips. Even proper training of police was not started for long. Till very recently the security forces had weapons much inferior to those of the terrorists. For long they were not provided such essential instruments as night-vision devices.

Solution

Those who say that the Punjab problem is only a law and order problem are wrong. Equally wrong are those who consider it only as a political problem. It is both and must be tackled simulta neously at both the fronts.

Immediately following steps are needed:

1. An offensive against terrorists must be a continuous offensive without any let up till their backbone is broken. Excesses must be avoided.
2. All except the killers and their organizers out of the Jodhpur detenus must be released unconditionally.
3. Those responsible for organizing anti-Sikh riots of November 1984 must be prosecuted.

4. All states including Punjab must be given more powers but no special status of any kind to it because the same will lead to a theocratic state.
5. An all party national level meeting to evolve the broadest possible consensus regarding territorial and river waters disputes. Prior to that or at the meeting all national parties must pledge that their state units will not be allowed to take contradictory stands and will be bound by the consensus. All must then go to the people of the concerned states and appeal to them to accept the same. Such a consensus will of course be arrived at keeping in view the national interests, in the spirit of give and take and without doing gross injustice to any state. This is the only way the spirit of Rajiv-Longowal Accord can be saved.

Secular and patriotic parties and groups must jointly as well as individually launch a new and powerful mass compaign at the grass root level to isolate separatist terrorists, against killings, against excesses, against the slogan of Khalistan and of Hindu Raj, for the above demands; against the misuse of religious places, against the slogan of revenge and retaliation, for separation of religion and politics, religion and state.

Of course, from joint platforms only jointly agreed issues must he taken up. There must be no attempt by anyone to exploit the joint platform against each other because that will stake any joint compaign impossible.

The experience so far has shown that the organized working class, and the agricultural labourers have not only not fallen prey to separatism, extremism and even communalism. These two have actively intervened in a big way at various critical junctures and have saved the situation.

Role of Parties

It is not intended to describe the role of various political parties. for reasons of space. It must however be mentioned that the left has played an outstanding role on its own (the two communist parties and some Naxalite groups acting independently and also jointly), by taking successful initiatives to unite all parties for joint campaigning on more than one occasion. All parties have paid a big price but the heaviest has been paid by the communists. By their sacrifices the communists have proved that they are not only internationalists but are fine patriots.

The CPI has also run a big campaign regarding the Punjab issue which in fact is a national issue involving the very future of the entire country, in a number of states other than Punjab. The Punjab Istri Sabha is the only mass organization which is doing work to provide relief to victims of terrorists on a non-communal basis. (The first place of course goes to the Shaheed Pariwar Fund of the Hindu Samachar group of papers.) Its scheme to give stipends to orphaned children to enable them to continue their education has caught the imagination of big sections. Funds are coming from all over India. A big part in the collection is being played by the units of the National Federation of Indian Women and many individuals belonging to different walks of life. This is not only good humanitarian work It helps the fight for defending and strengthening the unity-in-diversity of our country and our people.

Last but not the least. The question is not whether India will remain one or not. No power on earth can separate Punjab from India. The total failure of the terrorists even though helped by communalisms of the opposite hue to bring about Hindu. Sikh riots should convince all of the correctness of this assertion. The real question is how many more innocent lives would be lost before terrorism in Punjab is fully and finally defeated. The reply depends upon us all–or our response to the call of blood of innumerable innocent persons belonging to different political parties as well as to no party–Hindus as well as Sikhs, Muslims and Christians who have fallen during the last ten years.

9

Terrorist Violence in India

The modern European writers like Nicolo Machiavelli, Jean Bodin and Thomas Hobbes later conceptualized the notion of a modern sovereign state as something 'Fear' institutionalized, rationalized and hence justified. Calling State as 'The Buldgeon' with which the proliteriat shall wage its war, the great political philosopher of our times Karl Marx accepted and even underlined the role of 'Force' and 'Violence' in the theory of the Sovereign Nation State. The Lasswalian perspective of looking at politics as a crude game in which someone seeks to get something, somehow at some point of time does not preclude the need of terror or coercion as a basic instrumentality of the game. Modern political theory may argue to rule out the possibility of use of gun as an argument, but some sort of violent coercion has to have its place in the process of 'authoritative allocation of values' which Easton Calls the basic function of the political system.

Philosophical musings apart, this notion of political power or legitimate force or governmental authority, wielded by the sovereign state represents a 'legal instrumentality of action'; so very essential for the political survival of the system always and everywhere. Whether people can be kept terrified or they themselves perceive the terror of anarchy or authority is the central question which keeps bordering on the conceptual domains of 'volition', 'utility', 'general will' and now 'public interest'. Aristotle, the father of political science who predicted the possibility of revolutionary phenomenon or dissensions in the city states of Hellas linked them inversely with the dimunition of fear from the government which often culminates in the rise of terrorist groups in the body politic of the State. Machiavalli quite candidly uttered a universal political truism, when he blatantly maintained that a "Sovereign should be feared rather than loved" Hobbes, Hegel and Hitler might have their respective notions of coercion but terror does occupy a central place in their weaponary of the State.

The contemporary view of politics as a struggle for hegemony and domination of elite groups over disorganized masses in its ultimate tends to indoctrinate people and make the citizens reconcile to some sort of 'pattern maintenance'. The political systems, democratic or otherwise, do accept the manipulative role of politics in controlling the sub-systems of society. Both USA and USSR permit their political systems to regulate their economies, coordinate their belief structures and generate new cultural values of development and modernization. The national and international dimensions of the present day nation state system systematically concentrate upon the questions of sovereign identity, its defence and even expansion. The phenomenon of political nation state in the nonwestern world confronts a gruesome challenges of 'state Building' and 'Nation Welding' around the nucleus of political structure which Myrdal calls 'the soft state'! Burdened with the. colonial legacies of frightening dimensions, most of these new sovereign states in the third world find their nation state building efforts frustrated by unprecedented pressures of demographic explosions, cultural pluralism and international ideologies.

The ethnic, religious and lingual minority sub-groups in most of these developing countries find their newly won political independence at variance with their respective cultural identities, solidified over a period of centuries. In a country like India, where political nationalism has developed around colonial exploitation and negativism of communal partition, the cultural mainstream of national life has either been too elitist or stands ecologically polluted by strands of communal distrust and ethnic exclusiveness. Consequently, the battle between the political nation state and the society, culturally organized into sub-national groups results into inevitable jolts which a liberal and secular constitution often finds too shocking to absorb. The hope that the modern apparatus of the political state will ultimately take care of parochialism of the mediaeval Indian society bears a big question mark. As things stand the risks of disintegration of the largest democracy of the world are not very high, but the process of internal dissensions and external manipulations keep on encouraging the ambitious minority groups to manipulate and control the politico-cultural mainstream of national life. The innocuous non-issues are politicized in the name of minority grievances, minority identities and minority victimization , and the political process of nation building is hampered by rhetorical fantacies of Home lauds. Gorkhaland, Khalistan, Dravidisthan, Azad Kashmir, autonomous pockets in the North East are being paraded as dreamlands for which terrorist violence and insurgent battles are being resorted to as a part of political strategy.

They play in the hands of self-seeking leaders and alien powers who have vested interests in destabilization of the region and balkanization of the subcontinent. Terrorism as a weapon in politics is quite handy to these individuals and enemy states, which want to use terror for publicity or for dramatizing their so called minority cause, which in the present, has no public support. By fighting an imaginary war of the weak these terrorist and insurgent minority groups in India or even in Sri Lanka want to push the legitimate constitutional governments into defensive, so that they may be coerced to accept the unreason able. The nation building exercise in India or in any third world. country requires a cooperative endeavour by all groups to subordinate their sub-cultural interests to national consolidation. The minority politics when vulgarized to manipulate cruder power at the hustings activizes these sub-groups into fanaticism and fundamentalism. The terrorist tactics represent an articulate attempt to create missionaries, Messiahs and martyrs for a so called cause which can electrify the insecure and blinden the ignorant to fight under the leadership of self-appointed fascists. Terrorist violence as a tactic to sabotage nation building exercise in India needs an intellectual inquiry into its conceptual formulations to appreciate some of the violent operations of minority politics in the federal system of India.

Rice of Terrorism

Terrorism in politics represents a radical method, or a theory behind this method, whereby an organized group of saboteurs seeks to achieve its avowed aims through the systematic use of violence. In any theory of revolutionary change, the concept of terrorism can be distinguished from its allied concepts like 'intimidation', 'insurgency' and 'revolution'. Unlike the latter situations, the terrorist does not merely threaten injury to collect a ransom, nor does he plan to overthrow a government, even when circumstances offer a hope of success. Insurgency may be one of the objectives of the group, which employs terrorism, but the two phenomena are not necessarily linked at the ideological plane. Absence of pre-meditated plans and lack of painstaking preliminary preparations may in fact characterize both.

All terrorists primarily aim to are use the mass of the people to a realization that constituted authority is no longer safely entrenched or unchallenged. Their acts may be conceived as an advance notice of what may be expected from mass action. Death and destruction to them are not 'mere threats', but a part of programme of action. A terrorist is a combatant in the struggle between social groups and political forces, rather than in a fight between individuals. All kinds of social and political systems can be prone to this sort of combat.

Speaking realistically terrorism in politics is a weapon of blackmail, coercion and imposition of minority will against and upon a majority decision, legitimate or otherwise. All terrorists profess to have a laudable cause. Their missionary zeal and commitment operate under the assumption that sooner or later a majority of the people will recognize and support the course, for which constitutional means are not effective in the present.

Historically the Blanquists in France, Sin Fenners in Ireland and Bolshevics and Narodnya Volya in Tsarist Russia have employed terror as a chosen instrument of political action against their adversaries. Their conspiratory methods of scare and violence had their appeal in 'Romantic Messianism'. The theoretical formulations of these subversive activities were derived form the writings of Kropotkin and Brousee, who believed in the 'propaganda of the the deed' and 'educative and publicity value of terror' in human Society. A classic statement about the nature, scope, purpose and methods of terrorists appeared quite succinctly in the programme of the Executive Committee of Narodnya Volya in 1879. It reads:

> *The terrorist activity consists in destroying the most harmful person in the government, in defending the party against espionage... It aims to undermine the prestige of the governmental power to demonstrate the*

possibility of struggle... to arouse revolutionary. spirit of the people and their confidence in the success of the cause and finally to give shape and direction to the forces fit and trained to carry out the fight.

They take risks to publicize their cause and steadfastly work to expand and establish a popular base for the continuation of a movement. Actually, their immediate purpose is generally to add urgency to the problem. Being a hopeless minority they strive to present a desperate and cynical dimension of the problem to demoralize the rulers and ultimately to push them into a more cynical situation of counter-terrorism. Jallianwala Bagh massacre can be taken as an example in point. The frightening acts are intended to create a breakdown of law and order, which may intimidate people, and delegitimize a constitutional government. The psychology of mass insecurity may hasten institutional collapse.

The killers of Indian diplomat Mahatre, the captors of US hostages in Iran, the assassins of General Vaidya and Lala Jagat Narain, the killers of British policewomen at Libyan Embassy in London and the guerrilla fighters of PLO all had a common criminal weaponry of violence, advocated and justified as a noble cause, about which people are supposed to have sympathy, but arc not enlightened enough to feel inspired to other an organized fight.

As a revolutionary tactic, terrorism in world history has rarely succeeded. Governments have seldom retreated before acts of black mail. Barring a few examples of the former colonial world like Israel, the heroic or desperate acts of isolated individuals have by and large been unsuccessful in generating the phenomenon of revolutionary change, which presupposes a popular mass base.

Yet, it will be naive to assert that terrorism of 'Gun as an argument' in politics can be dismissed as something secondary or non-decisive especially when the chips are down. Its exclusive role may not be very potent but the context of intervening and inter-dependent variables can add to its apparent vehemence. The real strength of the terrorist force depends upon the state's capacity to hold on and refuse to get cowed down in sheer panic or alarm. Like terrorists the government also have to exhibit its risk-taking potential, especially when the leaders have fanatic followers, trained in the use of sophisticated weapons. The state of international complicity (if complicated by a free flow of funds and arms, made available to strengthen or contain political ideologies) can go a long way to give a prolonged lease of life to the already discredited or fading movements. Preemptive action, shock-threapy, dramatization of trivialities may keep the popular attention glued to a projected cause, but in its ultimate, the battle may prove self-defeating to the terrorists, who may fall into a trap of organizing terror, rather than a terrorist movement. History bears a testimony that dastardy acts of violence and mass killings, even when glamourized, may romanticize the liberal bourgeois, but they often leave the peasants or masses bewildered and cold. The illusion of making any cause venerable through the barrel of a gun is actually misreading Mao.

Islamic and Marxist Bases

International 'Terrorism' is not a sporadic phenomenon born in social misery or frustrations. It is rooted in the political ambitions and designs of expansive states or the violent groups that assert for identity. The terrorists habitually describe themselves as guerrillas, but all guerrillas are not terrorists. Actually they are irregular soldiers who wage war on regular military forces. The 'terrorist' choose to attack on weak and defenceless civilians, old men, women and children or any one except the soldiers against whom rapid they think they cannot tight. Contemporary terrorism began its growth in the sixties when it got-sparked off by an early success of two violent groups of terrorists. The PLO was the first to *introduce airline hijacking as an international weapon* to terrorize its opponents. The European radical faction was another group which carried out increasingly bold bombings, kidnappings and assassinations throughout the continents. These terrorist groups, seemingly independent of each other soon proliferated throughout Europe, Japan, North and South Americas and the Islamic middle east. But as the evidence got piled up it was discovered that the Arab PLO, the Iranian muzahedin, the ASALA, the German Barderminnhoj Gang, the Italian Red Brigades Army and several others were linked not only with one another but also with the, superpowers and the radical Arab regimes. After the expulsion of PLO from Beirut the captured documents revealed that it had a role in the terrorist ministration at Lebanon which was a training Centre and launching ground for what has come to stay as a kind of terrorist international. This collaboration between the Marxists and the Muslims was not accidental. The roots of modern terrorism can be traced to these two movements that have assumed international prominence in the second half of 20th century. The, Communist totalitarianism and Islamic radicalism have given modern terrorism its idological impetus and much of its material support. Both of them championed unbridled violence in the name of high causes and are hostile to democracy. Both these movements have found in terrorism an ideal weapon for waging a war against democracy.

The Targets

The targets of modern terrorism can be seen and found in Britain, Germany, Spain, Portugal, France, Italy, Israel, Japan, Sri Lanka and Latin America. The US nationals alone roughly account for one-third of the terrorist victims Since 1969. A network of professional terrorists seeks to weaken and demoralize democratic societies, by attacking their citizens, their leaders, their institutions and thereby disrupts their way of life and saps their political will. The terrorist attacks now kill and injure not one or two but dozens and hundreds at a time as has been the experience in Sri Lanka and Punjab. The terrorist activities assume international dimensions. when they are directed at foreigners or foreign targets and are aimed at influencing the policies of foreign governments. Criminals have used it to obtain ransom and other forms of private gains. The psychopaths have terrorized people for motives which they themselves have not fully understood. The bored, sadistic and weak-minded activists have terrorized innocent citizens to express their frustration and hatred in acts of symbolic protest and revenge against society. When politically motivated this coercive intimidation has. led to systematic murders and destructions. The threats of murder, and destruction are used to terrorize individuals, groups, communities and governments to concede to political demands.

The concern of terrorist activities in different parts of the world has assumed disconcerting proportions during last few years. The terrorist believe in the cult of the bomb and the gun–violence by all available means. Terrorism has come out in many shapes and sizes. A solitary individual may plant a crude home made bomb or a grenade or some other explosive in a shopping centre, at a bus stand, or in a cinema house or at a railway station. There can be fugitive groups which may plan kidnappings and assassinations of important personalities. Well-equipped and adequately financed organizations may use force to terrorize an entire or sizeable section of population of a country. All these categories of terrorists wreck vengeance against those whom they regard as oppressors, enemies and obstacles in the achievement of their goal. In pursuance of these goals, these desperate people adopt diverse tactics of which hijacking, blackmail, ruthless killings are the most common ones. Some of the effective terrorist groups, functioning in the present day world are:

1. Symbionise Liberation Army, US.
2. The Front de Liberation an Quebeck (Front of the Liberation of Quebec), Canada.
3. The Tupamaros of Uniguay and the Ejertico Revolucionario de Puelble (People Revolutionary Army) of Argentina.
4. The IRA of Ireland (killer of Lord Mountbatten).
5. The Badder Minhoff group of FRG.
6. The Red Brigades of Italy.
7. The Palestinian Guerrillas.
8. Arab Terrorist Group such as Black September Organization.
9. The Hukbalahaps of the Philippines.
10. Red Army of Japan.
11. The Khalistan Commando Force of India.
12. Liberation Tigers of Tamil Eelam of Sri Lanka.

The Tragic Tale of Terror

During the Munich Olympic Games of 1972 a dastardly act of terrorism occurred which killed several sportsmen from Israel. It aroused world wide anger. Since then intensive security arrangements are made to ensure protection to all the athletes and players in Olympic Games and other such events. In the year 1985 international terrorism claimed more than 600 lives in hijackings, bombings, assassinations and sabotage. Brian Jenkins, a terrorism expert calls the year 1985, 'the worst year for international terror.'

Hijacking of aircraft is a common form of the act of terrorism by certain groups because the passengers of the aircraft provide an alluring target for the criminals. The first hijacking incident occurred in 1930 when Perunian Revolutionary seized a Fokker F 7 aircraft on a domestic flight to drop propaganda leaflets. It was around this time that the word 'terrorism' came into vogue. The period 1968-72 with nessed a wave of hijackings touching the record figure of 1965 a year. In 1970 there was a major case of hijacking a plane by the popular Front Guerrillas for liberating Palestine. There were also cases of hijacking of Indian airlines flights when they were forced to land in Pakistan by the hijackers. A young Chinese from the mainland hijacked a British airways flight to Taiwan. In each case no passenger was hurt and the aircrafts were not damaged. The latest in the hijacking business are the Shi 'ite Fundamentalists. Their first operation threat was in Iran. Soon after the Shah was thrown out of power, the followers of Khomeini hijacked the entire American Lmbassy. Later Khomeini himself intervened to lift the seize. The Iran Shi'ites victory in humiliating the world's most powerful nation encouraged their coreligionists in other parts of West Asia. In the year 1965, some Iranian Shi'ite Fundamentalists siezed a Kuwait Airbus in Dubai in the air and killed two US passengers. They also took over a Transworld Airlines Flight in Athens and held about 48 US passengers at gun point. One of them was killed. The demand was to release 700 Lebanese Shi'ites detained by Israel. In the same year on 23 June the Air India plane *Kanishka* carrying 329 passengers from Canada exploded in the air, reportedly by an explosion of a time bomb placed by some terrorists based in Canada.

The Camper School

The terrorists hatched a conspiracy to kill Rajiv Gandhi, Prime Minister of India and some Indian VIPs during their visit to the United States in 1985. It was believed that they were trained in terrorism at Alabama, an institution run by Frank Camper. According to US columnist Jack Anderson, Iran is having a training camp for terrorists from different countries to hijack aircrafts and kidnap Americans. Saudi Intelligence report estimated that about 55 terrorists have studied hijacking in Iran in the year 1984.

They included Iranians, Iraqis, Tunisians, Moroccans, Egyptians and at least one Saudi. The Chief Instructor was a Palestinian guerrilla with good experience in hijacking. Similarly about the extremist activities in Punjab, there is strong suspicion about the existence of training camps in Pakistan to encourage transborder criminality.

Nuclear Terror

Crimes and criminals usually march with the times and adopt the latest inventions and available devices. It is believed that every country is vulnerable to nuclear terrorism, whenever it might actually occur. Since nuclear terrorism is a potential menace for the whole world, it needs to be tackled on a global scale. The nuclear powers themselves make a point to possess enough weapons to create a deterrent and to ensure safety for their respective territories. But there is always a danger of theft of nuclear materials and their misuse by mischief mongers. The US Government believes that, as in the case of world problems, nuclear terrorism, can also be taken care of by a collaborative strategy among the five nuclear weapon powers. In the summer of 1985, the USA signed agreements on nuclear terrorism with Soviet Union and France. The Moscow-Washington treaty signed, on 14 June 1985 in Washington, indicates that the superpowers are involved in seeking a consensus to the effect that terrorists who use or threaten to use nuclear weapons may be dealt with jointly and somewhat effectively. The establishment of an international police force to prevent thefts of nuclear materials along with other security measures like anti-terrorist squads have been debated and proposed to protect critical nuclear targets. Spread all over the world, since 1979 several State Governments have joined what may be described as 'League of Terror.' A study of international terrorism conducted in 1984-85 by the University of Israel criticized the western nations for taking recourse to terrorist methods while condemning them simultaneously when it hits their own interests. Experts maintain that terrorism perpetrated by countries for strategic objectives will continue to prevail in the coming decades. The abduction-cum-assassination of an Indian diplomat in Burmingham, the hijacking of an Indian Airlines plane to the United Arab Emirates and the killing of the British Deputy High Commissioner in Bombay and Russian diplomat at Delhi were among the significant terrorist incidents of the years 1984-85. The responsibility for the 27 November attack on Morn's Percy of British consulate in Bombay was claimed by a group calling itself the revolutionary organization of the Socialist Mulims. The target of Israel was PLO hqs. with the intention of killing its Chairman Yasser Arafat. Another tiny Asian country which is continuously affected by State Terrorism is Sri Lanka where there is regular fight between

Government forces and Sri Lankan Tamils resulting in the deaths of thousands of innocent civilians in Jaffna.

Indian Variant in Prospect and Retrospect

The terrorist activities in India were noticed for liberating India from the British Rule. At that time 'Terrorism' was distinct from other revolutionary, methods such as communism and Ghadar Movement. It denotes the commission of outrages which were comparatively 'Individual' in nature. The terrorists held the belief that Indian Independence can be brought about by a series of revolutionary outrages calculated to instil fear into the British officials and to drive them out of India. The movement took violent shapes in the then undivided Bengal and later on in upper India. M.N. Roy and Rasbehari Bose, the great revolutionaries made elaborate plans for a general uprising among Indian troops but the scheme could not succeed after the discovery of the plot. Later, the idea moved to Punjab, United Provinces, Delhi, Madras, Bihar and Orissa. In the later half of the nineteenth century, then Wahllabis, a puritanical Islamic sect steeped in fundamentalism, unleashed a wave of violence in India. In 1872 one of its members assassinated Lord Mayo, the Viceroy in Andaman Islands. The CPI in its second Congress held in Calcutta in March 1948 adopted an insurrectionary temper and organized violent activities on its. peasant fronts in Telengana and Kakdwip in West Bngal. Insurrectionary violence involving acts of Terrorism erupted in Nagaland over independence issue and later extended to Mizoram in 1966, Manipur in 1970 and Tripura in 1980. Extremists in CPI(M) whose activities began worrying even the party leadership in 1965, emerged a: a distinct stream in 1967 and formed the Communist Party of India (Marxist-Leninist) on 1 May 1969 in Calcutta. They indulged in all sorts of serious and violent activities liquidating, persons including police personnel in Calcutta and West Bengal. They declared police as a class enemy and the State governments have to suppress them in West Bengal, part of Assam, Tripura, Bihar, Orissa, Andhra Pradesh, Tamil Nadu, Kerala, Maharashtra and Punjab. Tripura in Eastern India was affected by terrorism in the eighties and passed under CPI(M) rule in 1984. The activities of extremists there, pose a threat to the national integrity of the college. Terrorism has attracted youngsters snore especially tile school and college students. The pre-Independence terrorists in Bengal, tire Nexalites in the late sixties and the terrorist in Punjab mostly comprise misguided but idealistic youths. Certain sections are apparently more vulnerable than others to the call of terrorism but it is also true that anti-social elements often became active in these movements to achieve their goals. Various kinds of revolutionaries, inspired by nationalist ideas, choose to tread the path of violence to ensure liberation of their motherland from foreign yoke. The so called terrorists have indulged in reckless killings for narrow, sectional and communal ends. During India's freedom movement revolutionaries like Bhagat Singh, Sukhdev, Rajguru, Surya Sen, Binay Badal Dinesh, Dhudiram and Bagha Johri and innumerable others played a heroic role. The Wahhabi Martyrs fought against colonialists in order to break the shackles of slavery.

Xeno and Homo Fighters

The hostility between a democratic system and terrorist techniques are basic. Actually, terrorism represents a kind of political violence which is directed against the basic values and fundamental national interests of the citizens in a modern democratic state. In the process it may join hands with dictatorships and totalitarian regimes because a terrorist has little respect for all orderly set-up based on rule of law. Like a sports person a terrorist has to be motivated to the core. He has to move in the right circle arid prove his utility by taking part in demonstrations and learn how to fight the police. The real hardcore terrorist groups simply order their trainees to kill some prize people on their hit lists. Those who can stand to it are asked to assume the role of a 'shaper'. He is the most dangerous and insidious kind of a terrorist. All sorts of people have been joining the terrorist ranks. Even, lawyers, intellectuals, peasants, criminals and highly trained recruits merely await orders to get activized. Things have come to such a pass that even literature exists on how to form terrorist groups and obtain funds by kidnapping and through bank raids or sabotage. This kind of literature is freely available in the United States and several other. Ariel Merraric has classified terrorist groups into two broad categories, viz. Xeno fighters and Homo fighters.

The *Xeno fighters* are the groups lighting against foreigners for achieving goals like withdrawal of foreign powers and realignment of political boundaries. They are not interested to get support of local pupulace of the country which is their target.

The *Homo fighters* fight for their own country. Their efforts are to overthrow the Government of the day and thereby achieve the desired political objective. They rely on popular support or at least on some basic support, in the community. They know that indiscriminate use of violence can be counter productive. The Italian Red Brigades, for example attacked on political VIPs and Government dignitaries rather than making indiscriminate attacks on members of the society.

Political Assassinations

There have been number of cases of political assassinations in the world and in India. To achieve political gains the terrorists have been inspired by political motivations, and have not spared political leaders and heads of the States. The examples are many and assassinations of Presidents like Abraham Lincoln, John Keneddy, Allande and Olaf Palme prove the point. These politically motivated killings selected the victims because the assassinations may cause a political impact. The assassination of Prime Minister Indira Gandhi by her own security men is significant because it generated public criticism and stirred thought. To ensure proper security of the important and influential political leaders it is necessary that the techniques adopted by the terrorist assassins are countered. It is a very difficult and delicate job because the terrorists have also improved and perfected their techniques of attack on the targets. In 1986 the British Prime Minister Mrs. Margaret Thatcher had a narrow escape when a bomb containing high explosive blasted and damaged some rooms of the hotel at Brigton where she was staying. Even the Scotland Yard could not nail the culprits.

Considerations for Security Administration

The major difficulty in the operations against the terrorists is the collection of intelligence about their plans, preparations, ramifications and international connections. Due to picking up 'agents' in the target it is often difficult to break the ring. The terrorists have to be really motivated and self-sacrificing. Such motivated persons who are not in active field are picked up and planted. Disgruntled persons who have come away are also picked up to avoid exposure. The communication between intelligence officer and the agents has to be indirect as well as cautious. The security administration has to keep several factors in view to strengthen the striking forces in the field. It should know that terrorists impelled by fanatic religious and ideological considerations Ore prepared for any sacrifice including suicide for the achievement of their goals. They are trained in the handling of sophisticated fire arms and WT nets. They have intensive training and are capable of planning and executing their operations. They may adopt various subversions, impersonations in the guise of security forces and political leaders to gain access to VVIPs. They can be highly mobile with diverse transport resources and are capable to employ hit-and-run techniques.

In the face of such highly organized terrorist movements, the security agencies have to adopt a much larger and stronger profile. They have to plan, develop and expand intelligence gathering because good intelligence alone is the best way to beat the terrorists. In the seventies the United States and Israel managed to thwart murderous attacks in the Middle East by penetrating into the PLO. While dealing with the terrorists, the ideological motivation poses the biggest problem. This can be met appropriately only by a concerted public relations drive. Unless a strong support base is made available both ideologically and in the practical field, the counter movement is not likely to make much headway.

Handling a terrorist crisis is a complex job. It is necessary to choose the right negotiator-someone who speaks the terrorist language must understand their history and culture. Negotiable flexibility helps in selective reprisals. Terrorism often has roots in deep seated political grievances and violence cannot be ended until these grievances are redressed or looked into.

Preventive Measures

To prevent the growing activities of terrorists a proper scheme on 'internal security' has to be adopted. The setting up of village defence parties, the assessment of forces for operational purpose and preparation of lists of important activists who can be identified and detained are the foremost tasks which should be strengthened by collection of intelligence. The plans and programmes of the terrorists, their hideouts, the persons or organizations helping them and the sources of arms and ammunitions and funds need to be checked and shadowed. The identification of the problems of local people, learning their language and respect for their customs can help in understanding the psychology of the terrorists. Tightening of search on the border check posts, on entry and exist of foreign terrorist, on fake passports and visas is a routine precaution. A foreign terrorist who has entered the country needs to be checked by intelligence agencies to the best of their capabilities. A foreigner who has been detained for violation of Foreigners Acts and Rules, must be interrogated by experts and a record check of his previous activities if any has to be made with warning circulars. Meticulous guarding by the security forces of the borders should plug the unauthorized entry of the foreigners. Obviously the Anti-Terrorist Act can be made more stringent. In 1987 the President of India promulgated an ordinance to replace the Terrorist and Disruption Activities Prevention Act incorporating some of the stringent measures required to deal with the terrorists. Internal security aims to provide measures for ensuring internal peace in the event of external aggression and internal disorder. These measures can be adopted at all the three stages, namely, the precautionary stage, the war stage and the crisis stage. To meet the challenge of terrorist activities, it is the duty of security forces and their leaders to keep the morale of the forces high. They should provive effective leadership by motivating and proper briefing of their force regarding the terrorists, on their actives, places of operation pand lans of action. Steps should be taken to set up village defence parties and home guards for protection and maintenance of reserve forces at the State, District and Sub-divisional levels. Proper coordination with CPOs, wireless net at places of disturbances, reviewing of arms and ammunitions with police and preparing a list of important activists can go a long way to achieve targets.

But then, a constitutional, legitimate and democratically elected National Government should exhibit calm courage, stable firmness and negotiating skill while dealing with this kind of political chicanery. Avoiding all appeasement, vulnerability and surrender it should encourage social apathy by taking away the wind from the terrorist sails. It has to evolve a short-range policy of effective police action and long term policy postulates for an enduring political settlement. The former demands a continuous and systematic review of field operations and their logistics, but the latter needs. precaution in cutting the criminal insanity to size. In no case the terrorists should be permitted to acquire ideological sympathy, mass support and popular respectability.

Indian Situation

The third world countries, including India are desparately struggling to maintain and defend their national identity. The heterogeneous character of their plural populations is a direct threat to their territorial integrity and national sovereignty.

In case of India, the democratic processes have negatively operated to weaken her capacity of crisis management. The insensitivity and unrepresentative character of the dysfunctional democratic institutions has further distorted the articulation of pressure politics of the bargain counters. The fading of the charisma of the second generation leaders at regional and national levels has changed the basic character of public protests and agitations in India. The urban culture and anomie situations have generated new waves of violence in public life of industrial towns. The poll politics at the hosting has given a complete new orientation of parochial loyalties which tends to harden the 'minority granules' not accepting the melting pot situation.

A military coup de etat or an all out revolution on or civil war or a party take-over on Maoist lines being ruled out in the present context of Indian history, perhaps India is in for an era of public disorders and 'Rim Land Insurgencies' of varying types. The economic squeeze, accentuated by social disorganization and continued demographic explosions may further rock the political system which does not seem to have developed a national consensus on live issues of regional disparities and minority discords.

The states on the north-east and north-west borders of India have shown violent manifestations of this phenomenon. Of course, the two situations obtained in Assam and Punjab are absolutely uncomparable, but the basic issues of 'minority identity' and 'majority backlash' in a polyglot nation State of India's diversity have to be confronted continuously and somewhat courageously. Unlike the Black Niger in America the Indian minorities have a historical sense of communal superiority. The partition of the country and a special preferential treatment situation of privileges in politics have unleashed a 'crisis of manipulations and expectations' during last four decades. Communal nuances apart, it is an exercise in balancing 'majority revivalism' and 'minority fundamentalism'.

The problem of Indian minorities has three levels of awareness (i) The grievance situation, (ii) The identity crisis, and (iii) The homeland dream through secession. If Sikhs in Punjab have the problem at the first level, it can be taken care of by poll politics, political negotiations and constitutional means. But if the problem, as perceived by the minority leaders, has attained the second level, then it reopens the basic question of the nature of 'secular polity', which cannot be legislated by any Parliament but shall ultimately be settled through political conventions over a period of time. Worse still, if the minority or minorities feel that their religious identity can have a political meaning only by having a 'Theocratic State' of Israel variety through secession or partition, then the Indian. wation state has no alternative but to preserve its borders.

TheAnandpur Sahib resolution talks of the first level problems, to which moderate Akali leaders have added the problem of Sikh identity. Upto this level the problems are mar geable -nd can be sorted out within the framework of the constitution. But then, if all this is a cloak for the third level demand, then the solution of the first two levels cannot be naive or acceptable as elusive tactics to buy time.

Terror, when handled by counter-terror, requires an extra-perceptivity. The sensitivity of violent actions by people or government usually has uncontrolled and far reaching ramifications. People should know that a slight mishandling of the terrorist conspiracy even by a legitimate government can sanctify criminality and erode fear, faith and respect for law. The inept and imprompt moves can be further exploited and a 'psychology of insanity' and 'fanaticism' may cause transfer of segmental populations, retarding economic growth and political development. Jalianwala baghs in a free India are inconceivable and no political expediency is worth a risk which may shake the very foundations of an incipient but emerging nation of the orient. The sovereign identity of many of the newly independent nations of Asia and Africa fore-warrants a concept of territorial integrity and its sacredness. Whether it is India or Sri Lanka the heart of the problem is to preserve the national borders.Simultaneously the State must endeavour to modernize the heterogeneous sub-groups of its medieval population along with an incremental democratization of its dysfunctional institutions. All this requires a bold attempt to strengthen the shifting centres of sovereign power in the midst of terrorist turmoil. The assimilation process of conflict groups without much political articulation and inbuilt participation generates newer demands of autonomy, homelands and secession of territories under one grievance or the other.

The experiment of developmental democracy in India has unleashed socio-political tensions, which besides being inevitable, bring irrational forces of violence into play. Negatively, there is nothing which can absorb the thrust of fissiparous tendencies of the development-oriented nation state system. Conversely, there is an unmanageable hiatus between 'the levels of rising expectations' and 'system's performance' at all fronts. The resilience and strength of the Indian political system ale being subjected to stress and the capacity to withstand trial and test through management of crises and chaos by developing extra-load bearing strength in the system. Every general election in free India has taken the live issues of communal conflicts and cultural discords right upto the grassroots. The articulation of pressure groups in poll politics at hustings has been rather weak. It has not generated any acceptable consensus to deal with coercive structures of power of the bargain counters. The charisma of regional and minority leaders has declined a good deal in past few decades and this has contributed to the insensitivity of the political system to constitutional and peaceful protests of the sub-groups, agitating for the ventilation of their perceived grievances. Conversely, the affluent sections of society have grabbed the 'lion's share' of the developmental cake. They have mastered the democratic art of clothing their economic aspirations under religiously sensitive and politically well articulated demands. The minority phobia of a plural society has further helped these secessionist groups to sanctify their aggrandizing missions to mobilize minorities against the democratic and secular mainstream of national life.

Assam, Punjab, Kashmir, Nagaland, Tripura, Gorkhaland and for that matter the whole of the north eastern border region is caught in insurgency born of turmoil. The specific causes and shades of grievance articulation and their protest manifestations are apparently different, but the recurrence of public agitations and recrudescence of political violence which has followed in their wake, establishes the fact that a peaceful and democratic social change in India stands obstructed in the operational processes of the political system. The minority issues which cry for a political Solution are being shelved through extra-constitutional means to buy time. This encourages the protesters to resolve them on the streets and in the temples, forcing the government to take recourse police and para-military methods. The fatiguing exercise tends to push the political system to an exhausting end, where from the wrath of the agitators and the police power of the state violently indulge in political terrorism and counter terrorism as a daily sport under stress of inevitability.

Nation building exercise in India is essentially an attempt to strengthen national integration the political aspect of which has been accomplished but the socio-cultural and economic components of which continue to generate unfinished struggles within the policy. The enormity of this challenge gives misgivings about the continuation of political integration of the Indian Nation State. In other words, the "Cultural sub-nationalism" of the sub-continent even after partition, continues to threaten 'political nationalism' and its viability to survive as a Nation state. The answer lies in economic nationalism and mass mobility which must ultimately overwhelm cultural sub-nationalisms of the Indian peninsula and give a new content and regional dimension to political nationalism to which the entire Indian sub-continent has really awakened after the second world war. Of course, there are innumerable 'ifs' and 'buts' and 'imponderables' in the prediction about the future of Nation States in the South Asian region but perhaps the evolutionary trend represents a mounting graph from cultural sub-nationalism to economic regionalism via political nationalism.

Hence, the historical war against the medieval parochial society has to be won by the modern nation State in India. The social forces which can be and perhaps are in league with the political power of the State in a democracy, can apparently put the government of the day to a positive position of disadvantage. The social tensions among various kinds of Indian sub-groups, especially among minority groups have manifested themselves in violent public agitations and insurrectionary activities against the federal state. Placed as they are in the political and social contexts of Indian society, the minority groups are too weak to organize insurgency or guerrilla warfares. Rebellion and civil war situations are also ruled out by the demographic spread of these groups in the politico. cultural framework of the country. The legacies of Indian history permit some of these minority groups and their leaders to conjure up images and harbour illusions to live in their hoary past. This past can never be relieved. Nor can they ever recreate it by the democratic power of the ballot box. Some of them may have genuine grievances but none of them can create mass disorders without inviting a risk to their own cultural survival. The political system can accommodate them only to a point for its incremental growth, but beyond that the threat of the majority backlash does not permit such compromises, which may fulfill the ill-conceived historical aspirations and bizarre cultural urges of the minority groups and that too to their entire satisfaction. Right now the nature, and use of the weaponry and the violent character of the minority protests against political authority of the nation state of India are being determined by the kind of leadership these groups have. Then, foreign complicity adds vebemance to this game of nation breaking for a bigger deal of destabilization of the subcontinent. Encouraged by this, these religious, linguistic and regional minorities of Indian federation often wish to induct political violence and terror in their desperate expressions of extra-constitutional protests for a radical change. Terrorism as a political weapon is apparently a prelude to insurgency, which hopefully wants to coerce a legitimate national government to succumb to the illegitimate demands of minority identity, autonomous minority state and ultimately minority homeland through secession.

10

Kashmir Question: Need for a Visionary Approach

The Times of India August 12, 1994

The turmoil in Jammu' and Kashmir because of militancy is now well into its fifth year. The toll has been enormous - thousand killed, including members of security forces; tens of thousands forced to leave their homes for refugee camps; crores of rupees worth of residential and other property destroyed; thousands of widows and orphans left to face a bleak future; trade and tourism almost completely disrupted, and deep wounds inflicted on the psyche of the Kashmiri community. By encouraging and financing training and arming peaceful Kashmiris to take to the gun, and move from their traditional cultural patterns to fundamentalism, Pakistan has rendered them a major disservice which will take decades to rectify.

Human Suffering

This aspect of human suffering needs to be highlighted, because many in the Capital tend to look upon Jammu and Kashmir merely as an interesting "problem" to be studied in academic seminars. In fact, it is human beings–mainly Indian citizens– dying; it is a whole cultural pattern disintegrating; it is the greatest challenge faced by

Indian civilisation since Independence. The basic question is--can we summon the reserves of wisdom and statesmanship needed to bring the situation under control through a negotiated political settlement, or are we going to look upon it only as a law and order problem to be tackled indefinitely by the security forces? People have often told me that Punjab took 10 years. Nagaland 15 years and, therefore, what was the desperate hurry about Jammu and Kashmir! Surely such an approach is not in keeping with our cultural traditions.

In the broader perspective of India's destiny, Jammu and Kashmir must be saved from its present agony, enabling us to devote our energies to playing our rightful role in the emerging global society. The great leaders and seers who inspired and guided our freedom movement envisaged India not merely as just another nation-state but as a powerful moral and spiritual force for world peace and harmony. We can fulfil that role only if we make a genuine efforts to sort out the problems in Jammu and Kashmir with understanding and compassion. If the present situation is allowed to drag on, not only will the suffering of the people and attrition of our security forces continue, but it could culminate in yet another armed conflict between India and Pakistan which, with upgraded weapons technology would be disastrous for both countries.

Despite everything that has happened over the last few years, some positive factors have emerged with the release of important political detainees, a general disenchantment with militancy among the people specially with the influx of heavily armed non-Kashmiri militants who are now threatening the Kashmiries themselves, and the turmoil within Pakistan. The two regions under Pakistan' control -- POK and the Northern Areas – are also driven by discontent which is manifesting itself increasingly in public demonstrations against the authorities. However, these factors in themselves are not enough to bring about a settlement. For that. some bold initiatives are needed, which must come from the Prime Minister himself. The displays the vision that distinguishes the statesman from the politician, this vexed and complex problem can be resolved.

There is a range of options for a possible political settlement, but clearly these involve addressing several dimensions separately and yet an integrated and holistic manner. These include Indo-Pakistani relations in terms of the Simla Agreement; the status of the two regions under Pakistan's control since 1949; the precise constitutional relationship between the state and the rest of India based on the Instrument of Accession signed by the Maharaja; the inter relationship between the three regions of Jammu, Kashmir and Ladakh; and a massive employment oriented economic package which must include the rehabilitation of Kashmiri migrants.

Key Element

The recent dramatic peace moves in West Asia show that when the time is ripe. Innovative and persistent diplomatic negotiations can achieve miracles. The key element here would be opening an urgent multi-level unconditional dialogue. This has to take place between India and Pakistan, between the emergent leadership in the Valley and the Center; among Kashmir, Jammu and Ladkh, and between India's areas and those in Pakistan's control. It is only such a wide-ranging series of dialogues that can pave the way for an enduring political settlement. The idea that if we let matters drift we will sooner or later revert to the pre-1989 situation is not acceptable to the Kashmiris or even, for that matter, to the people of Jammu and Ladakh whose long standing demand for effective regional autonomy has never received the attention that it deserves.

Another aspect which is not generally understood is that in the five years under Governor's and President's rule the democratic processes in Jammu and Kashmir have come to a complete halt. As a result there is not a single elected representative in the state today from the panchatats right up to members of the legislature and Parliament. This represents an unprecedented and unacceptable hiatus in the political process which cannot be allowed to continue indefinitely in a democratic nation.

Obvious Advantages

Jammu and Kashmir has, in fact. produced an impressive number of service officers and ciyil servants whose experience could have been utilised pending the re-establishment of democracy. There are obvious advantages in involving a substantial section of top officials who are aware of the special topography, cultural patterns and languages of the state. The present arrangements neither provide accessibility nor accountability, and make it almost impossible for the common man to interact with the administration, thus increasing alienation not only in the valley but even in the Jammu region.

Responsible senior people often complain that they have no access to the highest echelons in the present administration. Even the portfolios of the advisors who exercise all the powers of cabinet ministers are far from clear.

Unfortunately, there is a feeling that idealism is at discount at present. We are all supposed to be "realists" and "pragmatists" who should not get bogged down in "sentimentality" Yet that approach surely implies a failure from the broader civilisational point of view. Jammu and Kashmir is a crucial test for us– for our "firmness" and "strength" and for our wisdom and compassion. If we pass it, the light which is faintly visible at the end of the tunnel will become clearer. If we do not, then the journey into the heart of darkness will continute.

11

Caste Conflict: Its Causes and Resolution

History of the castes conflict in India is as old as the history of the castes itself in this country. As we know, the origin of the castes is found in the 'Purush Sukta' of the 'Rigveda' that Brahmin is born from the head of the Purush, Kshatriya from the arms of the 'Purush', 'Vaishya' from the middle part of the 'Purush' and the Shudra' from the feet of the 'Purush'. This hierarchy among these 4 castes emanated from the early period of Rigveda, the oldest scripture of the Hindus.

After the Vedas, a number of 'Purans' and 'Smritis' namely 'Manusmriti', 'Yagyavalkya Smriti', 'Gautam Sutra' etc. were written wherein the position status ofthe 4 castes viz. - Brahmin, kshatriya, Vaishya and Shudra were defined in the form of a code to be followed very strictly. The Shudras were not only placed at the bottom of this caste system but these codes provided segregation of the Shudras from the 3 higher castes along with very cruel and inhuman punishments for them unparalleled in the World History. Some of them are quoted here:

(1) Shudras are born to serve the 3 higher castes - Brahmin, Kshatriya and Vaishya, failing which the king shall punish and exile them out of the country.

(2) Shudras will eat the left overs of the 3 higher castes in lieu of the services rendered by them. They will wear old and torn clothes used by their masters and the Shudra-women prohibited from wearing gold and silver ornaments. Shudras were also not allowed to wear shoes.

(3) Shudras shall not possess any land and wealth and if they do it. their masters shall size their wealth, land etc. by force. They were prohibited from having their huts inside the habitats of the higher castes as they were regarded untouchable and inferior even to the animals.

(4) Shudras shall use only earthen pots utensils. They were forbidden from taking milk and ghee.

(5) The offence of killing Shudras shall be equated with that of killing dogs, cats, mongoose, crows and the like.

(6) Shudras were forbidden from learning of Vedas. If by chance they heard the Vedvani, molten lead would be poured into their ears, if they recite Vedas, their tongue shall be taken out and if they conduct in accordance with the Vedas, their heads will be chopped off.

There is a mention in the 'Bhagw:at-Geeta' too that Vaishya, Shudra and women-folk are all 'Pap-Yoni' and this was said by no less a person than Lord Krishna himself. This shows that the caste-conflict was caused by the ancient and religious scriptures from the ancient times in this country.

During the reign of Lord Ram, the Shudra Muni 'Shambook' was running a 'Gurukul' on the banks of Saryu river that was not liked by the higher castes, particularly the Brahmins of Ayodhya as cquel of which the Shudra Muni was killed by Lord Ram himself with a sword at the instance ofthe Brahmins. His only offence was that he was a Shudra, running a Gurukul of Shudra students and leading a life of 'Rishi' in devotion to God on the bank of holy Saryu river.

The great warrior 'Karn' of Mahabharat was not allowed to become Commander in Chief of the Kaurava army by 'Bhishma Pitamah' only because he was brought-up by a Shudra family. Although he was the eldest son of 'Kunti' the mother of the Pandavas, he was called Sootputra (Shudra) as he was flown away in river by Kunti, soon after his birth and was rescued and reared-up by a Shudra family.

The caste conflict in ancient India was not confined between the Shudras and the 3 higher castes only. According to our scriptures, the Brahmins and the Kshatriyas fought over the question of supremacy between the two for thousands of years. Lord Parashu Ram, the legendary Brahmin God, destroyed Kshatriyas 21 times entirely from this earth. Raja Venu, the ancient Kshatriya king was killed by his arch Brahmin enemies only because he was a Kshatriya.

'Visvamitra' the great Kshatriya Muni was not regarded as Brahmarshtr by Vasislitha the royal Brahmin Priest of Ayodhya though the former claimed himself as enlightened as the latter. It maybe remarked here that Vishwamitra was the Guru and mentor of Lord Ram and his brothers. But he was never regarded a Brahmarshi by the Brahmins. After a long and sustained war between these two castes for thousands of years, a compromise was however reached between Brahmins and Kshatriyas that hence forth the Kshatiyas will enjoy the kingship and the Brahmins will be their Royal Priests and Ministers in their kingdom. And also, all the posts of power and importance shall be held by the Brahmins, i.e. Brahmins will be *de-facto* rulers and Kshatriya kings will only reign on the advice of the Brahmin advisors.

Chhatrapati Shivaji, the great saviour and protector of Hinduism and Hindus from the onslaught of Aurangajeb known to be the crudest emperor against Hindus, was not regarded a king like other Kshatriya kings by Brahmins. Instead, he was called Chhatrapati and Brahmins of Maharashtra even refused to perform his Rajtilak. Consequently a Brahmin from Varanasi had to be sent for by him for doing the Rajtilak ceremony and he too did the 'Tilak" with the toe of his feet and not by his hands. This was done so by the Brahmin priests as the bravest Maratha king–Shiva ji did not belong to the so called high castes.

Swami Vivckananda, who revived and spread the Hindu religion in India and also outside the country, was first opposed by his fellow 'Sanyasis' from becoming the head of Swami Ramkrishna Mission, after the demise of Swami Ramkrishna since he was not a 'Dwij' i.e. –Brahmin, Kshatriya and Vaishyasaid to be twice born. But he had to be accepted as head of the Ramkrishna Mission since he was named as his successor by Swami Ram Krishan his guru and mentor, during his life time and Sharda Maa had also prevailed on the followers of Swami Ramkrishna in favour of Vivekananda. In his book Caste, Culture and Socialism" —Swami Vivekananda has said — " Shudras in India have long been exploited by the higher castes for thousands of years but now time has come to give them their due place and rights in the social, educational and political fields. It is the duty of the higher castes to and the exploitation of the Shudras as they are the true Indians who earn their livelihood by their own hands. The higher castes are dependent on them leading life of parasites. The Shudras being illiterate and uneducated have not awakened themselves as a result of which they are being exploited by the higher castes for their vested-interests. But when the Shudras wake-up, the higher castes will be blown-away by their single mouth wind. I have no doubt that the Shudras will rule over This country maintaining dignity of their community".

Government of India appointed "Backward Class (Mandal) Commission" in 1977 to identify the backward class communities and recommend measures for their uplift. The Mandal Commission, although submitted its report in 1979, but that was shelved as the recommendations were made on the basis of castes. Later on Janata Dal Government resolved to implement its recommendations in 1989 that 27% posts in the Government services shall be reserved for the backward classes who constitute 52% of the population of India. This resolution of the Janata Dal Government was vehemently opposed by the caste Hindus because the backward classes who are regarded as Shudras, were going to occupy 27% posts in the Government services which had been denied to them so for. The opposition was sponsored by the caste Hindus with a lot of hatred and violence as a sequel of which many innocent persons lost their lives.

Instances of caste conflicts are reported in the Newspapers practically every day the recent-one took place at Kumher in Bharatpur district of Rajasthan where a marriage procession of Jatava (Shudra) was not allowed to pass through the village of Jats. When the Jatavas persisted on taking-out their marriage procession through, they were assaulted violently by the Jats killing many of them. Nay, many houses of Jatavas were burnt by the Jats wherein several innocent Jatavas were burnt alive. A similar case was reported from one village of Agra district a few years back wherein several Jatavas were killed by the Jats of that area only because they dared to carry their marriage procession through the 'abadi' of the Jats. That is to say, the Jats are not prepared to allow the Jatavas along with the band of drums and horse and they also can not see the improved standard of living of the Jatavas and their economic betterments.

During the British rule over India, many communities of Shudras were declared as criminals under the Criminal Tribes Act whereby they were regarded criminals by birth and accordingly apprehended by the police and the higher castes as and when a crime was committed in their area irrespective of the fact whether the crime was committed by them or not. After India attained independence, this obnoxious Act was repealed and the carst while criminal tribes were scheduled as denotified tribes and several measures were taken for their rehabilitation on agriculture and various cottage industries. Notwithstanding their identification, the so called ex-criminal tribes are still regarded as criminals by the police and the caste Hindus as a result of which they continue to be apprehended and tortured by them on false pretexts and reports. To the contrary, the crime statistics shows the majority of the crimes are committed by the criminals belonging to the higher castes who were never scheduled as criminal castes and tribes.

Communal riots in India between Hindu and Muslims community, Sikhs and Muslims, Sikhs and Hindus and others are caused mostly due to the caste conflict. Violence is committed against the opposite community only because the offender-community is not willing to allow the opposite community to live in peace and coexistence. Most of these communal riots are instigated and provoked by the community leaders themselves.

In Bihar, the second most populous State of India, several armies have been formed on the caste basis namely - Bhoomihar Sena, Rajput Sena, Yadava Sena etc. These armies have been formed to suppress the Shudras who are getting awakened of their rights and demanding adequate wages for their labour. The high castes still want to continue the bonded labour by paying pittance to the Shudra laborers against the labour done by them in their fields. In desperation, the Shudras of Bihar have also started organizing themselves and relating the brutal assaults of the higher castes on them and this caste conflict in Bihar State is on the rise killing many of them and burning their houses in large number.

Dr. B.R. Ambedkar, one of the greatest sons of India saw and experienced agom of the caste conflict from the very beginning of his life. He tried his best to reform the Hindu Society but failed. The caste system, according to him, is mainly responsible for the caste and for the formation of castcless society. Unfortunately, he was opposed by the higher castes in this direction as the caste Hindus feared that they will lose their supremacy over the backward classes in the event of abolition of the caste. He led the movement for the basic human rights to the Shudras of this country who had been deprived of their human rights for the past thousands of years and in this struggle he had to suffer and sacrifice a lot. The untouchables were not allowed to enter the temples and draw water from the public tanks. Dr. Ambedkar himself was notallowedtoenter Hindu temples and draw water from the common tanks though he was said to be one of the most learned, distinguished and enlightened persons of the World and he also occupied the highest posts in the Government of India as a member of the executive council of the Viceroy of India and thereafter Law Minister of the independent India. As we know, Dr. Ambedkar led the 'Satyagrah' by drawing water from the public tank of Mhad and by entering the Kalaram temple of Nasik along with thousands of his followers, in which he received several blows and injuries on his person, inflicted by the caste Hindus. Ultimately, he succeeded in getting the right of entry of the untouchables in the temples and also the right of drawing water from the public tanks.

Thus, it is proved from the history of India and the ancient scriptures as well, that the major cause of the caste conflict has been the 'Varnavyavastha' i.e. the caste system of our society. This is why, Dr. Ambedkar laid great emphasis on annihilation of the caste system and introduction of intercaste marriages and intercaste dining between the various castes and communities of this country. About 2500 years ago, Lord Buddha also preached an equality and fraternity among the different castes and communities of the society. He did not believe in the hierarchy of the caste system in the society as his religion (Buddhism) is based on the equality, enlightenment and compassion. In fact Lord Buddha, though born in a royal family, rebelled against the prevailing caste system, producing caste conflict in the society. Dr. Ambedkar adopted Buddhism after renouncing Hinduism, since Buddhism does not recognize the caste system. To conclude, the path shown by Lord Buddha and Dr. Ambedkar is the best way against the caste conflicts i.e. formation of a casteless society on the foundations of equality, fraternity, compassion, enlightenment and social justice.

12

Impact of Terrorism on Indian Politics

In order to map the effects of terrorism on Indian democracy we must begin with a picture of the Indian democratic experiment. What stands at the heart of Indian democracy? The following key elements can be identified: liberal constitutionalism; civic nationalism; the devolution of power in a layered federalism; and group rights. Beyond this institutional structure, Indian democracy has been sustained by a political culture of tolerance and accommodation. In addition, there has been a suspicion (if not aversion) to the excessive use of violence to settle political disputes and dissent. Finally, Indian democracy has been sustained by a relatively "thick" conception of the political. Terrorism has corroded all these facets of Indian democracy by encouraging Indians to question the crucial building blocks of their democracy. Right-wing Hindu groups have taken advantage of this growing skepticism. Their rise is the greatest threat to Indian democracy.

The Nature of Indian Democracy

Since independence, India has evolved a complex set of institutions that, in effect, place limits on the power of the central and other government as well as potentially domineering social groups. At the core of the Indian political structure are four elements: liberal constitutionalism, civic nationalism, the devolution of power in a layered federalism, and group rights.

Constitutionalism is the promise that the government will deal with individuals and groups according to established principles, rather than arbitrarily A liberal constitution consists of principles that limit the authority and power of governments and protect individuals and groups against government tyranny or the tyranny of others, including social majorities of any kind which, by virtue of superior numbers, could override the rights and preferences of those who disagree with them. Liberal constitutionalism means that the system of government allows those who feel that their rights have been violated to seek justice and compensation. A liberal constitutional order usually is marked by checks and balances between government agencies so that no one institution can dominate and trample on the rights of citizens. The Indian constitutional system has all these elements — this is well enough known.

A second set of limits arises from the Indian commitment to civic as against an ethnic nationalism. Civic nationalism is the notion that citizenship is based not on ethnic attributes but rather on political attributes, namely, the willingness to abide by the values and rules of a common political order. Being Indian, in this view, is not matter of ethnic belonging, it is not something that is conferred on you because of your *ethnic* community; it is based, rather, on belonging to a particular *political* community by virtue of birth and later by virtue of one's own reason, You are Indian or part of the Indian political community by *choosing* to accept the political values and "rules of the game" prevalent in India. This does not mean that if you disagree with any particular value or rule you are disqualified from Indian citizenship: dissent within bounds is a value or rule that is part of the Indian political ethos. It docs mean, though, that if you disagree with the basic system of values and rules, you arc in danger of being un-Indian (in a legal sense). Even when someone docs disagree with the basic system of values and rules, this does not mean that he is thereby deprived of all rights. No liberal constitutional order can (or should wish to) deprive anyone--citizen or non-citizen–of all rights.

The third limit on government and social domination by any kind of rampant majority is the devolution of power in a layered federalism, which means that various units of government have rights and responsibilities that cannot be overridden by the central authorities, at least in the normal course of things. Indian federalism divides jurisdictions and powers between the central governments. Given that many of the states were created on the basis of the dominant language in an area (by the States Reorganization Bill and later legislation), the centre-state division of powers in effect gives *language* groups a good deal of autonomy at least in principle. In addition, in response to the problems of ethnic groups *within* states, which felt that the state governments were not treating them properly; various local councils have been created. Thus, there is an array of autonomous district or hill councils in Jammu & Kashmir, West Bengal, and the North-East, Another layer of Indian Federalism, in effect, was created by the panchayati Raj Acts of 1992 and 1993. According to these Acts, states must hold elections to panchayats and give the panchayats various power, including some financial powers. Many states have done this in the years following the passage of the Act. Some states have not yet done so, but the pressure on them to conform is growing. Here again is a means by which local aspirations can be satisfied in the sense that groups which feel alienated from the state governments could carve out a measure of autonomy over cultural and economic life.

The fourth limit on government and social dominance is the conferral of group rights, that is, rights that we enjoy as members of a community. The most important rights arc the rights of religious communities, language communities, and caste and tribal communities. Religious groups in India enjoy various group rights. They can run their own denominational schools. They can raise money for religious institutions free of tax. Most importantly, Christians and Muslims in particular have the right to their own personal laws. While the Indian Constitution commits the country to a Uniform Civil Code, it has been understood since Jawaharlal Nehru's time that a common code would only be written when the country's two largest religious minorities were ready to participate in its writing. In effect, therefore, Muslims and Christians have their own personal laws, a group right of considerable importance for both communities. Language communities in India also enjoy various group rights. The two most important of these rights are to have state of one's own, and to be educated in one's own language. The Indian states are, in part, organized on linguistic lines (some are delineated along tribal lines). The basic principles used by the States

Reorganization Act to redraw India's internal boundaries was language predominance. The "three-language formula", which in the 1960s resolved differences over the status of the national language and the regional languages, also reflects a group rights approach. Group rights of a different sort have been extended to caste and tribal groups as well. The most important of these rights are reservations. The reservations policy establishes quotas in three arenas—education, public employment, and political representation. These quotas are commensurate with the proportion of the Scheduled Caste (SC) and Scheduled Tribe (ST) population.

Indian democracy has rested not just on this political structure, but also on a particular kind of political culture. That political culture consists of three elements in particular: a valuation of tolerance, an aversion to violence, and a thick conception of the political, all of which arc interrelated. First of all, India 's political culture has featured a belief in tolerance. This does not mean that Indians are always tolerant. All it means is that Indians value what they regard as tolerance in public life, and believe that it is a political good. Tolerance means many things. On the whole, what it means to Indians is a sense of moderation in all things and a tendency not to take extreme positions. Second, related to tolerance is the aversion to violence in politics. Here again, I do not mean that Indians are stringently non-violent and scrupulously avoid intimidation and coercion. Rather, what I mean is that Indians frown upon extremism, and, in particular, the use of violence in politics, and they tend to condemn extremism and violence when they do occur. Finally, Indians have a "thick" conception of the political. Politics is not just a matter of making workmanlike collective decisions on what to do about various social problems; it is not mere policy making. It is also about process—it is about debate and dialogue. Politics is about forging a collective ethics, about articulating and understanding difference, about attempting to change people's minds, and, if necessary about agreeing to disagree. Tolerance and an aversion to violence are tantamount to saying that on some occasions people may simply have to agree to disagree. They are, therefore, vital to the thicker conception of politics, as much as this conception is vital to the prospects of tolerance and the aversion to violence. They are, all three, mutually reinforcing, if not tautologically related.

Effects of Terrorism

Terrorism and the response to terrorism have had a number of effects on Indian democracy. just the following may be noted: the miniaturization of the Indian imagination; the government's accretion of emergency powers; the devaluation of debate and dissent; the assault on liberals and the idea of liberalism; the spread of Hindu self-hatred; and the turn to a more managerial, technical view of politics. Together, these have encouraged the rise of the Hindu right, which threatens liberal democracy as nothing else has in India. It should be clarified here that when, in the following paragraphs, the phrase "the effect of terrorism" is mentioned, this is shorthand for "the effect of terrorism and the response to terrorism", because the harm to democracy has come not just from the acts of terrorists, it has also come from the actions of governments and citizens in responding to terrorism. The focus of this essay is, in fact, the latter, that is, the actions of governments and citizens. What *terrorists* have done to democracy is so palpable that it requires little elaboration.

The first effect of terrorism has been the militarization of the Indian imagination. The use of force against terrorism is at some level inescapable; no one except a Gandhian or pacifist would completely oppose the use of violence to control terrorism. Over the years, the amount of force the Indian government has used to combat terrorism in the borderlands in particular has been quite extensive (though never genocidal). Behind this willingness to use force is the militarization of the Indian imagination. Indians, increasingly have hardened their views on how to respond to terrorism. Calls on the government to be more "active" than "passive", to be "proactive" rather than "reactive" are part of this militarization. The tolerance of human rights abuses and the dismissive attitude towards those who talk about human rights are signs of the hardening of Indian attitudes, Even a casual survey of the Indian press and television is revealing on this score. Anyone who raises doubts about the efficacy of violence is dismissed as a "liberal", at best a fuzzy-headed do-gooder, and at worst all "antinational" it does no good to retort that India has consistently used violence against terrorists (from the fight against the Naga rebels in the I 950s onwards), and that it is simply inaccurate to characterize the Indian state as "soft". Violence — the determination to use violence-increasingly permeates our imaginations. The people want their leaders to use violence. Violence is seen as a more or less natural part of politics: it is a way of communicating, if an extreme one. Violence is also seen as intrinsic to the state: how can one have a legitimate and effective state without the ability and willingness to use violence? Violence is cathartic and emancipatory. The people arc thrilled at the use of righteous violence (in the films, television, and literature). Those who have been wronged and oppressed can only break out of their chains by using violence. The question is no longer "why violence"; it is "why not more violence" against those who fight us? That counter-violence has virtually never succeeded in eradicating terrorism does not convince. Indians are coming around to the view that it is a measure of political maturity to use violence, and that it is only the naive Indian political class that has not understood this basic political fact.

A second effect of terrorism is the granting of emergency powers to the government. Over the years, the Indian government has passed a series of anti-terrorist bills. These include the Armed Forces Act, the Terrorist and Disruptive Activities Act (TADA), and, most recently, the Prevention of Terrorism Act (POTA). All democratic constitutions have emergency provisions. The Indian constitution is no exception. The central government can declare a national emergency and curtail rights and liberties during the emergency period, as it did during 1974-77. It can also suspend State governments under Article 356 of the Constitution. Over the years, it has done the latter with some frequency. The various anti-terrorist bills have only added to the draconian elements of the Indian Policy. These Acts enable the government to make preventive arrests, to hold detenus without trial for long periods of time, and to protect government officials and agencies from prosecution in the course of counter-terrorist operation. Quite apart from the damage this has done to the country's efforts to control terrorism (by threatening and alienating the very people the government is trying to protect and integrate), the Acts have harmed the cause of democracy by increasing the impunity and immunity of the state.

A third effect of terrorism has been the way in which debate and dissent have been constrained. Both the terrorists and the government have been responsible for this. The terrorists have used violence or the threat of violence to intimidate ordinary citizens, citizens' groups (e.g. NGOs), government officials, political leaders, and the media. The government too has used violence and intimidation. It is true, of course, that the terrorists, on the whole, were the instigators, and the terrorists and the Indian government should not be equated in this respect. Nevertheless, the government also has played a role in curbing free expression. It is clear enough that the media, for instance, must be cautious in reporting and analyzing terrorism. The government has many instruments at its disposal in dealing with errant journalists and news organizations. One of the most worrying aspects of the problem is self-censorship. Individuals and organizations stif1c themselves even before they have been warned or targetted. This is not surprising or indefensible: no one wants to confront either terrorists or governments. Still, self-censoring is a long-term problem for a democratic political culture.

A fourth effect of terrorism has been the assault on liberals and liberalism. As noted earlier, the word liberal is now an accusation (right up there with the accusation that someone is "secular"). It is a reproach that few want. There are many reasons for the devaluation of liberalism in India over the years. Colonialism harmed the cause of liberalism. If British liberalism could tolerate, if not actively propagate, colonial subjugation and rule, it was difficult for Indian nationalists to hold liberalism up as the political creed of independent India. That India's post-colonial rulers managed to fashion a liberal polity after Independence is impressive, but it is interesting that, Nehru and some others apart, they could scarcely ever utter the word liberalism in their public utterances. Liberalism was also a favorite bugbear of the political left in India, which saw liberalism and democracy as a bourgeois construct that legitimized the domination of an elite class (Now the left sees in liberal democracy the only hope of checking the surge of the Hindu right). The left was joined in its contempt for liberal democracy by the Hindu right. The RSS and its various camp followers would abolish liberal democracy if they could. For them, it is another foreign import, along with Marxism, that prevents them from thing India into a *Hindu Rashtra* (the English language is another such import). Terrorism has damaged the liberal cause further. Even liberals wonder if liberalism is enough when they are confronted by terrorism. Some liberals have become illiberal over the years, arguing that liberalism cannot work in the face of terrorist violence, and that those who stick by liberal tenets are idealistic or foolish. The Hindu right, in particular, has used the fact of terrorism to pour scorn on liberalism and to win converts by arguing that liberalism is appeasement and passivity, that the terrorist menace grew because liberals were in power and did little to combat it (which is not true—just as the accusation that liberals are anti-religious is not true).

One of the related effects of the Hindu right's accusations has been an increasing sense of self-hate, particularly amongst Hindus. The Hindu right has argued d1at terrorists have been emboldened by the passivity of Hindus, who are unwilling to fight back. Hindutva ideologues have castigated Indians/Hindus for not having a sense of history, of territoriality of political unit); and of strategy. The Hindu right has charged the Congress Parry, and Nehru most of all, with not having protected India against both external and internal threats. In their view, India has been weak and reactive in dealing with national security threats. Nehruvian idealism and internationalism were foolish and naïve. They perpetuated the slave mentality of Hindus encouraged by centuries of Muslim and British rule. This critique has gone home. A sizeable number of a Hundus, particularly from amongst the educated middle class, have come round to exactly this view (which only confirms that a little education can be a very dangerous thing), and no amount of counter-argumentation seemingly will persuade them otherwise. Nehru is not the only object of their anger. Mahatma Gandhi, also, is objectionable to this educated middle class. It was not so many years ago that a popular film dealing with Gandhi's assassination drew loud cheers from Delhi audiences. The cheering broke out during the scene depicting Gandhi's assassination. The audience was clearly on the side of the killer, Nathuram Godse, and clapped and hooted derisively during the crucial scene. Behind the celebration over Gandhi's assassination was the sense that India's various fallibilities and difficulties arise from Gandhiansim.

Finally, terrorism has had the effect of promoting a "cult of action" and propagating a view of politics as managerial and technical. Political discourse in India is marked as never before by a vocabulary of actions and decisions. There is a constant refrain suggesting that the government of the day is not doing enough. Any discussion that moves beyond "what is to be done" immediately runs into comments that suggest impatience with "theoretical discussions". Politics is merely in this "pragmatic" view, about hard-headed, practical-minded decisions, a managerial and technical "policy science". If there is a problem, there must be a solution. If a solution has not been found, then the government and political leaders must lack something -- acumen, honesty, imagination, strength. Responsibility for the awful state of things is never with the citizenry, with ordinary Indians, in all walks of life. It is always the fault of those in positions of authority. If terrorism has not been eradicated, it is because someone is just not clever enough, industrious enough, honest enough, or brave enough. India, therefore, needs better managers and technocrats. This is a terribly thin conception of politics, and it will not sustain a vigorous democracy. Such a managerial, technical view of politics could well end up in authoritarianism, with voters rewarding those who promise to bring in a pragmatic utopia. Patience is the hallmark of statesmanship, good sense, and moderation.

The militarization of the Indian imagination, the steady accretion of extraordinary powers, the stifling of dissent and debate, the rising assault on liberals and liberalism, the growth of Hindu self-hate, and political managerialism and impatience are both reflecting and shaping a cultural nationalist conservatism that is shaking liberal democracy to its roots. This conservatism has little time for the regime of democracy and the democratic political culture described at the top of this essay. It is no respecter of liberal constitutionalism. It is hostile to civic nationalism. It is convinced that the devolution of power can only be a tactical convenience in its own rise to power: as long as there arc coalition partners to be had at the state level, who for partisan reasons would rather be with the right wing, it is worth talking about devolution of power. The day the coalition is no longer useful, it is unlikely that the Hindu right will have any time for coalitions and the sharing or devolving of power; indeed, a centralized, hierarchical conception of rule, which is a right-wing fantasy everywhere, will then be installed. This cultural nationalist conservatism also has no time for' group rights other than Hindu group rights; minority group rights, in its view, arc a form of "appeasement", contain the seeds of political mischief, and, to adapt Arthur Schlesinger's phrase about the United States, will led to the "disuniting" of India.

Nor do these conservative forces have any love for tolerance and accommodation, which they mistake for — or misrepresent as — confusion, indecision, and immaturity. The aversion to violence, in their grammar, is mere cant and cowardice. And the thicker conception of politics that has played such an important role in India's politics over the past one hundred and fifty years is, for them, simply a cover for prevarication and doubt. Indians should be gelling on with things (the most importing thing being the construction of a Hindu majoritarian "Ram Rajya") whereas they are afflicted by dilatoriness and timidity I suggested earlier that a thicker conception of politics is about forging a collective ethics, about articulating and understanding difference, about attempting to change people's minds, and, if necessary about agreeing to disagree. The conservative cultural nationalists already "know" what collective ethics Indians should agree on. They insist on articulating and understanding difference insofar as their point of view gets an airing (eventually to drown out all other different voices). They are not, contrary to what their missionaries say interested in debate and dialogue as a way of truly changing people's minds-they will impose their mind when they have clawed their way to unassailable power. Their understanding of debate is not dialogical; it is propagandistic. Debate, in their view, is an occasion for sparing and denunciation. They support the notion of "agreeing to disagree" as long as this allows them to do what they want-there will be little space for agreeing-to-disagree when power is decisively in their hands.

Conclusion

Terrorist violence has not abated much since the terrible events of 11 September 2001. Indeed, the roll call of attacks inside and outside Kashmir since then is an impressive one: the Kashmir Assembly Parliament, Kaluchak, the Amarnath pilgrims, the Akshardham temple, and the Raghunath temple. In addition, there was the assassination of the All- Party Hurriyat Conference leader, Abdul Ghani Lone. Not with standing the presence of the US in Afghanistan and Pakistan, terrorists operating from Pakistan and within Kashmir have not been cowed, India's military mobilization from January 2002 onwards also did not have a great dissuasive effect on terrorism. We can, therefore, expect terrorism in Kashmir to continue (even though there is evidence of a reduction in cross border infiltration). So also in the North-East-and most specifically in Assam, Nagaland, Manipur and Tripma — there is likely to be more violence. While there are signs of amelioration in Nagaland-the Indian government and the NSCN (I-M) arc negotiating there is still a long way to go in this turbulent region of the country.

The anti-democratic trends listed in this essay are not all directly traceable to terrorism. Having said that, terrorism has deepened the travails of Indian democracy. The rise of the Hindu right is not a function simply of terrorism, yet terrorism has certainly played a major role in strengthening the right. The rise of the right is the greatest threat to liberal democracy. How fast and how far the right advances in India is unclear, but this is a crucial moment in its development.

13

Role of Media in Terrorism

Terrorism has been defined as the use of violence when its most important result is not the physical and mental damage of the direct victims but the psychological effect produced on someone else. Terrorism also involves in addition to the act, the emotion and motivation of the terrorist. Violence may lead to death, injury or destruction of property, or deprivation of liberty. It becomes terror when the significant aim is not to attain these ends but through these, to terrorize people other than those directly involved. The distinction between terror and violence is not an absolute one. There may be violence Inked with terror in which the intention is to harm the direct victim, but the assault may be linked to an act of terror which either preceded or followed it. In this context whether a hijacking is an act of terror depends upon what the intent of the hijacker is—whether to escape or to create terror as an ancillary effect. The trait characterizing this type of terrorism is the sense of absolutism felt by the terrorist. Terrorism in the service of an absolute value has a kind of psychologically reinforcing effect.

All terrorism is not politically motivated. Criminals have used it to obtain ransom and for other forms of private gain. Matters are complicated by the fact that criminals and psychopaths often clothe themselves in political slogans of justification and by the propensity of terrorist movements to recruit assistance from and collaborate with the criminal underworld. Political terrorism may be described as coercive intimidation. It is the systematic use of murder and destruction, and the threat of murder and destruction in order to terrorize individuals, groups, communities or governments into conceding to the terrorists' political demands. It is one of the oldest techniques of psychological warfare. A primary target for terrorization is selected, the objective is determined and credibility is established by convincing the target that the threat can actually be carried out. The victim or victims may not be the primary target and the aim may in fact be, "Kill one, frighten ten thousand." The terrorist wants a lot of people watching rather than d lot of people dead. This may hold good for the rare cases of 'pure' terrorism such as mass hostage situations, but repressive and revolutionary terror often results in the massacre of large numbers of people. Terrorists are also consumed with hatred against a 'perceived' enemy and often deliberately attempt mass slaughter in public. This was in fact advocated by the pioneer German terrorist theorist, Johannes Most in the 1880's. Consequently terrorism is also to be viewed as "the use, or threat of use, of violence by an individual or a group, whether acting for or in opposition to established authority, when such action is designed to create extreme anxiety and/or fear-inducing effects in a target group larger than the immediate victim with the purpose of coercing that group into acceding to the political demands of the perpetrators. Terrorism is, as the nineteenth century anarchists claimed 'propaganda by deed' and in Brian Jenkins more recent formulation "Terrorism is theatre". Terrorism is aimed at the people watching not at the actual victims.

There is also a link between propaganda and terrorism. Propaganda has been defined as any information, ideas, doctrines or special appeals disseminated to influence the opinion, emotions, attitudes or behaviour of any special group in order to benefit the sponsor either directly or indirectly. Terrorism also seeks to influence a mass audience in a way intended to benefit the sponsor But while terrorism has a singular purpose—inducing fear and uncertainty, propaganda can and does serve every imaginable purpose from religion to politics to commerce. Yet terrorism is also a sub-species of revolution, which is a struggle for power—the key to which is popular allegiance, whether given voluntarily or out of fear. The objectives of terrorism can only be reached by a complex psychological military process in which propaganda and violence are like a boxer's two fists. This operational propaganda needs to he better understood because without it terrorism would be more easily defeated and less effective.

A critical factor in the development of political violence and terrorism is information. Changes in technology have increased the speed and ease of communications. Information that once influenced only a limited area may now affect societies throughout the world.The repercussions of one event or idea now spread across the globe so quickly as to make it difficult to respond to the proliferation of reactions. Faster communications have also tightened functional interdependence. Increased information broadens perspectives, desires and interests. Once aware of what other groups have, a group may desire the same things for itself). During the fifties, Cite Libre, a progressive French Canadian review drew similarities between Quebecs situation and the colonial struggle. When the colonial struggles succeeded, frustration among French Canadians increased and some resorted to terrorism to attain their goals. The process of modernization and communication causes a society to become vulnerable to external factors and may even expose it to information whose influence may be destabilizing. A society's sensitivity to external influences can also stem from its identification with the outside forces. The increase in kidnappings and hijackings since the mid-sixties is another example of the volatile influence of informational flows. The upsurge in terrorist attacks must be linked partially to the international flow of information because it not only provided events and involved groups with enormous publicity and even sympathy, but also inspired other groups to try similar acts. The Quebec terrorists, imitating the Tupamares, kidnapped two officials while the Croatians and Moluccans copied the hijackings of the Palestinians.

Two basic motivations for the use of terrorism as a strategy include the fact that overwhelming balance of forces between th rebels and their opposition may offer the former no other option. Here terrorism is the weapon of the last resort and is used by militant minorities who feel themselves driven at last to have recourse to violence in the service of their cause-where the inequality of forces between them and the government is such that victory for themselves in open warfare is out of the question. The transnational flow of information through the media may provide dissidents with the spark that will cause them to resort to terrorism. Once the terrorists had resorted to violence, their selection of tactics and ideology has been critically influenced by the transnational flow of information that publicized and sensationalized certain terrorist activities and movements. Dissidents may use terrorism to gain publicity for their cause and increase the interest and support of their own community and international society. The range of communication has enabled terrorists to accomplish this goal as their activities and demands are quickly dispensed via international communications. Terrorists, cognisant of the power of international communication will attempt drastic and even vicious acts of terrorism to get extensive international publicity and exposure for their grievances. Undoubtedly the plight of the Palestinians would have received less attention in recent years had Palestinian militants not resorted to hijackings, kidnappings and murder. The world today offers an attractive setting for terrorist acts. We live in times where technology has made possible both the magnification of violence and also created complex and vulnerable targets for that violence. It has become far more alluring for the frantic few to appear on the world stage of television than remain obscure guerrillas of the bush.

The media consisting of the press, radio television and even films is an indispensable communications link of modern industrial: society. The media serves economic and sociopolitical interests in the collection and dissemination of information. Electronic technology's emergence makes the diffusion of information more extensive and rapid than over before. Society's easier access to and reliance on media renders their psychological impact more persuasive than ever before. The power of the Fourth Estate for good or evil is unquestionable. Often modern mass media has resolved situations with which conventional political machinery is unable to cope. Since the 1950.

An even more potent medium than the press or radio, television, leas reached into most houses across the globle, bringing drama, entertainment and a real life immediacy to life situations to which the viewer can relate. Television cameras have reached far into the hearts and minds of men and women.

These facts have not escaped the attention of those who use violence to obtain media coverage, The correlation between the escalation of global terror-violence in the past twenty years and the, innovations in media technology that facilitate rapid dissemination of information to large audience is not a coincidence. The correlation illustrates the symbiotic relationship between terrorism and the media. The terrorists rely on the media to further their terror inspiring goals and the media use terrorist acts as necessary or rewarding news items. For the terrorists the media is the indispensable carrier of the Message. The transmission of that message in the form and manner dictated by the terrorists is scarcely less important, to him than the accomplishment of the act he desires to publicize.

Much of terrorist activity attractive for the media is that it is often carried out for audience entertainment. The Iranian students who kept American diplomatic personnel hostage in Tehran were experts in managing to attract world attention. It is the dramatic appeal that makes terrorism the glamorous growth industry that it is and will remain as long as the mass media, under the guise of information, entertain their public at prime time with stories of terrorism and titillate the imagination of an increasingly passive public.

Mass media man becomes the main agent of "mythological instruction." Due to the necessity to entertain for maximum audience pseudo-participation mass media not only glorifies violence but favours cinematographic solutions. The earlier relationship between reality, its reporting and picturing in the mass media has been reversed ; now it is the mass media relationship that produces reality and strongly suggests presumably viable, popular options. More and more do we want solutions to national problems based on the fashion of Errol Flynn, John Wayne or even Amitabh Bachchan.

This creates a dilemma for the media. There are those who claim not only a sacred right but a veritable duty to publish anything newsworthy. Can such extensive licence be appropriately claimed where public interest is involved ? The freedom to publish rests on "the need to know"—should it not be limited by the other public interest in denying the use of the media to those who would damage the common weal ? However as events have proved, "The terrorists is an urgent suitor; if he cannot get what he seeks by seductive means, he will not hesitate to attempt rape. The real problem seems to be uncertainty on the part of the media whether to play coy handmaiden or harlot."

Present day terrorism is a direct consequence of modern mass communication. The terrorist has always been publicity hungry. Barbara Tuchman cites the case of Luchini, the anarchist killer of Empress Elizabeth, who was an avid collector of newspaper clippings and longed to kill somebody important enough to get into the, papers. Cooper cites the case of Arthur Bremer, who attempted to assassinate American Presidential candidate George Wallace. Recently Doordarshan's national network allowed a convicted murderer condemned to death in Jaipur his last wish of appearing on television, an event seen all over the country. The prospect of standing alone for a moment on the cent restage is fatally attractive to many tormented minds and will continue to do so.

But organized terrorism has truly been able to exploit the media, particularly television. The members of Baader Meinhof gang in West Germany have seen themselves the true masters of this. This was revealed in the events following the sensational kidnapping of the West Berlin mayoral candidate, Peter Lorenz. The nation's television screens served the master plan of the kidnappers for 72 hours. It was the gangsters who programmed the mass media.

This ability to capture the media and through it national and international attention has not only changed terrorist's tactics but also his perception of his role and potentialities. Terrorist attacks are planned to attract the attention of the electronic media and the international press. Taking and holding hostages for instance, increases the drama. These theatrics have become possible because the wider stage is set and the audience is waiting. Television camera crews and hordes of press reporters are a standard part of the event. It is difficult to imagine any important terrorist action taking place without them. Media travels to where the action is and this is expected of them. What gives rise to concern is not the presentation of news, but the manner of their presentation. "Media publicity tends, very often to favour the terrorist side of the drama they represent. It is in the nature of television as a medium that it tends to favour the revolutionary side."

Whereas in the Lorenz incident the media may draw some sympathy on loosing control, none can be given when the media itself rushes headlong into the arms of the terrorist. The media becomes an active participant in the event and not a mere detached recorder of it. There have been many events in which the press, film producers and television have cooperated in publicizing terrorists activities. A reporter from *Der Spiegel* actually accompanied members of the Bader Meinhoj gang in an attack on a house in Hamburg. Here the media representative was in effect in collusion with dangerous criminals. There has been similar collusion between British and American media representatives and the Irish

Republican Army. The recent controversy over the attempt to ban the BBC TV documentary "Real Lives : At the Edge of the Union" by Mrs. Thatcher arose over the filmed interview with Martim McGuinness, a leading IRA terrorist in the documentary. This was part of Mrs. Thatcher's plan to starve terrorists of "the oxygen of publicity."

Films too have been made attempting to give the "spurious justification" so essential for the terrorists movement. Violence by the terrorists, by this argument is a reluctant but inevitable reaction to violence by the state. Costa Graves' film "State of Siege" (1973) portrayed Tupamaro violence as a justified reaction to America's political and economic domination of Uruguary, a domination which the film alleged, introduced torture to that country. Similarly Reinhard Hauff's film "Stammheim — The Trial" (1986) reportedly grants legitimacy to Baader Meinhof atrocities by portraying the suicides of convicted terrorists as "state terrorism." In both cases the justification theme merges with guilt transfer, because audiences are required to see authority in a worse light than the terrorists.

Terrorism like advertising, increases the effectiveness of its messages by focussing on spectacular incidents and by keeping particular issues alive through repetition. Carlos Marighella in his "Minimanual of the Urban Guerrilla" states that "The coordination of urban guerrilla action, including each aimed action, is the principal way of making armed propaganda."

These actions carried out with specific and determined objectives, inevitably become propaganda material for the mass communication system.

Bank assaults, ambushes, desertions and diverting of arms, the rescue of prisoners, executions, kidnappings, sabotage, terrorism and the war of nerves are all cases in point.

The war of nerves or psychological war is an aggressive technique, based on direct or indirect use of mass means of communication and news transmitted orally in order to demoralize the government.

In psychological warfare, the government is always at a disadvantage since it imposes censorship on the mass media and ends up in a defensive position by not allowing anything against it to filter through.

The utilization and manipulation of the media as directed by Marighella and others have been followed by practically all terrorist movements. They have sought not only to spread fear among the primary target, but also publicize their discontent as well as their ideologies with a view to making their violent deeds appear heroic.

Whether acts of terror violence are committed by individuals against a state or are state sponsored terror violence against individuals, the perpetrators' strategy involves the use and instrumentalization of media. State sponsored terrorism often reduces media exposure of repressive violence while non-state sponsored violence seeks maximum exposure.

Ideologically motivated terror violence from below is the weapon of those who are too few or powerless to achieve their objectives through the conventional political process. Technology has made the media an indispensable device by which an individual or small group can magnify their power over society within a short period of time and with relatively little effort.

The mass media performs five basic functions. These are informational, judgemental, educational interactional and recreational. Moreover, news must be timely—or else it will become outdated. To be newsworthy an event must also be unique. It must deviate from the routine monotony of every day existence. An adventure, specially mane involving violence is certainly newsworthy. News often requires an event which affects the lives of those being informed of it. An incipient war, a tax rise or a crime wave are newsworthy since it affects the reader, viewer or listener directly. Terrorist activities are by nature newsworthy because they affect our lives.

Ideologically motivated terrorism usually operates on three levels each having. its own goal. The primary stage is an attack against a suitable target, the secondary is tile dissemination by the media of tile ideological claim or terror inspiring effect of the act and the third is the achievement of the desired power outcome. Each of these objectives are interrelated in the perpetrators reliance on the media to attain his ends. The choice of the tactical target is usually directed against highly visible targets and conducted dramatically to draw media attention and maximize the impact. The media conscious perpetrator also attempts to manipulate the media so that his grievance or ideology may be portrayed as desirable or inevitable. In an excellent piece Crelinsten attempts to explain terrorism as a struggle over access to the communication structure. The terrorist act is a claim for attention, for recognition as a participant in tile political process and ultimately for legitimacy as a valid representative of a particular political cause. Tile terrorist becomes a political actor who by the use of Violence is participating in a particular political discourse. Crelinsten basis his analysis on a detailed study of even newspapers in Quebec, Canada when Quebec separatist activitists acting under the name of *le Front tie liberation Quebec* (FLQ) kidnapped a British diplomat, James Cross and a Quebec Cabinet Minister Pierre Laporte in October 1975. Data sources for the media coverage also revealed that electronic media, particularly the radio played a central role in the development of the crisis. In fact two Montreal radio stations came to be known as the electronic 'mailboxes' for the two terrorist cells, each of which sent the majority of their communiqués to one of the two stations. In this crisis the superior power of tile state was sufficiently challenged by the terrorists' actions which were reflected in the change in the pattern of press coverage. When the state reasserted its authority by a display of power, press coverage also shifted to a pattern consistent with the restoration of the balance of power to the state!

Four major problems associated with media coverage of terrorism emerge. The reporting of acts of terrorism may encourage others to engage in such conduct. This is described as the contagion hypothesis. The public success of a particular group may encourage the group to repeat its acts to focus public attention to itself or its ideology. This may goad less successful groups to commit increased or more daring acts of terrorism. The spotlight of media attention may be an irresistible lure to violence for certain individuals. Many examples of criminal education through media presentation of crime have been recorded. In India violence and crime in films has undoubtedly triggered off violence and increased crimes in the country. Research in the area generally supports the proposition that the contagion effect of terrorism leads to imitation by other groups especially when previous terrorist acts have been successful.

In contrast, media coverage of terrorism may instead have a cathartic effect on potential terrorists. Media coverage may dampen an individual's enthusiasm if it successfully portrays the failure of terrorists acts due to effectiveness of law enforcement.

The most pervasive problem associated with media reporting of terrorism is the climate of intimidation it generates, a general fear of victimization spoiling the quality of life and destahili7ation of' social institutions. Repetitive dissemination of terrorist acts produces this impact Media mediates between a man and his environment particularly in a complex society. Media coverage of terrorist violence enhances dysfunctional media-created anxiety which enhances the perceived power of the terrorist not only in his own eyes, but also in the eyes of the public.

The immunization effect can manifest itself in three ways. The first resulting from continuous media coverage of violence in general and terrorism in particular heightens public tolerance and acceptance of violence and terrorism as a way of life. Consider how mush violence we have been seeing on Doordarshan of late in the news particularly regarding the events in Burma, Israel and students protests in Seoul. Most of us sit down to dinner during the news and do not react to it adversely at all.

The second manifestation of this is the portrayal of terrorists as "crazies" alien to our accepted frame of reference and therefore society is unable to control them. The third results from the abstract and impersonal portrayal of terrorism and its harmful effect. As society becomes immune to violenoe two consequences are possible—the level of violence necessary to elicit a terror-inspiring effect increases in order to overcome the dulled perceptions of the public and more persons may resort to violence or terrorism. This in turn increases the contagion and immunization effect.

Public immunization is not a foregone conclusion of media coverage of terrorism. It may result in increasing public opposition to such behaviour. What the terrorist wants is enough balanced media coverage to produce immunization and not outraged media coverage to trigger an opposing social reaction.

Social researches and policy makers all over report that viewing of televised violence by children encourages antisocial tendencies and aggressive behaviour. Media is also in the business of making profit. The media today is in the business of selling attention. Terrorist events are newsworty and dramatic. When news reporting becomes a commercial product aimed at its attention-getting potential, excessive coverage is given to violent dramatic events in disproportion to their actual significance.

Terrorists are well aware of the competition between news organizations, their desire for 'scoops' and quest for larger audiences which foster reliance on sometimes questionable reporting techniques. Reporters do not merely report the news, they often become subjective participants in it. Terrorists take advantage of this in their attempt to manipulate the media. When commercial and competitive factors displace judgement in the coverage of terrorist incidents, the media loses control and becomes a hostage itself.

Television has acquired an infinitely more powerful means of communication than anything known earlier. With television not only are the senses of sight and hearing fully occupied out every emotion is caught up and involved. Terrorists consequently have a particular affinity for gaining access to television since the bias is inevitably against established authority and on the side of the revolutionaries.

Media coverage of a terrorist attack often gives rise to three areas of conflict between police and the media. The first involves media dissemination of information tactically useful to the terrorist while an attack is under way. Being isolated, the terrorists equip them selves with receivers which allow them to listen to news broadcast. In the process the media may unwittingly serve as the intelligence arm of the terrorists when they broadcast vital information involving hostages or strategy involving law enforcement officials.

Media interference may exacerbate the situation by impending the negotiating process. Another problem which arises is that of crowd control during the coverage. Police chiefs generally view these problems as being serious. The 1977 Summer survey revealed that 93°% of police chiefs believed that live television coverage of terrorists acts encourages terrorism. None wanted terrorist acts to be telecast live.

Media and law enforcement have necessarily to cooperate to tackle the issues. In India the problem of the role of media has to be looked at a little differently. Both television and the radio are state controlled. However as pointed out continuous violence on Doordarshan immunizes the effect of violence and the persistent inability to stem the terrorist probably has a contagion effect too. The press has access to other sources of information but obviously the impact of the written word is limited. Being a largely illiterate society where the television network is 'booming' and entering increasingly into our lives the government should be aware of the potential impact of television even if it is controlled by the state.

The media has to report objectively and accurately about terrorists acts lest the public panic and lose trust and confidence in both the press and the government. Attempts to impose media blackouts will not only lead to rumour-mongering but perhaps force terrorists to escalate the levels of violence in order to attract more attention. Conversely since a major goal of terrorism is to undermine authority an unjustifiable limitation of free media will ultimately lead to the victory of terrorism. Given the nature and complexity of modern terrorism the determination of a proper role for the media should not be left to their judgement or to unilateral decisions of the law enforcement agencies. The threat of contemporary terrorism necessarily regains the openness, understanding and cooperation of society to deal realistically with this major area of public concern. The recent controversy over the public debate over the material allegedly sympathetic to the terrorists in the 'Ajit' newspapers in Punjab illustrates the need for mature political debate on the issue.

14

Terrorism in South Asia: Bangladesh

Terrorism has become a threat to humanity. While the act of terrorism is very unevenly distributed over the world in terms of its nature, intensity, and coverage, its negative impact is spread both over the developed and the developing countries, directly and indirectly. Terrorist acts not only discourage economic activity by threatening the safety of life and property; they also damage the overall investment environment of a country by creating turmoil and anarchy. LDCs and developing countries, which are striving for development with poor resource bases, can hardly afford such a cost of terrorism.

South Asia is a region of LDCs and developing countries. South Asian countries (except Afghanistan) have been performing much better in terms of economic growth compared to the average performance of the low-income countries. Some of the countries have already graduated from the status of LDC to that of developing countries. However, these countries had even better potential: some of these economics could have stood at the same level as the newly industrialized countries (NICs). During the early 1960s the economic conditions of the South Asian countries were similar to those of many NICs. The potential of the South Asian countries could not be fully realized for many reasons, including terrorism. Terrorism is a common phenomenon in this region, although the nature of terrorism is not identical across the South Asian countries.

Nature of Terrorism

Terrorism, by nature, is very difficult to define. The old adage, "One man's terrorist is other man's freedom fighter" is still alive and well. For the purpose of our analysis of the cost of terrorism, we take the' FBI definition, Terrorism is the unlawful use of force or violence against persons or property to intimidate or coerce a government, the civilian population, or any segment thereof, in furtherance of political and social objectives." James M. Poland's view is that "terrorism is the premeditated, deliberate, systematic murder, mayhem, and threading of the innocent to create fear and intimidation in order to gain a political or tactical advantage, usually to influence an audience." While terrorism is usually meant to be an act of an organized group of people, or small groups of miscreants, it may also be government-controlled or directed. Similarly while terrorist activity is sometimes confined within some locality, the scope of terrorist activity may also be extended beyond the national boundaries. The nature of terrorism in the present world is summarized in Fig. 14.1.

		Government Controlled or Directed	
		Yes	**No**
Scope	Nation	Domestic Terrorism	State Terror
	Regional/ International	International Terrorism	State-Sponsored

Fig. 14.1: Nature of Terrorism

Terrorism in Bangladesh

Bangladesh is a country with a virtually homogeneous society. There is some ethnic diversity, basically due to very small numbers of tribal inhabitants in the Chittagong Hill Tracts (CHT) and some other parts of the country Bangladeshis are, by nature, peace-loving people. Bangladesh has set up a unique example of communal harmony although some scattered incidents took place after the general election of 2001, mostly due to political motivation. In general, terrorism ill Bangladesh is not as severe as that in some of the other countries in South Asia. This does not, however, mean that Bangladesh is free of it. Bangladesh also has had to bear a large cost arising from terrorism.

Several types of terrorist activities have been observed in Bangladesh. The most severe type of terrorism is associated with activities of the groups who arc ideologically and politically motivated. This includes: (1) the activities of outlawed political parties, (2) the threat from the terrorist group of fundamentalists, and (3) the terrorism in the CRT Right after Independence, an activist group became involved in terrorism that was politically motivated to establish communism in this country It targeted the rich people who had accumulated wealth within the capitalist system. Direct action against those people, they believed, would ease the path towards establishing communism. Initially, they were organized as a political party. The Government of Bangladesh outlawed this parry at some point. Since then, this group started to be involved in terrorist activities. Although their terrorist activities were scattered around many parts of the country, they were more organized in the south-western part of the country. Fortunately, the activities of this terrorist group have been declining in recent years. However, they are still very active in the south-western parts. Many of the killings and bomb attacks in the past few years were believed to have been conducted by this terrorist group. The majority of the people in Bangladesh believe in the religion of Islam. They are basically peace-loving Muslims who do not support any terrorist activity Despite this, a very small group of Islamic fundamentalists who had been alleged to be involved in many terrorist activities in the past few years also exists. This group, the Harkat-ul-Jehadi-eIslami, is committed to establishing Islamic *Hukumat* [rule] in Bangladesh. This extremist group is believed to have close links with Pakistan. It was also believed to have close ties with tile Taliban. However, the activities of this group were marginal and guite scattered in Bangladesh. It seems that the presence of this Islamic fundamentalist group got more propaganda than its real existence. Lately, tile terrorist activities of this group have virtually ceased. The natives of the CHT had been fighting to establish their rights and "independence" since the early 1970s. They were organized in political parties and militant groups to fight against Bangladesh. Since then, they have carried on many terrorist activities in the Hill Tracts area. The government signed a peace treaty with them (the CHT Accord) in 1997. which brought the hope of establishing peace in that region. However a subgroup of theirs remained discontented with the treaty The accord promised the tribes restitution of their land, greater participation in the government, and a reduction of the presence of Bangladesh military force in the CHT. However, the accord did not solve many of the outstanding questions, and the implementation of the treaty ran into snags, so the full potential for peace, development and coexistence between the tribal and the settler segments of the region's inhabitants remained practically unrealized. Within the tribal community, there is persistent tension between the pro- and anti-peace accord groups. In February 2001, three foreign nationals were abducted in the forest of Rangamati districts and were kept hostage for a month until they were rescued by a commando action. According to Indian government sources, terrorist groups such as the United Liberation Front of Assam (ULFA), the All Tripura Tiger Force (ATTF), and the National Liberation Front of Tripura (NLFT) run several base camps in the jungles or CHT areas and Sylhet, which has become a point of discontent in the bilateral relationship between India and Bangladesh.

The most common terrorism in Bangladesh is the activities of miscreants, which is associated with deterioration in the law and order situation. The miscreants use violence with the civilian population to have unlawful possession over their money and property. The "*mastans*" [hooligans] use threats, physical torture, and force on innocent people to compel them to surrender to their unlawful will. A severe unemployment problem, inf1ux of illegal weapons, patronage from political parties, along with the inadequate, inefficient and corrupt role of the law enforcing agencies are responsible for the rise of general mastanism in the country. The common people of Bangladesh have become captive to the miscreants.

In addition to these two major types of terrorism, political confrontation also gives rise to terrorist activities. Even though Bangladesh has started its journey on the path of democracy, there is a higher degree of political instability as the democratic and institutions are severely undernourished. Two major political parties seem to be very stubborn and intolerant to each other. There are frequent calls for hartal and other destructive programmes due to political fragmentation and conflicts. Sometimes, political programmes give rise to terrorist activities like bomb attacks or setting fire to property. Even the members of the law enforcing agencies sometimes become so brutal with the suspects, who may even be innocent people, that it could also be categorized as a type of terrorism.

Cost of Domestic Terrorism on the Economy of Bangladesh

General *mastanism* and the associated terrorist activities of the miscreants have the most negative impact on the economy of Bangladesh. Businessmen arc oppressed by the high incidence of toll extraction by the political and local miscreants: they arc alleged to be forced to pay involuntary tolls at every stage of business operations. It increases the cost of doing business directly or indirectly and lowers business competitiveness. New investment in productive activities is heavily discouraged, because of the up-front involuntary tolls that have to be paid to the miscreants when any one goes for a new construction or a new establishment. Sometimes, peoples' lives are jeopardized if they hesitate to pay tolls to miscreants. The overall law and order situation in Bangladesh is far from satisfactory.

As explained in the earlier section the political confrontation may give rise to destructive programmes that may lead to terrorist activities like bomb attacks or setting fire to property: These destructive activities not only hamper the profitability of existing production activities, they also reduce the incentive to invest in this country. More importantly, terrorist activities by miscreants, along with political violence have created a negative image about the investment potential in the country to both local and foreign investors. Although private investment in this country started to increase since the early 1990s due to economic liberalization, the investment/GDP ratio became stagnant in recent years. Similarly there was a massive inflow of FD I in the mid-1990s. However, the FDI is showing an alarmingly declining trend lately (Table 14.1). Growth of general terrorism and the poor image of the country are the important factors behind this poor performance ofinvestt1lent in recent years.

Table 14.1: Investment Scenario in Bangladesh in Recent Years

	Private Investment as% of GDP	Foreign Direct Investment (in million US$)
1997-98	15.31	249
1998-99	15.5	198
1999-2000	15.6	194
2000-01	15.9	174
2001-02	16.1	41 (Jul-Feb)

Although Bangladesh has been enjoying a moderate growth rate in recent years, a recent study (by this author) shows that there is a huge discrepancy in the level of development and economic growth rates across different regions in Bangladesh. Investment activities are highly concentrated in the capital city and a few other major cities in Bangladesh. Investors do not feel equally safe in investing in all areas of Bangladesh. One of the main reasons for concentration of investment in the major cities is the relatively greater presence of the law enforcing agencies and relatively less pressure for "tolls" from local miscreants. Thus, the growth of terrorism by the local *mastans* has also contributed to the unequal regional development of the country. Private investment had also been lower in the districts of CHT and the south-western parts of the country where the terrorist groups were more active. This point is substantiated by the state of per capita bank advances in different divisions and selected districts in Bangladesh (Table 14.2). Bank advances may be a good proxy for private investment. It is quite evident that bank advances are very unevenly distributed across different regions of the country. Per capita bank advances are quite low in the districts of the CHT. The same is true for the districts in the south-western part of the country.

The CHT is one of the regions with the most potential in terms or its resource base and capacity to have a positive impact on the overall development of the country. This is the region where most of the country's forest land is located. The region has enormous natural resources. It is famous for its natural beauty However, the potential or its own development is far from having materialized. Terrorist activities in that region are one of the important factors in this regard. Development in the hill tracts area has been achieved basically through government initiative. Private investment is much lower in this area. Foreign investors arc also very interested to take part in extraction of natural resources and contribute to development in this region.

Table 14.2: Per Capita Bank Advances in Selected Districts and Regions of Bangladesh

(Taka in '000s, as on 30 Sep 2001)

Bangladesh	5.706
Dhaka Division	11.834
Chittagong Division	4.908
Khulna Division	3.344
Bandarban*	2.180
Rangamati*	1.175
Khagrachar*	0.625
Bagerhat**	1.093
Chaudanga**	1.312
Jhenedah**	1.457
Magura**	1.023
Narail**	1.253
Satkhira**	1.526

* District in the Chittagong Hill Tracts Area.

** Districts in the south-west part of the country.

Source: "Scheduled Bank Statistics", Bangladesh Bank

The 11 September terrorist attack allected our economy in many other indirect ways. First, the US resorted to help from Pakistan to carry on the war against the Taliban of Mghanistan. In return, Pakistan received some additional benefits from the US regarding export of RMG, which the country otherwise would not have received. As a result, many orders for RMG were diverted from Bangladesh to Pakistan. Thus, the gain of Pakistan was achieved at the cost of LDCs like Bangladesh. Imposition of restrictions on US visas for the citizens of countries like Bangladesh may also have some negative impact. First, it might lower the inflow of remittances to Bangladesh. Second, it may minimize the exchange of knowledge, and deprive prospective Bangladeshi students from receiving modern education.

Foreign investment depends not only on the image of a country, but also on the image of the *region*. Terrorism in the South Asian region may have some negative impact on the economy of Bangladesh as well by discouraging FDI.

Conclusion

Terrorism has become an important concern in recent years. Although the severity of terrorism is less in Bangladesh compared to some other South Asian countries, it still incurs heavy costs on the economy. Domestic terrorism has increased the cost of doing business, reduced competitiveness, and diminished the image of the country as a good place for investment. Terrorism by miscreants due to general weakness in the law and order situation is supposed to have the most widespread negative impact on the economy. On the other hand, terrorism by Islamic fundamentalists, mosdy being propaganda, also results in a negative image for foreign investors and tourists. Terrorism in the CHT is a great hindrance for the development of this region, as all as its potential contribution to the economy has been rendered null and void. Bangladesh is also negatively affected by regional and international terrorism.

Although sometimes there is confusion between terrorism and the acts of freedom fighters by counter-groups, it is true that such activities cause huge economic costs to the society. Hence, Bangladesh and all other nations should seriously work to minimize terrorist activities. Dialogue must be encouraged instead of force, where possible. The overall law and order situation must be improved through reforming the police force and rejuvenating the legal system, which would help curb terrorist activities by miscreants.

15

Terrorism and Democracy: Pakistan's Perspective

Introduction

Terrorism in many cases is rooted in economic deprivation, a sense of social or political injustice, or a narrowing of the mind induced by ideological indoctrination. The terrorist often claims that his action is an expression of his political or religious beliefs or retaliation because of injustice to him.

In recent years, in a number of cases terrorists have emerged from relatively afl luent countries. Yet, it is noteworthy that the Taliban, who were integrally linked with the Al Qaeda, predominantly came from poverty-stricken Afghanistan. Those Tlliban terrorists who were recruited from religious seminaries (*madrasas*) in Pakistan also came from the poorest sections of Pakistan's society. Therefore, poverty can be as fertile a breeding ground for terrorism as a sense of political injustice.

Combat *vs.* Preventive Diplomacy

The key feature of the war against terrorism that distinguishes it from wars between states is that the location, and sometimes the identity of the enemy is uncertain. Even less certain is which individual or group of individuals is going to become an enemy in future to cause the feared mega-destruction. Therefore, in the prosecution of such a war, military combat and preventive diplomacy are intimately linked. If, in the past, war was "the conduct of politics by other means", today politics is perhaps essential to the conduct of war itself. Preventive diplomacy as a complement to combat was first tused in second-century Rome when Marcus Aurelius Caesar secured the Roman Empire through convivial economic and political arrangements with potentially hostile tribes and warlords on the margins of the Roman Empire. Today, given the peculiar nature of the war against terrorism, preventive diplomacy may be even more important than in ancient Rome.

Pakistan has played a crucial role in the combat operations conducted by the coalition against the "Taliban and Al Qaeda elements in Afghanistan and the tribal belt along its border. Equally important is the configuration of economic, social and political force in Pakistan to determine whether it can effectively provide the logistical and political support to the war against terrorism in the future. Therefore, in examining the linkages between combat and preventive diplomacy Pakistan may be an important case study.

State Policy in the Zia Regime and the Rise of Islamic Fundamentalism

In Pakistan's case, the socio-political roots of terrorism as well as those of the current economic crisis can be traced to the Zia regime in the period 1997 to 1988. These tendencies developed further during the decade of the 1990s, when a historically unprecedented growth in poverty combined with an undermining of democratic institutions. The aim of is to analyse the interplay between the rise of militant religious groups, government poverty during the last two decades spanning Zia's military regime and the subsequent decade of democracy.

In the absence of popular legitimacy, the Zia regime used terror for the first time in Pakistan's history as a conscious policy of the government. President Zia-ul-Haq publicly stated: "Martial law should be based on fear." In the same vein, Malik wrote: "Terror struck into the hearts of enemies is not only a means, it is the end itself." The Minister for Labour and Manpower, Lt. Gen Faiz Ali Chishti, declared the same policy objective regarding those who dared to dissent: "The enemies of Islam must be hunted down and killed like snakes even when they are offering prayers. In the pursuit of this policy, the democratic constitution of 1973 was set aside and draconian measures of military courts, arbitrary arrests, amputation of hands and public lashing were introduced. Pakistan's society, by and large, was historically characterized by cultural diversity, democratic aspirations, and a religious perspective rooted in tolerance and humanism. This was one of the reasons why the founding father, Quaid-e-Azam Muhammead Ali Jinnah, conceived of Pakistan's Polity a democratic and pluralistic, with religious belief to be a matter concerning the individual rather than the State.

> *You may belong to any religion or caste or creed... that has nothing to do with the business of the state We are starting with this hll1damental principle that we arc all citizens and equal citizens of one state... Now, I think we should keep that in front of us as our ideal and you will find that in the course of time Hindus would cease to be Hindus and Muslims would cease to be Muslims, not in the religious sense, because that is the personal faith of each individual but in the political sense as citizens of the state.*

President Zia-ul-Haq, in attempting to restructure such a State and society into a theocracy, undertook two kinds of initiatives. First, measures were desigl1cd to subordinate to executive Authority, the institutions of state and civil society such as the judiciary and the press, which, if allowed to function independently could check governmental power. In the case of the Judiciary, its essential powers to scrutinize the legality of martial law or the orders of military courts were abolished. The judicial protection against arbitrary detention of a citizen embodied in the right to habeas corpus was eliminated for the first time in Pakistan.

In the case of the press, President Zia-ul-Haq gave a pithy statement of Martial Law Policy: "Democracy means freedom of the press, Martial Law its very negation. The pursuit of this policy, press control measures were introduced. The government constituted committees at the district level to ensure that articles repugnant to the ideology of Pakistan were not published. Those members of the press who had refused to acquiesce faced state repression. A number of newspapers were banned and journalists were arrested and given flogging sentences by military courts.

The second set of measures towards a theocratic State sought to inculcate obscurantist views and induce a narrowing of the human mind. It involved a suspension of the sensibility of love and reason underlying the religious tradition signified in Pakistan's folk culture.

In the absence of a popular mandate, Zia claimed that his mission to bring an "Islamic Order" in Pakistan had divine sanction: " I have a mission given by God to bring Islamic Order to Pakistan. Advocacy for a theocratic social order was conducted through the state-controlled television and press. Individual and group behaviour and society were sought to be controlled through the enforcement of coercive measures such as the amputation of wrists and ankles for theft, stoning to death for adultery, and 80 lashes for drinking alcohol. Apart from this, in 1984 a law was passed to officially give women an inferior status compared to men. In August 1984, the government began a national campaign involving the direct physical intervention of the state in the personal life of individuals. For example, the Nizam-e-Salat Campaign was launched through the appointment of 100,000 "Prayer Wardens" for rural and urban localities. The task of these state functionaries was to monitor religious activities of individuals and to seek their compliance in religious practices.

The institutional roots of "Islamic Fundamentalism" were laid when government funds were provided for establishing mosque schools (*madrasas*) in small towns and rural areas, which led to the rapid growth of militant religious organizations. This social process was catalysed by the Afghan war. As Gen. Zia moved towards the construction of a theocratic State and brutalized civil society, his isolation from the people as a whole was matched by increased external dependence. He sought political, economic and military support from the US by offering to play the role of a front-line state in the Afghan guerrilla war against the occupying Soviet Army. Accordingly Pakistan obtained a package of $3.2 billion from the US in financial loans and relatively sophisticated military hardware. Moreover, with support from the US, Pakistan was able to get additional fiscal space by getting its foreign debt rescheduled, and increased private foreign capital inflows. These official and private capital inflows played an important role in stimulating macroeconomic growth in this period.

As the Zia regime engaged in a proxy war, some of the militant religious groups together with their associated madrasas were provided with official funds, training and weapons to conduct guerrilla operations in Afghanistan. While they helped fight the war in Afghanistan, the religious militant groups were able to enlarge the political space within Pakistan's society as well as in its intelligence and security apparatus. Since the late 1970s, with the steady inflow of Afghan refugees into Pakistan and its use as a conduit for arms for the Afghan war, trends emerged to fuel the crisis of civil society.

1. A large proportion of the weapons meant for the Afghan guerrillas filtered into the illegal arms market in Pakistan;
2. There was a rapid growth of the heroin trade.

Powerful *mafia*-type syndicates emerged which conducted the production, transportation and export of heroin. The large illegal arms market and the burgeoning heroin trade injected both weapons and syndicated organizations into the social life of major urban centres. At the same time, the frequent terrorist bombings in the Frontier province together with a weakening of State authority in parts of rural Sind, undermined the confidence of the citizens in the ability of the State to provide security to life and property. Increasing numbers of the underprivileged sections of society began to seek security in various proximate identities, whether ethnic, sectarian, ***biradari*** or linguistic groups.

From 1987 onwards, sectarian violence mushroomed in the Punjab province (which till then had been relatively peaceful) and later spread across the country. The phenomenon of large-scale sectarian violence conducted by well-armed and trained cadres was closely associated with rapid growth of *deeni madrasas* (religious schools). While historically such schools merely imparted religious knowledge, in the late 1980s a new kind of *deeni madrasa* emerged, which engaged in systematic indoctrination in a narrow, sectarian identity, and inculcated hatred and violence against other sects. In 1998, there were 3,393 *deeni madrasas* in the Punjab alone, and 67 per cent had emerged during the period of the Zia regime and after. The number of Pakistani students in these *madrasas* was 306,500 in the Punjab. Between 1979 and 1994, many of the amdrasas were receiving financial grants from zakat funds. According to an official report of the police department, a number of *madrasas* were merely providing religious education. Yet, as many as 42 per cent of them were actively promoting sectarian violence through a well conceived indoctrination process. The students (predominantly from poor families) were given free food and lodging during their term at the madrasas. As poverty increased in the 1990s, the burgeoning madrasas provided a growing number of unemployed and impoverished youths with the security of food, shelter and an emotionally charged identity: a personality that felt fulfilled through violence against the "other".

As the new kind of sectarian madrasas emerged and grew during the Zia regime, so did sectarian violence. The number of sectarian killings increased from 22 during the 1987-89 period to 166 during the 1993-95 period. Thus, violence against the "other" became both the expression and the emblem of the narrowed identity.

The mobilization of these narrow identities involved a psychic disconnection from the wellsprings of universal human brotherhood within the Islamic tradition. Its liberating elements of rationality and love were replaced in the narrowed psyche by obscurantism and hatred. Violence against the "other" became an emblem of member-ship within these identities. Thus, civil society divorced from its universal human values began to lose its cohesion and stability.

Economic Growth and the Prelude to Recession

The rapidly growing debt servicing burden together with a slowdown of GDP growth and government revenues that had occurred at the end of the Bhutto period (1977) would have placed crippling fiscal and political pressures on the Zia regime but for two factors: (1) the generous financial support received from the West; and (2) the acceleration in the inflow of remittances from the Middle East, which increased from US$0.5 billion in 1978 to US$3.2 billion in 1984. These foreign capital inflows cased budgetary and balance of payments pressures, and thereby enabled the Zia regime to undertake the policy of building a theocratic State.

Although the GDP growth rate during the Zia period did increase, yet this higher growth rate could not be expected to be maintained because of continued poor performance of three strategic bctors that sustain growth over time:

(1) The domestic savings rate continued to remain below 10 per cent compared to a required rate of over 20 per cent;

(2) Exports as a percentage of GDP continued to remain below 10 per cent and did not register any substantial increase; (Table 15.1);

(3) inadequate investment in social and economic infrastructure.

As defence and debt servicing expenditure increased, the Annual Development Programme (ADP) through which much of the infrastructure projects were funded, began to get constricted. For example, ADP expenditure as a percentage of GDP fell from an average of 7.4 percent in the Z.A. Bhutto period (1973-77) to 6.2 per cent in the Zia period. (1977-88).

It is not surprising that when the cushion of foreign loans and debt relief was withdrawn at the end of the Afghan war, the underlying structural constraints to GDP growth began to manifest themselves: debt servicing pressures resulting from the low saving rates, high borrowings and balance of payments deficits related with low export growth and poor infrastructure, combined to pull down the GDP growth into a protracted economic recession in the 1990s.

Poverty, Politics, and Terrorism in the 1990s

The decade of the 1990s was marked by a protracted economic recession, a historically unprecedented increase in poverty, and a deteriorating law-and-order situation. There was a sharp decline in the growth rate of GDP from 6.3 per cent in the 1980s to 4.2 per cent in the 1990s. During the decade of the 1990s, political instability historically unprecedented corruption of the top leadership, and the worsening law-and-order situation had a significant adverse effect on private investment and GDP growth. Yet, these factors merely accentuated the tendency for growth to slow down as a result of structural features of the economy that were manifest even in the 1980s. The failure of successive governments in this period to address the deteriorating infrastructure and the emerging financial crisis further exacerbated the unfavorable environment for investment. (Investment as a percentage of GDP declined from 18 per cent in the period 198892 to 16 per cent in the period 1993-97.) This decline in investment was accompanied by a decline in the productivity of capital, thereby accentuating the decline in GDP growth rate. The sharp decline in the GDP growth rate was accompanied by an unprecedented increase in poverty. In terms of the calorific norm, the percentage of the population below the poverty line increased from 17 in 1987-88 to 32 in 1999-2000. While one-third of the population was hungry the majority of the population was deprived of access to basic services such as education, health, sanitation and safe drinking water.

Pakistan's demographic age profile shows that as much as 49 per cent of the population is below 18 years of age. These young men and women arc living in families, which in one-third of the cases are hungry where the elders arc predominantly sick and without adequate medical treatment. In most cases, the young women and men arc not only subject to the pressures of hunger and untreated illness in the family; but have few prospects of education or employment. These are desperate circumstances, which in some cases are inducing suicide, and in many otl1ers constitute the social base of religious violence. *Madrasas* linked to armed militant groups which provided food, shelter and a sense of group identity therefore, found ready recruits in this period. During the 1990s, acute political stability combined with official tolerance of armed religious groups, gave them an opportunity to increase recruitment and enlarge their political constituencies, particularly in the provinces of NWFP and Baluchistan. (In these provinces, large sections of the Population had kinship and ethnic tics with communities across the border in Afghanistan.) As the Taliban regime consolidated its hold over Afghanistan during the 1990s, it found loyal support from some of the armed militant groups functioning in Pakistan.

After 11 September the Government of Pakistan wisely joined the international coalition in the war against terrorism. Courageous policies were undertaken by the government to provide logistical support to coalition forces fighting in Afghnistan.

Conclusion

Pakistan is at the crossroads today. It can emerge as an enlightened, moderate and modern Muslim country that can make a significant contribution to world peace and human civilization in the twenty-first century. Pakistan's society has a deep-rooted tradition of religious tolerance, and is imbued with universal values of humanism. It has a talented and creative human resource base. For Pakistan to actualize its great human potential, it is necessary to strengthen the institutions of democracy and to undertake a process of rapid economic development. Poverty must be quickly overcome, and access to education, health, transport and housing must be provided to those currently deprived of these basic facilities.

Terrorism, at a psychic level, involves a divorce from the wellsprings of reason and humanity that give to the individual his sense of wholeness and relatedness with others. If Pakistan is to avoid becoming a breeding ground of terrorism in the future, then poverty and illiteracy must be overcome. This is necessary to enable its people to love and reason rather than hate and kill.

16

TERRORISM IN SOUTH ASIA: PAKISTAN'S PERSPECTIVE

Introduction

The terrorist act of 9/11 and the ensuing "war on terrorism" waged by the US and its Western allies have impacted, among others, on development of democracy in a number of developing countries. This is discernible more in Pakistan, that assumed the role of a front-line State in the "war against terrorism", than in any other country.

Three international power centres, namely, the United States, the European Union, and the British Commonwealth made conscious efforts to influence and shape events aimed at the restoration and revival of democracy in Pakistan. The approach adopted by each one of them for this purpose has been different. In particular, we observe this difference in approach between the US on the one hand, and the EU and the Commonwealth on the other. The present paper proposes to look at the following questions. What has been the attitude of these power centres towards Pakistan's democratic odyssey? How does one explain the asymmetry in attitudes on their part in the matter? Finally, how does one explain the abandonment of democracy in favour of security?

Asymmetry of Attitudes

As the curtain rose on 9/11 when the terrorists struck on the Twin Towers and the Pentagon, Pakistan was already under military rule since October 1999 following the coup d'etat engineered by Pervez Musharraf against the government of Nawaz Sharif. Soon after the coup, President Musharraf become more or less a pariah in the international community because of the changed international atmosphere on the question of authoritarian rule since the end of the Cold War. The extent of Musharraf's untouchable status can be gauged from the fact that when President Bill Clinton visited South Asia in March 2000, the made a stopover of merely five hours in Pakistan, as compared to five days iii India. Additionally, the refused to be photographed shaking hands with Musharraf and gave all insulting lecture to the Pakistani nation oil die virtues of democracy.

The attitudes of the EU and tile Commonwealth were no different from that of the US. No head of state or government from the EU considered Musharrfa's Pakistani worth visiting. All proposed talks between the EU and Pakistan on economic cooperation and trade were put on hold. As to the Commonwealth, in pursuance of the Harare Declaration, it decided to suspend Pakistan's membership of its ministerial councils.

This was how the three international power centres were treating Pakistan oil the eve of the horrendous events of 9/11. The terrorist attack oil the Twin Towers on that fateful day, however, changed everything, including their attitude towards Pakistan. Pakistan, which had been the staunchest supporter of the Taliban regime in Afghanistan in the wake of the 9/11 incident, effected a complete somersault, and, responding to Bush's threat of "with us or against us", decided to join the American-led coalition against terrorists. The change in the attitude of Musharraf paid immediate dividends, as international pressure on him to return his country to civilian rule eased as government leaders from the US and West Europe made a beeline to Islamabad to lend Support and succour to him. The mail who, a little while earlier, stood ostracized in the international community, was overnight accorded recognition and legitimacy by the same powers. It is noteworthy that when on 6 October 2001, the eve of the first air strikes against Afghanistan, Musharraf extended his tenure as the Chief of Army Staff (COAS) for an indefinite period, there was not a squeak of protest from the concerned quarters.

As the "war on terrorism" progressed, Musliarraf was rewarded by a number of goodies and incentives by the West with the view of encouraging him to stay the course. For example, Pakistan was given an aid package of $600 million, increased access for its textiles to the American and European markets, liberal and enhanced IMF loans, debt profiling for part of the $36 million loan, and debt swap by sonic countries for an equivalent amount of spending in the social sector, and restoration of economic and military assistance by the US, which is ill the process of being given practical shape Additionally, sanctions of various kinds, some of which had been imposed against Pakistan for almost three decades and were still in force, were lifted. Incidentally, they were basically of two kinds: nuclear programme related, and democracy related. In the first category fell those imposed under the Symington, Glenn, and Pressler Amendments, and those imposed in 1998 following the nuclear test in response to similar tests by India. In tile second category, which needs special mention here, fell sanctions imposed under Section 508 of the US Foreign Operations Appropriation Act following the Musharraf coup. It is noteworthy here that the economic or military. assistance which Washington was forbidden to extend under the democracy-related sanctions as stated above is in the process of being restored.

Conscious of his indispensability to tile West, Musharraf decided to give himself a five-year tenure as president. For this purpose, he opted for a referendum. According to Article 41 of the 1973 Pakistan Constitution, the president is to be elected by members of both the houses of parliament and the four provincial assemblies. The Constitution, in Article 48(6), provides for referendum, but this is to be used in order to elicit public opinion on a matter of national importance, and not for the purposes of elections to tile presidency. Despite the unambiguous position in the matter, Zia-ul-Haq (and before him Ayub Khan) resorted to, this gimmick to get himself elected as president. Following in the footsteps of his worthy predecessors, Musharraf too got himself elected for a five-year term through this dubious device. Additionally; the whole exercise was more fraudulent than that indulged in by his predecessors. There was no list of voters :at the polling booths, and anybody could vote anywhere (parks, government offices, railway stations, bus stops, petrol stations, hotels, political party offices, etc.), the only check, according to tile government's own claim, being indelible ink put on the voter's thumb. The government claim of 56 per cent participation by the electorate was vehemently contested by tile opposition parties. Government servants Nacre under orders to vote, and at bits and railway stations and airports, among other places, people were made to vote before embarking on their journey. Those calling for boycott were promptly arrested. The US attitude against this manifestly undemocratic practice was one of nonchalance, as the American administration officials were of the opinion that it was up to the people of Pakistan and the Pakistani courts to decide cm the beast way to move towards restoration of democracy. White House spokesperson Ari Fleischer articulated thus feeling by stating that "it's our understanding that Pakistan's constitution allows for referenda. But we believe the constitutionality of this referendum should he open to review by tile country's courts.

As opposed to the US, the Commonwealth ministers made a statement ill which they unambiguously criticized the referendum. The EU was so upset with the deceitful manner in which the whole exercise was conducted that members of the European Parliament declined to approve the EU-Pakistan accord after several members voiced scepticism over the referendum's legality. John Cushnallan, the parliamentary rapporteur on Pakistan and subsequently head of EU's Observer Group during the parliamentary elections of 10 October, termed it as "wholly inappropriate and in conflict with the Pakistan Constitution". The Musharraf Government, as mandated by the Pakistan Supreme Court, decided to hold elections to the national and provincial assemblies on 10 October. However, these were far from being free and fair, because of large-scale rigging during and before the polls.

The Musharraf Government took a large number of measures, which unmistakably fell in the category of pre-poll rigging. For example, by the order of 23 June, it bareed non-graduates from contesting elections. This was not only violative of the Pakistan Constitution, but also of Article 21 of the Universal Declaration of Human Rights and Article 25 of the Covenant on Civil and Political Rights. On 22 August the Musharraf Government issued an order that barred a court absconder from contesting elections. There was an apprehension that it was Benazir Bhutto-specific, which proved right, as subsequently the Election Commission (EC) rejected her nomination papers for elections to the National Assembly. On 19 October, the military government, through an amendment to the Representation of the People Ordinance, 2002, . made it mandatory for anybody desirous of contesting the Senate election to come himself/herself for filing the nomination papers.

On 6 July, the Musharraf Government issued still another order that barred twice-elected prime ministers and chief ministers from a third term. This was indeed a strange measure in a parliamentary system. The purpose behind the order appeared to stop Benazir Bhutto and Nawaz Sharif from becoming prime ministers. It is noteworthy that following the elections, the government clarified that the foregoing order did not exclude an individual who had been chief minister twice but was now candidate for the prime minister's slot. The purpose of the clarification was to cover Mir Zatullah Jalnali, who had twice been chief minister and was then a candidate for prime ministership.

On 9 October, hardly six hours before the polling, the Legal Framework Order (LFO) was amended so that independent can didates could join any political party within three days after the publication of their names in the official gazette. The purpose behind the amendment was to help the government-supported party, PML(Q). Resultantly, out of 29 independent Members of the National Assembly, 18 joined the King's party.

There were credible reports of certain government agencies which successfully pressurized some vulnerable candidates of the PPPP and PML(N) to join the PML(Q) the King's party, or become independent candidates. A number of civil servants reportedly openly loped the PML(Q), and the police in Punjab was reportedly, instructed to support the latter. The provincial governments reportedly doled out 1.5 million rupees to the pro-government *nazims* to help PML (Q).

Regarding rigging on the polling day, it was plentiful. Some glaring examples, some of which were listed by the European Union Observer Group, were as follows:

1. There was abuse of state resources in favour of the which the EC failed to stop, throwing its independence in doubt.
2. The EC's code of conduct for political parties, issued prior to the commencement of the election campaign, allowed processions which arc traditionally one of the most important

means of campaigning, which, however, was subsequently banned.

3. There were two kinds of abuse of state resources: the illegal use of public infrastructure (buildings, vehicles, etc.), and pledges about future development projects. The public authorities from nazims to the senior level of government servants were actively involved in partisan electioneering.
4. The State-owned PTV Khabarniama devoted 6 hours and 20 minutes to election-related news from 15 August to 9 October. The duration of coverage for the main parties was as follows; PML-Q (44 minutes), MMA (36 minutes), PPPP (29 minutes), GNA (13 minutes), PML-N (13 minutes), PTI (10 minutes), and MQM (8 minutes). The news broadcasts consistently promoted the government's views on election-related activities. The administration had a free hand on the state television to criticize the behaviour of past political rulers. President Musharraf made an inappropriate election-eve address to the nation.
5. At a number of polling stations, voters were turned away because their names could not be found on the register.
6. The secrecy, of the vote was compromised at a number of polling stations. In addition to polling-day rigging, through the LFO, President Musharraf brought about certain amendments in the Constitution, such as tile provision of the National Security Council (NSC) and tile restoration of Article 58(213), both of which undermine the sovereignty of Parliament. With these changes, it was highly unlikely that power would be transferred from the military to civilians, and real democracy restored.

As to the Commonwealth, which three years earlier had suspended Pakistan from its ministerial councils following the Mushiarraf Coup d'etat, maintained the suspension pending further assessment of the functioning of its democratic institutions. While appreciating tile positive role that Pakistan played war the war against terror, it observed: "We will have to wait what powers the parliament and the government that emerges end up having before a final decision".

Reasons for Asymmctry of Attitudes

Here, tile question arises as to why there has been an asymmetry, of attitudes on the part of the three power centres towards development of democracy in Pakistan. This is explained by three factors. To begin with, the abandonment in the wake of the 9/11 gory incidents of the strident attitude by the US towards the Musharraf Government for putting the clock of democracy back in Pakistan is attributable to the fact that the latter was directly affected by it. It was, in consequence, prepared to do anything to protect itself As opposed to this, since the EU and the Commonwealth, though deeply concerned with the event, were not directly touched by it, they refused to show flexibility in the matter. In other words, whereas the US decided to downgrade democracy in favour of security, tile EU and the Commonwealth refused to do so by continuing to accord top priority to democracy.

Second, whereas the US constitutes a single country, the EU and the Commonwealth are composed of a motley group of states. This affects their decision making. Thus, it is easier for the US to change its policy, as it does not have to consult other powers; this is not true about the EU and the Commonwealth, as they have to evolve a consensus to reach a decision. Third, the US enjoys flexibility in deciding the democracy vs security debate in a given situation, as there is no rigid, written, binding obligation in the matter; notwithstanding the claim of morality as constituting an important component of its foreign policy. This is not the case with the Commonwealth, which is bound by the Harare Declaration agreed upon by consensus. The EU situation is no different, as democracy constitutes the binding force in the relations between its 15 members. The case of Turkey, which was excluded from being given the status of a candidate for a long period, amply proves the point.

From the foregoing, it is obvious that, in spite of the fact that tile EU and the Commonwealth kept up a relentless pressure on the Government of Pakistan by severely criticizing the way it conducted the elections and the referendum and by taking concrete steps against it, their influence in the development of democracy was minimal. The US, on the other hand, by going along with the undemocratic policies of Musharraf was instrumental in bringing about distortions in the development of democracy in Pakistan. This certainly shows a measure of tile influence that the sole superpower is able to exercise in the world.

Reason for Abandonment Democracy

Finally, as far as the question of the abandonment of democracy in favour of security is concerned, the US and its apologists justify it on the ground that the battle against global threat to liberty which is posed by Islamic fundamentalism, cannot be won without it. This has been termed as the principle of lesser evil. In this respect, Churchill's famous dictum is cited in which he stated that "if I were told that the devil were on poorer terms with Hitler, I should find myself making an alliance with hell". When we examine this argument, we realize that examples are galore where diflcrcnt American administrations throughout American history sacrificed democracy at the altar of its security. While doing so, it often invoked highfalutin principles (such as the defence of liberty and freedom) for jettisoning democracy, as exemplified through American support extended to generals in Vietnam, Mobutu of Zainc, Pinochet of Chile, etc. In reality, this justification constituted the *good* reason, whereas the real one related to the promotion of security, which is quite often economic in nature. For example, the American decision in the 1980s to support Gen. Zia-ul-Haq's Pakistan as a front-line state in the Western attempt to dislodge the Soviets from Afghanistan was, in reality, meant to secure oil supplies from the Persian Gulf region rather than the liberation of the Afghans, which was trumpeted at the time as the real objective of the whole exercise. The current "war on terrorism" is similarly increasingly being viewed by objective observers of the situation as the American attempt at the outset of the new millennium to have access to the remaining energy resources of the world, rather than a crusade against the dark forces of obscurantism and authoritarianism, as portrayed by the Bush Administration.

Summary

This is attested to in the case of Pakistan, which, from being a pariah state because of sanctions imposed by the US, the EU, and the Commonwealth, in the wake of the 9/11 terrorist attack overnight became the most sought after state in the world. The internal struggle for democracy was, thus, overshadowed and overwhelmed by external forces.

We observe, however, a difference of attitudes on tile part of the US on the one hand and the EU and the Commonwealth on the other. The US abandoned democracy in favour of security, whereas the EU and the Commonwealth refused to do so. Given tile preponderant US influence in tile world, it has amply contributed to the distortions in Pakistan's democratic development.

There are three factors which explain the asymmetry in the attitudes of the three power centers. The first relates to the fact that the US was directly affected by the events of 9/11, which was not the case with the EU and the Commonwealth, Second, the US, being a single state, could bring about a change in its foreign policy more easily than the EU or the Commonwealth, which are composed of several states whose consent for any corporate decision is absolutely indispensable. Third, the US, in the democracy vs security debate, does not have to follow a rigid, written, binding guideline. In the case of the Commonwealth, the Harare Declaration does not leave much room for manocuvre, whereas the EU does not enjoy flexibility in the matter because of the status of democracy as a binding principle in the relations of its members.

Islamic Revival in Pakistan

The Weberian approach emphasizes the ideological vitality of Islam as an autonomous political force. It argues that Islamic ideology has often been a focal point in situations involving social and political conflict, foreign encroachments, and attempts to restore purity in dogma and rites. Invocation of Islam in times of crisis has numerous historical precedents in Muslim societies. The millcnarian, puritanical, revivalist, and pre-modern religious reform movements which emerged in various Muslim societies after the beginning of the eighteenth century share features with the present movements.

The second approach situates Islam and the Muslim societies in the context of world historical forces and explains Islamic revivalism as one response to modernization and economic change. Some sociologists have related Islamic resurgence to the powerful comeback of religious ideologies, the worldwide re-awakening of religious identities, and the "re-enchantment" of the world as a reaction to modernity.

The third approach finds the basis for the variations in different Islamic revivalist movements in their relationship with the state and religious structures; their diverse doctrinal resource-base; their social bases of support, their constituencies, and their patterns of alliances; their relationships with the dominant power structures of society; and above all, the conjunction of ferees that define the character of the regimes in specific Muslim societies.

Despite apparent similarities in their orientations towards problems of Islam and social change, revivalist movements in South Asia and the Muslim World are not unified and monolithic. Their differences are more important than their similarities. Although Islamic revivalist groups everywhere in the Muslim world strive for the restoration of the puritanical values and practices of early Islam, their programmatic emphases owe their origin to the local social forces. Each of these groups carries the distinctive marks of a unique social and political environment within which it operates. While intellectual developments in other Muslim societies and international events that affect all Muslims have their impact on South Asian Muslims, their influence is mediated .by indigenous forces.

A case in point is the impact of the Iranian revolution in Pakistan. The Iranian revolution was enthusiastically supported by the leading revivalist group in Pakistan, the Jama'at-i-Islami, as a triumph of Islam over secular forces. Later, when this revolution encouraged Shi'ite militancy in Pakistan, which was perceived as an obstacle in the way of Pakistan's own program of Islamization, enthusiasm waned. In Bangladesh, where there are no Shias among indigenous Bengali Muslims, the attitude toward the Iranian revolution has remained indifferent.

Islam as an Ideological Basis of the State

This understanding was articulated in the "Objectives Resolution" which was passed by the first Constituent Assembly of Pakistan in 1949 and later became an ideological preamble to all the subsequent constitutions of the country. This relationship of Islam .to Pakistan has assumed such an orthodox status that secular and socialist political parties do not dare challenge it. The existence of a broad consensus on the inseparability of Islam and Pakistan-popularly known as the "Pakistan ideology"—has thus helped groups to press their demands and agitate for an increased role for Islam in public affairs. Islam is thought not only to be the ideological basis for the state of Pakistan but also fundamental to the nation's very existence. Without Islam the state would lose its identity, disintegrate, and perish. Propagation of an ideology other than Islam – be it secularism, socialism, communism, or Western liberal democracy – would be treason against the state.

Islam as a Legitimating Factor for Existing Power Relations

Since the very inception of the new state, Pakistan's rulers have used Islam to legitimize their authority which was, more often than not, derived from the coercive apparatus of the state rather than from popular support. Since the majority of the regimes came into power through extra-constitutional means, their claims to legitimacy were dubious. As a result, these regimes depended on Islam as a source of legitimacy. The chaotic parliamentary regime, Ayub Khan's development-oriented government, Yahya Khan's transient government, Zulfikar Ali Bhutto's populist corporatism, and Zia-ul-Haq's conservative authoritarianism all benefited from the same tactics. In each phase, Islamic ideology was invoked, albeit with varying emphases, in order to legitimize not only the authority of the incumbents but also their contemporary policy goals. A degree of political stability was thus achieved at least in the short run (Ahmad 1981).

Like several of its predecessors the Zia government has sought to elicit the moral commitment of the people by linking the destinies of Islam and Pakistan with that of the military regime. Zia maintains that the military rule has been vital for the preservation of Islam and Pakistan. Thus, the trinity of Islam, Pakistan, and the military regime become one and the same thing. The new election law of September 1979 provided that no politician could propagate "any opinion or act in a manner prejudicial to the ideology of Pakistan" or would express views "defaming or ridiculing the . . . Armed Forces".

When a pro-government politician from Karachi was assassinated in 1982, Zia declared that the assassins were "enemies of Islam." The crux of Zia's case against his opposition is that since the elements identified with the opposition arc ideologically leftist or secularly oriented, they have no legitimate claim to power in an Islamic state. In 1980, addressing the Councillors of Multan district, President Zia declared: "Pakistan was achieved in the name of Islam, and Islam alone could provide the basis to run the government of the country and sustain its integrity...The present government would provide opportunity to others to serve the country after it achieved its objectives... (but) no un-Islamic government would be allowed to succeed the present regime".

The use of Islam has thus created a situation in which religious interests have become indistinguishable from purely political interests and the regime's need for legitimacy. The road to salvation has become the road to power as well.

This convergence of salvation and power is also evident in an ingenious argument about the ideological affinity and undifferentiated character of the institutions of an Islamic polity. According to this argument, the armed forces are not a separate corporate group. The ideological affinities that run through the civilian executive, the legislature, the judiciary, the bureaucracy, and the military transcend artificial institutional boundaries. If all the "load-bearing pillars" of the society are motivated by the same ideological considerations and adhere to the same ***Shariah***, which is the "guiding and controlling spirit" of every section of the population, the distinction between civilian and military rule can not arise.

Islam has been used to seek the support of the religious political parties and to create a constituency among the lower middle class of the Punjab, urban Sind, and the Northwest Frontier Province. This constituency participates in religious festivals and rituals; in the newly created religious institutional network of zakat, uslir, and the islah-i-mu'ashra (reformation of society) committees; and in government-organized religious gatherings such as the Milad-un-Nabi and the qirat and na'at competitions. Zia's policies and rhetoric have appealed to the religious sensibilities and economic interests of this stratum whose support is regarded as critical to the stability of the regime. His promise to protect the sanctity of chador (literally, "the veil") and chardivari ("the four walls of a house"), symbols of women's honor and private property, touches a vital chord.

Similarly, the introduction of Shariah, especially its penal laws; the organization of zakat and ushr systems; the establishment of a network of religious institutions in association with the ulama; and the recent legislation prohibiting the Qadianis (or Ahmadis)-a heretical group founded in early twentieth century Muslim India-have reinforced the regime's claims to political legitimacy.

Zia's Islamic revivalist commitment may be quite genuine but it is difficult to isolate the elements of personal piety and subjective commitment from the political benefits. Whatever degree of genuine religious enthusiasm and revivalist zeal one may be able to identify in Zia, he has used popular Islamic symbols to legitimize his continued grip on political power and to safeguard the interests of the social forces which constitute its bases of support.

Islam as a Vehicle of Protest

One must not think that rulers have a monopoly over the instrumental use of Islam. The Iranian revolution is a prominent example of the use of Islam as a vehicle of protest. In Syria the Muslim Brotherhood is engaged in a fierce struggle against the Ba'athist regime in the name of Islam. Islamic groups in Egypt, Iraq, Turkey, Tunisia, and Indonesia protest the corrupt and un-Islamic character of the rulers.

The most outstanding example in Pakistan of this delegitimizing role of Islam is the I977 Nizam-i-Mustafa {System of the Prophet Mohammad) movement. As a result of tins movement, a militant alliance between the jamaat-i-Islami and certain conservative ulama groups undermined the secularly-oriented regime of Zulfikar Ah Bhutto. At the time of the 1977 elections, various religious political groups formed the Pakistan National Alliance (PNA) which campaigned on the central theme of the introduction of the Nizarn-i-Mustafa and stirred up an unprecedented religious enthusiasm during and after elections.

The Nizam-i-Mustafa movement featured the effective use of Islamic revivalist ideals and symbols by discontented groups for whom religious concerns and material interests converged under the umbrella of Islamic fundamentalism. Even Prime Minister Bhutto during his last years had succumbed and introduced Islamic measures in order to widen his sources of legitimacy and to will support. In 1974, for example, Bhutto declared the Ahniadis to be non-Muslims. And his last bid to establish his Islamic credentials was to ban alcoholic drinks, gambling, dancing, horseracing, and dance clubs in May 1977.

As an incumbent Prime Minister Bhutto enjoyed enormous advantages, including control of the mass media and the educational institutions. These enabled him to publicize widely the Islamic orientation of his government and the services he had rendered to the cause of Islam. He also had at his disposal—and to some extent used—the huge financial resources of the state to court the religious establishment, including the extensive network of the state-controlled *Auqaf* or religious institutions which had been taken over by the government during President Ayub Khan's rule.

The fact that the power to confer Islamic legitimacy was in the hands of those whose vital economic, status, and ideological interests he had earlier so vehemently challenged, however, proved to be a serious obstacle in Bhutto's search for Islamic credentials. Even if he had succeeded in winning over the orthodox religious establishment—and his Minister for Religious Affairs had in fact chalked out an elaborate programme for Bhutto's second term to circumvent the militancy of the *ulama* using both persuasive and coercive measures-it would not have necessarily guaranteed automatic acceptance of his claims to Islamic legitimacy. The initial opposition to Bhutto, articulated in Islamic religious idioms by the jama'at-i-Islami, came from the lay Islamic activists of the lower middle classes and not from the *ulama*. Given the relative lack of a structural hierarchy in Islam, incumbents have severe limitations in using the Islamic "card". A Muslim ruler who has successfully incorporated the "professional" religious establishment into state structures may still be vulnerable to opposition by equally legitimate lay and popular Islamic forces. The relative success of General Zia in establishing his Islamic legitimacy can be explained in part by his strategy of seeking certification for his Islamic authenticity from both the "professional" religious establishment as represented by the *ulama* and the *Mashaikh* (sufi leaders), and the popular, lay Islamic forces as represented by the Jama'at-i-Islami.

Islam and National Integration

Another factor which has contributed significantly to the political salience of Islam in Pakistan is its role as a major source of national integration in a society characterized by considerable ethnic, linguistic and cultural diversity. At the time of independence, the constituent units of Pakistan (East Bengal, Punjab, Sind, Baluchistan, and the North West Frontier Province) had very little in common except Islam. It was Islam which became the basis for the Muslim League's appeal to the diverse Muslim regions of British India to join together in a common struggle for Pakistan.

The fact that Pakistan was not created in the name of ethnicity, language, or geography, but rather on the basis of Islamic solidarity, albeit expressed in the idioms of Muslim nationalism was perceived as an important potential asset for the prospects of national integration by both policy makers and intellectuals. It was believed that an emphasis on Islam in official rhetoric and the incorporation of Islamic values in public policies, especially in the fields of education, culture and mass communications, would weaken the parochial loyalties of ethnicity and language. As a result, the bonds of unity among various regions of the new state would be strengthened. The historical experience of early Islamic empires was invoked as a paradigm for contemporary Pakistan to show how diverse ethnic groups and regions united into a single political community on the basis of over-arching loyalty to Islam.

East Bengal—later renamed East Pakistan and now Bangladesh—was seen as a test case to demonstrate the effectiveness of ideological bonds in a situation where the differences in ethnicity, language, ecology, demography, and culture were acute. The two wings of the country, which were separated by over one thousand miles of hostile Indian territory, shared very little with each other except Islam. But the founders of the nation were convinced that the geographical remoteness and other differences would not in any significant way obstruct the processes of national integration if the people of both wings would continue to relate to each other on the basis of Islamic brotherhood. The emphasis on the role of Islam as the major integrative factor increased even more so in the 1960s when Pakistan witnessed a marked assertion of centrifugal, fissiparous forces based or ethnic identities and regional demands. The emergence of regional reverberations and separatist tendencies was seen as further reason to promote Islamic ideology as a basis for national solidarity. But as was evident from the subsequent developments, emphasis on the religious aspect alone to the exclusion of other more tangible ones would not ensure national unity. As Nurul Huda, then Finance Minister of East Pakistan, put it in 1965:"... it would be unfair to expect that our spiritual bonds through Islam will be so strong... that we shall forget all our disparities and will still remain united... as a nation".

The secession of Bangladesh in December 1971 clearly demonstrated that Islam, although necessary for the creation of Pakistan consisting of two separate regions with distinct ethuolinguistic identities of their own, was still not a sufficient factor for sustaining their continued unity in the absence of other policy measures. The failure of the national political elite and the intellectuals to link Islam to more mundane issues such as the equitable distribution of economic resources among the various parts of the country and the enfranchisement of the politically alienated sectors of society, ultimately led to a situation in winch Islam itself came to be seen by the deprived regions as an instrument of exploitation.

However one may interpret the experience, or rather the failure, of national integration in East Pakistan, the fact remains that it left an indelible mark, both before and after the breakup of the country, on the popular consciousness about the importance of Islam as a national political ideology. Before the separation of East Pakistan, it was the fear of the disintegration of the country which had acted as a propellent for Islam. In the aftermath of the separation, the faith m the efficacy of Islam as a basis for national unity for the remaining portion of Pakistan seems to have grown even stronger. It is in this context that one can describe the current wave of Islamic revivalism in Pakistan as a post-1972 phenomenon. The traumatic events of the 1971 civil war and the humiliating defeat of the Pakistani forces fighting for national unity at the hands of India had powerful psychologically unsettling effects for the people of the then largest Muslim state in the world, which often prided itself as the "fortress of Islam."

After the initial shock of the disintegration of the nation had been absorbed, there followed what may be called a period of introspection and soul-searching this renewed quest for authenticity and national identity coupled with self-criticism as a result of the mortifying encounter with the Bengali separatists and the Indians in East Pakistan, led to the reaffirmation of Islam as both a personal succor and a national ideology. The Islamic groups were quick to seize upon the opportunity and point out that East Pakistan was lost only because the people had not been good Muslims in their personal as well as collective behavior. They also accused the rulers of neglecting Islam as a source of public policy, a fact which, in their view, had led to the emergence of a wide variety of anti-national forces in the country. According to this formulation, the secession of East Pakistan was therefore not a failure of Islam but of the un-Islamic policies and conduct of the rulers.

India and Bangladesh

Although this chapter focuses on Pakistan, it is instructive to make some brief comparative references to the Indian and Bangladeshi cases of Islamic revival.

Unlike Hinduism and Sikhism which are spatially confined to South Asia, Islam has transcontinental connections. Thus, Muslims in Pakistan, India, and Bangladesh are not only affected by developments and experiences of one another but also by developments in the Middle East. Before the drawing of new political boundaries in 1947 and then again in 1971, the Muslims of South Asia had shared a, common religio-political experience and had participated together in socioreligious and cultural movements of sub-continental scope. Even today, the majority of the Pakistani and Bangladeshi *ulama* in leadership roles consists of those who were trained in places like Deoband, Farangi Mahal, Rampur, and Baeli in India. The two major grassroot revivalist movements, the Jama'at-i-Islami and the Tablighi Jama'at, are truly subcontinental movements with their activities and branches spread all over Pakistan, India, and Bangladesh.

In an article entitled "India: Ahmad argued in 1980 that untouched by the recent developments in Iran and Pakistan as well as in other countries of the Muslim World... The recent resurgence of Islamic revivalism has not struck a sympathetic chord among Muslims in India". It, however, one is not looking for those manifestations of Islamic revival in India which are usually identified with countries like Iran and Pakistan, the isolation thesis with regard to the Indian Muslims would become untenable. One cannot, obviously, expect the Indian Muslims who constitute only about 11 per cent of the total population, to launch an Islamic revolution (as in Iran) or make demands for the establishment of an Islamic state (as in Pakistan). Even from the perspective of the state, the political role of Islam is limited. Since India is a secular state, the Indian state authorities make very little use of religion as a legitimating force. Whenever they do feel such a need, they prefer to use Hindu symbols to legitimize their authority and programs. Islamic symbols are only used while dealing with the Arab world and at international Islamic conferences in order to authenticate India's Islamic credentials vis-à-vis Pakistan's.

The Muslim community of India-estimated to be 80 million in 1984 is probably the largest minority in the world. Despite its complex and highly differentiated structure in terms of socio-economic stratification, cultural, linguistic, and geographical dissimilarities, and diversities of political affiliations, the Muslim community has exhibited, over the years since the partition, an impressive unanimity of views on certain identity symbols derived either directly from their religious tradition or from the cultureal history of the early British period.

The current wave of Islamic revivalism in India can be traced to four unrelated factors: (1) the failure of the old guard of Indian nationalism, both from the modern Muslim educated elite and from the traditional religious establishment of Deoband, to help solve the "communal" problems of the Indian Muslims in the post-independence era; (2) the 1971 Indo-Pakistan war and the break-up of Pakistan which finally brought home the truth to the Indian Muslims that they were on their own and could no longer look toward Pakistan for any possible help, even moral help; (3) the post-1973 oil boom and the subsequent migration of a large number of Muslims, especially from the south, to the countries of the Middle East, which brought substantial amounts of remittances to the families left behind; and, (4) the increasing militancy of the right wing Hindu revivalist movements, both cultural and political, whose slogans emphasized an integral relationship among "Hindi, Hindu, and Hindustan."

Unlike in Pakistan, the Islamic yearning in India finds expression in two types of movements. First, there are the more strictly religious movements such as the Tablighi Jama'at, Muslim Youth Movement (MYM), Students Islamic Movement (SIM), and the Jama'at-i-Islami. Within the community, their emphasis is on Islamization, i.e., to "purity" the beliefs and practices of their co-religionists in order to bring them closer to the teachings of Islamic orthodoxy as enunciated in the Quran and the Sunttah of the Prophet. With respect to the rest of Indian society, their activities are centered on the reassertion of Muslim religious rights and identity as represented by such issues as the Shah Banu case and the Babri Masjid case.

Second, groups like the Muslim League, the Muslim Union League, Itehad-ul-Muslimeen, Majlis-i-Mashawarat, the Muslim Majlis, Ta'amir-i-Millat, and the Islamic Council of India, represent the increasing attempts of the Muslim political elites of various regions to find a focus for effective political mobilization and to enhance the economic autonomy of the Indian Muslim community.

With the exception of the Tablighi jama'at which eschews politics and the "worldly" concerns of the community as a matter of policy, one can witness in recent years an increasing convergence of and cooperation between the purely religious revivalist movements on the one hand and the community-oriented groups on the other. The dominant thrust of their joint activities is building autonomous educational and economic institutions. Promotion of education is given the highest priority in the revivalist agenda. Funds from Middle Ease remittances and local sources are invested to create an educational infrastructure which combines Islamic and general education as well as technical education. The idea is to provide the Muslim youth with Islamic religious education which is not available in government schools and also to prepare them for gainful employment in various sectors of economy. The mushrooming of Muslim educational organizations in recent years is reminiscent of the great educational revival in Muslim India at the turn of the century. According to one estimate, educational organizations like the All India Muslim Educational Conference of Aligarh, All India Muslim Educational Society of Calicut, the *Al-ahmeen* Educational Society of Bangalore, the Hamdard Educational Society of New Delhi, the *Deeni T'alimi* Council of Lucknow, the Kerala Muslim Education Society, and dozens of other local organizations have established more than 500 educational institutions in recent years.

Islamic revivalism has also manifested itself in building autonomous economic institutions by the Muslims. Facing certain structural barriers in obtaining credit from the government controlled banks, many Muslim communities, especially in the south, are establishing their own cooperative banks, cooperative societies, *Bait-ul-Mals, zakat* funds, and interest-free (profit and loss sharing) credit societies in order to finance business initiatives by individual entrepreneurs as well as to invest in activities of collective economic benefits. In those cities of North India where there is a big concentration of Muslim artisans and craftsmen- such as Moradahad, Agra, Faizabad, Aligarh, Mirzapur, Varanasi, Lucknow, Tonk, and Jaipur--a large number of Muslim artisans' guilds and cooperative societies have been established both for generating credit and for marketing the products. As a result of these efforts—some of which owe their origin to the Bahuguna ministry in 1974—there is some evidence of the emergence of a Muslim petit bourgeoisie in these traditional centers of Muslim artisans. It is also interesting to note here that these are precisely the cities which have witnessed the worst and most violent communal riots in recent years.

The Islamic revival in India is not confined only to building parochial institutions and strengthening the religious moorings of the community. It is also related to efforts toward participating more fully in the political life of the country and sharing responsibility for its social progress and economic development. Only through participation in the national political process can Muslims face the problems and the discrimination to which they are subjected, bring them to national attention, and make them part of the national agenda. It was this realization that became the basis for the formation of the Ail India Muslim Majlis Mashawarat, a coalition of various Muslim political parties and religion-educational organizations.

At the level of ideas, the Indian Islamic scene also offers an interesting example of how a reiigio-political movement tends to articulate its ideology in two different political contexts. The case in point is that of the Jama'at-i-Islami of Pakistan and jama'at-i-Islami of India. Founded in 1941 by Sayyid Abul A'la Maududi one of the most prolific writers and systematic thinkers of the twentieth century Islam, the Jama'at propounded a program of action which clustered around four major points: (1) to elucidate the teachings of Islam with reference to the contemporary social, economic and political situation; (2) to create an organization of highly dedicated, disciplined, and righteous people to form an inner core of Islamic revival; (3) to initiate, at the level of civil society, changes that arc conducive to the transformation of human society and (4) to establish an Islamic state which would implement the Shariah (Islamic law) and would direct and manage all affairs of the society in accordance with the Islamic scheme of things.

When the Jama'at became formally organized into two separate entities at the time of partition in 1947, the Pakistani Jama'at took the establishment of an Islamic state as the most imporant means for creating the order envisaged by Islam while the Indian Jama'at, finding itself in a secular constitutional framework, expunged all references to the goal of establishing an Islamic state from its programme of action. According to the Jama'at-i-Islami of Pakistan, Islam does not admit any division between religious and public affairs. Hence, the Islamic state is not a matter of choice but a fundamental obligation of Islamic way of life. This state which is based on the political and legal sovereignty of God is to be governed by people of clear Islamic vision, commitment, and character. The Jama'at-i-Islami of India, in contrast, had no choice but to abandon the idea of an Islamic state. It was, however, able to find a convenient justification for its revisionist ideology in the original critique of its founder, Sayyid Maududi, against the creation of Pakistan, i.e., the geographical delimitation of Islamic *umma* in the territorial confines of Pakistan would delay the growth and spread of Islam as a universal message. The Indian Jama'at has thus successfully avoided the question of establishing an Islamic state as it was articulated in its original constitution of 1941 by emphasizing the concept of the worldwide Islamic *umma* and the Indian Muslims being an integral part of it. According to the Two Nation theory of the Muslim League, the Muslims who chose to remain in India should be considered as members of the same Muslim nation which had established a separate homeland for itself, namely Pakistan. The Jama'at-i-Islami of India has sought to resolve this anomaly by disassociating the notion of the Muslim nation from the state of Pakistan and, instead, relating it to the concept of universal *ummah Islamiya*. This is not only a politically safe conceptualization but is also intended to provide the Indian Muslims with an enormous psychological sense of security and strength in their immediate environment of numerical and political weakness. What is most interesting to note is that while the Jama'at in Pakistan denounces secularism as "an evil force" and "the greatest threat to Islam" the Jama' at of India is equally vigorous in defending secularism as "a blessing" and as "a guarantee for a safe future for Islam" in India.

The only area where the Islamic revival in India has taken a radical political stance and where the slogans of the Islamic state have been publicly raised is Kashmir. This Muslim majority state exhibits an increasing convergence of political forces representing the old-style Islamic fundamentalists of the Jama'at-i-Islami, Islamic radicalists "following the line of Imam Khomeini," and secessionists of the People's League, jammu and Kashmir Liberation Front, Mahaz-i-Azadi, and Liberation League Both the Jama'at-i-Islami and Al-Jihad movement, clandestine organization influenced by the ideology of the Iramian revolution, have used Islamic revivalist idioms to proclaim their rejections of the political status quo in

Kashmir and to demand the right of self-determination for the Kashmiri Muslims While the Al-Jihad movement talks about the "Islamic revolution" in Kashmir as the "primary objective" of the organization and "the only way to liberate" jammu and Kashmir. The Jama'at-i-Islami and its student wing believe that Islamically-inspired political mobilization of Kashmiri Muslims would culminate in the establishment of an Islamic state in Kashmir. The March 1987 election alliance between the National Conference and the Congress(I) in Kashmir was prompted, in part, by what Prime Minister Rajiv Gandhi described as "the dangers posed by the dark forces of religious fundamentalism" in the state.

In the case of Bangladesh, Islamic revival can be studied within the context of the conflict between the religious and ethnic identities of Bengali Muslims. While Bangladesh was created on the basis of modern secular nationalist thought and a deep sense of a separate Bengali identity, it was nevertheless dependent upon the religious experience of the Bengalis. With the creation of Bangladesh, ethnicity apparently triumphed but not necessarily at the cost of a permanent damage to Islam. A brief look at the major trends in the political loyalties of the Bengali Muslims in the recent past indicates that the focal points of their collective identity have been in a state of constant tension. During the 1930s and 1940s, the Bengali Muslims identified themselves as "Muslims" and participated in the creation of a separate Muslim homeland along with the rest of the Indian Muslim community. During the 1950s and 1960s, the tension between their Islamic-Pakistani identity on the one hand and their Bengali identity on the other, expressed itself in controversies associated with the ideological character of the Pakistani state, federal-provincial relations, national language, and distribution of national resources. But even during the 1960s, the Bengali Muslims of East Pakistan did not see any inherent contradiction between their being good Muslims and their demand for cultural and linguistic autonomy.

17

TERRORISM IN SOUTH ASIA: SRI LANKA'S PERSPECTIVE

The chapter begins with a discussion of the processes of ethnic and social-class competition and conflict operational in Sri Lankan societ and then goes on to analyse the Tamil secessionist insurrection. Subsequently, it analyses the statements of a significant political leader and his part on the causes which underlay the Tamil secessionist insurrection. In spite of this prescience (of which these statements are illustrative examples), Sri Lankan governments could not develop a coherent set of policies which could led to a Resolution of the ethnic conflict. In the following section, it is argued that acknowledgement of underlying causes is the first but also one of the most difficult steps that a government needs to take. The chapter then goes on to briefly examine the dilemmas which governments face when confronted with insurrections, and why they avoid acknowledging underlying causes.

Underlying Systemic Processes: Ethnic and Class Competition and Conflict

Sri Lanka is a country with scarce resources, a growing population, and a relatively underdeveloped economy. The fruits of development have not sufficiently reached the majority of the people and poverty is widespread. Both ethnic groups and social classes compete for all manner of resources—land, water, credit, employment, education, urban space, and housing. This competition manifests itself in the marketplace, in government departments, between government officials and the public, in schools, public debates in newspapers, neighborhoods, universities, and in numereus other contexts. This process of competition is a *systemic* and incessant phenomenon, and will continue in the foreseeable future.

The intensity of competition has steadily increased over time along with the increase in population and the increasingly complex social-class divisions which have emerged in tandem with modernity, and now, increasingly, globalization. Most importantly, there is intense competition between ethnic groups for political representation and power. Political power is in many ways the most sought after "resource", because through it *all* other resources—land, water, urban space, religious space, access to government credit, access to employment, etc.—can be accessed, made available, or appropriated. The competition for political power is seriously problematical, because there is no consensus on the Constitution the fundamental law of the land. From Independence onwards, Sri Lanka has been unable to devise a stable and sustainable constitutional framework within which processes of political and economic competition can be regulated in a peaceful and democratic manner. The country has up to date, functioned under three different Constitutions—the Soulbury Constitution bequeathed by the British (1948-72) which gave the island a "dominion" status, the 1st Republican Constitution (1972-78), and the 2nd Republican Constitution (1978 onwards). Sri Lanka is presently faced with serious constitutional problems which will need the eminent of a fourth constitution or (at the very least) substantial constitutional reforms. This "constitutional restlessness" is symptomatic of deep and hitherto irreconcilable disagreements between and within all ethnic groups as to the fundamental constitutional basis on which the country is to be governed. It is within the context of unfulfilled development needs, poverty, and incessant competition for all resources and the intensifying competition for political power that violent insurrections—secessionist in one case and social-class in the other-emerged within Sri Lanka.

Ethnic competition and conflict, and social-class competition and conflict underlie intra-state conflict in Sri Lanka. Both ethnic and class competition have been under way at least from the early nineteenth century. Sri Lankan society is composed of diverse ethnic groups. Religion and language, singly or combined, are the primary markers of ethnic identity. The four major ethnic groups in the island arc the Sinhalese (74 per cent of the population), Sri Lanka Tamils (12.7 per cent), upcountry Tamils (5.5 per cent), and Muslims (7.1 per cent). In terms of religious distribution, the percentage is Buddhists 69.3, Hindus 15.5, Muslims 7.6, Christians 7.6, and other religions 0.1.

All ethnic groups contain class divisions. Neither ethnicity nor class can be derived from the other, and neither should be given analytical preference. Ethnic identity in Sri Lanka is a combination of religion, language, some elements of culture (including childhood socialization), combined with collective economic interests. While economic interests are in important constituent element of ethnic identity, the yearning for political rights, collective security, and the opportunity for social and cultural expression are no less significant. Ethnic identity has evolved through time in tandem with political mobilization. The action of the state (which include military and police actions) have also influenced this evolution. Class identity stems from complex processes of class formation which have been under way due to changes in the economy over several centuries. Class formation was accelerated by the shift from state welfare capitalism to the liberalization of the economy and market-driven growth from 1977 and, in the last 10 years or so, by globalization.

The collective interests of ethnic groups and social classes are articulated through tile political party system. Left-wing class-based political parties have, on the whole, been less successful than ethnic political parties. All the major ethnic groups arc politically mobilized throtigh political parties. The two major political parties—the United National Party (UNP) and the Sri Lanka Freedom Party (SLFP) are identified with the Sinhalese, even though the, both have had numbers of Muslim and Tamil supporters. Although both have attempted to project themselves as incorporating all ethnic groups, both have had to respond to the electoral gravitational pull of the Sinhalese electorate. When first established in 1946, the UNP was able (to a limited degree) to incorporate members of all ethnic groups, although the leadership of the party was, of course, in the hands of

Sinhalese. In contrast, in 1951 the SLFP began on all unequivocal pro-Sinhalesc platform. This platform was phenomenally successful among Sinhalese voters in 1956. The UNP could not remain unaffected by the SLFP's success. Over the following turbulent decade the UNP gradually lost its multi-ethnic orientation due to tile competition posed by and the need to emulate tile SLFP. The UNP and the SLFP have continued to compete—for the votes of the Sinhala electorate, often accusing each other of "betraying" Sinhala interests, thereby adding to the difficulties of arriving at compromises with the other minority ethnic communities.

Faced with tile reality of political power becoming more and more concentrated in the hands of the Sinhalese after Independence, Sri Lankan Tamils have also mobilized politically along ethnic lines. The parties of the 1950s were the Illankai Tamil Arasu Kadchi (ITAK, "Lanka Tamil State Party", otherwise known as the Federal Party), and the Tamil Congress (TC). Through subsequent schisms and amalgamations, the 'Tamil United Liberation Front (TULF)' emerged in tile 1970s as the foremost parlianlentaiy party of the Sri Lankan Tamils. The Tamil secessionist tendency spawned many Tamil guerrilla groups in the 1970s and early 1980s, including the Liberation Tigers of Tamil Eelam (ME), Eelam Revolutionary Organisation of Students (EROS), Tamil Eclam Liberation Organisation (TELO), People's Liberation Organisation of Tamil Eelam (PLOTE), and Eelam People's Revolutionary Liberation Front (EPRLF). But of these, only the LTTE has continued to prosecute the secessionist insurrection.

Upcountry Tamils have a unique trade union-cum-political party called the Ceylon Workers Congress (CWC), which has worked in several coalition governments to further their collective interests. Until the 1980s, the Muslims found political representation within the UNP and (to a lesser extent) the SUP Although many Muslims continue to support these two parties, from the mid-1980s a number of Muslim ethnic parties have emerged, among which the Sri Lanka Muslim Congress (SLMC) is the most prominent.

In the 1950s and 1960s two left-wing parties—the LSSP (Lanka Sama Samaja Party) and the CP (Communist Party)—had some support among tile urban working class, but were unsuccessful in the face of escalating ethnic mobilization. From the mid-1990s Janatha Vimukthi Peramuna (JVP People's Liberation Front) has transformed itself from an insurrectionary movement into the main left-wing party. Its attempts to mobilize people across ethnic lines have been largely unsuccessful, and its support base retrains predominantly Sinhala. In sum, where ethnic identity is pitched diametrically against class, it is ethnic identity which has usually emerged victorious. This does not mean that class identity and consciousness have ceased to exist, merely that they have been over determined by the strength of ethnic mobilization.

Social-class insurrections were launched on two occasions by the JVP, a movement which arose from within then majority Sinhala ethnic group. The first insurrection (April-May 1971) was relatively easily suppressed in around six weeks, although with the loss of 5,000-10,000 lives. The second (mid-1987 to 1989) was more protracted, and lasted two and a half years and resulted in about 60,000 deaths and disappearances. The second JVP insurrection effectively ceased at the end of 1989, now more than 14 years ago. From 1994 onwards, the JVP has entered mainstream politics and has participated in many electoral and democratic political activities. At present, the JVP has 16 members in Parliament and many more at the provincial council and local government levels.

The Tamils Secessionist Insurrection

The Tamil secessionist insurrection posed/poses by far the most serious politico-military challenge to the unity of tile post-colonial Sri Lankan State. From February 2002 onwards, a cease fire has been in existence between the LTTE and the government, peace negotiations have begun, and a peaceful settlement may ensue. During negotiations, the LTTE stated that it may agree to a settlement within a federal state. "Posed" is used to flag the many cumulative political, military and economic consequences of the insurrection which have now embedded themselves in tile polity and society; "poses" is used to mark the possibility that the insurrection play re-ignite in the future (no assumptions are made in this paper regarding a durable peace settlement in Sri Lanka).

The Tamil secessionist insurrection aims to establish a separate state called "Tamil Eelam" in the northern and eastern provinces of Sri Lanka. It rejects the territorial and political unity of the (Sinllala-dominated) Sri Lankan State. The insurrection is a complex politico-military process arising from ethnic competition and violence between Sri Lanka Tamils and Sinhala exclusivists, and the (Sinhala-dominated) post-colonial State. On a number of occasions, the possibility of a negotiated settlement existed, but none of these attempts bore fruit. The intensification of the insurrection also occurred consequent to various governments' efforts to counter the insurrection through the massive (and ill-conceived) use of military force alone.

The political estrangement of Sri Lankan Tamils from the (Sinhala dominated Sri Lankan State is the fundamental process which gave birth to the secessionist insurrection. This estrangement began to intensify in the mid-1950s when the "Sinhala only" legislation was enacted and with the occurrence of anti-Tamil riots in 1956 and 1958. Political ideas which promoted secession were active among Tamils from at least the 1958 riots onwards.

The armed activities of the secessionist insurrection began in 1972 along with the formation of the Tamil New Tigers (TNT) and the perpetration of various acts of political agitation-including the burning of government owned transport buses—against the then government's new Republican Constitution of 1972. The violence was on a (relatively) low level of intensity during these initial years. The early targets were Tamil politicians who were hostile to tile secessionist project, and Tamil policemen who—because of their language skills and knowledge of the inner workings of the ethnic group—were seen as threats to the embryonic guerrilla organizations. The nascent guerrilla groups of the early 1970s started with a handful of Tamil youths. The weapons were shotguns, revolvers, and locally manufactured hand bombs. A great deal of verbal persuasion and coercion occurred within the Tamil community, interspersed with rare occurrences of bodily harin and assassination. The intensity of violence was low, and the government at the time did not realize that an insurrectionary process was underway. Throughout these years, a gradual process of political radicalization occurred within the Tamil community. The five main groups (LTTE, EROS, TELO, PLOT, and EPRLF) which emerged during these years were the result of the perceived (and actual) ineffectiveness of Tamil parliamentary parties. In 1976, the Tamil parliamentary party, the TULF, itself responding to pressures from a politically roused Tamil electorate, adopted a secessionist programme for the general elections of 1977. In the aftermath of the 1977 general elections, anti-Tamil riots occurred which serve to increase the alienation of the Tamil people, which in turn led to a further increase in support for the secessionism.

Consequent to increased insurgent activities in the first half of 1979, President J.R. Jayewardene placed Jaffna under emergency regulations and handed over control to the Army. In July 1979, he sent a brigade-strong Army contingent to Jaffna, and ordered its commander to "wipe out terrorism" in six months. The Artily contingent duly carried out a series of high-intensity "internal security" operations, which included a considerable amount of torture, incommunicado detention, and a small number of extra-judicial killings and disappearances. Many Tamil insurgents crossed over and found sanctuary in Sonth India during this period. In December 1979, the contingent commander reported to President Jayewardene that the mission had been successfully completed. This was far from the case, as the insurgents had merely made a tactical retreat.

In 1981, anti-Tamil riots of a (relatively) small scale occurred followed by the pogrom-cum-riots of July 1983. After 1983, the insurrection escalated to a qualitatively much higher intensity. This pogrom-cum-riots proved immensely beneficial to the secessionist calls and served to swell the guerrilla organizations with thousands of new recruits. No Political reforms aimed at addressing the grievances of the Tamil people were formulated or effectively implemented during these years.

From 1983 to 1987, the government carried out a series of military actions (mostly "cordon and search" and high-intensity internal security operations), but these were not undergirded by a coherent overall strategy which included political reforms which addressed Tamil grievances. Consequently, the insurrection relentlessly increased. A considerable amount of internal displacement of Tamil civilians occurred due to the military operations; extra-judical executions and incommunicado detention were also used by the security forces in their (vain) effort to suppress the insurrection. Some efforts were made at arriving at political reforms which would address the Tamil grievances, but these efforts proved filtile. By 1986-67, the tension between the LTTE and the other four groups also broke into the open and violent intcrnccinc killings began among them. The LTTE was determined to become the hegemon and sole secessionist guerrilla organization — a status which it achieved over the subsequent years.

In May-June 1987, President Jayewardene's Government embarked upon a large-scale military operation in the Jaffna Peninsula. Although the operation made some territorial gains, it was a failure in terms of overall strategy because it precipitated direct Indian intervention July 1987 via the Indo-Lanka Accord. The accord was the culmination of a "Track II" policy, whereby the Indian government covertly assisted secessionist insurgent groups while it concurrently exerted overt pressure via diplomacy on the Sri Lanka government to make concessions. As a part of the terms of the accord, the Sri Lankan Armed Forces were compelled to retreat to the positions from which they launched the operation. Under the terms of the accord, all the armed groups except the LTTE agreed to search for a solution for the Tamil people's problems within an undivided Sri Lankan State.

In October 1987, fighting began between the LTTE and the Indian forces. From 1987, it was the LTTE alone which prosecuted the secessionist insurrection, and consequently the LTTE's strategies and tacties on the one hand and the secessionist insurrectionary process on the other gradually became synonymous with one another. During 1987-90, the Indian forces and the LTTE were involved in a great deal of fighting in the north and cast of the island. While the main cities of the north-east such as Jaffna, Trincomalee, Batticaloa, and Amparai and many other smaller urban centres were under the control of the Indian forces, the LTTE withdrew into the jungles in the north an cast and carried out guerrilla operations. The IPKF carried out several large-scale operations which combed the jungles of the Vanni, but were unable to decisively defeat the LTTE. In June 1989, the LTTE and the Sri Lanka government agreed to cease fire, whereupon the Sri Lankan president requested the Indian government to withdraw its forces. In due course, the Indian forces left the island in March 1990.

In late 1994, the Peoples' Alliance (PA, a coalition led by the SLFP) was voted into office. This new government attempted negotiations, but these too proved fruitless. The LTTE withdrew from the cessation of hostilities in April 1995, and subsequently widespread fighting of a very high intensity occurred between the LTTE and the security forces. While the government made several attempts to formulate a political reform package, nothing could be endorsed by Parliament or implemented. The period 1995-2001 witnessed a great deal of military operations of an unprecedented high intensity. During Operation Riviresa (the government's capture of Jaffna pPninsula), the LTTE fought on a semi-conventional basis and ultimately withdrew to the Vanni area (the largely jungle area immediately south of the Jaffna Peninsula) of the northern province.

During the course of Operation Jayasikuru, the government tempted to capture the A-9 main road which runs through the centre of the Vanni. This attempt proved fruitless, because over a period of two and a half years (May 1997 to November 1999), the LTTE successfully resisted the Armed Forces' attempts to move northwards and link up with Jaffna peninsula. During November 1999-May 2000) the LTTE launched a large-scale counter-offensive which, in its southward thrust, pushed the Army back to Vavuniya from where it had started in May 1997, and in its northward thrust overran the Elephant Pass Army base and came near the outskirts of Jaffna city The Army counter-attacked and was able to push the back to the Kilali--Eluthumadduval-Nakarkoyil area in the Jaffna peninsula. 'I6 date, the region downwards from Kilali-Nakarkoyil to Vavuniya, approximately 100 km to the south, remains under the control of the LTTE.

International published sources estimated that in 2000-01, the LTTE had 6,000-7,000 armed cadres at its disposal. It is the author's estimate, however, that the figure was closer to 10,000 at that time. These cadres would also have been supported by many thousands of part-time supporters who provided logistic, medical, food preparation, administration, vehicle and weapon repair, intelligence, and numerous other types of assistance. After the February 2002 cease fire the LTTE has kept on recruiting cadres.

The Tamil secessionist insurrection has undergone many changes over the last three decades. The rebellious secessionist tendency initially originated and grew within the womb of democratic Tamil political parties like the Federal Party and the LTTE. The insurrection has outlasted numerous political, diplomatic, and military developments in both Sri Lanka and India during these decades, as well as four Sri Lankan governments, namely the 1970-77 (SLFP coalition), 1977-88 (UNP), 1989-94 (UNP), and 1994-2001 (SLFP coalition). Since January 2002, a new UNP Government has been in office, and, as mentioned earlier, consequent to a cease-fire agreement in February 2002, detailed negotiations have begun between the government and the LTTE.

From a political-military perspective, tile most important characteristic of the Tamil insurrection general, and the LTTE in particular, has been tile ability to wage protracted guerrilla warfare. Such warfare has proved extremely difficult for both the Sri Lankan State (from 1972 onwards) and tile Indian State (during 1987-90) to cope with. It is this ability to wage protracted guerrilla warfare which has also differentiated the Tamil insurrection from the two JVP insurrections. Furthermore, the LTTE have also demonstrated over the last 10 years their capacity to face—and oil sonic occasions defeat—the Sri Lanka Army in large-scale conventional-type military operations. A prime example of the latter is the LTTE's successful defense against Operation Jayasikuru (May 1997 to November 1999), and its counter-attack (November 1999-May 2000) which brought it to the outskirts of Jaffna city. Operation Jayasikuru was launcltcd by the government in May 1997, and its objective was to move northwards on the A-9 road from Vavuniya and link up with the Army in the Jaffna peninsula. The operation was the largest that the Sri Lankan Armed Forces have ever launched, and the attacking force, which eventually constituted five Army divisions (totalling, about 25,000 personnel) plus police, Navy and Air Force personnel whose mission was to hold the ground captured by the Army. Four divisions were involved in the effort to move northwards from Vavuniya along A-9, while the fifth division based in Kilinochchi-a town on the route to tile peninsula—tried to move downwards along the A-9 road. Both prongs of the operation were fiercely resisted by the LFFE. It took the Army's southern thrust 16 months of fighting to reach, in September 1998, a town (Mankulam) which was approximately halfway to tile Jaffna peninsula. But even this proved ephemeral, as the LTTE attacked and overran the Army's base at Kilinochchi during that same month. The fall of Kilinochchi effectively ended any hopes for Jayasikturu's success. The operation was officially terminated by the government in December 1998.

By the above, It is not meant to imply that the LTTE were expcrts in guerrilla and conventional-type warfare from its beginnings in the early 1970s. To the contrary, their initial actions were amateurish and they committed mistakes. But as the insurrection unfolded and political mobilization of the 'Tamil People continued, the characteristics of protracted guerrilla warfare gradually evolved, and later, by having to deal with the large-scale military operations of the IPKF (1987-89) and the Sri Lankan military (1990-2001), the LTTE developed the capacity to fight semi-conventional warfare.

Parallel to its military operations, the LTTE have been adept at exploiting all governments' errors. LTTE political cadres carried out, and continue to perform, a great deal of political mobilizational work among Tamil civilians in areas under both LTTE and government control. The LTTE military cadres have developed fighting capabilities at sea and against aircraft; on land, the LTTE have developed potent quasi-conventional military capabilities. The organization has comprehensively penetrated tile Tamil community and any Tamils who oppose the LTTE are dealt with ruthlessly bite Tamil diaspora has been systematically organized and generates large amounts of funding with which arms and other equipment are purchased.

The Impact of Intrastate Conflict

The insurrections have had widespread economic and political consequences for Sri Lanka. If we consider economic costs first, one of the earliest assessments of the total cost during the period 1983-88 arrived at a figure of US$4.2 bilhon. This was a large sum for a developing country and was equivalent to Sri Lanka's total capital expenditure for the entire three-year period 1986-88. This damage assessment does not include the period up to 1983, nor the culminating year, 1989, of the second JVP insurrection, nor the subsequent highly destructive phases of the Tamil secessionist insurrection (June 1990 onwards).

The Institute of Policy Studies (IPS) has analysed the cost of the Tamil secessionist insurrection for the period 1984-96. Total direct government military expenditure was Rs. 287.5 billion, rising to 6 percent of GDP and 21.6 per cent of the government budget by 1996. Total cost of the conflict considered under direct an indirect costs was 1,168 billion. This amounted to US$21 billion (at the 1996 rate of exchange), which was a huge burden for a relatively poor Third World country to carry. It should be noted that the above figures too are incomplete. They do not include the five-year period 1997 to 2001, when a large number of military operations took place during which a great deal of additional funds were consumed and equipment for 1927-2001 would have been at least a further Rs. 200 billion.

In 2000-01, a sequence of events occurred which brought the economic crisis to head. First, as mentioned earlier, during November 1999-May 2000, the LTTE counter-attacked the Army in the Vanni and also captured significant territory in the Jaffina peninsula itself. They heavy losses in men and equipment compelled the then government to dramatically increase military expenditure by US$350 million. This unscheduled expenditure decreased funds available for development and also increased the public debt: "the massive increase in war expenditure in 2000 was mostly responsible for the large increase in public debt that year". In the subsequent months, the government carried out a range of military operations in Jaffna which culminated with the unsuccessful Operation Agni Kheela in April 2001. Second in July 2001. The LTTE attacked Sri Lanka's sole international airport and destroyed civilian passenger aircraft and Air Force helicopters and attack aircraft. This attack led to increases in international insurance premiums and grievously affected the country's export and import trade. Concurrently, the global recession too had begun to affect the country's highly export-oriented economy. Third came the impact of the deepened global recession consequent to the attacks on the USA on 11 September As a result of this sequence of events, in the latter part of 2001, the country underwent a period of negative growth for the first time since the great depression of 1929-30. As of February 2002, the country was in serious economic difficulties, with the public debt of Rs. 1,414 billion exceeding GDP by 13 percent.

The secessionist insurrection and the government's counteractions have also had numerous direct and indirect macro-political consequences, of which the political alienation from the state of a large proportion of Tamils is the foremost. This alienation has developed to such an extent that a considerable number of Tamils consider themselves a separate nation that requires a state of its own. A second macro-political consequence has been the political, military, and administrative weakening of the Colombo-centred, unitary, Sinhala-dominated post-colonial State. A new State structure which includes a great deal of devolution – be it asymmetric devolution, a federal State or a confederal State-is needed if the State is to remain even loosely united. The shape and character of the final constitutional and political arrangements cannot be anticipated at present. The Colombo-dominated centralized unitary state, however, will need to undergo change.

The secessionist insurrection has resulted in numerous human rights violations, including extra judicial killings, "disappearances" torture, and incommunicado detention. The insurrection is said to have led to the loss of at least 60,000 lives, half of them civilians. Tens of thousands have been injured and approximately 800,000 were internally displaced (some of whom are now gradually reclaiming their lands and homes subsequent to the post-February 2002 cease-fire). Political violence on this scale has had its inevitable negative repercussions upon society and polity.

Political Prescience; No Effective Policies

The primary process which underlies the Tamil secessionist insurrection is the persistent alienation of large numbers of Tamil people from the (Sinhala-dominated) post-colonial Sri Lankan government and State. The 1956 "Sinhala Only" Act, the anti-Tamil riots of 1956, 1958, 1977, 1981 and 1983, the restricted access to Inrblic-sector employment and university education, and the competition for land in the eastern province are all factors which contributed to this alienation.

The Sri Lanka government's primary project should have been to develop and implement policies to regain and retain the allegiance of the constituency, viz., the Tamil people, from within whom the secessionist insurgent movement arose. Accordingly, government should have given the highest priority to first understanding the underlying grievances of the Tamil people, and then developing appropriate policies which addressed these grievances. Military and police measures should have been used—conceived and implemented in a manner appropriate for intra-state conflict only in support of such an overall project.

The insecurity faced by ordinary Tamils was a potent factor in the development of the secessionist insurrection. The security of Tamil people should have been a fundamental concern of all governments. The government and State should have protected Tamil civilians, and should have been seen to be doing so. On the contrary, Sri Lankan governments have paid scant attention to the security of its Tamil citizens: the anti-Tamil riots of 1977, 1981 and 1983 revealed to most Tamils the precariousness of their security. For instance, the 1983 programme-cum-riot was effectively brought under control only six to seven days after the rioting began; this was a profound dereliction fo the government's fundamental duty to ensure security of life and limb to its citizens. Apart from such well-known instances like the 1983 events, however, consider the issue of persistent emigration of hundreds of thousands of Tamils over the last 20 years: not a single government has officially expressed regret at this phenomenon. The Tamil people should have been reassured of their status as citizens of Sri Lanka, and policies should have been designed and implemented to wean them away from the secessionist trend. Military and police operations which merely subjected Tamil civilians to death displacement and injury had a completely counterproductive effect in countering the secessionist insurrection. Collective "punishment" of Tamils, e.g. the pogrom-cum-riot of 1983 and the numerous extra judicial killings and disaperances which have taken place during these years were counter-productive to the government's cause.

Were Sinhala political leaders unaware of the dangerous political consequences of alienating Tamils? Were they unaware of the dangers which could arise to both the security and stability of the country as well as its citizens? In the following paragraphs statements by UNP stalwart J.R. Jaycwardene (in 1956 and 1966), and the UNP manifesto of 1977 are quoted and discussed. (It needs to be clarified immediately that J.R. Jayewardene's statements are used as illustrative examples of political prescience, and because of the central position he came to occupy during 1977-88 when the secessionist insurrection escalate. Both major political parties, the UNP and SLEP, and their leaders have played a crucial role in the escalation of the Sinhala Tamil ethnic conflict in Sri Lanka.)

As already noted, it is now widely accepted that the "Sinhala Only" language policy introduced by the SLEP-le coalition of 1956 was a significant milestone in the conflict between the Sinhalese and the Sri Lanka Tamils. This policy was widely debated in Parliament and the press at the time. In early June 1956, a few days before the Bill was presented in Parliament, Jayewardene released a statement to the press in which he said:

> *No Government should and could make Sinhalese the official language trampling down file language rights of over a million of the permanent residents of the country. It cannot thrust to the wilderness the cherished language of these people. The doors of the public services should not be closed to the thousands of youth who did not know Sinhalese for no fault of their own. Surely that was the way to sow the seeds of civil war. [...]*

> *There was genuine fear in the minds of all minorities, Tamils, Muslims, Burghers and others with regard to the proposals of the Government. [...] Mr. Bandaranaike had (sic) still time to shake off the shackles with which he had been bound and to save the country from long years of unnecessary strife and even bloodshed (Ceylon Daily News, 4 June 1956: 5, "J. R. Jayewardene on Sinhale Bill"; emphases added).*

In this statement, J. R. Jayewardene stated that the language rights of non-Sinhalese should not be "trampled". He connected the "Sinhala Only" language policy with restricted access to public sector employment—which was a part of the political agenda of those who advocated the policy and correctly anticipated that the public sector would become an enelave for the Sinhalese. He then went on to imply that the resultant alienation could lead to civil war, thereby correctly anticipating the political radicalization of hundreds of educated Tamil youth in the 1970s and early-1980s. Second, Jayewardene correctly recognized and acknowledged that all minority ethnic groups were genuinely fearful of the then (SLFP-led coalition) government's policies; third, he anticipated a long and protracted period of conflict and bloodshed and used the ominous term "civil war" to describe that possibility. These were perceptive political insights to have had in June 1956. It need to be noted that when Jayewardene made his statement, the formal establishment of the LTTE (in 1976) was still 20 years into the future, and LTTE leader Velupillai Prabhakarn, born in November 1957, was one and a half years old.

Lest it be thought that the UNP had better position on the language issue, in the same speech Jayewardene stated that:

> *The United National Party accepted "Sinhalese as the only Official Language" at the Kelaniya sessions and made it one of its election promises. If it was returned to power this promise would have been implemented but not in the manner the present Government was acting (ibid.).*

Whether a UNP Government's policies would have been qualitatively different from the SLFP Government's, and whether Tamils would have been less alienated from the government, and accordingly whether Sinhala-Zamil relations (1956-2002) would have been substantially different are moot points. The point which is relevant to our present purpose is, however, that J. R. Jayewardene had correctly identified prior to the actual enactment of the Bill the inherent potential for serious internal conflict. It needs to be noted here that many other politicians too—Sinhales, Tamils and Muslims—from across the political spectrum cautioned the then government against the enactment of this Bill. J.R. Jayewrdene is mentioned because of the immense power and opportunity he and his government had during 1977-88 to deal constructively with the ethnic conflict.

In any event, the "Sinhala Only" Bill was enacted on 5 June 1956, while outside the Parliament building Tamil legislators were involved in a peaceful satyagraha demonstration in opposition to the Bill. These legislators were assaulted by supporters of the government. That evening, itself anti-Tamil riots began in Colombo, and ill the ensuing days the riots spread to areas of tile eastern province. In 1957, Mr. Bandaranaike and Tamil political leaders arrived at an agreement (the "Bandaranaike-Chelvanayakam Pact."), but parties which opposed the government foremost of which was the UNP-mobilized the Sinhala electorate against the Pact. Mr. J.R. Jayewardeneh played an important role in the opposition campaign. The political tensions generated during this campaign contributed to the next bout of and-Tamil riots which occurred in 1958, this time throughout the island, with at least 400 Tamils killed and tens of thousands displaced. Smaller and less well-known inter-ethnic clashes too occurred over the subsequent vicars. The 1961 satyagraha campaign launched by Tamil parliamentarians resulted In a great deal of political mobilization of Tamils, and agitation and hostility against Tamils within the Sinhalese community. Although riot always violent, there existed a great deal of tension between the Sinhalese and the Tamils during these years.

The UNP won the general elections of 1965, and J.R. Jayewardene was appointed Minister of State. In April 1966, lie gave an important speech at the Annual General Meeting of the Planters Association. During the course of his speech (which outlined tile then government's proposed plans for economic development and touched on a great many other subjects), he said:

> *When we assumed office last year we were faced firstly with the problem of national disunity. For the last ten years there has been some form of civil war going on between the two major communities of the country.*

Here, J.R. Jayewaredene is consistent with his analysis of 10 years earlier. He again uses the menacing term "civil war", and per iodizes the "war" as having begun in 1956. While in 1956 lie mentioned the *possibility* of civil war, in 1966 he refers to "civil war" as a phenomenon which had already been under way for tile pervious 10 years. While it is acknowledged that politicians are wont to make hyperbolic statements-indeed rhetorical flourishes are a part of their stock-in-trade—and though there was an clement of exaggeration in Jayewardene speech, there was also a significant element of foresight encompassed in these statements of 1956 and 1966.

The UNP's 1977 election manifesto was an important document, prepared tender the UNP's leadership, which, at that time, in addition to J.R. Jayewardene also included R. Premadasa, Lalith Atliulathmudali, Galnini Dissanayake and many others. This docuinent was prepared during 1970-77, and included many subjects which were under discussion by the UNP leadership during the entire period they were in opposition (i.e., 1970-77). The UNI"s leadership would leave keenly observed the many incidents which indicated the gradual escalation of the Tamil insurrection—the assassination of some Tamil policemen and some Tamil politicians had already begun by this time. Most important of all was the "Vaddukkoddai resolution" of 1976 where the TULF, the main Tamil parliamentary party; decided on a policy of secession. The TULF was responding to intense political pressure from secessionist political currents within Tamil society—the embryonic secessionist insurgent groups and some of its own party members.

Clearly, a significant degree of secessionist political mobilization was under way within Tamil society by that time. This mobilization posed a grave threat to the unity and security of the entire country and its people. Any mature political party aspiring to form a government should have been prepared to examine the grievances of any section of the people. This is precisely what the UNP Manifesto, as a written text, did. In relation to the problems faced by Tamils, the manifesto made a comprehensive set of promises to the Tamils:

> *The United National fatty accepts the position that there are numerous problems confronting the Tamil speaking people. The lack of a solution to their problems has made the Tamil-speaking people support even a movement for the creation of a separate State. In the interest of national integration and unity so necessary for the economic development of the whole country' the Party feels such problems should be solved without loss of time. The party, when it comes to power, will take all possible*

steps to remedy their grievances in such fields as: (1) Education; (2) Colonization; (3) Use of Tamil language; (4) Employment in the public and semi-public corporations. We will summon an All-Party Conference as stated earlier and implement its decisions (Abeynaike 1987: 296; emphases added).

The manifesto incorporated an unequivocal acknowledgement that the Tamil people faced numerous problems, and that the absence of solutions to these problems had led to the emergence of a movement to create a separate State. Very significantly, the manifesto explicitly acknowledged the relationship between underlying grievances and the secessionist insurrection. Acknowledgement of this linkage was/ is the *sine qua non* for any process of negotiation and conflict resolution.

This acknowledgement, however, remained as text and was not translated into policy. After coming to power, President Jayewardene did not convene the All-Party Conference (APC) as promised. A unique opportunity for resolving tile conflict was lost. If the APC lead been convened and the manifesto's promises had been realized (at least to a moderate level) and implemented during 1977-82, then it *could* have begun a political process whereby the problems faced by Tamil *could* have been gradually resolved. With five-sixths of the parliamentary seats, the that UNP Government dominated the legislature to such a degree that it could have enacted at will any legislation which was necessary to enable any "political reform package" that happened to emerge through a process of negotiation. The government could amend the Constitution when and where necessary (which it did on many occasions during 1977-82, but never as the result of the enlightened reasons which underlay its own manifesto). Most important of all, President Jayewardene's leadership of the UNP was unquestioned. He dominated the party, the government the state to a degree that no other president has since been able to, and lie also had more than two-thirds control of Parliament. The APC was not convened and eventually, with the occurrence of the July 1983 riots the secessionist insurrection escalated to a qualitatively higher level, and the opportunities which existed during 1977-82 were lost.

Dilemmas Faced by Government Confronted by Armed Challenges

The early manifestations of insurgency are looked upon with hostility by most governments, and the commonest initial reaction is to resort to the (seemingly) easier option of coercive actions via the police and the military. Very little attempt is made to understand – and even less to acknowledge – grievances which underlie the insurrection. As the initial acts of rebellion are on a small scale and seem insignificant, governments anticipate easy and quick victories.

However (provided the insurrection has some depth of popular support), police and military actions (which are invariably heavy-handed) serve to deeper the political alienation of the people and results in the exacerbation of the insurrection. The use of force alone-which earlier seemed the easiest option – is often revealed as having been self-destructive to the government's cause. Police and military measures often (inadvertently) pave the way to the exacerbation of an insurgency. In the initial years, when recognizing grievances and developing appropriate policies would do the most good, most government are loath to acknowledge grievances. Later, when they do acknowledge them, they may have to make far more serious concessions than they would have had to if acknowledgement and negotiations lead begun earlier. Sri Lanka's experience of tile last 30 years clearly bears this out.

A sustained insurrection lays bare fundamental fault lines within society. These fault lines can he ethnic competition and conflict, social-class competition and conflict, or diverse religious identities. The problems that these fault lilies generate cannot be dealt with by force alone. Appropriate political reforms are necessary supported, where appropriate, by police and military measures, provided such operations they are done carefully with the appropriate level of force.

Why are government to acknowledge any grievances articulated by significant ethnic, religious and/or any other types of minorities? Because, First, in most instances such grievances have some basis in fact, and, second, the governments. Acknowledging the factual bases of a grievance could have far-reaching consequences: the ethnic, social-class, or religious constituencies which support the government often take great exception to any recognition being given to the grievances of other minority ethnic, class, or religious constituencies. The development of suitable policies pose further problems: here again, the constituencies which support the government can take exception to the new policies and could oppose the government. A great deal of dissension and turbulence can arise within a polity consequent to a government trying to develop policies which address minority ethnic, religious, or class constituencies in society: Therefore, due to such reasons it is far easier for most governments—at least initially—to use force alone. Very few governments can resist the temptation to do so.

Does the imperative to prepare a "political reform package" imply that a government is somehow a "captive" of the insurgent's cause, and thereby, indirectly a hostage of the insurgent's civilian base? To some degree this is the case: insurrections are symptoms of very real conflicts and problems within society; between ethnic groups and/or social-classes on tile one hand and governments and States on tile other. While the term "captive" is strictly not applicable, the term "policy imperative" would be more appropriate. A government facing an insurrection needs to look at the pressures it is subjected to as being analogous to other policy imperatives—economic developmental, social welfare, health policy, educational policy; etc.—which impinge upon it during the course of normal governance. These are imperatives which it must give heed to if it is to govern successfully: Choices have to be made—sometimes of a very difficult nature—and compromises arrived at, but no government questions tile need to address these issues.

Some Comparative Reflections for International Security

At present, serious problems of security bedevil the international community. The events of 11 September 2001 have led to the political, diplomatic and military galvanization of the United States, Britain and the rest of Europe to an unprecedented degree. South Asia and the adjacent Middle East occupy centre stage in the present context. The political and military mobilization of Islamic fundamentalism—some instances as State policy, while in other instances through non-state insurrectionary groups—is incessantly underway in the Middle East and South Asia. Two of tile most intractable and dangerous disputes (both of which have tile capacity to precipitate wider regional insecurity and conflicts) are located within these two regions—the Palestine—Israel dispute, and the Kashmir dispute.

There is wide international recognition that the Palestinians have some reasonable grievances. These grievances have to be addressed in a balanced and reasonable fashion. The consensus that has now emerged within the international community is that a Palestinian state needs to be established. Although in the past many Palestinians repudiated the existence of tile state of Israel, during the last decade a large segment of Palestinians have come to accept the existence of Israel. The end to Israeli settlements in the occupied territories and the formation of an independent Palestinian state is an urgent task. Serious negotiations towards this objective, however, have not even begun. In the meantime, the unresolved issues continue toy generate enormously violent Islamic fundamental political tendencies within the Palestinian people, and these feed into the wider regional network of Islamic fundamentalism. It is possible that Weapons of Mass Destruction (WMDs) could be used—with devastating consequences for regional and global security-in tile years ahead it this conflict is not resolved. It is time that the fundamental issues in the Palestinian-Israeli conflict were given attention by the international community, and appropriate political reforms formulated.

The Kashmir dispute also needs a lasting and sustainable solution. Here again, the fundamental issues underlying the dispute be they of the Kashmir people, the Indian government, or the Pakistani government—have to be addressed. Serious negotiations towards this objective, however, have not even begun. In the meantime, the unresolved issue continues to generate violent Islamic fundamentalist and Hindu fundamentalist political tendencies within Kashmir, Pakistan, and India, respectively: Unexplained terrorist attacks and bomb explosions take place within both India and Pakistan. Each accuses the other of being responsible for the attacks oil their soil. The possibility of an India-Pakistan war (which could include the use of WMDs) cannot be discounted. It is time that the fundamental issues in the Kashmir dispute were given attention by the international community; and appropriate political reforms formulated.

Both disputes arc now more than 50 years old. If the present situations are allowed to continue, these disputes could, theoretically; continue into the future for a further similar period. The cost in human suffering and regional instability would be high.

Summary

When compared to the above regional disputes, the Sri Lankan conflict is relatively simple and, therefore, direct comparisons cannot be made. However, some general insights such as the following thay prove useful. First, tile need to acknowledge underlying grievances at the earliest possible time. Obviously easier said than done—with each dispute involving several different states and regional strategic concerns. However, this vital initial phase cannot be deferred indefinitely—sooner or later it will arrive on the agenda. The later it arrives, the greater will be the other problems and issues that it brings along with it. This will make the formulation of reform programmes that much more difficult. Second, delay heightens the level of violence and provides extremists time, recruits, and opportunity to introduce new weapons and tactics into the conflict. Delay also provides time and opportunity for wider and deeper political mobilization with unforeseen (and unforeseeable) consequences.

The Tamil secessionist insurrection need never have developed in Sri Lanka to the level it did during 1977-2001. If the grievances of the Tamils had been given at least some acknowledgement and suitable political developed, it would have possible to have been possible to have resolved the conflict at an early phase of its development. Each year that passed, every anti-Tamil riot that occurred, each instance of large-scale internal displacement and human rights violation that occurred made the insurrection that much more intractable. Ironically, in the present negotiations between the government and the LTTE (2002-03), issues such as the creation of a federal state—an option which was considered unacceptable to most Sinhala politicians—have now arrived on the negotiating table. That the "Tamils have legitimate grievances and that these need to be addressed have now been widely accepted in government, media, and society. By this, it is not implied that a negotiated solution is at hand, or that the conflict will not re-ignite in the future. Merely, that underlying grievances which had been identified decades ago arc on tile political agenda once again, and are still the ones which will need to be addressed.

It may be that Ill tile case of international security text the time has come to begin tile task of seriously examining the arguments and grievances underlying insurgent and anti-state movements which impinge on regional and global security. This does not mean that it is compulsory that any and all of these grievances be accepted. It is entirely possible that after examination it is found that in some cases no compromises are possible.

BUDDHIST REVIVALISM, NATIONALISM, AND POLITICS IN MODERN SRI LANKA

Introduction

There are indeed some common features in all forms of modem religious revival, whether fundamentalist or merely resurgent. The first is the striking potential for politicization—socialist, radical, conservative, and reactionary. Indeed some scholars see in Islamic fundamentalism a natural division into radical and traditional forms, a division which is a central element in the politicization and political impact of Buddhist revivalism in Sri Lanka. Secondly, most forms of revivalism spring from the grassroots of society, quite often from the mass of citizens, and are led by the alienated and frustrated, in brief, by those with a grievance against the powers that be in the political system. Thirdly, most forms of fundamentalism and religious revivalism are:

> *Not religion as contemplation or a private experience of divinity; but religion as the essence of a culture, the binding brotherhood transcending material need.*

Thus speaks V.S. Naipaul, turning his sceptical eye on the political face of religious fundamentalism in its current manifestation in the United States. He captures the essence of the problem with elegant lucidity.

The Buddhist commentarial tradition and its works of classification and analysis are similar to many of the scholastic traditions of other major world religions. To that extent, there is a "fundamentalist" strand in Buddhism. All religions have basic scriptures which preserve the message of the founder or founders of that religion. Buddhists generally consider the *Sutta Pitaka* to be the original message of the Buddha. Thus we may speak of the importance of the "word of the Buddha" and its special place in early Buddhist tradition. But the strand of fundamentalism in Buddhism was never a prominent one. Indeed, through a kind of "internal criticism," the Buddha's teachings on their own present a corrective against fundamentalism as found in its Islamic and Christian forms. The *Kalama Sutta*, for instance, urges the would—be Buddhist not to accept anything merely because it is found in the scriptures or sacred books, because it is a traditional belief, because it is the opinion shared by large numbers of people, or because of the prestige the teacher enjoys.

The Buddha refers to three kinds of thinkers: traditionalists who depended on scriptural tradition; rationalists who relied on logic and reason; and the experientialists whose strength lay in personal knowledge and meditative experience. He identified himself with the third group. This view provides a corrective to fundamentalism in religion, as docs the strong pragmatist strand in Buddhism.

Fundamentalism in Islam and Christianity has at its core a "back to the inspired word of God" ideology in which the Koran and the Bible supply the all-sufficient guide for every condition and circumstance of life. The Buddhist tradition shifts the focus of attention from the book to the individual's own verification of the truth. The ultimate judge in these matters is thus the contemplative individual and his search for the truth in which the word of the Buddha and its inner meaning are but guides or, to change the metaphor, merely signposts on the path to wisdom.

Buddhist fundamentalism, then, is a contradiction in terms. The more appropriate term is Buddhist revivalism, and that is what we use in this chapter.

The German Indologist, Heinz Beehert, observed that the Buddhist societies of South and Southeast Asia are "historically conscious" societies. The reference was to Sri Lanka, Burma, and Thailand, all of them old societies with long and troubled histories. Sri Lanka's is the oldest Buddhist society in the world, and the country carries a huge burden of historical memories that have powerfully affected the link between religion, nationalism, and politics in modern times.

The legacy of that colonial experience common to both Sri Lanka and Burma is the confrontation between Buddhism and the intrusive Western culture, civilization, and Christian religion. In Sri Lanka that intrusion and its inevitable tensions with indigenous religions began in the middle of the sixteenth century with Portuguese influence and, later, Portuguese rule in the littoral. Portuguese colonialism was very much the child of the counter-reformation. If its emphasis on the principle of *cujus regio illius religio* perpetuated a central feature of the Sri Lankan political system – since the local link between state and religion had originated as long ago as the third century BC – the zealotry and harsh intolerance which characterized the imposition of Roman Catholicism on Sri Lanka were something new and unfamiliar. Sri Lankan society and civilization had seldom confused the obligation to encourage adherence to the national religion with the suppression of other faiths.

Sri Lanka provides one of the most striking illustrations of the truth of Anthony Low's comment that "Empire was as much a religious as a political or economic or ideological problem." Christianity, Roman Catholic and Protestant, came to the island with the three Western powers—Portugal, Holland, and Great Britain—which from the mid-sixteenth century controlled parts of Sri Lanka (Portugal and Holland) or the whole of it (the British). As successive official religions, Roman Catholicism, Calvinism, and Anglicanism each had a special relationship with the ruling power which provided it with prestige and authority. Converts to the prevailing orthodox version of Christianity— especially under the Portuguese and the Dutch—came to be treated as a privileged group. Severe restrictions and, often, penalties were imposed on the practice of the traditional religions—Buddhism, Hinduism, and Islam. These were severest under the Portuguese; the Dutch widened the scope of these restrictions to include Roman Catholicism as well. Forced conversions increased the numbers of adherents of the official religion. Once again, these were more frequent and the pressure most persistent under the Portuguese.

The colonial state under Portuguese rule in Sri Lanka, the *Estado*, was a Roman Catholic one. The role of religion in the state system was no less significant under the Dutch, despite the fact that the maritime regions conquered by them from the Portuguese were administered by a commercial company, *Vereenidge Oost-Indisdie Compagnie* (V.O.C.) or the Dutch East India Company, as it was known. At the time of the conquest of the Dutch possessions in the island by the English in 1795-96, the majority of the citizens of these territories were classified as Protestant Christians. With the more relaxed outlook of the English, the superficiality of conversions to the Dutch Reformed Church was amply demonstrated when most people returned to their traditional faiths. Once the legal restrictions" on the Roman Catholics were removed between 1806 and 1829, they emerged as the largest of the Christian groups in the island, a position they retain today. Conversions to Roman Catholicism under the Portuguese thus stood the rigorous test of persecution under the Dutch and the disdain and indifference of British officialdom.

The link between state and Christianity continued in the early years of British rule in the maritime regions of Sri Lanka, although the attitude to the Anglican Church—theoretically the established Church—infinitely more complicated once the British gained control over the whole island between 1815 and 1818 with, the conquest of the Kandyan kingdom, the last of the independent Sinhalese kingdoms.

With the absorption of the Kandyan kingdom, the British confronted one of the most perplexing and intricate problems they were called upon to handle in Sri Lanka: the definition of the state's relations with Buddhism. The undertaking given by the British in 1815, through the Kaudyan Convention about the status of Buddhism was unambiguous: "The Religion of Boodhoo [sic] professed by the Chiefs and inhabitants of these Provinces is declared inviolable, and its Rites, Ministers, and Places of Worship are to be maintained and protected." When he sent a copy of the Convention to the Colonial Office, Governor Sir Robert Brownrigg explained to his superiors in Whitehall that he had been obliged to consent to "an article of guarantee couched in the most unqualified terms" because it was vitally important to quiet the apprehensions of the Kandyans about their religion. Only by making it clear that the fifth clause of the Convention would be scrupulously observed could the British gain the adherence of the *bhikkhus* (members of the Buddhist order, the *sangha*) and chiefs. These guarantees were softened considerably through a Proclamation of 11 November 1818 after the suppression of the Kandyan rebellion of 1817-18, but even so they were by no means repudiated.

From the outset, the attitude of the British rulers towards Buddhism was an ambiguous one, veering towards reluctant adherence to the letter of the treaty rather than to its spirit, and the requirement of positive support. As we shall presently see the link between Buddhism and the state was severed in the 1840s under Evangelical pressure. The historical significance of this could scarcely be exaggerated, for it marked the severance of the traditional bond between the state and the national religion that had lasted for over 2,000 years almost without interruption from the earliest days of the ancient Sinhalese kingdom. The withdrawal of the traditional patronage accorded to Buddhism, and the consequent loss of precedence and prestige, deeply disturbed and often excited the indignation of Sri Lanka's Buddhists.

The disestablishment of Buddhism was part of the common colonial heritage in Sri Lanka and Burma, even though the strength and durability of Christianity set Sri Lanka apart from Burma where Christianity was a minority religion in every sense of the word. Thailand, in contrast, escaped colonialism's grasp during the nineteenth century and the *sangha* there, far from being disestablished, was brought closer to the government. By the early twentieth century, the links between the monarchy, state, and Buddhism in Thailand had mobilized,

> *the concept of nation and the older symbols of kingship and religion ... as a safeguard against colonialism.*

King Wachirawut one of the principal monarchical ideologues of this traditional Theravada notion of a link between state and religion, sought to reaffirm and revitalize

> *The traditional Thai religio-political belief that the prosperity and progress of the nation is closely related to the prosperity of Buddhism, and that the religion and the king constitute the moral foundations of the nation-they are inseparable.*

Representatives of Buddhist interests in Sri Lanka refused to acquiesce in the unilateral decision to sever the link between the colonial state and Buddhism. Even if they were reconciled to the impossibility of the restoration of that link in its original form, they continued to insist that some institutional and legislative mechanism be devised to protect the property of Buddhist institutions from adverse consequences after the precipitate severance of the link in 1847. An assurance had been given in the 1840s and 1850s that some such institutional machinery and legislative mechanism would he established took nearly fifty years before this promise was met so pressure for its fulfillment was a principal Buddhist demand during the second half of the nineteenth century.

The British, for their part, would not go back to the *status quo ante* 1840 by restoring the formal link between the colonial state and Buddhism. But by the 1870s they began to see advantages to themselves in an accommodation with Buddhism that would be mutually beneficial. This pragmatic concession to political realities eventually resulted in a formula which provided for a special concern, if not a distinctive position for Buddhism in the colonial polity. This notable example of British pragmatism at work had unusually significant long-term effects. When pressure for the restoration of the link between Buddhism and the state continued after Sri Lanka achieved independence in 1948, Sri Lankan politicians adapted and elaborated upon this formula. It was embodied in the constitutions of 1972 and 1978 as a substitute for the elevation of Buddhism to the position of the state religion.

The second theme to be emphasized in this introductory section is the size of the Christian community and its powerful influence under British rule. Although Roman Catholics and Protestants in Sri Lanka together never numbered more than one-tenth of the population during the period of British rule and in the early years of independence, that proportion was significantly greater than in British India where Christians numbered only about two percent of the population. More important, the Sri Lankan Christians—nine-tenths of whom were Roman Catholics—were also, quite unlike their Indian counterparts, a privileged group with a larger number of persons of elite status than any other religious group in the country.

The extent to which Sri Lanka's Buddhist movements were affected by their perception of Christian dominance is seldom considered in analyses of the nature of Buddhist revivalism in Sri Lanka, but it affected them in a number of ways: in the high priority given to eliminating sources of Christian privilege, especially in education; in the conscious and unconscious imitation of the techniques and mechanisms adopted and used by Christians to popularize their faith: and above all in the passionate quest for a redress of grievances accumulated over the many centuries of Christian domination, a quest which often served to distort perceptions and to heighten a sense of historic deprivation.

The peculiar demographic configuration resulting from the overwhelming numerical dominance of the Roman Catholics within the Christian community had a distorting effect on the relationship between the Christian minority and the rest of the Sri Lankan society. For much of the first half of the nineteenth century, the Roman Catholics had little influence on official policies and attitudes. The pace was set by the Protestants in general, and not necessarily the elite Anglican group. But over time the Roman Catholics asserted themselves and, with numbers very much on their side, the interaction between Christianity and the indigenous society was often very complex.

Buddhism in Sri Lanka, 1870-1920: Recovery, Resistance, and Rehabilitation

The fifty years after 1870 marked a period of religious ferment in the island, especially in its littoral regions. The revival of Buddhism, Hinduism, and Islam was contemporaneous with the vigorous recovery of Roman Catholicism. Unlike the recovery of Roman Catholicism in Sri Lanka and South Asia, the Buddhist revival and its impact on the country are now very familiar territory to scholars and students of Sri Lankan affairs There are three significant aspects of the Buddhist revival in Sri Lanka: the recovery of self-confidence; the resistance to missionary enterprise; and the rehabilitation of the surviving institutional structures of Buddhism. The first and third of these followed upon the second, the successful challenge to a powerful but divided missionary movement which by the middle of the nineteenth century seemed poised to obliterate the traditional religions as comprehensively through peaceful means as the Dutch had done through repressive legislation and the social and economic pressure directed to that end by the governing commercial company and its officials.

The period reviewed here had two distinct phases with the governorship of Sir Arthur Gordon forming a convenient dividing line. One sees a distinct duality in the processes of Buddhist recovery, between those who sought to and were indeed encouraged to operate within a non-political framework which accepted the preeminence of British rule, and the more radical forces which sought to politicize the movement and to assert the primacy of Buddhism within the Sri Lanka polity.

In the first phase the issues seemed more clearly focused than in the second, but that clarity came from a reluctance to be drawn into political activity. The emphasis was on resisting missionary activity and the use for this purpose of techniques and instruments of propaganda popularized by the missionaries themselves: public debates, tracts, pamphlets, newspapers, and of course the educational process through schools established and controlled by the Buddhists themselves Pressure for restoring a link between Buddhist institutions and the state was a hardy perennial in the "politics" of Buddhist revival. There was pressure to restore at least part of the Buddhist heritage, whether the recognition of Vesak (the annual celebration of the birth and death dates of the Buddha) as a national holiday, or the protection of the archaeological treasures at Anuradhapura and Polonnaruwa from encroachment by non-Buddhists and by state institutions. The problem of education and the complications it posed to the state and to Buddhists illustrates the increasingly politicized revivalism. In the last quarter of the nineteenth century, the state's responsibility for the provision of educational facilities was clearly if somewhat narrowly defined; the state was to concentrate its energies on vernacular education. The major role in education was conceded to the Christian missions. Protestant missions initially reaped the benefits of this decision because of the superior organization of their educational programmes. One of the most striking developments of this period was the phenomenal increase in the number of state-aided missionary schools, of which very soon a substantial number were Roman Catholic.

The challenge to the superiority of the Protestant missions in the field of education came first from the Roman Catholics, then from Buddhists, Hindus, and Muslims. The credit for the recovery of Roman Catholic self-respect and self-esteem in Sri Lanka was due, in large measure, to the efforts of the redoubtable apostolic delegate, Msgr. C.A. Bonjean, especially in the sphere of education. From 1860 on Bonjean conducted a purposeful campaign for a denominational system of education with a conscience-clause safeguarding the religious scruples of those who did not belong to the religious denomination which ran the school; a system of state grants in support of schools controlled by the various religion-groups; and for the neutrality of the state in religious affairs.

Indeed, the revival of the indigenous religions was inextricably bound up with the expansion of the Roman Catholics' own educational activities. Without quite ceasing to be the battleground of rival Christian groups—largely Protestant versus Roman Catholic, education became the focus of growing "nationalist" opposition to the Christian missions. The Roman Catholics came to control a stake in education which overshadowed that of the Protestants, but by the 1880s the very effectiveness of their success brought them into constant conflict with the increasingly militant Buddhists. This confrontation between Roman Catholics and Buddhists broke out into sporadic acts of violence. The first such episode was in 1883 in a suburb of Colombo. On that occasion the aggressors were Roman Catholic and the victims Buddhist. There were subsequent clashes in and around Colombo where a resurgent Buddhist revival clashed with a well-entrenched Roman Catholic minority. Unlike the clash in 1883, none of these clashes resulted in loss of life but they spread to other parts of the littoral. In the first decade of the twentieth century sectarian conflict occurred in the town of Anuradhapura. In 1903 vigorous Buddhist protests against encroachment by government institutions, non-Buddhist traders, and religious organizations into the ruins of the ancient city led to violence which included the destruction of a recently established Catholic church.

The Buddhist revival of the last quarter of the nineteenth century posed awkward difficulties for the colonial government in the sensitive area of relations between state and religion. Opinions expressed by the more articulate Buddhist activists of this period ranged from a nostalgic adherence to the traditional position of Buddhism in the Sri Lankan polity, to a realistic demand for some institutional mechanism for supervising the properties of Buddhist institutions, to the more controversial views of men like the Anagarika Dharmapala (1864-1931) described as "visual[izing] the restoration in modern Sri Lanka of an ideological state in which the rulers... would be totally identified with Buddhism".

Because the Buddhist movement did not present demands for constitutional or administrative reform which constituted the two main points of interest in the incipient formal political activity of the day—Governors like Sir William Gregory (1872-77) and Sir Arthur Gordon (1883-90) were inclined to regard it with sympathy and sought an accommodation with it. Whatever the motive behind this attitude there was no mistaking the advantage to the Buddhist movement. A breakthrough came first over establishing the crucial principle of the state's neutrality in religion. It came with studied deliberation, and moved from one precedent to another. Gordon went beyond this principle to accept that the state had a special obligation towards Buddhism, a judicious patronage of Buddhism which could easily be transformed into a special responsibility towards that religion. With this acceptance the Buddhist breakthrough was consolidated (de Silva 1981).

The state's neutrality in religious affairs was asserted so often in the mid-1850s and thereafter was demonstrated in a manner at once open and vigorous by the disestablishment of the Anglican Church in 1881. With that the separation of church and state was very nearly complete.

Gordon, reviving an initiative attempted by Gregory, broke through the barriers of bureaucratic inertia and missionary opposition to give the Buddhists some satisfaction over this long-standing grievance. This he did in 1888 through proposing an ordinance of considerable complexity. There was opposition to this bill both within and outside the Legislative Council, but order steered it through to Colonial Office approval in 1889, though not without some concessions to his critics. The ordinance of 1889 was important because of its principles rather than for its impact on the problems it was devised to remedy. It proved to be too complicated and cumbersome, and it did not eliminate or even significantly reduce corruption and peculation among the trustees of these temporalities. The Buddhist movement regarded this state of affairs as an intolerable scandal, a blot on the reputation of Buddhism, and continued to agitate for stronger measures to eradicate it. In response to this pressure and in recognition of the validity of the charges leveled by Buddhist activists the colonial government in the early years of the twentieth century decided on fresh legislation to prevent, more effectively than in the past, misappropriation of trust property.

By this time, the Buddhist movement was pitching its demands higher. It anted the state to assume direct responsibility for the administration of Buddhist temporalities and urged that there be, more positively, a formal link between the state and Buddhism. There were also more vigorous expressions of growing impatience with the Roman Catholic presence in places regarded as historic sites of Buddhism whether on the coast, or more passionately at Anuradhapura which—along with Polonnaruwa, the other ruined capital of ancient Sri Lanka—was now a prominent place of Buddhist pilgrimage. There was dissatisfaction over the establishment of government buildings in such locations. This bitterness triggered the Anuradhapura runs of 1903. The leader of the agitation at Anuradhapura was Harischandra Walisingha, an associate of Anagarika Dharmapala and a man who shared his views on the restoration of Buddhism to a place of primacy in the Sri Lankan polity.

The frequency of Buddhist-Roman Catholic clashes—in which the Buddhists became die more aggressive party—diminished in the early years of the twentieth century. But religious conflicts arising from attempts to restrict Buddhist processions continued to cause trouble, not so much from the Roman Catholics as from the Muslims.

Attempts to reassert the traditional rights of Buddhists in this regard precipitated the Sinhalese-Muslim riots of 1915.

By the turn of the century the Buddhist movement had gained great self-confidence, Its leaders turned their attention to what was regarded as one of the great social evils of the day, and one associated with the processes of westernisation: intemperance. They confronted several contradictions. For one thing the manufacture and distribution of liquor — largely arrack — were controlled by Sinhalese capitalists, many if not most of whom were *karava* Christians (Roberts 1982). Secondly, there were also Buddhists of the same and other castes who had large investments in the liquor industry. Thirdly, to the British government, excise duties were a legitimate source of state revenue. While there was an increasing awareness of the evils attendant on excessive alcohol consumption, there was too a reluctance to endanger a valuable source of revenue by the wholehearted pursuit of temperance objectives. The Buddhist movement had no such inhibitions. By the turn of the century temperance activity was a vitally important facet of the religious revival. Some or the money that went into the support of temperance agitation came from wealth amassed in the liquor trade, conscience-money from Buddhists who thus repudiated a lucrative source of income. There were many prominent Buddhists in this category and it was often the case that they had inherited fortunes wholly or partly based the arrack trade.

By the first decade of the twentieth century, the Buddhist temperance agitation had spread tar and wide, especially in the Sinhalese areas of the Western and Southern Provinces. The response evoked was such that there were hopes that it would develop into a political movement. On occasion, temperance agitators indulged in criticism of the government by associating it with the evils of intemperance. Diatribes against foreign vices and Christian values were cleverly scaled down into more restrained and subtle criticisms of a "Christian" government. Although the temperance agitation gave added momentum to the Buddhist movement, it afforded only a tentative and astutely restrained introduction to formal political activity. The politicization of the movement seemed the logical and inevitable next step, but this was never taken. Equally significant, the mass grassroots support which the temperance agitation achieved came without the assistance or involvement of such political organizations as existed.

The colonial authorities in the island cither ignored these political organizations or treated them with studied contempt, although many British administrators in Sri Lanka were perturbed by temperance agitation. Recognizing that the Buddhist revival in its newest manifestation through temperance agitation could, potentially, disturb the hitherto placid political life of the island, they viewed the proliferation of temperance societies with the utmost suspicion. In this mood of deep suspicion and fearing the worst they reacted to the Sinhalese-Muslim riots of 1915 with an unwarranted ferocity. They mistook these riots as the precursor of a more formidable political movement of opposition to the British.

Despite its persistently vehement anti-Christian tone, one of the most interesting features of the Buddhist revival of the late nineteenth and early twentieth centuries was the extent to which its organizational apparatus came to be modeled on that of the Protestant missionary societies. The Buddhist movement had absorbed Victorian Protestant ethical ideas, the missionaries' rules of sexual morality as regards the conduct they prescribed for the laity, their ideas on monogamous marriage and on divorce. These were woven into the framework of ethics which came to constitute part of the popular Buddhist culture.

As regards Dharmapala himself, despite a pronounced antipathy to the Christian missions, his early education in the mission schools appears to have left its mark on him. His techniques of propaganda were modeled, consciously or unconsciously, on those used by the missionaries against the Buddhists, to the point where one might claim without much exaggeration that the new Buddhist revivalist was old missionary writ large. He was an unabashed advocate of a Sinhalese Buddhist domination of the island, and his propaganda bore a remarkable similarity to that of the great champion of Hindu resurgence in western India, Bal Gangadhar Tilak. Dharmapala lacked the political acumen and organizational skills of Tilak, and as a result his political program remained inchoate. His religious campaigns had a more compelling attraction for the rank and file of the Buddhist movement, though these too might have left a more indelible mark, had they not been the irregular forays which, in retrospect, they appeared to be. Nevertheless, his religious programs were never without political overtones.

One point needs special emphasis. Dharmapala grasped, as few of his contemporaries in Sri Lanka did, the significance of the emerging force of the reawakening of national consciousness in Asia. In his career as a Buddhist activist he never lost sight of the need to set the Buddhist revival in Sri Lanka within this wider framework. That he did not altogether succeed in the attempt is less important than the fact that the effort was regularly made. Part of this re-awakening process involved, almost inevitably, the downgrading of Christian missions in order to demonstrate that their work was not so much

> *The sharing of an inestimable treasure, but an unwarranted imposition from without, inseparably associated with the programme of the Colonial powers.*

The Interwar Years: The Buddhist Movement and the Search for the Center

Buddhist activists of the interwar years either could not or chose not to direct the groundswell of religious enthusiasm generated through the temperance movement into an overtly political programme. After the riots of 1915, Dharmapala's brand of Buddhist militancy receded to the background for over two decades. The reasons lie in the field of politics rather than in any decline of interest in Buddhism. Indeed in this same period a firmer institutional structure and a more complex organizational network was devised for the Buddhist movement.

The Buddhist Theosophical Society (BTS), which played a decisive role in the Buddhist revival of the last quarter of the nineteenth century, provided the nucleus of the Buddhist movement. Its main emphasis was on the organization and administration of Buddhist schools so new organizational machinery was required for social work and consciousness-raising. The model chosen for emulation was the Young Men's Christian Associations (YMCAs). As in contemporary Burma, Young Men's Buddhist Associations (YMBAs) were established, the first YMBA having been established in 1898. The YMBA units in the island were brought together in 1918 to form the All Ceylon Congress of Buddhist Associations which in 1940 changed its name to the All-Ceylon Buddhist Congress. By this time it was the most prominent, as well as the most articulate, of Buddhist pressure groups.

With the exponents of Buddhist "radicalism" unable to make much headway either as lay leaders or more directly in the political sphere, the leadership went by default to more conservative men. These reflected a new mood of caution and restraint. A crucial feature of this period was that the principal Sinhalese political leaders were also lay leaders of the Buddhist movement. F.R. Senanayake (1882-1925) and D.B. Jayatilaka (1868-1944), the two most prominent of these leaders, kept as tight a rein on their religious institutions as on the newly established Ceylon National Congress. They set the tone in Buddhist activism from about 1918 when, together with C.A. Hewavitharana, a brother of the Anagarika Dharmapala, they helped form the All-Ceylon Congress of Buddhist Associations. F.R. Senanayake was dominant till his untimely death in the last week of December 1925. Thereafter Jayatilaka assumed that role until his own retirement in 1943. As a result of this change in both national mood and leadership of the Buddhist movement, the Christian minority and the Christian missions found themselves under less pressure for a reduction of their privileges and a diminution of their customary prominence in Sri Lanka's public life. Yet they themselves were more indecisive than they had been in the past. This noticeable lack of self-confidence ended their expansionist phase. Instead they adopted a policy of contraction and occasional retrenchment of their activities. In retrospect the interwar period was the most decisive phase in the reconciliation of the Christian minority — or at least its influential Protestant sects — to a diminished role in public affairs, if nor yet to a ready acceptance of Buddhist dominance in the Sri Lanka policy (de Silva 1986:63-83).

The Christian missions could no longer afford to dissipate their energies in sectarian disputes. Most of them recognized the need to close ranks in the face of a resurgent, if temporarily quiescent, Buddhism. The coordination of activity which characterized the Christian missions in this period did not, in general, encompass the Roman Catholics. The latter stood aloof from other Christian groups and resisted every attempt to promote Buddhist interests at the expense of the Christians. They became the strongest defenders of the *status quo*, especially in education, which brought them into regular conflict with the Buddhist movement.

The interwar years, especially after 1931, saw a rapid transformation in the country's constitutional status. Three successive increases in the size of the national legislature occurred in 1920, 1923-24, and, most significantly, in 1931 when universal suffrage was introduced for the first time in a British crown colony. Politicians of the first (1931-1935) and second (1936-1947) State Councils, unlike their predecessors of the reformed Legislative Council of the 1920s became subject to the pressures of a democratic electorate. Buddhist pressure groups could now work through the electoral process to influence the election of supporters to the national legislature and this they proceeded to do. No Buddhist had been elected to the Legislative Council in the 1921 general election (when the electorate was around four percent of the population; all elected representatives of the Sinhalese were Christian. In the elections of 1924 the cry of "Buddhism in danger" was raised in a number of constituencies in which Buddhist candidates faced Christian opponents. It had the desired effect of ensuring the election of a large number of Buddhists. The situation changed dramatically with the introduction of universal suffrage. At the general election of 1931, the first under universal suffrage, 38 Sinhalese were returned to the national legislature of 50 elected members. Of these, 28 were Buddhists or claimed to be, since it was now politically advantageous to be a Buddhist. Thus the Buddhists had a clear majority in the legislature for the first time.

Sinhalese Buddhists were awakening to a new political awareness. The very nature of democratic "parliamentary" politics produced political groups which sought to build a political programme emphasizing the traditional cultural and religious patterns associated with Buddhism. The most notable of these groups was S.W.R.D. Bandaranaike's Sinhala Maha Sabha. There are few doubts now about the viability of religio-cultural nationalism as a major political force or more importantly of its appeal to a democratic electorate. But in the 1930s its potentially divisive effect on a plural society such as Sri Lanka deterred the moderate leadership in the Board of Ministers—the duumvirate of D.B. Jayatilaka and D.S. Senanayake—from enthusiastically supporting such a programme.

The Sinhala Maha Sabha had no such restraints. They urged a Sri Lankan polity essentially Buddhist and Sinhalese in orientation. In the late 1930s it took issue with the premier political organization of the nationalist elite, the Ceylon National Congress, on the latter's concept of a "Ceylonese" national entity wherein ethnic and religious minorities retained their distinctive identities while conceding to the Sinhalese Buddhist majority a primacy in the Sri Lankan polity.

The duumvirate drew a distinction between a government in which the Buddhists were a predominant influence and a Buddhist government. The former they preferred and were indeed committed to it because, quite unlike the latter, it was compatible with the requirements of their negotiations on the transfer of power as well as their personal inclinations. The latter they strongly opposed because of its political implications. In doing so they successfully postponed what now appears to have been an inevitable confrontation between the more militant sections of the Buddhist movement and those who were committed to the maintenance of a secular state, to a careful demarcation of the boundaries between state power and religion, and to a scrupulous observance of those boundaries. The moderating influence of D. B. Jayatilaka, the most prominent Buddhist leader of this period, is most significant in this regard because of his dual role as elder statesman in both political and religious affairs. D. S. Senanayake lacked his scholarship and was seen—and preferred to be seen—as a political leader rather than as a lay leader of the Buddhists. But his commitment to die principle of Sri Lanka as a secular state was even firmer than Jayatilaka's.

What the moderate leadership in the national legislature sought to do, and did successfully for a while, was to embark on a policy of redressing Buddhist grievances on a piecemeal basis through *ad hoc* measures. They sought a central position between the diehard defenders of the status quo (who could rely on the support of the British administrators) and the proponents of a speedy implementation of a comprehensive program of change. Significantly the issue of Buddhist temporalities was settled very early. Ordinance 19 of 1931 conceded the demand which Buddhist opinion had made for several decades for state intervention in and supervision of the management of the properties of Buddhist institutions by trustees both lay and "clerical." Then again there was the ordinance approved by the State Council in 1942 for the preservation of the sacred city of Anuradhapura. It was based on sober necessity but it was also the culmination of a half century's pressure and agitation to protect the holy places of Buddhism from any further encroachment by state institutions, by public and commercial establishments, and by places of worship belonging to persons of other faiths, especially the Christians.

These, however, were relatively simple, straightforward issues which did not need complex legislation nor lengthy negotiations with parties likely to be adversely affected by the change. There were, in fact, no such parties. It was easier, therefore, to give Buddhist activists satisfaction over these long-standing grievances of theirs than it was to be over education policy. The educational issues involved were both complex and complicated by conflicting interests. There was also another significant difference: on education policy powerful vested interests put up a dogged defence of the *status quo*. The most striking feature of the schools system was precisely the one to which the Buddhists took strongest objection, namely the dominance of the Christian schools. That dominance was no longer as overwhelming as it had been in the last quarter of the nineteenth century, but the schools system had long been feared as a means of religious conversion.

These fears persisted and tended to divert attention away from the more constructive achievements of the missionaries in education. If the mission schools were seldom designed for purposes unrelated to evangelization, their students nevertheless did find new vistas of secular knowledge and their intellectual horizons were widened, quite often well beyond the scope intended for them by those who organised their education.

If the Buddhists opposed the existing schools system because of its dominance by the Christian minority, others opposed it for quite different reasons. To these latter the most objectionable feature of the educational system was its elitism. These emerging radical forces, joined after the mid-1930s by Marxist groups, combined with the Buddhist movement in seeking a reconstruction of the education system. They sought to make its benefits more accessible to all and to bring it under greater state supervision. The Buddhists, of course, were not as committed as were the radicals and Marxists, to a secularization of education, but this issue did not divide them from the forces of radicalism in their common struggle against the defenders of the *status quo* in education.

This alliance between Buddhists and radicals was an uneasy one, but it was strengthened by the emergence of a new force in Sri Lankan Buddhism. The political *bhikkhus* (Buddhist monks) began to play a conspicuous and very effective role in this struggle against Christian dominance over education. This phenomenon of politicized *bhikkhus* appeared for the first time in Sri Lanka in the 1930s nearly twenty years after its appearance in Burma and thirty years before its appearance in Thailand. The theme of political *bhikkhus* and their impact on Sri Lanka's politics will be discussed later, but their intervention during the struggle over education reform helped to clarify some issues, such as the need for expanding educational opportunities, but caused confusion over others, such as the emerging link between radicalism and secularism. It also raised new issues such as the form and nature of the connection between state and religion in a multi-ethnic society. For all their radicalism these political *bhikkhus* were just as insistent as the traditional *bhikkhus* on the elevation of Buddhism to the status of the most visible symbol of Sri Lankan nationalism.

The debate over educational policy during the interwar years has been reviewed in several recent books. Three particular features arc germane to the issue of religion and politics. First-, the most far-reaching and controversial change was the proposal for a system of "free" (i.e., "free" of tuition fees) education at all levels: primary, secondary, and tertiary. Had "free" education been confined to the state schools there would have been little opposition from the denominational interests. But the state was anxious to extend the benefits of the new scheme to students in denominational schools. For this purpose the system of financial assistance provided to the latter schools by the state—its grants-in-aid—was to be revised. The state would continue to afford a maintenance grant and pay the salaries of teachers in the denominational schools, provided that they made "free" tuition available to their pupils. The Christian missions regarded these new financial arrangements as a potent threat to their interests. Only the elite mission schools could survive without grants-in-aid from the state. Absorption into the new scheme of "free" education posed the dangers of increased state interference and bureaucratic control.

Second, the determination of the Minister of Education, C.W.W. Kannangara, to carry through this policy of far-reaching reforms was resisted not merely by the Christians and the "denominational" interests, but also by influential colleagues in the Board of Ministers itself, the most notable of whom was D.S. Senanayake. The peculiar constitutional structure introduced in 1931 gave individual Ministers (or for that matter backbench legislators) much greater influence over the determination of policy and the introduction of legislation than under a cabinet system. Therefore Senanayake could warn his colleagues in the national legislature about the financial implications of these reforms and about the danger of precipitate changes damaging the existing education system rather than improving it. He also pointed out the potential damage to the whole fabric of relations among the country's various ethnic and religious groups. But he could not prevent the adoption of this legislation. Indeed while he opposed it in many ways, he did not vote against it. However, he softened its impact on the existing system by setting a time table for implementation of the reforms which was considerably longer than the advocates of these reforms had wanted. As a result, education remained an area of controversy.

Third, the opposition to the "free" education scheme came mainly from the Roman Catholics. It is ironic that the bitterness of the Buddhists against the injuries and neglect suffered at the hands of Christians during the period of western rule should be directed against the Roman Catholics rather than against the Protestants who, for the preceding two centuries, had enjoyed special favors from the imperial powers. That bitterness remained a factor in Sri Lankan politics until the early 1970s.

Political *Bhikkhus* and Politicized Buddhism

Had the Sri Lankan political establishment been aware of developments in contemporary Burma they would have been better prepared to understand and cope with the phenomenon of political *bhikkhus* when it first appeared in Sri Lanka. But they were not. To be fair, not many in the Buddhist movement itself knew much about tlie links between nationalism and Buddhism in Burma where, to a greater extent than in Sri Lanka, the defence of Buddhism became a powerful form of nationalist expression. Among the leaders of Burmese Buddhism were nationalist *bhikkhus*, the earliest and most famous of whom was U. Ottama

> *who provided modernistic elitist aspirations for independence with roots in traditional folk Buddhism.*

Inspired by Gandhi and his non-violent movement for India's independence, Ottama had returned from India in 1921 and sought to introduce these ideas to Burma. He was soon arrested by the British for his advocacy of independence for Burma and spent several years in jail for his nationalist agitation. Another political monk was U. Wisara who died in a Rangoon jail in 1929 after a hunger strike. Burmese Buddhist monks were involved in and indeed led the anti-Indian strikes of the 1930s. Saya San, an ex-monk and nationalist leader who led a revolt against the British, failed in this enterprise, and paid for his failure with his life.

Burma, as Sarkisyanz point out was thus the

> *only Tiieravada Buddhist country to reach independence through a revolutionary mass movement during an acute crisis of traditional culture. Among her striking acculturation phenomena is Buddhist-Marxist syncretism.*

The so-called "*political bhikkhus*" first appeared on the Sri Lankan scene in the late 1930s when a group of young radicalized *bhikkus* from the Vidyalankara *pirivena* (educational institute attached to a temple) in Kelaniya near Colombo led an attack on Christian privileges in the educational system. They enthusiastically supported the reforms initiated by C. W. W. Kannangara. Such support also provided an opportunity to discredit the opponents of these educational reforms within the Board of Ministers and the national legislature, the most prominent of whom was D. S. Senanayake himself.

One of the radical *bhikkhus*' main contributions to this campaign was their consistent effort to enlarge the area of battle. They sought to displace the Sri Lanka political elite itself and not merely the Christian religious elite. While the lay leaders of the Buddhist movement were not inclined to reject their support in this latter battle, they were quite often greatly embarrassed at the attempt to widen the range of the conflict to include the Sri Lankan political elite, the emerging establishment led by D. S. Senanayake. Most of the leaders of the Vidyalankara pressure group had studied in India, often in Bengal, when they had been drawn into the political struggles of the subcontinent. Many had gone to India at the invitation of the Anagarika Dharmapala in order to aid his ultimately futile campaign to win a secure position for Buddhism in India. Thus these political *bhikkhus* were products of: Dharmapala, the Buddhist nationalist *par excellence*.

Of the *bhikkhus* who went to India in the 1930s and 1940s five are of very substantial importance. They are: Udakandawaia Sarauankara (1902-1966), Naravila Dhammaratana (1900-1973), Hedipannala Pannaloka (1903-1953), Walpola Rahula (1907-), and Bambaranda Siri Sivali (1908-1985). All of them were associated with the Vidyalankara *pirivena*, and all of them imbibed in Bengal the current orthodoxies of Indian nationalism as well as Marxism. On their return they turned to political activity with the newly established Marxist party, the Lanka Sama Samaja Party, and other radical forces. All of them became prolific pamphleteers intent on introducing to a Sinhalese readership the radical and Marxist notions then current in India. Three of them became committed Marxists who saw no contradiction between their calling as *bhikkhus* and the advocacy of Marxist solutions to the country's problems: Udakandawcla Saranankara, a founder-member of the Ceylon Communist Party; Naravila Dhammaratana; and, Hedipannala Pannaloka who became Vice-Principal of Vidyalankara in 1945.

The Vidyalankara *bhikkhus* won their political spurs in the notable success they achieved in their first real political struggle: the campaign to have the education proposals of the 1940s accepted by the State Council, the national legislature, in 1943-47. From its outset their campaign provoked considerable opposition from the more orthodox Buddhists, lay and clerical, even from those who otherwise welcomed their support in the struggle to reform the education system.

At issue was the role of the *bhikkhu*. Was he to renounce the world or seek to reform it? There was no doubt where the sympathies of the Vidyalankara *bhikkhus* lay on this issue. They would reform the world, not renounce it. Among their most prominent critics was D.S. Senanayake himself and J.R. Jayewardene, the present President of Sri Lanka, who was then a backbench member of the State Council for Kalaniyaein which constituency the *pirivena* was located. They expressed deep concern at the political involvement of the *bhikkhus*, who breached what were regavded as age-old rules and practices governing the behavior of *bhikkhus*.

In response to mounting pressure from this quarter the *bhikkhus* compiled a statement clarifying their position. This document entitled "Bhikkhus and Politics" was approved unanimously by the teaching staff of their institution and released to the public on 13 February 1946. It was a defiant restatement of their position. The Vidyalankara declaration asserted that it was,

> *nothing but fitting fur the bhikkhus to identify themselves with activities conducive to the welfare of the people-whether these activities were labelled politics or not — as long as this activity did not impede the religious life of the bhikkhu.*

It went on to state,

> . . . *today bhikkhus by being engaged actively in education, rural reconstruction, anti-crime campaigns, relief work, temperance work, social work and such other activities are taking part in politics. Such activity they noted was approved of by the society at large. It was only when certain vested interests were threatened that the cry 'bhikkhu polities' was being raised.*

The declaration added that,

> *It is incumbent on the bhikkhu not only to further the efforts directed towards the welfare of the country, but also to oppose such measures detrimental to the common good. For example, if any effort is made to obstruct the system of free education, the great boon which has been recently conferred on our people, it is the paramount duty of the bhikkhu not only to oppose all such efforts but also to endeavour to make it a permanent blessing.*

They took their campaign to the country by launching a news paper which first appeared on 14 March 1946 and came out thereafter at irregular intervals. They published books and pamphlets on a variety of themes congenial to their cause, both to propagate their views as well as to raise funds for their campaigns. The most significant publication to emerge from Vidyalankara at this juncture was a polemical work by Walpola Rahula written to demonstrate that the *bhikkhus* had always played an active role in the educational, cultural, social, and political life of the community. In support of this theme Rahula selected material from Buddhist scriptures and from the long history of Buddhism in Sri Lanka and India. The point was made that the bhikkhu's role had never been a narrowly defined personal quest for salvation, but rather a life of service to the community. That service assumed a variety of forms, including political, when circumstances warranted it. The modern *Bhikkhu* who is aware of that heritage and aware too of the contemporary decline in national and religious affairs would regard it as his duty to arrest that decline. It was a powerful restatement in the Sri Lankan context of arguments that Burmese counterparts of Rahula had popularized in Burma. Significantly Rahula's book written in Sinhalese bore the title *Blriksuvage Urumaya* for the *Heritage of the Bhikkhu*. This latter was its title when it appeared nearly thirty years later in an expanded English version which time Rahula enjoyed an international reputation as a Buddhist scholar and as the author of an excellent introductory work on Buddhism.

What impact did the political bhikkhus of Vidyalankara have on the rapidly changing political scene of Sri Lanka at the transfer of power? Following their triumphant intervention in the "Free Education Bill" campaign they launched a political movement in earnest. They followed the Marxist parties in their opposition to the policies on the transfer of power adopted by the Board of Ministers under the leadership of D. S. Senanayake and in particular the acceptance of the status of a Dominion within the British Common wealth for Sri Lanka. On 6 January 1947 at a meeting held in the Kelaniya temple a statement of policy which came to be called "The Kelaniya Declaration of Independence" was adopted. It affirmed that

> *We, the Sangha of Sri Lanka . . . do hereby declare and publish on behalf of the people that Sri Lanka claims its right to be a Free and Independent Sovereign State, that it has resolved to absolve itself from all allegiance to any other power. State or Crown, and that all political connection between it and any other state is hereby dissolved ....*

During the election campaign of 1947 the radical *bhikkhu* stalwarts such as Walpola Rahula, Kalalalle Ananda Sagara, and Kotahene Pannakitti were prominent speakers at the meetings organized by the Marxist parties against the newly formed United National Party (UNP)-the successor to the Ceylon National Congress-led by D. S. Senanayake. Two seats in which they were most active were Kelaniya and Mirigama. The UNP candidates in these two scats, J. R. jayewardene and D. S. Senanayke, had expressed very strong opposition to *bhikkhus* involving themselves in political activity. Both of them won their seats, the latter more easily than the former. The *bhikkhu* activists went on to claim that the substantial increase in Marxist representation in the new Parliament owed much to their own campaigns. In so doing they greatly exaggerated the importance of their role in the election campaign. Unlike their Burmese counterparts Sri Lanka's Marxist-oriented political *bhikkhus* were a minority group. For all their eloquence and political vitality they were neither the spearhead of a nationalist movement nor of Sri Lankan radicalism. In campaigns to change social policies their pressure had been more effective, but their coordination of activity with the more orthodox groups in the Buddhist movement provided the really decisive factor.

A prominent and influential *bhikkhu*, Yagirala Pannanda, argued in 1947 in the Vesak number of the *Sinhala Baudhaya*, the foremost Sinhalese-Buddhist journal of the day, that Buddhism must be protected against the destructive forces represented by the political *bhikkhus*. He said,

> *In the past so many attempts had been made by impious bhikkhus to destroy the sasana. Their attempts, however, came to nought. Even those bhikkhus never considered the Buddha as an equal. They never Stated that nirvana was unnecessary.*

He accused them of seeking the destruction of Buddhism in order "to foster the religion of Karl Marx."

The All Ceylon Buddhist Congress, the leading lay Buddhist organization in the country, expressed some concern about bhikkhu participation in politics. Yet its criticisms were more circumspect than someot the orthodox bhikkhus. Thus at the 26th Annual Session of the Congress its President, Professor G. P. Malalasekera, expressed Ins disapprobation with considerable restraint and hi measured tones,

> *Some bhikkhus today maintain that they have entered the political field in order to eradicate social inequalities. . . . Some among them even state that in effecting such a revolution even the abrogation of certain precepts of bhikkhus' discipline is permissible. . . but these bhikkhus must realize that when they received ordination they took a vow pledging to maintain those precepts.*

There was, unmistakably, a sting in this last sentence. Malalasekcra was by now the leading lay Buddhist leader. A highly regarded Buddhist scholar, and one of the leading campaigners for education reform, his exposition and defence of the orthodox attitude on the role of the *bhikkhu* in society could not be as easily brushed aside as were the effusions of less erudite defenders of orthodoxy.

All this dovetailed neatly into the campaign waged by the political establishment of the day against the Marxists and the radical political *bhikkhus*. It also enabled D. S. Scnanayake to divert attention away from the wider issue of a closer association of the new state with the Buddhist religion and the restoration of its traditional patronage along with the precedence and prestige that would accompany such patronage. He thwarted all efforts to abandon the concept of a secular state and the principle of the state's religious neutrality. He succeeded to the extent that in 1948, despite some Buddhist displeasure over the continued prestige and influence enjoyed by the Christians, there was little evidence of the religious turmoil and linguistic conflict which were to burst to the surface after 1956.

For nearly a decade after 1947 the issues which the Buddhist activists of the 1940s and the Vidyalankara *bhikkhus* had raised lay dormant, but not extinct. The confrontation between the advocates of a secular state and those who sought to underline the primacy of Buddhism and the Sinhalese in Sri Lanka-and sought also to redress the grievances of the Buddhists about the slights, injuries, harassment, justice denied, unfair treatment, and curtailment of historic privileges inflicted on them during three centuries of western rule—was renewed in the mid-1950s. For beneath the placid surface of the late 1940s and early 1950s religio-ethnic sentiments were gathering momentum and developing into a force too powerful for the existing social and political institutions to accommodate or absorb.

The radical and reformist zeal winch one saw among die Vidyalankara *bhikkhus* in the 1940s appeared to have lost some of its spirit in the years after independence. Some of the more active and articulate *bhikkhus* who led the campaigns" of the 1940s were now absorbed in other ventures including the tedium of administration and teaching in pirivenas and other religious establishments. Others had abandoned their robes. And yet others—most notably Walpola Rahula—had left the island.

The year 1951 is crucial in this regard. It saw the establishment, by S.W.R.D. Bandaranaike, of a new political party, the Sri Lanka Freedom Party (SLFP), which vowed to espouse the Sinhalese-Buddhist cause. Bandaranaike resigned his Cabinet position in the first post-independence government and crossed over to the opposition. The second event is less well known but just as significant. This was the publication in April that year of the resolutions adopted at the and annual sessions of the All Ceylon Buddhist Congress under the Presidency of Professor G.P. Malalasckera. The resolutions were published along with a memorandum, as a pamphlet entitled *Buddhism and the State* and addressed to I). S. Senanayake as Prime Minister of Sri Lanka.

The memorandum stressed the

> *. . . disappointment, almost resentment, growing among the Buddhists with regard to the present position of Buddhism in [Sri Lanka]. . . the present Government... is legally and morally bound to protect and maintain Buddhism and Buddhist Institutions. The Buddhists feel,*

however, that our present rulers have shown a marked reluctance to acknowledge this fact....

Although politicians were not

slow to exploit the unique position which [Sri Lankan] enjoys among the nations of the world, by reason of her proud heritage of Buddhism and Buddhist culture... [they] have shown no earnest desire to rescue Buddhism from the great state of neglect to which it has been deliberately reduced by foreign rulers of this country not to secute for the Buddhists the paramount position which should be theirs in the life of the nation.

This theme of restoring Buddhism to "the paramount position of prestige which rightfully belongs to it" was repeatedly emphasized in this document, and along with it the demand that the Buddhists "be given all-out assistance to rehabilitate themselves and to resuscitate their Institutions . . . ." The document asserted that "it is incumbent upon the present government of Free Lanka to protect and maintain Buddhism . . . . " and added that the "definite steps to be taken by Government to discharge this duty and obligation is a matter for decision after thorough investigation by a competent Commission."

The final paragraph of the memorandum made a specific request: that "measures be taken at once" to provide the Buddhist religion with an "autonomous constitution." "For this purpose," the memorandum went on

[the Buddhists] ask for the immediate enactment of an Act on lines similar to the Buddha Sasana Act 1312 B E (1950) of Burma, relevant extracts from which are given as an Appendix to this [document]. To secure the enactment and implementation of such an Act, they ask that a Buddha Sasana Department he forthwith established under a suitable Ministry by the Government of [Sri Lanka].

These demands were to be repeated with greater frequency but not with any greater clarity over the next few years. While the government in power tended to ignore them, they attracted wider and stronger support from the Buddhist public with each passing year.

In the first years after independence one of the major preoccupations of the government was the need to establish a sense of a Sri Lankan nationalism on territorial lines. D. S. Senanayake's government was intent on subordinating ethnic differences to the common goal of strengthening the foundations of nationhood through the establishment of a stable equilibrium of ethnic forces within Sri Lanka's polyethnic polity. He would give no satisfaction to the All Ceylon Buddhist Congress and, indeed, rejected its demands. He did not concede even the need for a Commission of Inquiry to report on the state of Buddhism. But politicized Buddhism was already a powerful force which would upset the equilibrium of forces he bad set up. When Bandaranaike moved out of the government he was essentially seeking to exploit this new force and to give the Sinhalese-Buddhist majority, long dormant, a political institution for the fulfillment of their aspirations. This was the role of the SLFP.

From the outset the new party offered a home to those who rejected the concepts of a polyethnic polity, of a Sri Lankan nationalism, and of a secular state. It welcomed to its ranks bhikkhu activists, and some of them held positions of influence in its executive committee. Among them were Mapitigama Buddharakkhita, the Vihamdhipathi (the chief *bhikkhu*) of the Kelaniya temple and an alumnus of the Vidyalankara *pirivena.* and *bhikkhu* Talpavila Silavnmsa, who had a solid base of support in the city of Colombo.

There were other centers of support for the SLFF among the *bhikkhu* activists. There was, for instance, the Sri Lanka Vidyalaya located in Maradana in the heart of the city of Colombo. Its head, *bhikkhu* Baddegaina Wimalawamsa, had great influence among and strong support from the Sinhalese traders and the people of the area. Wimalawamsa was one of the most effective activists for the Sinhalese Buddhist cause. As pamphleteer and propagandist there were few to equal him in the zeal with which he conducted his campaign against the Christian minority and its influence m public life, especially education. Equally important was the support he received from Buddhist activists in government departments who saw the Buddhist movement as a means of reducing if not undermining the continuing dominance of religious and ethnic minorities in the bureaucracy. Among his strongest supporters were *bhikkhu* Henpitagedera Piyananda, his vice-principal at the Sri Lanka Vidyalaya, and *bhikkhu* Davamottave Amarawamsa soon to earn a reputation for his platform oratory and highly emotive speeches.

Their political ideology was at best a vague populism, mixed with a deep and abiding nationalist fervor. They were themselves avowedly political *bhikkhus*, but their activity was less vulnerable to the criticisms directed at the Marxist *bhikkhus* because it was rooted securely within the conventional tradition of twentieth century Buddhist activity in Sri Lanka. They worked in tandem with the lay Buddhist leadership. They also cooperated with the Vidyalankara *bhikkhus*.

The mid-1950s marked a critically important watershed in the recent history of the island. Against the background of the 1956. Buddha Jayanthi, the worldwide celebration of the 2500th anniversary of the death of the Buddha, an intense religious fervor became the catalyst of a populist nationalism whose explosive effect was derived from its interconnection with language. Language became the basis of nationalism, and this metaifiorphosis of nationalism affected both the Sinhalese and Tamil populations. Buddhism and Sinhala were so closely intertwined that it was impossible to treat either in isolation.

The crucial significance of the renewed link between language and religion was that Buddhist activism, which had been directed so far against the privileged position enjoyed by Christianity and Christians in Sri Lanka, shifted its attention to the Tamil minority as well. Buddhist activists and the Sinhalese-educated intelligentsia had seldom, in the recent past, exerted influence on a national scale. They felt that they had been unjustly excluded by the English-educated elite from a share of power commensurate with their numbers, and that rewarding careers were closed to them by the pervasive dominance of English as the language of administration. Concentrating their attention on the superior educational advantages enjoyed by the Tamil minority, they set their sights on the demolition of the language settlement arrived at in 1945-44 wherein both Sinhalese and Tamil should eventually replace English as the national languages. They insisted instead on its replacement by Sinhalese alone, or "Sinhala only." the slogan which became the main plank of the coalition of parties set up by Bandaranaike in anticipation of the general election of 1956. "Sinhala only" campaign brought together a formidable array of forces which had hitherto been unable to unite in support of a common programme: the Sinhalese school teachers, Ayurvedic physicians (practitioners of traditional herbal medicine), Sinhalese writers, and above all the bhikkhus.

The *Buddha Jayanthi* offered Buddhist activists the opportunity to appeal over the heads of the government and the political establishment of the day directly to the people for a restoration of the traditional convergence of nation, religion, and ethnicity—Sri Lanka, Buddhist, and Sinhalese. However, the government and its critics were both confronted with the political implications of a situation in which the advantages of this convergence in sustaining a national identity and self-confidence were negated by the vocal dissent of minority groups who rejected this facile identification of sectional--albeit majoritarian—with national interests.

The crux of the problem was that while the political system had accommodated itself since 1931 to the fact of Buddhist-Sinhalese predominance, other areas of public life lagged far behind in adjusting to that demographic reality. In the mid-1950s a concern for the enhancement of the status of Buddhism became, in the millenarian atmosphere of the *Buddha Jayanthi*, the prime determinant of a process of change whose main thrust was the extension of the predominance established by Sinhalese Buddhists in the political sphere into all other areas of activity.

The religious confrontation that erupted was between the Buddhists and the Christian minority, in particular the Roman Catholics. Because of linkage between the linguistic nationalism of the Sinhalese and the religious resurgence associated with **Buddha Jayanthi**, it was inevitable that there would be intensified pressure for a closer association of the state with Buddhism and even for the declaration of Buddhism to be the state religion.

Buddhism and Buddhist interests had suffered and, in the perception of Buddhist activists, still suffered from the decline in status and prestige that had occurred under colonial rule. The drive by the Buddhist leadership—a coalition of laymen and *bhikkhus*—to restore their influence in national life commensurate with the historic position of Buddhism in the Sri Lankan polity gathered momentum in the mid-1950s. The position of Buddhism and Buddhists had improved quite substantially at independence and in the first decade after independence, but these advances only served to emphasize the narrowing gap between aspiration and achievement and give it an exaggerated salience.

Thus, despite the education reforms introduced in the 1940s, Christian schools still retained much of the prestige and influence they had enjoyed in the days of British rule. The preponderance of Christians and other minorities, especially in the higher bureaucracy, in the professions and in public life, remained intact although under increasing pressure. While the balance was shifting in favor of the Sinhalese Buddhists, this process was inevitably slow and seemed to be in measured stages. As a result, Buddhist activists were not only thoroughly dissatisfied with the pace at which the balance was shifting, but they also attributed the survival of the privileged position of the Christian and other minorities to the existing rules of the political game. These were presumed to bear a heavy and unfair bias against the Sinhalese Buddhists.

> *There was .it this time a common belief in all Buddhist countries that this anniversary [would] initiate a great revival of Buddhism throughout the world when the Buddhist way of life and thus universal peace prevail.*

Buddhism was being hailed as a new political force. The Sn Lankan Buddhist leadership found, to their great disappointment, that U Nu's Burma had emerged as the pre-eminent Theravada Buddhist country. The Buddha Sasana Council and the Ministry of Religious Affairs established by U Nu in 1950 were regarded by the All Ceylon Buddhist Congress as appropriate models for Sri Lanka. In 1951 U Nu had decided on a more ambitious project which would emphasize the international aspects of the Buddhist revival: the decision to convene the Sixth Great Buddhist Council. Convened in 1954 and lasting for two years, the council established Rangoon as the center of international Buddhism by attracting Buddhists from all over the world as well as from the five main Theravada Buddhist nations: Burma, Thailand, Sri Lanka, Laos, and Cambodia. It completed its work in May 1956, by which time Buddhism appeared to have established itself as the new global political force U Nu had envisaged:

> *The significance of the Sixth Great Buddhist Council had many dimensions, national and international, religious and political, its implications for government, Sangha, and laity were profound. The council's greatest significance was symbolic; it dramatized in unforgettable fashion the government's commitment to the promotion of Buddhism, which was regarded as an essential component of the Burmese national identity.... The council, while it had special meaning for the Burmese, was also a demonstration of the solidarity of all Theravada Buddhists and, in a more limited way, of all Buddhists. In one sense it was an expression of resurgent Buddhist Asia in the post-colonial era, pointing to the spiritual bankruptcy of the Christian West in failing to achieve world peace and reasserting the validity, vitality, and relevance of the message of the Buddha...*

In Sri Lanka, S. W. R. D. Bandaranaike successfully channelled the religious discontent of the Buddhists into an election campaign which swept the UNP out of office in April 1956. His decisive victory was a significant turning point in Sri Lanka's history, for it represented the rejection of a Sri Lankan nationalism based on an acceptance of pluralism as an essential feature of the democratic system which D. S. Senanayake had striven to nurture. Instead the SLFP victory introduced a more populist nationalism which was at the same time fundamentally divisive in its impact on the country because it was unmistakably Sinhalese and Buddhist in content.

In this emphasis on the presumed unifying influence of the religion, culture, and language of the majority, there was a remarkable similarity in objective, methods, and even political styles between Sri Lanka under Bandaranaike (and later on under his wife and successor Sirimavo Bandaranaike) and Burma under U Nu. The latter desperately sought to use Burmese culture and the Buddhist religion to give the fragile post-colonial Burmese state a sense of national unity. On a long term basis this program was not unviable, but the time span required had to be measured in decades, not years. For example, Thailand had taken a century or more to work out a similar policy of national unification of Tai states and the hill peoples within a Thai-Buddhist polity. There these policies achieved remarkable success, although sonic resistance has come from Thailand's minute Malay-Muslim minority. In Burma the resistance to these policies was wider, stronger, and seemingly more effective in thwarting them.

A second point is equally significant: the essence of this programme in Burma and Thailand is an assimilationist policy. In Sri Lanka, on the other hand, none of the governments since independence has deliberately or consistently followed assimilationist policies. The attitude to the minorities has been embodied in a mixture of policies, sometimes emphasizing national integration, and sometimes recognizing the advantages of a pluralist approach. Above all, there has been no conscious attempt to assimilate the diverse minority groups in the country to the dominant Sinhalese-Buddhist culture.

The minorities, needless to say, did not see things in this light. While they did enjoy an advantageous, if no longer a privileged, position in public life, this was threatened by the pervasive influence of a politicized Buddhism. For the achievement-oriented Tamil minority, the implications of the change in language policy forced upon them in 1956 seemed starkly clear. The Tamils were disproportionately represented in public sector employment as clerks, teachers, and technicians, and in the professional services as doctors and engineers as well. Their advantageous position in government employment had been a point of contention and division in politics since the 1930s. Tamils saw the change in language policy as heralding the beginnings of hard times ahead in the competition for such employment. The rules of the game had been changed to their disadvantage. More importantly, once language became the determinant of ethnic identity, as it did with the transformation of nationalism to a linguistic form, there were fears that the new dominance conferred on the Sinhalese language would lead to an erosion of the Tamils' ethnic identity through a policy of assimilation. While these fears were exaggerated, when not imaginary, the fact remains that the Tamils were extremely vulnerable and exceptionally sensitive to changes in language policy.

The language conflict in Sri Lanka was generated by the campaign to elevate Sinhalese to the status of the national language. The "Sinhala only" campaign brought together a formidable array of forces which had hitherto been unable to unite in support of a common programme: the Sinhalese school teachers, *ayurvedic* physicians, Sinhalese writers, and the *bhikkhus*. On 4 September 1954, a meeting convened by the Sinhalese teachers' association, the Lanka Jatika Guru Sangamaya, brought these groups together in a federation of five associations (including representatives of peasants) which came to be called the Pancha Maha Bala Mandalaya. Significantly the chairmanship was offered to and taken by *bhikkhu* Kiriwattuduve Pragnasara, then principal of the Vidyalankara pirivena.

The Pancha Maha Bala Maudalaya was formed to intensify pressure on the government, but the full force of its fury first fell on the two Marxist parties, the Trotskyist Lanka Sania Samaja Party and the Communist Party. Both at that time were firm supporters of a policy of parity of status for Sinhalese and Tamil as national languages. These two parties had introduced a motion in Parliament calling for a declaration on these lines. To explain their stand to the public they organized two public meetings at the Colombo Town Hall, on 12 October 1955 by the Communist Party and on l6 October 1955 by the Lanka Sama Samaja Party. Both meetings were broken up by "Sinhala only" activists led by *bhikkhus*. In a bid to mobilize even wider support for the cause of Sinhalese as the sole national language, the Pancha Maha Bala Mandalaya organized an oath-taking ceremony at Anuradhapura on 29 October 1955. The symbolism of choosing Anuradhapura as a site for this ceremony was unmistakable. A motorcade that left from Colombo proved to be triumphal procession and the ceremony, presided over by *bhikkhu* Kiriwattuduve Prajnasara, attracted an enormous crowd.

The committee issued a pathbreaking report on 4 February 1956. It contained a detailed exposition of the disadvantageous position of Buddhism in the mid-twentieth century and blamed this on the cumulative effect of several centuries of foreign rule and on the neglect of post-independence governments of Sri Lanka. The demands it made on behalf of the Buddhists were an expansion of those which were presented for the consideration of D.S. Senanayake's government in 1951 through the previously mentioned memorandum entitled "Buddhism and the State." The report made it abundantly clear that the redress of Buddhist grievances was a matter of the utmost urgency and that this could only be achieved through the political process. The fact that the report was presented to the "People of Lanka" and not to the government signified that in the committee's view the solutions lay with the former. The English version of the report carried the title: *The Betrayal of Buddhism*.

How the two major parties, the UNP and the SLFP, both hurriedly changed their language policy to one endorsing "Sinhalese only" has been dealt with in detail in many monographs. The SLFP's change of policy came .it its annual conference held on the 17 December 1955 at Nittambuv.i in S. W. R. I). Bandaranaike's own electorate. The resolution calling for the change was moved by *bhikkhu* Mapitigama Budtlharakkita.

To fight the elections the SLFP had formed a coalition with a number of smaller political groups. This coalition, the Mahajana Eksath Peramuna (MEP) or the People's United Front, issued its election manifesto on 7 March 1956. It pledged to make Sinhalese the sole official language of the country, to accept the recommendations of the Buddhist Committee of Inquiry, to foster ayurveda, and to reorganize the system of education in accordance with national culture.

The MEP coalition scored a decisive victory but found the implementation of its policies a matter of the utmost difficulty. This was especially so with regard to language. The government sought to reconcile its commitment to make Sinhalese the sole national language with the political and indeed practical necessity to make some concession to the Tamils about use of their language. Extremists on both sides made this reconciliation almost impossible to achieve. Every concession to the Tamils was fought bitterly by forces within the SLFP, led by *Bhikhhus*, as well as by opponents of the government such as the UNI'. Thus the years 1956 to 1958 were years of turmoil and violence, of race riots, and of long periods of rule under emergency regulations as the armed services and police sought to restore law and order.

Much of the agitation against compromise on language policy and against concessions to the Tamils was organized and led by *bhikkhus*. The most notable of such instances occurred on 9 April 1958 when a group of *bhikkhus* led by *bhikkhu* Baddegama Wimalawamsa organized a sit-in on the lawn of the Prime Minister's private residence in Colombo. They compelled Bandaranaike to tear up an agreement he had reached on language policy and related nutters with S.J.V. Chielvanayakam, the leader of the principal Tamil political organization, the Federal party.

Two major concessions were made to the Buddhist activists at this time. First there was the creation of a Ministry of Cultural Affairs in 1956 with N. Q. Dias, a senior civil servant as its first Director. His background of militant Buddhist activism set the tone of this new administrative unit. Amid attempts to promote indigenous literature and the traditional arts and crafts its major concern was the promotion of Buddhist activities.

Second, there was the elevation of the two principal seats of Buddhist learning, Vidyodaya and Vidyalankara, to university status in 1958. This decision was *an ad hoc* one, in the nature of a quick, if not desperate, remedy for an impossible situation; it was a classic instance of how not to establish universities. The two new universities began as non-residential arts colleges teaching in Sinhalese. This format was devised to accommodate the large number of students taught in Sinhalese who found the doors of the University of Ceylon closed to them. More to the point, the government's original intention had been to confer university status only on the Vidyalankara *pirivena* in recognition and appreciation of its long record of service in the cause of establishing a socialist government. But the government yielded to pressure from the sister institution,

Vidyodaya, founded two years earlier (1873) than Vidyalankara, when it appealed for similar status.

By this time the triumph of linguistic nationalism had made pressure for stronger links between Buddhism and the state, and for a corresponding reduction if not eradication of Christian influence in the Sri Lankan polity, almost irresistible. There was pressure for the elevation of Buddhism to the status of the state religion. In 1951 the All Ceylon Buddhist Congress had gone on record as saying that:

> *A great deal of deliberate confusion has been caused by the cry that the Buddhists want their religion made the State Religion in Free Lanka. The Buddhists have made no such demand. But the Buddhists do want legislative enactments enabling them to manage. their own affairs efficiently, by means of an autonomous constitution with legal sanctions. This concession is made by them because they recognize the undesirability of the Government, as at present constituted, controlling the internal affairs of any religion.*

There were no such inhibitions in 1956-57 about the elevation of Buddhism to the status of the state religion. But the new government was entangled in the coils of the language crisis of 1956-58 and preferred to delay consideration of this controversial issue. The means adopted for this delay was the appointment of the Commission on Buddhist Affairs that the All Ceylon Buddhist Congress had asked for 1951. The publication of the report of the Committee of Inquiry appointed bv that Congress in 1955-56 and which report the government was pledged, through its election manifesto, to adopt and implement complicated the issue. Was not this new Commission superfluous?

When in February 1957, Bandaranaike proceeded to appoint the Buddha Sasana Commission, its terms of reference were seen to be much wider than that of its non-official predecessor of 1955-56. The term *sasana* itself was one of infinite flexibility, encompassing as it did the institutions, property, including monastic lands, and the rights, obligations, duties, and privileges of the *bhikkhus*. The term generally covered doctrine as well, but that seemed less relevant on this occasion. It had something to satisfy everybody. Advocates of institutional reform could regard it as a mandate for modernization; adherents of the *status quo* were encouraged to believe that there was no inherent incompatibility between their interests and those of the reformers.

The task before this Commission of *bhikkhus* and prominent Buddhist laymen was the unenviable one of reconciling these obviously conflicting interests. Looked at in historical perspective, it was an attempt by Buddhist activists to identify the issues and set out the solutions to the problems that emerged from the severance of the historic link between the state and the Buddhist religion which had occurred in 1840. British Governors of the colony and Sri Lankan politicians alike had come up against the impossibility of returning to the *status quo ante* 1840. For all of them the religious neutrality of the state was a major premise of their thinking; and for many of them—including men like Gregory and Gordon, D.B. Jayatilaka and D. S. Senanayake—the only adjustment possible to the reality of the burdens of past history and perceptions of national destiny seen as an unfolding of Buddhism's inextricable links with the state was a pragmatic recognition of a special status for Buddhism. To recognize this officially was worrisome enough in the context of those tunes; to spell out a policy of action based on this was as problematic in the years 1948-56 as it had been under British rule.

The terms of reference of the Buddha Sasana Commission included an examination of the implications of the general but vague principle of "according Buddhism its light ful place in the country," to which the government was publicly committal The commission was also asked to make recommendations for a reform of the *sangha*, one of the crucially important aspects of the ruler's, and the state's, traditional responsibility in regard to the maintenance and protection of Buddhism as the national religion, and one which had been in abeyance since the fall of the Kandyan kingdom in 1815.

Bandaranaike was all too aware of the legal and constitutional difficulties to be overcome if Buddhism were to be declared the state religion. Above all there was the formidable hurdle of section 29(2) (c) of the Soulbury constitution which laid down that no law enacted by Parliament shall: "... confer on persons of any community or religion any privilege or advantage which is not conferred on persons of other communities or religions." It was not at all certain that the legislature would provide the special majority required for the purpose of overcoming this constitutional obstacle.

There was a greater chance of success with regard to the quest for increasing state control over the schools, in brief, for a completion of the work begun in the 1940s. There was strong support for this reform from Marxists and other left-wing groups. But the Minister of

Education, W. Dahanayake, was adamantly opposed to a takeover of the schools run by the Christian missions and other religious organizations. And he had the support of the Prime Minister. It would appear that the government was not at all eager to get embroiled in another contentious issue while coping with the political fallout from the language crisis.

Meanwhile, the coalition of forces that had done so much to ensure the success of Bandaranaike's own political career was crumbling in the face of the turmoil that had characterized the last: two years (1958-59) of his administration. *Bhikkhu* activists were divided on a number of issues, and some of the most prominent among them—most notably the *viharadhipathi* of the Kelaniya temple, Mapitigama Buddharakkhita—had become controversial because of their involvement in the ugly factionalism within the Sri Lanka Freedom Party (SLFP), of which they were such visible members. Many of them were also prominent opponents of some of the key social and economic reforms initiated by the left-wing members of Bandaranaike's cabinet. Among the most noteworthy of these acts of opposition was the agitation against the *Paddy Lands Acts of 1958*. The *bhikkhu* opposition came principally from the two powerful and wealthy chapters of Malwatta and Asgiriya, the principal representatives of monastic landlordism.

The Buddhist public was now becoming increasingly soured by the spectacle of *bhikkhus* engaging in political infighting, and using pressure for financial gain—for kinsfolk if not for them selves-through influence-peddling and the manipulation of bids for contracts. Their disgust turned into deep consternation and shock when the Prime Minister was assassinated on 26 September 1959. The chief figure in the conspiracy to murder Bandaranaike was Mapitigama Buddliarakkhita, and the actual shooting was done by another *bhikkhu*, a close associate of the principal conspirator the assassination of Bandaranaike, with its powerful mix of political and sordid commercial motives, not to mention other even more distressing factors, underlined as nothing else did so sharply before or alter, the perils involved in *bhikkhus* engaging in partisan politics. Never again did *bhikkhus* wield the same influence in political affairs as they did in the years from 1943 to 1959.

The assassination of Bandaranaike provided reformist groups among Buddhist activists the opportunity they so desparately needed to initiate moves for far-reaching institutional reforms in the *sangha*.

But the political confusion that followed on his death prevented any such initiatives. There was nobody to provide the leadership in converting the upsurge of revulsion against the excesses of the political *bhikkhus* into a constructive program of reform of the sangha. In the meantime, political energies were devoted to coping with the shattering impact of Bandaranaike's death, and with the two general elections of March and July 1960.

The Triumph of Orthodoxy, 1960-1986

At the time of Mrs. Bandaranaike's accession to power, the process of elite displacement, Christian by Buddhist, had stopped well short of the objectives set by Buddhist activists in the mid-1950s. That considerable progress had been made towards the achievement of these objectives daring this period only rendered the survival of Christian privilege all the less palatable to them. The struggle for supremacy was now resumed. Her husband, despite his anxiety to restore to Buddhism the traditional patronage accorded to it in precolonial times, had not been able to do much in this sphere. Furthermore, he was unwilling to endorse the demand that Buddhism be raised to the status of the state religion. As the new leader of the SLFP, Sirimavo Bandaranaike pressed ahead in seeking to satisfy some of the demands of Buddhist activists. She was intent on continuing the language policy initiated by her husband, and on doing so with as few concessions to the Tamil minority as possible. She displayed greater rigidity on principles underlying this policy than he may have showed had be been alive. Even more important, although the times seemed hardly propitious to enlarge the area of conflict from language to religion and education as well, she embarked on this two-pronged attack on behalf of Sinhalese-Buddhist interests. At that stage, she was not interested in the complicated question of the status of Buddhism in the Sri Lankan polity. It was education reform and the completion of the changes initiated in the 1940s that absorbed her attention.

When the recommendations of the Buddha Sasana Commission were published late in 1959 they proved to be immediately controversial. Among their principal recommendations was the creation of an incorporated body with wide powers over the *sangha*, empowered to regulate entry into it, the education and residence of *bhikkhus*; it would also regulate their engagement in social and political activities, and in paid employment outside of their temples.

That body was also empowered to adjudicate disputes between *bhikkhus*, especially on matters relating to succession as heads of temples, issues on which *bhikkhus* generally sought legal remedies in the civil courts. Among the other areas of activity which would come under its purview were: the collection of funds for temples and Buddhist activity, the building of temples, and publications relating to Buddhism.

There was considerable irony in this opposition because historically the Siyam *nikaya* has had close links with secular authorities since its inception in the eighteenth century. It generally has sought centralized control over the order of *bhikkkus*—which was more or less what the Buddha Sasana Commission report recommended—while the other *mikayas* had emerged into autonomous existence partly because there was no central authority to regulate the affairs of the sangha in colonial times.

Despite the opposition from the more orthodox *bhikkhus*, the new government could well have embarked on an implementation of a programme of Buddhist institutional reform. Mrs. Bandaranaike's government had other priorities, and it turned to these. Thus, a historic opportunity was missed for lack of the political will to seize it and exploit its potential for a purification of the *sangha*. Had these recommendations of Buddhist institutional reform been implemented, Sri Lanka may well have today resembled Burma and Thailand as regards the status of Buddhism in relation to the state.

To move into educational reform was certain to engender conflict with the Roman Catholics in Sri Lanka. But Mrs. Bandaranaike calculated on support from the Marxist and other left-wing groups in Parliament and outside it which may not have shown the same enthusiasm for moves to make Buddhism the state religion. For them state control over education was a desirable end in itself. The Buddhists, however, saw it as nothing less than the restoration of a balance that had been tilted far too much in favour of Christians. Indeed, they looked upon the existing education system as the fountainhead of Christian privilege in Sri Lanka. The fact that the vast bulk of the mission schools were almost totally dependent on governmental finances, while in all but a handful of them the great majority of students were Buddhists, made it nearly impossible to meet the arguments of the advocates of state control.

Once again the Roman Catholics led the resistance and bore the brunt of the attack. Though all the religious groups—including the

Hindus and Muslims, not to mention the Buddhists themselves—were affected by the decision to bring the state-aided secondary schools directly under state control, the Roman Catholics were the biggest losers. Most of the state-aided denominational schools accepted the painful decision to be absorbed by the state. A few big schools, mostly Roman Catholic institutions in the urban areas, decided to retain their independence by becoming private institutions without the benefit of state aid. Deprived by law of the right to levy fees from their students, they maintained their precarious existence under very severe financial handicaps. The long drawn-out Buddhist agitation for state control over education had, at last, achieved its goal.

The constitution afforded no protection to the minorities against these changes in language and education policy, though they were adversely affected by both. The constitutional obstacle of Section 29(2)(b) would not operate as long as legislation was so framed that there might be a restriction in fact but not in legal form, and the restriction was made applicable to all sections of the community and not to a specific group. (When S. W. R. D. Bandaranaike's *Official Language Act*-the "Sinhala only" Act, as it came to be called—was introduced in the Mouse of Representatives in 1956, the Speaker ruled that it was not a constitutional amendment and therefore required only a simple majority.) Nevertheless, the proven ineffectiveness of Section 29(2)(b) as a check on encroachments on the interests of the minorities did not make that clause any more palatable to Buddhist activists. They continued to view it as an ostentatious concession to minority influence, and persisted in an agitation for its elimination. Indeed, one of the reasons given, in 1972, for the adoption of an autochthonous constitution rather than a revision of the Soulbury constitution was the need to eliminate this clause.

An abortive *coup d'etat* in 1962, in which the leaders were Roman Catholic and Protestant officers of the army, navy, and police, further strained relations between Roman Catholics and the governmental had the double effect of reviving the sagging popularity of the government and, more important, of providing justification for the government to support Buddhist activists in their campaigns against the Roman Catholics and their influence in public life—in the bureaucracy, in the armed services and police, and the national press.

In the course of Mrs. Bandaranaike's first (1960-64) term of office, the primacy of Buddhism and Buddhists in Sri Lanka's political system and public life had become a reality. Significantly, this achievement was won by the lay Buddhist leadership within the government and governing party, and outside it, and not by the *bhikkhus* whose contribution was by now very limited. This is not surprising considering that the sangha in general had suffered a grievous loss of prestige after the assassination of S.W.P.D. Bandaranaike and had not sufficiently recovered to return to their pre-1959 level of political activism and influence. The absence of *bhikkhus* on political platforms in the election campaigns of March and July 1960 was notable. With the abortive *coup d'etat* of 1962, *bhikkhu* involvement in politics resumed, but the scale of this involvement was limited and its nature was different in that the *bhikkhus* were no longer almost entirely on the side of the SLFP and its allies. The *bhikkhus* themselves were sharply divided with some of the most prominent political *bhikkhus* of the mid-1950s having switched their political loyalties to the UNP.

The issues in dispute in this realignment of political forces demonstrate the ambiguities inherent in the uneasy and shifting relationship between Buddhist activists and the new government. In the response to the recommendations of the Buddha Sasana Commission there were contradictory impulses between the lay and *bhikkhu* leadership of Buddhist revivalism. On the whole the lay leaders responded more positively to these proposals but, bereft of a strong political leadership committed to their implementation, they lacked the nerve to campaign for them in the face of almost unanimous opposition from the *bhikkhus*. As Kemper points out

> *Even the prospect of making Buddhism once again the state religion in the cases of Sri Lanka and Burma has met with unlikely opposition.*

He quotes Tambiah's well-known work on Thai Buddhism (Tambiah 1976:527) which observes that

> *The allied problem faced by Sri Lanka and Burma is that restoration of religion by the state implies also the attempted regulation of the sangha by the state, a proposition that is antithetical to those monastic interests that have come to cherish the decentralized autonomy resulting from [the] British disestablishment of religion.*

Opposition to these recommendations was by no means limited to the *bhikkhus* of the Siyam *nikaya*. The main recommendations of the report were those that concerned them, and there was no attempt to consider implementation of these important ones. But an attempt was made to introduce some minor changes which would have affected the *bhikkhus* opportunities of employment and conditions of service in the state sector. These provoked so hostile a response from *bhikkhus* readily identified as political *bhikkhus* that they were immediately withdrawn, thus demonstrating that the political *bhikkhus* had not entirely lost their influence in secular affairs. Some of the more vocal were permanently alienated from the SLFP as a political party.

As for governments and political leaders within governments and the major national parties alike, the interaction with Buddhist activists, both lay and *bhikkhu*, called for great delicacy in practice because all parties were subject to conflicting pressures. Thus, the SLFP's coalition with the Trotskyist LSSP negotiated in 1964 provoked determined opposition from many of the political *bhikkhus*. Some of the latter were quite prepared to tolerate the association as long as the gains of the immediate past were not threatened, and the new Marxist allies of the SLFP scrupulously refrained from providing evidence of any such threats like advocating generally a secular state. However, not all their critics were won over or even mollified by this seemingly accommodative attitude. The coalition government's attempts to bring the national press under state control led to a renewal of fears that Marxist influence within the government was inherently erosive otf Buddhist values. The SLFP sought to break the press monopoly held by Lake House which was politically associated with the UNP. Buddhist activists found common cause with the SLFP because they perceived that institution to be a stronghold, perhaps an impregnable stronghold, of Christian influence on public life. The LSSP shared the SLFP's attitude to Lake House, and enthusiastically joined forces in a bid to bring it under state control. But this combination provoked the opposition of a section of the political *bhikkhus*. The opposition to this assault on the freedom of the press was led by the UNP.

The ambiguities in the relationship between Buddhist activism and the government were revealed afresh with the return of the UNP to power in 1965 at the head of a coalition. In opposition the UNP had opposed the educational reforms of 1960-61; in office there was no relaxation of the restrictive measures against which they had voted nor any concessions to the Roman Catholics despite the pledge given to them in 1967. In a bid to prove its *bonafides* on Buddhism the government introduced the *poya* holiday scheme under which the weekly holiday was based on the phases of the moon while the traditional Christian *sabbath* holiday was abandoned. Once more U Nu's Burma was the model emulated, with total disregard of the impact this variable weekend scheme would have on Sri Lanka's trade links with the rest of the world. Despite the acquiescence of the church hierarchy, the *poya* holiday also caused some discontent among the Roman Catholics—without any compensating support from the Buddhists for the UNP.

Bhikkhus in politics and political agitation was a constant factor during this period. A young *bhikkhu* was killed when the police opened fire on a mob demonstrating against the government's proposals to introduce regulations to give effect to the *Tamil Language (Special Provisions) Act* which Bandaranaikc had piloted through Parliament in 1958. The SLFP under his wife's leadership now opposed these regulations when the new government introduced them in January 1966. Buddhist activists were divided politically, but a large section of them opposed the regulations and demonstrated against them in their customary role of articulators of the people's aspirations. But even if this particular form of involvement in politics received approbation from a large section of the Buddhist public, other instances of political *bhikkhus*' patent disregard of the tolerable limits of partisanship served to revive public memories of the excesses committed by the political *bhikkhus* during S. W. R. D. Bandaranaike's government. In April 1966 a leading political *bhikkhu* linked with the SLFP, *bhikkhu* Henpitagedera Gnanasiha, was closely associated on charges of complicity in an attempted *coup d'etat*.

The government sought to construct a new policy for interacting with the Buddhists. Its central feature was an attempt to emphasize the role of what may be termed the "establishment" in the *sangha* since the two *Mahanayakes* (chief *bhikkhus*) of the Malvatta and Asgiriya chapters of the prestigious Siyam *nikaya* were acknowledged as the principal articulators of Buddhist opinion and as the most authentic representatives of Buddhist interests. In doing so the government took a calculated risk, but there was the undoubted advantage that the Buddhist public widely accepted these *bhikkhus* in this role. Because of their political non-partisanship this acceptability rose in inverse proportion to the perceptible decline in the prestige of the politically active *bhikkhus*. Their leadership also had a formal and institutional aspect to which the political bhikkhus could never aspire. The two *Mahanayakes* were traditionally the highest dignitaries of the *sangha*, and the government's new policy buttressed their status with some tangible and some intangible forms of official recognition. The tangible forms included two official residences for them in Colombo. The intangible but very-conspicuous form included the practice for all appointees to important official positions in government and public life to make ceremonial courtesy calls on the two *Mahanayakes* in Kandy.

Also in 1966-67 in a gesture symbolic of a decline in status, the two *pirivena* universities of Vidyalankara and Vidyodaya were converted into secular institutions and the *bhikkhus* who headed these two universities lost much of their patronage and influence. Beneath this avowed design to secularise these institutions there was also much irony and individual ambivalence in the choice of the first Vice-Chancellor of Vidyodaya under the new dispensation: it was none other than Walpola Rahula himself.

The official recognition and buttressing of the orthodox *bhikkhus* did not inhibit their interventions on political issues whenever an occasion demanded. Throughout the last two decades *bhikkhus*, including the two *Mahanayakes* of Malwatta and Asgiriya, have generally taken a strong stand on issues involving relations between the Sinhalese majority and the Tamil minority, a stand which reflected an instinctive ethnic nationalism. There was general opposition to the concessions on language made to the Tamils in January 1966, but on this occasion the *bhikkhus* played a subsidiary role in a campaign led by politicians and laymen. The opposition was stronger among the political *bhikkhus* of old than among the more orthodox *bhikkhus*. The latter's opposition to the District Councils scheme envisaged by the government in 1967-68, however, was more vocal because it coincided with concessions, made at about the same time to the Indian residents in Sri Lanka about their citizenship rights.

The defeat of the UNP in 1970 and the return to power of Mrs. Bandaranaike at the head of the center-left United Front coalition saw the final phase of the process of redressing Buddhist grievances and establishing Buddhist ascendency in the Sri Lanka polity. This phase was all the more significant because it marked support from the principal Marxist parties of the country which had hitherto taken pride in their commitment to the concept of a secular state. The new Republican Constitution of 1972 read as follows:

> *The Republic of Sri Lanka shall give to Buddhism the foremost place and accordingly it shall be the duty of the state to protect and foster Buddhism while assuring to all religions the rights guaranteed by section 18(l)(d).*

When this proposal was originally made in the Constituent Assembly, its supporters included the UNP. This time there was no opposition from the Christians in general or the Roman Catholics in particular. When the 1972 constitution was replaced by a new one in 1978 under a UNP regime this same principle was incorporated in the second republic's constitutional structure. The innovation introduced in 1972 came at a time when the Roman Catholics had themselves embarked on a change of policy in their attitude to other religions. Their increasing acceptance of religious pluralism allowed the Vatican Council of 1963-65. All this occurred without any attempt by the SLFP to change its education policy. The government, nevertheless had become much more conciliatory to the Roman Catholics. Equally significant, when the UNP government which came to power in 1977 adopted the second Republican Constitution in 1978, the status – the "foremost place" – accorded to Buddhism in the previous constitution remained unchanged.

In both instances the governments concerned were operating within the limits of the formula adopted in the late nineteenth century by the British governors Gregory and Gordon. The formula proved to be elastic enough to cope with the pressures of Buddhist activists for a special status for Buddhism within the Sri Lankan polity, without making it the state religion on the Burmese model. However, in 1978 the All Ceylon Buddhist Congress urged that Buddhism be declared "the State Religion." Other less prestigious, if not less vocal, Buddhist organizations proposed that the constitution should require that the President, the Executive Head of State, be a Buddhist. Nonetheless the UNP government remained content with sustaining the primacy of Buddhism in the Sri Lankan polity at the level established in 1972, a primacy which fell distinctly short of declaring Buddhism to be the state religion.

Even so the position accorded to Buddhism was much too elevated for some non-Buddhists who complained that the constitution "does not prohibit the state from providing munificent financial assistance to Buddhism or from placing restrictions on the efforts of other religious organizations to propagate their faith" (cited in Wilson 1980:103). The opposition to this special status for Buddhism no longer came from the Roman Catholics on religious grounds, but from spokesmen for the Tamil minority on political grounds.

By the late 1970s Buddhist activism was but a shadow of the vibrant force it had been in the previous seventy years. Partly this was because many of the issues about which Buddhist activists had agitated had been settled very much in their favour.

While most of the gains of the mid-1950s and early 1960s were securely established, others were lost. The most conspicuous example of the latter was the abandonment of the *poya* holiday scheme in July 1971. Almost all political parties supportd this move, including the UNP itself which had originally introduced it. Significantly, the SLFP-led coalition took the initiative in a matter in which a section of the sangha and some lay Buddhist activists adamantly opposed the abandonment of a change for which they had had long agitated. Again the concessions on the levying of fees which had been promised the Roman Catholics by the then UNP-led coalition in 1967 came at last in 1978. With them, too, came wider government financial assistance to schools run by religious minorities, largely Christian, but also Hindu and Islamic, all of which lay outside the national schools structure. This bold initiative aroused surprisingly little opposition from Buddhist activists. The apparent equanimity with which—Buddhist activists accepted this decision is evidence of changed priorities in their demands and their perception of the potential harm to the interests of Buddhists and Sinhalese. The Roman Catholics, it would appear, have ceased to be regarded as a threat to Buddhist interests—perhaps because the former have accepted the political reality of Buddhist dominance in Sri Lanka.

Despite all the contradictory impulses set off by Buddhist activists, they have seldom engaged in any direct pressure for assimilating minorities into the Sinhalese-Buddhist culture. In this Sri Lanka provides a contrast to the other major Theravada Buddhist states of Burma and Thailand. Buddhist activism in Sri Lanka has been directed mainly at the redress of historic grievances, at the restoration of a status and prestige lost in the years of imperial rule, and at the purposeful elimination of the privileges of a powerful Christian minority, rather than at any efforts at assimilation of minorities. Unlike Burma or Thailand, there has been very little Buddhist missionary activity in Sri Lanka among minority groups. Even where a minority is eminently vulnerable to such proselytization, as for example the depressed caste Tamil plantation workers, Roman Catholics rather than the more powerful Buddhist *sangha* have been resourceful in converting them. For a time efforts were made by Buddhist groups to convert some of the depressed caste Tamils in the northern province to Buddhism, but such efforts were neither consistent nor persistent. Nor did they yield any substantial results by way of large numbers of converts.

Marxist and radical critics of Buddhist activism often question the latter's lack of interest in social issues, in particular the condition of the urban poor. Buddhist activism is charged with a lack of social conscience. There is some justice in this criticism, but again this lack of interest in social issues is more apparent than real. Buddhist pressure groups working through successive governments have been among the most powerful influences in the establishment and consolidation of a welfare state in Sri Lanka.

Buddhist activism in Sri Lanka is currently concentrating its energies on Sri Lanka's ethnic tensions. This has had the effect of reviving the importance of the two *Mahanayakes* of Malwatta and Asgiriya both as officially accepted representatives of Buddhist opinion and as legitimate guardians of Sinhalese interests. But they were only the most prominent among other representatives of the *sangha* invited to participate at an All Party Conference in January 1984 to devise measures for a resolution of the island's ethnic problems. The other *bhikkhu* representatives included the heads of the Amarapura and Ramanna nikaya (sects) and of small splinter groups of the Siyam *nikaya* itself—the Kotte and Kalyani factions.

Two other Buddhist *bhikkhu* leaders attended as well. The first was *bhikkhu* Madihe Pannasiha, of the Amarapura *nikaya*, who enjoys national recognition as a politically independent but pugnacious upholder of Sinhalese interests. The other special invitee was none other than Walpola Rahula who now lives mostly in Europe but still enjoys a national status. Because of his position as an internationally renowned scholar, he has been Chancellor of Kelaniya University since 1979. In the aftermath of the ethnic disturbances of July 1983 and at the All Party Conference, he became at once the principal spokesman for Buddhist interests as well as an eloquent voice for moderation and pragmatism. In one of the rich ironies that characterize Sri Lankan politics, his presence and prominence owe much to the persuasive skills of President Jayewardene, his erstwhile opponent of the 1940s when Rahula was the most articulate of political *bhikkhus* while Jayewardene was a rising star of the post-independence political establishment.

The All Party Conference had other significant participants representing all the major religious groups in the country. Hindus, Muslims, and above all the Christians were invited to send delegates, and did so. It was indicative of how far Sri Lanka had traveled since the religious controversies of the past generation. The Buddhists were secure enough in their position of primacy in the Sri Lankan polity to have Roman Catholic and Protestant Christian representatives engaged in an essentially political process of developing a national consensus on the current ethnic crisis.

Significantly no representatives of religious groups were invited to join the second of the major national conferences on Sri Lanka's ethnic conflicts. Held in Colombo in 1986 it was deliberately restricted to political parties and was called the Political Parties' Conference. It provides a telling demonstration of the point that the country's political leadership often disregards the wishes of the *bhikkhus* when the national interest, as that leadership perceives it, or political expediency, demands. The *bhikkhus* enjoy considerable influence among the people as representatives of Sinhalese-Buddhist opinion and, where a threat to the gains of the post-independence period is perceived, they become, in all but name, a permanent second chamber in Sri Lankan politics. The *bhikkhus* wield a significant if not always decisive influence over national policy.

Radicalized political *bhikkhus* arc no longer the revitalizing force they were in the 1930s and 1940s. Each passing decade brought a few into prominence but they have tended to be individuals working in isolation rather members of a cohesive group. The lay leaders of the Buddhist movement demonstrate this same loss of vitality.

18

Terrorism in South Asia: Nepal's Perspective

Terrorism refers to a strategy of using violence, social threats, or coordinated attacks, in order to generate fear, cause disruption, and ultimately, bring about compliance with specified political, religious, or ideological demands. The targets of terrorist attacks typically are not the individuals who are killed, injured, or taken hostage, but rather the societies to which these individuals belong. Terrorism is designed to subvert existing political atmospheres, often with the aid of the mass media's influence.

A total of 2,105 persons, including 1,584 Maoists, were killed in the year 2003 across Nepal, after Maoist insurgents called off the seven-month-old cease-fire on August 27, 2003. The cease-fire was originally announced on January 29, 2003. Fatalities were relatively low in the first eight months of the year - with 115 persons killed in January, 32 in February and between March and July, just nine. However, 84 persons lost their lives in August, largely due to the build-up of tensions and eventual collapse of the cease-fire. The total number killed in the insurgency substantially increased in the subsequent four months with 509 killed in September, 525 in October, 370 in November and 461 in December. Total fatalities for the year stood at 2,105, as against 4,896 in 2002.

While the exact cadre strength of the Maoists is difficult to estimate, official figures put their numbers at 5,500 combatants, 8,000 militia, 4,500 cadres, 33,000 hardcore followers and 200,000 'sympathisers' in early 2003.

At the third round of peace talks which began on August 17, 2003, between the present Government under Prime Minister Surya Bahadur Thapa and the Maoists in the western Nepalese town of Nepalgunj, the Government presented a 'concept paper' which included suggestions for changes in the country's administration. While the 'concept paper' conceded two key Maoist demands, for a roundtable conference and an interim government, the Government held that reforms demanded by the Maoists for elections to a Constituent Assembly could be introduced through amendments to the present Constitution. The Government suggested that political parties be included in the roundtable to discuss the reforms and the Maoists be included in an interim government that would hold elections to a new Parliament, which could, in turn, endorse the decisions of the roundtable.

The Maoists, however, rejected these proposals, dismissing them as 'cosmetic changes'. The third round of talks continued for another two days in the Maoist hotbed of Dang district. However, the Constituent Assembly issue could not be resolved and on August 27, 2003, the Maoists withdrew from the truce and violence again erupted in Nepal.

The year also witnessed a change of regime in Nepal during the period of the 'peace talks'. On May 30, 2003, the caretaker Government under Lokendra Bahadur Chand resigned, amidst pressure from the growing anti-monarchy agitation launched by Opposition political parties. King Gyanendra appointed Surya Bahadur Thapa as Prime Minister of Nepal on June 4, 2003, after turning down the proposal for premiership for Madhav Kumar Nepal (then secretary general of CPN-UML) jointly put forward by the five agitating political parties.

At the first round of peace talks held on April 27, 2003, by the Chand Government, the Maoists submitted a 35-point socio-political-economic agenda which outlined three main issues: Interim government, elections to the Constituent Assembly within six months and the formation of a joint army of the Royal Nepalese Army (RNA) and the Maoists.

Those who participated in the talks included Maoist leaders Baburam Bhattarai, Krishna Bahadur Mahara and Ram Bahadur Thapa. Government negotiators included the Minister for Physical Planning, Narayan Singh Pun, and Minister for Communications, Ramesh Nath Pandey. The Maoists had earlier withdrawn from the 'introductory talks' on April 21, 2003, demanding discussions on 'substantive issues'.

At the second round of talks held on May 9, 2003, the Government accepted two of the Maoist demands: restriction of the RNA's movement within five kilometers of their barracks and release of detained senior Maoist leaders. Though, on May 16, 2003, Government spokesperson Narayan Singh Pun accepted the agreement with the Maoists on the restriction of the Army's movement, the then Premier, Lokendra Bahadur Chand, rejected it. On December 18, the Government announced a general amnesty programme to the Maoists and urged them, their relatives and associates to eschew violence and surrender with or without weapons before February 12, 2004.

In the year 2002, 4,896 persons, including 3,992 Maoists, 666 security force personnel and 238 civilians were killed across Nepal.

Fatalities in Moaist Insurgency, 2003

	Civilians	SF Personnel	Maoists	Total
January	15	20	80	115
February	2	3	27	32
March	0	0	0	0
April	0	0	1	1
May	0	0	0	0
June	1	0	4	5
July	2	0	1	3
August	2	24	58	84
September	72	65	372	509
October	41	62	422	525
November	24	76	270	370
December	55	57	349	461
Total	**214**	**307**	**1548**	**2105**

Fatalities in Maoist Insurgency, 2002

	Civilians	SF Personnel	Maoists	Total
January	27	13	164	204
February	19	199	289	507
March	18	23	303	344
April	18	103	382	503
May	2	46	975	1023
June	3	11	255	269
July	4	4	112	120
August	14	3	205	222
September	57	154	452	663
October	14	7	144	165
November	42	79	567	688
December	20	24	144	188
Total	238	666	3992	4896

The Emergency, imposed in November 2001 after the first attacks by the Maoists on the Army following the breakdown of peace talks, had to be renewed every three months by the Parliament and eventually lapsed on August 25, 2002. However, since May 2002, when Parliament was dissolved following differences within the ruling Nepali Congress party, the Emergency was extended through an ordinance.

After the Emergency ended, the Maoists stepped up their activities and began to concentrate on Kathmandu. The capital appeared increasingly vulnerable, with frequent bombing incidents, as well as a large number of attempts that were foiled by the security forces.

The Government concluded that the Maoists had been emboldened by the lifting of the Emergency and began dropping hints that the Emergency could be clamped again. The Opposition parties, however, disagreed with the Government's assessment, although they remained committed to elections in November 2002. Things, however, changed dramatically in the first week of September 2002. The Maoists blew up a police post in East Nepal on September 8, and overran a district headquarters in western Nepal the very next day. More than a hundred people, including soldiers, armed police, civil police and civilians were killed, while the Maoists also suffered an equal number of casualties. The attacks, which came after a lull of four months, surprised the political establishment in Kathmandu. It was believed that the Maoists were on the run considering the cumulative reverses they had suffered. The loss of Maoist cadres in engagements with the Army; reports of surrenders by Maoists and their sympathizers; India's assurance that its territory would not be used as a safe haven by the Maoists, were all thought to have delivered hard body blows to Maoist operational capacities. The attacks sent a clear message to the Government that the strength of the Maoists was not to be underestimated.

Earlier, after a little over an year of its appointment on July 22, 2001, King Gyanendra dismissed the elected Sher Bahadur Deuba-led Government on October 4, 2002, calling Deuba 'inept' in handling the Maoist insurgency. The King assumed executive powers, and his promise of appointing an interim 'national government' did not materialise under the former Prime Minister and palace loyalist, Lokendra Bahadur Chand. Elections to Parliament were deferred indefinitely.

Rigorous training by ex-armed forces personnel have honed the military skills of the Maoists to the extent that their strikes are now characterized by detailed planning and deadly precision. Attacking during the night, the guerrillas have graduated to targeting district headquarters as well. In one such attack, on November 14, 2002, hundreds of insurgents overran the Jumla district headquarters, Khalangha Bazzar, and killed at least 37 police personnel. The insurgents first attacked the airport and then two police establishments and Government offices, killing the chief district officer, Damodar Pant, and two others. To deal with the attackers, reinforcements of Army troops and night vision helicopters were rushed in. On the same night, 23 police personnel were shot dead in the Gorkha district. Earlier, in a prolonged gun battle on October 27, the state forces eventually repulsed the rebels who had stormed the Rumjatar Airport in the Okhaldhunga district. Thereafter, the insurgents attacked the District Police Office, where 32 of them were killed, while two SF personnel lost their lives.

The largest number of SF casualties in major rebel attacks were during September and February 2002. Forty nine SF personnel were shot dead in the attack on the police post at Bhiman in Sindhuli district on September 7, 2002, while in a second attack on September

8, in Sandhikharkha, the district headquarters of Argakanchi, 68 SF personnel were killed. Sixteen SF personnel lost their lives in an attack on the Bhakundebeshi police station in the Karve district on February 4 and 97 SF personnel were shot dead on February 16-the highest number of SF casualties on a single day during year 2002-when rebels stormed the Saphebagar airport in the Accham district and the Army barracks in Mangalsen town. In another major attack on April 11 at two police posts at Satbaria and Lamahi in the Dang district, insurgents killed 84 SF personnel. In another attack launched on May 7, which extended into the next day, rebels killed 70 SF personnel at the base camp at Gam village in Rolpa district. On December 17, Maoists insurgents killed 11 soldiers in separate land mine blasts in Kapilavastu and Bardiya districts.

Fatalities in Major Clashes between Secrity Forces and Maoist Insurgents, 2003

Date	Civilians	Security Forces	Maoist Insurgents	Place
January 29			13	Gulmi
August 25			10	Nauthar village in Lamjung district
August 26			7	Melbote area of Panchthar district
September 2			11	Pasagaon area of Lamjung district.
September 5			10	Karnali bridge in the Bajura district
September 7			20	Ghartigaon in the Rolpa district
September 8	8			Kathmandu
September 17		5	57	Bhagawn area of Rolpa district
September 18			28	Panchthar and Accham districts
September 22			18	Udayapur, Banke and Nuwakot districts
September 23			15	Kailali, Barida, Taplejung and Panchthar districts.
September 25			11	Surket, Kailali, Dadeldhura and Rupandahi districts
September 27			12	Chitapokhari in the Khotang district

Date	Civilians	Security Forces	Maoist Insurgents	Place
September 30			35	Katahira police post in the Rautahat district.
October 11			125	Kusum in the Dang district
October 12		13	25	Bhalubang police barrack in Dang district
October 13			12	Doti district
October 15		2	25	Accham district
October 16			16	Chhatwal in the Sarlahi district
October 28	2	7		Sishuwa Police Post at Danda Nak in Kaski district
November 2		20		Simara in the Bara district; Parsa district
November 8			7	Sainpashala in Bhajhang district
November 12			12	Baijapur in Banke district
December 2			12	Palpa, Argakanchi, Panchthar Sarlahi and Dang districts
December 3		6	25	Bandaul and Pandaun areas of Kailali district
December 4			12	Palpa district
December 5 - 6			14	Khotang, Sindhuli, Dolakha, Bardia, Taplejung, Panchthar and Okhaldhunga
December 6			19	Khotang district
December 11, 12 and 13			48	Dailekh, Khotang, Udaipur, Rolpa and Dang districts
December 14		11	35	Aurahi in the Mohottari district and Biyako Lekh in the Dailekh district
December 15			15	Rolpa, Palpa, Ramechap, Kavre and Dhading districts
December 17		10		Dhankhola in the Kapilavastu district
December 25			16	Solokhumbu, Dhading, Dolakha Ramechhap, Okhalgundha, Rasuwa, Jhapa and Khoakharka districts

Fatalities in Major Clashes between Security Forces and Maoist Insurgents, 2002

Date	Civilians	Security Forces	Maoist Insurgents	Place
January 27			21	Sankranti Bazaar, Terhathum district
February 4		16	1	Bhakundebeshi police station, Kavre district
February 16	4	98	41	Sanphebagar airport, Accham district; Army barracks, Mangelsen town
February 20			46	Acham, Doti, Kailali and Dailekh districts
February 21		33	4	Sitalpati police station, Salyan district
February 21			37	Surkhet district
February 23			67	Kalikot district
March 13		6		Sanghachowk, 40km away from capital Kathmandu
March 17			69	Insurgents' training camp, Gumsa, Rolpa district
March 25			13	Rolpa
April 7			13	Kothiyaghat jungles, Bardia
April 11		84	150	Satbaria and Lamahi police outposts, Dang
April 14			17	Dang-Pyuthan border
April 27			18	Khotang
May 2			32	Dhagal, Dang-Kailali districts border
May 2-5		4	548	Maoist training camp, Lisne jungles
May 7-8		70	150	Security force base camp, Gam village, Rolpa
May 27		5	188	Security force base camp, Khara, Rukum district
June 12		4	51	Damachour, Salyan district
August 20		1	30	Thawang village, Rolpa
September 7		49	50	Bhiman police post, Sindhuli district
September 8	25	68	267	Sandhikharka, Argakanchi district
September 23		3	74	Rolpa

Date	Civil-ians	Security Forces	Maoist Insurgents	Place
October 27		2	32	Rumjatar airport and district police office, Okhaldunga district
November 14	3	37	55	Jumla district
November 14		23	63	Gorkha district
November 22			50	Thulo Kavre, Lamjung district
November 24			50	Lamjung district
December 29			25	Salyan, Surkhet, Dailekh and Rasuwa districts.

In a high profile terrorist act, the Maoists on March 13, 2002, shot dead six police personnel detailed for the security of Taranath Ranabhatt, the Speaker of Nepal, 40 kilometers from the capital Kathmandu, but the Speaker's vehicle was not in the convoy. In another high profile attack, the house of the former Chief of Staff of the RNA, Garud Shumsher J.B. Rana, was targeted on January 25, 2002, in Bara district, southern Nepal. The senior-most SF personnel killed by the insurgents was Armed Police Force Inspector General Krishna Mohan Shrestha, who was shot dead at Pattan, in the Kathmandu Valley, on January 26, 2003.

Nepal Terrorist Groups - Communist Party of Nepal-Maoist

Formation

The Communist Party of Nepal-Maoist (CPN-M), currently a proscribed outfit, was formed in 1995 following a split in the Communist Party of Nepal-Unity Centre. A radical faction led by Pushpa Kamal Dahal alias Comrade Prachanda and Baburam Bhattarai set up the CPN-Maoist and denounced the Communist Party of Nepal (Unified Marxist-Leninists) or the CPN (UML) and other mainstream communist factions as renegades' and 'revisionists' due to their participation in the parliamentary process. It resorted to an armed struggle on February 13, 1996, by attacking police stations in the Rukum and Rolpa districts in northwestern Nepal and thereby declaring a 'People's War' in Nepal.

Earlier, various communist groups had actively participated in the People's Movement of 1989-90 operating under the umbrella organisation of United National People's Movement (UNPM). However, after the conclusion of the People's Movement, these groups were not satisfied with the multi-party democratic system under constitutional monarchy. In order to contest the May 1991 elections, they formed a two-tier organisation, revolutionary front and political front, known as the Communist Party of Nepal-Unity Centre and United People's Front of Nepal (UPFN) respectively. The UPFN emerged as the third largest group in the Parliament and also performed well in the local bodies' elections of 1992. Gradually, however, ideological and personality clashes led to the disintegration of Unity Centre and the UPFN split into two factions, led by Nirmal Lama and Niranjan Govind Vaidiya at one end and Comrade Prachanda and Bhattarai on the other end. Subsequently, the decision by Prachanda not to participate in the 1994 elections led to the creation of CPN-M in 1995 as an underground outfit.

Objectives

The Maoists announced a 'People's War' on February 13, 1996, with the slogan "let us march ahead on the path of struggle towards establishing the people's rule by wreaking the reactionary ruling system of state." They strongly believe in the philosophy of Mao Tsetung that "Political power grows out of the barrel of a gun." They also draw inspiration from the 'Revolutionary Internationalist Movement' and Peru's left wing extremist guerilla movement, the Sendero Luminoso (Shining Path). The radical communist parties from different parts of the world have provided ideological sustenance for the Nepali Maoists.

The 'People's War' aims to establish a 'New Democracy' in Nepal and constitutes an "historical revolt against feudalism, imperialism and so-called reformists." The immediate reason given by the Maoists for declaring the 'People's War' was the failure of the Nepalese Government to respond to a memorandum presented by its representatives to Prime Minister Sher Bahadur Deuba on February 4, 1996. The memorandum listed 40 demands related to "nationalism, democracy and livelihood". These included among others the abolition of royal privileges and the promulgation of a new constitution, and the abrogation of the Mahakali treaty with India on the distribution of water and electricity and the delineation of the border between the two countries.

Leadership, Cadre and Command Structure

The chief of operations of the CPN-M is its Chairman, Pushpa Kamal Dahal (better known as Comrade Prachanda). He is also Chairman of the 'Central Committee', Member of 'Standing Committee' and 'Supreme Commander' of the People's Liberation Army.

Another front ranking leader Baburam Bhattarai heads the political wing of the Maoists called the United People's Front (UPF). Bhattarai alias Lal Singh @ Jitbir @ Mukti Manab, a 'Politburo and Standing Committee' member, is reportedly responsible for planning and foreign affairs, and was co-ordinator of the dialogue team in 2003. According to the Nepal Police Website, he is in-charge of mid central command (since 3rd cc meeting in September 2004).

Mohan Pokharel Vaidya @ Kiran @ Agam, a founder of the party and a 'Politburo and Standing Committee' member, is widely reported to be the political ideologue and is also in-charge of the Kathmandu valley and eastern central command. Another important Maoist leader is Post Bahadur Bogati @ Diwakar @ Ranadhoj who serves as a 'Politburo and Standing Committee' member and is also in- charge of the western central command.

Ram Bahadur Thapa alias Badal @ Lakhan @ Bhimsen @ Prem, another 'Politburo and Standing Committee' member, is reported to be special central command in-charge. Krishna Bahadur Mahara @ Amar Singh @ Chattan, who acts as the Maoists' spokesperson, is in-charge of the 'Foreign Section (India)'.

The top-level commanders of the insurgents include among others, Yan Prasad Gautarri alias Alok, Chitranarayan Shrestha, Shashi Shrestha, Hisila Yani, Man Bahadur Mahara, Santhosh Bura, Lekhraj Bhatt, C.P. Gajurel. In the political wing, the important Maoist leaders include, Comrade Parvati (a nom de guerre of Baburam Bhattarai's wife Hsila Yemi), Matrika Yadav, Deb Bahadur Gurung, Krishna Dhoj Khadka, Rekha Sharma, Rabindra Shrestha, Bamdev Chhetri and Mumaram Khanal.

The apex military institution of the Maoists is the Central Military Commission of the Communist Party of Nepal (Maoists), which was constituted in 1998.

Government estimates provided in early 2003 on the CPN-M strength indicated that there are approximately 5,500 combatants,

8,000 militia, 4,500 cadres, 33,000 hard core followers, and 200,000 sympathizers.

The main fighting and support forces consist of Magars, Tharus, Janjatis (Gurungs, Rais, Limbus, Tamangs, Dalits, Brahmins and Chhetris, the last two also providing the political and military leadership). Among the Maoist fighters - about 60 per cent - are deployed in the mid-west and west in their strongholds. Another 10 per cent are in the far west with around 10 percent in Gorkha, the rest is located in Kathmandu valley and east of it.

A considerable number of retired Gurkha soldiers of the British and the Indian Army inhabit many of the Maoist-affected areas and Nepalese security agencies have suspected that these former soldiers along with those retired and deserters from the Royal Nepalese Army (RNA) have/are involved in training the insurgents.

Women have been prominent in the recruiting profile. Available reports indicate that one-fifth to one-third of the cadre and combatants may be women. Reportedly, every village has a revolutionary women's organisation. According to a Jane's Intelligence Review report of October 2001, there are usually two women in each unit of 35-40 men, and they are used to gather intelligence and act as couriers. Baburam Bhattarai was quoted as saying in Spacetime on April 18, 2003, that fifty percent of cadres at the lower level, thirty percent of soldiers and ten percent of members of central committee of the outfit were women. Durgha Pokhrel, Chairman of National Women's Commission, who visited more than 25 Maoist-affected districts, stated on July 3, 2003, during a talk delivered at the Nepal Council of World Affairs that percentage of women cadres could be as high as forty. A women's group, the All Nepal Women's Association (Revolutionary), is alleged to be a front outfit of the CPN-M.

The All Nepal National Independent Students' Union (Revolutionary), or ANNISU-R is the student wing of the Maoists. Its membership comprises students from school to the university level. The general success in all the strikes called by ANNISU-R, especially in the educational institutions, (at present it is also one of the key student organisation in the anti-King agitation) shows the strong hold of the organisation. According to a report of June 2003, the ANNISU-R comprises approximately 400,000 members.

Reportedly, weaponry in their possession include AK-47 rifles, self-loading rifles, .303 rifles, country guns, hand grenades, explosives, detonators, mortars, and light machine guns. Nearly 85 per cent of these weapons are reportedly looted from the police and RNA.

Structurally, the CPN-M consists of the standing committee at the top, followed by the politburo, central committee, regional bureaus, sub-regional bureaus, district committees, area committees, and cell committees. The Politburo issues directives with the assistance of an approximately 25-member central committee. The main armed component reportedly consists of six guerrilla battalions, which launches military action in response to instructions relayed through their individual chief commissars (one per battalion), who are central committee members. The politburo and standing committee reportedly formulate most of the political and strategic policies. The standing committee, with approximately ten members, is the most powerfully body in the CPN-M. There are five regional bureaus: eastern, central, Kathmandu valley, western and international department.

Organisational Structure of the CPN-Maoist

Party	People's Army	United Front
Standing committee	Central military commission	United people's district committees
Politburo	Regional military commissions	United people's area committee
Central committee	Sub-regional military commissions	United people's village committees
Regional bureaus (five)	District military commissions	United people's ward committees
Sub-regional bureaus (in some places special sub-regional bureau)	Included in this are: Temporary battalion	
District committees	Companies	
Area committees	Platoons	
Cell committees	Squads (separate people's militias also exist under united village people's committees)	

Areas of Operation

The guerrillas operate to varying degrees in 68 of the 75 districts that comprise Nepal. Their influence varies between moderate to extreme in these districts. In the districts of Rolpa, Rukum, Jajarkot, Salyan, Pyuthan and Kalikot in mid-western Nepal, Government presence is limited to the district headquarters with the rest of each district under Maoist control. The Nepalese Home Ministry has designated these districts as 'sensitive class A'. Nine districts, namely Dolakha, Ramechhap, Sindhuli, Kavrepalanchowk, Sindhupalchowk, Gorkha, Dang, Surkhet and Achham, are classified as 'Sensitive Class B', while 17 'Sensitive Class C' districts are Khotang, Okhaldhunga, Udaypur, Makwanpur, Lalitpur, Nuwakot, Dhading, Tanahu, Lamjung, Parbat, Baglung, Gulmi, Arghakhachi, Bardiya, Dailekh, Jumla and Dolpa.

The Maoist insurgency initially commenced in the three districts of Rolpa, Rukum and Jajarkot and eventually spread throughout Nepal. Maoists have very strong bases in Western and mid-Western region and partially in Eastern region.

External Linkages

According to available information, the Maoists of Nepal have well-established linkages with Indian left-wing extremist organizations, primarily with the People's War Group (PWG) and Maoist Communist Centre (MCC). The first signs of contacts were reportedly registered during 1989-1990, when the two groups started collaborating in order to expand their influence. Towards this end, they began the process of laying a corridor, which is now widely referred to as the Revolutionary Corridor (RC) extending from Nepal to across six Indian States, including Bihar, Chhattisgarh, Jharkhand, Andhra Pradesh, Orissa and Madhya Pradesh. This entire area has been identified in Maoist literature as the Compact Revolutionary Zone (CRZ). The CRZ was organized by the Nepal and Indian members of the Naxalite (the popular term for left-wing extremism in India- the movement originated in Naxalbari [hence the term Naxal] in the State of West Bengal in the late 1960s) Movement, in a meeting at Siliguri in the Indian State of West Bengal during August 2001.

Gradually, the interaction between Maoist insurgents and the PWG increased with the sharing of knowledge about guerilla warfare, bomb manufacturing techniques and arms training. Nepalese Maoists had sent their delegates to the March 2001 Congress of PWG held at Abuz Marh in the Bastar region of Chhattisgarh. The establishment of CRZ gave a wider space and platform for all the proscribed Nepal and Indian left-wing extremist organizations to strengthen their bases in both the countries.

The more radical forces in South Asia, including both the PWG and Nepalese Maoists, are members of the Revolutionary Internationalist Movement (RIM). In July 2001, about 10 extreme Left Wing (Maoist) groups in South Asia formed the Coordination Committee of Maoist Parties and Organization of South Asia (CCOMPOSA), in which the Nepalese Maoists, PWG, MCC, Purbo Banglar Movement (Bangladesh), Communist Party of Ceylon (Sri Lanka) and other Indian left-wing extremist parties became members. The appearance of graffiti in remote villages in Naxalite-strongholds, in Rayakal and Mallapur mandals (administrative unit) of Karimnagar district in Andhra Pradesh, hailing CCOMPOSA points the spread of the idea of a common front of left-wing extremist groups in South Asia. Moreover, the Central Committee of the Maoists, in late-January 2002, passed a resolution stating that it would work together with the PWG and the MCC in fighting the ban imposed on the latter two organisations in India, under the Prevention of Terrorism Act, 2002. A year earlier, in 2001, the Maoists had sent a senior leader named Gaurav as a fraternal delegate to attend the 9th Congress of the PWG. Reports indicate that the Maoists and the PWG have also formed the Indo-Nepal Border Region Committee to coordinate their activities in North Bihar and along the India-Nepal border.

For quite some time, the Maoists have also been working closely with the MCC for unification, consolidation and expansion of Maoist movement in India and across South Asia. A careful examination of expansion of Naxalite activity in Bihar in the last two years would reveal that the growing linkages between the MCC and the Nepali Maoists are part of their larger strategy to create a 'Compact Revolutionary Zone' stretching across Andhra Pradesh, Chhattisgarh, Jharkhand, and Bihar to Nepal. The porous Bihar-Nepal border, the general breakdown of rule of law, poor governance and incapacity of the police force provides a context for these left extremist groups to operate with ease.

In February 1996, the MCC Central Committee had reportedly published a paper welcoming the Maoist movement in Nepal. Reports of April 2000 indicated that the MCC and Maoists were holding joint training camps in Hazaribagh and Aurangabad. In September 2000, MCC leader Pramod Mishra is alleged to have visited Nepal for extensive discussions with Maoist leaders. In December 2001, the MCC and the PWG, in their joint meetings, held in the Jharkhand forests, resolved to support the Maoist insurgents in Nepal. In the same year, the MCC, PWG and Maoists formed an "Indo Nepal Border Regional Committee" to coordinate their activities in the border areas.

The porous Bihar-Nepal border is easily permeable. Bihar has eight districts and 54 police stations situated on the border. In the recent past, the Bihar police have arrested a number of Nepalese Maoists in the border districts of West and East Champaran, Sitamarhi, Sheohar and Madhubani. Taking advantage of a general breakdown of law and order, the Nepalese Maoists have reportedly set up bases at several places along the border. Reports indicate the existence of training camps in the forests of Bagha in the West Champaran district, which has emerged as a safe haven for the Nepalese insurgents. The Bihar police also suspect that some top leaders of the Nepalese Maoists, including Baburam Bhattarai, were/are hiding in Bihar.

Not much is known about the Maoist links with other militant or left-wing extremist groups operating in India, besides that they are linked to a few Naxalite groups through CCOMPOSA. Besides, a left-wing extremist group, the Communist Party of India--Marxist-Leninist (CPI-ML) Janashakthi, which has a marginal presence at least in six Indian States, but is very active in isolated and limited number of pockets in Andhra Pradesh, expressed support to the Maoists. It is a co-signatory, along with 41 other left-wing extremist groups ranging from South America to South East Asia, to resolution that 'condemned and opposed the malpractice of the fascist state of Nepal' and demanded 'life security' for imprisoned Maoist cadres, leaders and sympathisers.

The Maoists, with the help of Pakistani Inter Services Intelligence (ISI), have been attempting to establish links with Naxalite groups such as the PWG and the MCC by using the Siliguri corridor in West

Bengal. Media reports of December 29, 2002, indicated that three members of a Maoist-affiliate, All Nepal National Free Students' Union-Revolutionary, were arrested at the Siliguri bus station, while on their way to Bihar to attend a meeting convened by the PWG.

The growing influence of Nepalese Maoists in other parts of India was unearthed after four of its cadres were arrested in West Bengal on February 26, 2003. The arrested Maoists confessed during interrogation of their plan to use West Bengal as a corridor between their areas of domination in India and Nepal. Darjeeling and Siliguri are the important transit routes. Also they are in a process of consolidating their presence in West Midnapore district, Bankura and Purulia especially in North Bengal with the help of Kamatapur Liberation Organisation (KLO).

The substantial population of nearly eight million Nepali residents in India (primarily in Sikkim, Darjeeling, Siliguri, Shillong, Dehradun, Himachal Pradesh and Gorakpur-Lucknow belts) have established a countrywide organization called the Akhil Bharatiya Nepal Ekta Samaj (ABNES). It was banned under the Prevention of Terrorism Act (POTA) in July 2002 by the Government of India. ABNES was registered with the stated objective of securing unity among immigrant Nepalese residing in India and working for their welfare. However, it gradually became involved in subversive activities and began to function as a front for the Maoist insurgents of Nepal. It is also believed that the organization is working for the idea of a greater Nepal.

There is also some reportage about the Nepalese Maoists' links with insurgent groups active in India's North-east like United Liberation Front of Asom (ULFA), Kamtapur Liberation Organisation (KLO), Gurkha National Liberation Front (GNLF) and Gurkha Liberation Organisation (GLO).

Though the exact nature of the relationship is not known, the Maoists are also reported to have some links with the Liberation Tigers of Tamil Eelam (LTTE) in Sri Lanka. However, it is suspected that the Maoists have received arms training from the LTTE operatives in the past and this may be continuing. Links between these two may have been facilitated through the PWG, which has a record of co-operation with the LTTE in arms procurement and training (especially in the use of Improvised Explosive Devices). The arrest of Chandra Prakash Gajurel alias Gaurab, a member of the Maoist politburo, at Chennai airport in Tamil Nadu in August 2003 while trying to travel to Europe to lobby for a political solution to the seven-year-old insurgency in Nepal needs to be seen in this context.

Major Incidents of Terrorist Violence in Nepal, 1999-2006

2006

April 23: Five Maoists, one SF personnel and three civilians were killed in an attack by the Maoists on security bases in Chautara, headquarters of the Sindhupalchowk district.

April 7: At least four Maoists and two civilians were killed after Maoists attacked security bases in the Butwal and Kapilavastu districts.

April 5: Five police personnel and four Maoists were killed during clashes at Malangwa, headquarters of the Sarlahi district.

March 30: Two SF personnel and one Maoist were killed during clashes at Bagmati checkpoint bordering the Sarlahi and Rautahat districts.

March 22: Two Armed Police Force personnel and three Maoists were killed at Urlabari in the Morang district, when the latter attacked security forces escorting a vehicle that was carrying money from the Urlabari branch of Rastriya Banjiya Bank.

March 21: Nine police personnel and three Maoists were killed when the latter attacked the Ilaka police post at Birtamod in Jhapa district.

March 20: 13 soldiers were killed during a Maoist ambush in the Dapcha area of Kavre district

March 10: Seven soldiers were killed during clashes with the Maoists in the southern part of Ilam district

March 8: Two soldiers were killed and another injured when Maoists opened fire at security forces near the district postal office of Bharatpur in Chitwan district

March 6: Two civilians, three security force personnel and four Maoists were killed in a Maoist attack at Ilam district headquarters.

February 28: Eighteen Maoists and 11 SF personnel were killed in a clash at Panena, a bordering area between the Arghakhanchi and Palpa districts.

February 27: Three SF personnel and a civilian were killed when Maoists attacked a team of troops at Kavre Bhanjyang area in the Kavrepalanchowk district.

February 9: Sixteen SF personnel, four Maoists and a civilian were killed at Rambhapur area along the Sunwal-Butwal section of the Sidhhartha Highway in Nawalparasi district, when the Maoists attacked security personnel who had reached Rambhapur to remove roadblocks put up by the former.

February 7: Five soldiers were killed and three sustained injuries when Maoists launched a massive attack in Dhankuta targeting the district administration office, regional administration office and all security agencies in the district.

February 7: Five SF personnel and a Maoist 'section commander' were killed when Maoists attacked a patrolling team at Simaltar in the Triyuga municipality of Udayapur district.

February 7: Five persons are killed when the Maoists attacked a RNA base camp and the Panauti municipality office in Kavrepalanchowk district.

January 31: Eleven SF personnel and four insurgents were killed in a Maoist attack at Tansen, headquarters of the Palpa district.

January 27: 11 Maoist insurgents and two SF personnel were killed in a Maoist attack on the joint security base at Hatuwagadhi in Bhojpur district.

January 24: Two security force personnel, one Maoist and a civilian were killed and four SF personnel sustained injuries when Maoists launched simultaneous attacks in the Nepalgunj town of Banke district.

January 20: Six police personnel were killed and four others sustained injuries when Maoists launched simultaneous attacks on the BP Chowk security check post, Jamunaha Police Post and the Customs Office in the Nepalgunj town of Banke district.

January 14: Twelve soldiers are killed and eight persons sustain injuries in a series of attacks carried out by the Maoists at different police posts of the Kathmandu Valley.

January 11: Seven police personnel are killed in a Maoist attack at Dhangadhi, headquarters of the Kailali district.

January 6: Three Armed Police Force personnel are killed and another sustained injuries when Maoists opened fire targeting a patrol party at Bhairahawa in the Rupandehi district.

January 5: Three police personnel were killed and two injured in a Maoist attack on an Armed Police Force security check-post at Ranjha chowk in Nepalgunj.

2005

August 27: Seven persons travelling in a passenger bus from Kathmandu to Dang were killed and three others sustained injuries in an explosion at Surai Naka section on the Mahendra highway at the border of Kapilvastu and Dang districts.

August 26: Five SF personnel were killed and two others were injured in an IED explosion at Khairanpur in the western district of Kapilavastu.

August 22: Four police personnel are killed and four others sustained injuries when their vehicle struck a landmine at Manigram in the Rupandehi district.

August 7: Approximately 50 troops are killed during a Maoist attack on a RNA base at Pili in the Kalikot district.

July 22: At least seven RNA personnel are killed in an ambush laid by the Maoists on a security patrol team near Goltakuri Rajkot in the Dang district.

June 25: At least 12 soldiers are killed during a Maoist attack on an army patrol team at Khandaha in the Arghakhanchi district.

June 24: At least eight Royal Nepalese Army personnel and one police personnel are killed by the Maoists at Pandhare in the Bhojpur district.

June 19: At least five soldiers are killed during a Maoist attack on various Government offices and security forces' bases at Diktel, headquarters of the Khotang district.

June 14: Maoists kill seven family members of a police personnel, including three women and a one-year old child, at Attariya in the Kailali district.

June 10: Six soldiers and two civilians are killed during a Maoist attack on a passenger bus near Narke river in the Mangaltar area of Kavre district.

June 6: At least 36 civilians and three soldiers are killed and 72 persons sustain injuries in a landmine blast triggered by the Maoists at Mudhekhola in the Chitwan district.

Maoists kill seven security force personnel and injure at least 12 others during an attack on a patrol team at Masuriya jungle in Kailali district.

May 6: Maoists kill Nepal's top Hindu leader Narayan Prasad Pokhrel, chairman of the World Hindu Federation (Nepal chapter), at Dudharachha village in the Rupandehi district.

April 23: Five children are killed and three others sustain injuries during a bomb explosion allegedly triggered by the insurgents at Pakhapani in the Rolpa district.

April 16: Maoists kill ten civilians, including a child, at Baragdawa in the Somni area of Nawalparasi district.

April 9: Insurgents attack the District Police Office, an Army battalion, district prison and also burn some Government offices at Charikot, headquarters of the Dolakha district, and freed some 30 prisoners from the prison.

March 6: A group of Maoists kill five civilians, allegedly members of an 'anti-Maoist retaliation group', at Kudarmatewa village in the Kapilavastu district.

March 4: Insurgents set ablaze and destroy 11 Government buildings, including those of the police, district administration and the general post office at Sandhikharka, headquarters of the Arghakhanchi district.

February 27: At least 10 soldiers are killed and an equal number sustain injuries during separate Maoist attacks in the Bara and Solukhumbu districts.

January 26: Five troops are killed and eight people sustain injuries in a Maoist ambush at Bhyaple along the Baglung-Pokhara highway in Parbat district.

January 19: At least 23 security force personnel are reported to have died at Barbote in the eastern district of Ilam.

January 2: Five police personnel are killed and six others sustain injuries during a Maoist attack on an Army patrol team at Bangaon along the Mahendra highway in the far-western district of Kanchanpur.

January 1: At least 12 soldiers are killed during a clash with the Maoist insurgents at Malbase on the Koshi Highway in Dhankuta district.

2004

December 22: Five soldiers, five civilians and eight Maoists are killed and several others sustain injuries when a group of insurgents attacked an army patrol at Karnali-Chisapani in the Bardiya district.

December 15: At least 21 Royal Nepalese Army (RNA) personnel are killed at Sisnekhola in the Sidwara VDC area of Arghakhanchi district.

December 4: Six security force personnel are killed and three others sustain injuries when Maoist insurgents attacked an army patrol near Surai Naka along the Mahendra highway in the western district of Kapilavastu.

November 21: At least 10 soldiers are killed at Khimdi in the Pandaun VDC area of Kailali district.

November 17: Eight Armed Police Force personnel are killed, a dozen others are injured and over two dozen were reported to be missing after Maoist insurgents detonate landmines at Khari Khola along the Mahendra highway in Banke district.

August 26, 2004: A group of 50 armed Maoist insurgents shot dead a former Chairman of Dhanusha District Development Committee and Rashtriya Prajatantra Party (Nationalist) leader, Badri Bahadur Karki, in the Bharatpur area.

August 2, 2004: Maoist insurgents have reportedly killed the former Mayor of Guleriya Municipality, Rajendra Shrivastav, in Bardiya district

July 5: Twelve police personnel and a civilian are killed in a land mine ambush laid by the Maoist insurgents at Bindhyabasini village in Parsa district.

June 14: At least 22 security force personnel are killed and 16 others sustained injuries in a landmine explosion by the Maoist insurgents at Khairikhola in the Banke district.

May 9: During a Maoist attack on a passenger bus, eight security force personnel and seven civilians are killed at Mainapokhari in the Dolakha district.

April 4: At least nine police personnel are killed during a Maoist attack on the Yadhusha police post in Danusha district.

March 20 - 21: In a Maoist attack on the District Jail, Office of the Chief District Officer and Army Camps at Beni Bazaar in the Myagdi district, at least 51 security force personnel, including 33 Royal Nepalese Army (RNA) personnel, and 20 civilians are killed.

March 3: Maoists insurgents, numbering around approximately 1500 to 2000, attack Nepal Telecommunication Towers and kill 32 security force personnel in Bhojpur district.

January 15: Maoist insurgents kill the Mayor of Birgunj and member of the Rastriya Prajatantra Party (RPP), Gopal Giri, at Bahuaari in the Birgunj district.

2003

December 17: Maoist insurgents kill 11 soldiers in separate land mine blasts in the Kapilavastu and Bardiya districts.

November 15: Four security force personnel, including Brigadier General Sagar Bahadur Pandey, are killed and nine others sustain injuries in an ambush by the Maoist insurgents at Bhainse in Makwanpur.

November 5: Maoist insurgents detonate a bomb outside the Crown Prince's palace (Nirmal Niwas) in the capital Kathmandu. However, no fatalities are reported.

November 2: At least ten security force personnel are killed and six others injured in an ambush by Maoist insurgents at Simara.

October 28: Seven security force personnel and two civilians are killed during a Maoist attack on the Sishuwa Police Post at Danda Nak in Kaski district.

September 12: Maoists kill six civilians in the capital Kathmandu.

September 8: Eight civilians are killed and 12 others sustain injuries in bomb explosions at six places in the capital Kathmandu.

January 26: Armed Police Force chief Krishna Mohan Shrestha, his wife and bodyguard are killed in an attack by Maoist insurgents in Kathmandu.

January 23: Two police personnel are killed and 20 more injured in an ambush laid by Maoists in Girighat, Surkhet district.

January 3: Maoist insurgents kill five security force personnel at Gawar, 350km west of Kathmandu.

2002

December 18: Insurgents attack a police post in Koilabas, Indo-Nepal border, Dang district, and kill six police personnel injure two more.

November 14: Intense clashes occur between security forces and Maoists in Jumla and Gorkha. Insurgents, numbering several hundreds, attack Jumla airport and two police establishments and other government offices killing Jumla Chief District Officer Damodar Pant and two civilians Also, 33 policemen and four soldiers are killed in the clashes in Jumla, while the insurgents lose at least 55 cadres.

23 police personnel are killed during clashes in Gorkha.

Insurgents kill former Member of Parliament Chakra Bahadur Chaudhary of the Communist Party of Nepal--United-Marxist-Leninist (CPN-UML), at his residence in Dhangadhi.

October 27: Insurgents attack the Rumjatar airport, Okhaldhunga district. The chief of the security forces stationed there, a Captain in the Army, and two more troops are killed.

September 28: Maoists attack the Phaplu airport tower causing a damage of NR 2 million.

September 13: Nine police personnel, traveling in a jeep, are killed in an ambush laid by Maoist insurgents near the Mahendra Highway, Siraha district.

September 12: Insurgents set-off an explosion and destroy the residence of Minister of State for Local Development Duryodhan Singh Chandhary at Padsari, Rupandehi district.

September 11: Insurgents attack and damage the residence of former Minister of State Bhakta Bahadur Rokaya at Mahat in Jumla, and separately set-off explosions at the home of former Minister Netra Bikram Thapa.

September 10: Maoist insurgents blast the residence of Hom Nath Dahal, spokesperson of the Nepali Congress faction headed by Prime Minister Sher Bahadur Deuba, in Okhaldungha.

September 8: 49 police personnel are killed and 21 more injured in an attack by a group of an estimated 1,100 Maoist insurgents in Sindhuli district at the Bhimad police post.

A group of an estimated 3,000 insurgents, in the Argakhachi district headquarters town of Sandhikharka, kill 68 SF personnel and raze to the ground all government offices in the town.

July 5: Ten persons are injured in a bomb explosion at the headquarters of Prime Minister Sher Bahadur Deuba's faction of the Nepali Congress party in New Baneswore area, Kathmandu.

February 17: 48 Royal Nepal Army troops and 49 police personnel are killed by Maoists in Mangalsen (Acham district) clashes.

2001

December 27: Maoists set off an explosion and damage the residence of Assistant Law Minister Nagendra Kumar Raya in Phulparasai village, Sarlahi district.

December 23: Insurgents destroy the private residence of Cabinet Minister Chiranjivi Wagle in Chitwan district.

December 19: The house of Water Resources Minister Narayan Sharma Poudel, in Chitwan district, is set ablaze by Maoists.

November 23: Maoist insurgents break the ongoing truce by attacking the Army barracks in Ghorai, Dang district, killing 14 soldiers and injuring 30 others. Separately, the insurgents attack the airport in Surkhet and blow up a private-owned helicopter, besides damaging two more helicopters stationed at the airport.

July 7: Insurgents set off explosions near the private residence of Prime Minister Girija Prasad Koirala at Biratnagar. However, no one is killed or injured in the incident

April 1: At least 300 Maoists attack a hilltop police post in Rukum district and kill 31 police personnel, besides injuring 11 and abducting 23 more.

February 3: Maoist insurgents ambush the convoy of Chief Justice Keshav Prasad Upadhyay, who narrowly escapes the attack, in Chhyasatti, Surkhet, 500km west of the capital Kathmandu. Six others, including a judicial officer, are killed in the attack.

2000

September 24: 1,000 Maoist insurgents attack and demolish the district administration headquarters and a branch of the Nepal Rashtriya Bank in Dunai, Dolpo district.

June 8: 1,600 Maoist insurgents surround a police post manned by 53 personnel in Jajarkot district and attack with mortars and bombs. Nine police personnel, seven civilians and 21 insurgents are killed in the incident.

February 7: Maoists waylay a bus in Dolakha district carrying Polish tourists and rob them of approximately US$ 5,000 in cash. This is the first major incident by Maoists targeting foreign visitors.

1999

April 19: Maoist insurgents explode bombs at the office of the Election Commission and of Gorkhapatra, the largest circulated Nepali newspaper, in Kathmandu.

March 5: Communist Party of Nepal--Unified-Marxist-Leninist (CPN-UML) leader Yadu Gautam is assassinated by Maoist insurgents

19

Cooperative Environment for Dealing with Terrorism

The chapter summarizes some of the lessons derived from three decades of experience in dealing with political violence in Sri Lanka, and argues that the Sri Lankan experience can provide many lessons on to how not to deal with political violence. Its focus will be South Asia. The chapter then argues that a human security framework needs to be established which can combine the objectives of state security with the promotion of human security.

Characteristics of Modern Terrorism

Although a draft text is now being prepared by the United Nations of a definition of terrorism, there is still no consensus. The UN, whilst attempting a comprehensive definition of terrorism, delineated some broad characteristics of the phenomenon.

> *Terrorism is, in most cases, essentially a political act. It is meant to inflict dramatic and deadly injury on civilians and to create an atmosphere of fear, generally for a political or ideological (whether secular or religious purpose. Terrorism is a criminal act, but it is more than mere criminality.*

To overcome the problem of terrorism it is necessary to understand its political nature as well as it is basic criminality and psychology.

An understanding of the linkages between politics, modernity, criminality; and psychology are essential in creating a new security framework. Often, these linkages are not understood, and narrow definitions of state security lead to an accentuation of the problem.

Conflicts will not disappear from the planet, nor is there any likelihood that they will diminish. As long as conflicts remain, political violence will be used by those who feel disenfranchised. It is my argument that the twenty-first century will witness new types of conflict, which are both ethno-political and systemic in character. Some of the systemic conflicts will not be based on territorial claims.

The Political Nature of Violence

Identity conflicts will become the dominant from of conflicts in the years to come. Identity conflicts have something to do with both context, and a searth for meaning. They came into ascendancy a long time ago, with the beginning of the French Revolution and with the birth of nationalism. Today, they have received a new salience after the demise of the Cold War and remain the most intractable conflicts in the world today. The ascendancy of identity conflicts is a result of many factors. Imagined communities are a fact of modernity. Globalization and the global village have different impacts on different communities. Modern means of communication can lead to instant communications and mobilization worldwide. Other reasons which have been given for the ascendancy of identity claims are that, increasingly, group claims are seen by communities as a basic human right, with the demand for representation and sharing power equitably. The presence of diaspora and cross-border affiliations and networks, and easy access to arms are bur a few reasons found in the literature. The primary factor for the increase in salience of identity conflicts is the manner in which the state responds and mediates these identity claims. Often, the state exacerbates these conflicts through the use of indiscriminate state violence.

Another interesting aspect of these developments is the notion of catastrophic terrorism where the targets are large numbers of civilians through the use of chemical, biological, radiological, or nuclear weapons. A distinct form of terrorism, which has hit centre stage, is the terrorism associated with the demonization of the US as a hegemonic superpower, where all citizens of the US and its allies are targets of attack. Distinctions, therefore, need to be made on the political context in the use of violence. The current war declared by Al Qaeda forces against US hegemony is a modern phenomenon whose aim is not the achievement of state power in one single country. These conflicts are not based on the struggle for a territorial unit. Unlike the military political structures of ethno-political movements whose organizations were monolithic with a single line of command, modern organizations are loosely formed networks, which are transnational in nature. The existence of imagined communities worldwide provides networks for raising funds and extension of activities. Systemic conflicts of this nature will become more prominent in the years to come. A small and well-knit group with access to state of the art technology' and easy access to weapons of mass destruction has the capacity to destroy entire cities and intlict huge damage on populations. This is why the Security Council has now given prominence to non-state actors being a major threat to international security.

What we know about ethno-political violence is that it has significantly changed its character. There is a need to study the political economy of internal conflicts so as to understand the complexities which are inherent in such conflicts. A fundamental change after the Cold War has been that the sources of financing of international terrorism have undergone a profound change. Before the Cold War, the US, the former Soviet Union, China and other regional powers such as India and Pakistan trained, financed, and supported organizations which acted as a proxy to their global or regional interests. Today new patron-client relationships are being developed with uneasy alliances with ever-expanding international criminal networks. These criminal networks, whether they are based on narcotic smuggling and drug trafficking, money laundering, sale of weapons, the smuggling of people and children, and trafficking of women around the world constitutes a grave threat to global security. In some countries such as Russia and Colombia, they behave as a parallel government, with relationships to ethno-political movements in the region. New important features stand out with regards the capacity of such coalitions to bypass national governments and to operate independently on a global scale.

Another aspect is the deliberate abuse of civilian populations, Civilian populations are stripped of assets and used as human reservoirs, both to attract outside emergency relief, and to procure fresh recruits for armed factions engaged in protracted internal conflicts. The loss of external support has caused such movements to look for alternative venues for income generation. The looting, money laundering, and extortion of local population groups are highly disruptive for local livelihood systems, and mostly result in a transfer of assets from civilians to armed factions engaged in such violent conflicts.

The technology that is currently being used by such groups is also more lethal and aimed at killing large numbers of citizens. Whether it is an airplane being converted into a human missile, or a suicide bomb that detonates in a crowded environment, the aim is to inflict large-scale damage to citizens, The suicide bomb has become a low-cost technology which can be used anywhere, whether it is a restaurant, a subway a supermarket, or a crowed market place. This technology today is capable of being developed very easily and is exported to other conflict zones. No country will be a safe haven from the reach of terrorism. Whether it is a seaside resort as in Bali, or the Parliament as in India, or a central bank as in Sri Lanka, the lethal hand of terrorism will strike without warning. What is distinctive about the suicide bomber is that the recruitment to political terrorist movements is very popular. Although originally the age group of the suicide bomber was between the ages of 18 and 28, today both men and women, the rich and the poor irrespective of age join such suicide squads. Studies on the psychology of the suicide bomber are also very revealing. It is certainly not economic impoverishment, or alienation from society which are at the root of the psychological dimension. Studies demonstrate the intense feelings of humiliation and anger at the perceived injustice brought upon them by their opponents and the sense of martyrdom given to them by their community which are at the heart of this phenomenon.

The risk of the proliferation of nuclear and biological weapons is a cause for grave concern. Strengthening the system of surveillance and monitoring becomes imperative. The fear of a rogue state obtaining access to weapons of mass destruction haunts the minds of many in the security establishment. What is even more alarming is the outcome if a small and well-placed group obtains access to such weapons.

Another concern, which has arisen in the last decade or so, is the proliferation and easy accessibility of small weapons, which help to fuel civil wars. Over the last decade, this problem has been recognized, and a Group of Experts has been established within the UN. Many regional workshops have been held, and standards are being discussed on how to monitor and regulate these flows in the grey market. Small-arms transfers are more difficult to detect, and there are very powerful lobbies such as in the US which refuse to accept the necessity of universal standards being adopted.

The privatization of security is another serious concern. The inability of weak states to protect their security from internal threats has given rise to a variety of private security establishments, which can be a grave threat to the country as well as its neighbours. The best example is the private corporation Executive Outcomes, which was originally based in South Africa. Today, it is a worldwide network of mercenaries, which offers its services to weak states and corporations. Its connections with lucrative diamond mines as in Angola and Sierra Leone as a trade-off for services rendered is well documented.

The Psychological Aspects of Terrorism

The UN has rightly drawn attention to the psychological aspects of terrorism. The psychological aspects of this phenomenon of denial need to be clearly borne in mind. In a situation of intensive globalization, the revolution of expectations and the feelings of relative deprivation are normally seen as a source of violence. Lindner argues, however, that deprivation is a superficial answer. She suggests that deprivation has many facets poverty, low status, or marginalization, but it does not automatically lead to violence The question must be as to what it is that transforms deprivation into unbearable suffering of a kind that triggers the urge to retaliate with violence. She suggests that feelings of humiliation are the answer. "Feelings of humiliation may lead to acts of humiliation perpetrated on the perceived community setting off cycles of humiliation in which everybody who is involved feels humiliated, and convinced that humiliating the humiliated is a just and holy duty." Whether it is the Israel-Palestine conflict, or the conflict between the Government of Sri Lanka and the Liberation Tigers of Tamil Eelam (LTTE), or the current global war between the US and

Al Qaeda, the psychological aspect of humiliation plays a significant role.

Lindner suggests that feelings of humiliation come about when deprivation is perceived as illegitimate, an imposition of lowering or degradation, one that cannot be explained in constructive terms. She goes on to explain that feelings of deprivation have much to do with modernity; where the universal message of human rights and equality creates the conditions for a sense of deprivation.

> *We live in a world that is listening to the message of human rights that indicates that every human being has a right to live in enabling circumstances; that equality is the ruling idea and not hierarchy; that every person has an inner core of dignity that ought not be lowered. In the first instance it strengthened feelings of humiliation, because inequalities and deprivation that were accepted before turn into unacceptable acts of humiliation perpetrated by the powerful on the less powerful.*

The point that is made here is that relative deprivation is an important concept, but it is not sufficient. Humiliation alone, however, is not enough, since humiliation requires a means of expressing itself through a process of mobilization. And it is this connection between humiliation and mass mobilization that leads to genocide, gross human right violations, and political violence, and is given legitimacy.

Post-11 September and Security Dilemmas

The post-11 September situation has precipitated a strategic shift in security thinking. The US has argued that the current global security, threats require a new paradigm shift in interstate relations, where the interdependence of the global system must be emphasized. Whilst the main thrust of the US-led coalition is to isolate and destroy the threat from the Al Qaeda network; it also uses this to enlarge its influence in many parts of the world. In this sense, many regions will be brought under the strategic umbrella of US security interests. Post-11 September also meant that the threat to the state is no longer conceived as external, but as the enemy within. In a multi-ethnic society such as the US, profound changes will occur in the surveillance of its own citizens. Where foreign adventures helped the Bush Administration buttress its vulnerable domestic base, post-11 September, national security has justified an increase in executive power even in areas unrelated to military operations. Executive power over law and enforcement has grown quickly, worrying those Americans who still believe in the separation of powers.

The commitment of the Bush Administration to regime termination in Iraq will have catastrophic consequences not only for Iraq, but also for the rest of the world. Evidence from the 1991 war indicates that it is highly likely that the Iraqi regime will use all available military means, including chemical and biological weapons, if its very survival is threatened. The Iraqi regime is one of the most despotic and authoritarian states in the world today: Its record of using nerve gas against the Kurds, the unilateral attack on Iran which took the lives of over a million people, and the attack on Kuwait are well-known ro the people. But whether unilateral action by a single country can deal with this phenomenon, violating international law and bypassing the UN is the issue.

According to President Bush's theory of the three evils, Iran and North Korea may also become focal points of destabilization. One of the key factors in targetting Iraq is that Iraq is the second largest producer of oil. With the depletion of oil reserves within the US, the quest for a continuous source of supply of oil becomes imperative to the current thinking of the Republican party of the US. Saudi Arabia has become a questionable ally; and cannot be relied on after the involvement of its citizens in the events of 11 September. The destabilization and balkanization of Iraq will be the first step in restructuring political relations in the Middle East as a whole.

Whilst 11 September provided the US with the moral authority to create the broadest possible coalition against terrorism, the invasion of Iraq will be the opposite. It will question that moral authority. The overwhelming majority of the world's population opposes the invasion of Iraq. The Security Council is deeply divided, and NATO is split down the middle. The US and the UK may decide to take unilateral action. Countries will be persuaded to support the US due to duress and leverage, which the US uses as the sole superpower and hegemon in the world today. One likely outcome may be that the unipolar status of the US as the number one superpower with a transatlantic alliance will be pitted against a multipolar axis based on Germany, France, and Russia. The consequences of this invasion will have profound implications for international relations in the years to come. The US and its allies will lose the moral high ground upon which they relied for legitimacy.

Asia and Terrorism

There are many reasons why Asia would become vulnerable to new forms of violence. The interplay of identity and modernity provides a fertile ground for new conflicts to emerge. What we know about terrorism is that it is changing its character, and that Asia will be the most vulnerable in the years to come. Asia accounts for 75 per cent of all terrorism casualties worldwide, while the southern belt is a theatre for terrorism, insurgency, and separatist violence that is very high compared with any other part of the world. The list of countries in this southern belt is Afghanistan, Pakistan, Uzbekistan, Tajikistan, Chinese-ruled Xinjiang and Tibet, India, Nepal, Sri Lanka, Bangladesh, and Burma. In South Asia alone, the annual number of fatalities in terrorist violence is again the highest in the world. Endemic ethnic conflicts, ideological conflicts, conflicts over resources and conflicts over governance, therefore, pose a serious threat to stability and interstate relations. In this sense, what we are witnessing today is multiple conflicts where the ideological, ethnic, and governance issues are often intertwined.

But the fundamental reason is to be seen in the failure of the nation building experiment by the political elite to meet the aspirations of the people. The failure of governance is a distinct feature of many of the states in the region. Further, the nature and character of the state is under contest. The state is under contest by multiple forces ranging from fundamentalist forces to ethno-political violence.

The regional dynamics need also to be seen within the assertions of US supremacy in South Asia, where each of the countries within the region is searching for a new patron-client status with the US. The Indian Ocean will become a high-security zone and a base for refuelling and protection of US interests. Since 11 September, India has shown its willingness to cooperate with the US in a common security framework. The nuclear standoff between India and Pakistan, the cross-border tensions, which exist between the two countries, constitute major obstacles to building a cooperative framework. Further, the turbulence in Pakistan and its ethno-religious composition means that future threats to its security are ever-present.

The fact that Pakistan has a nuclear arsenal and is vulnerable to regime change could make Pakistan a potential rogue state. In India, the programmes committed against Muslims in Gujarat, and the blatant connivance of the state in encouraging this outrage against the Muslim community will also have widespread repercussions in India and elsewhere. The civil war in Nepal continues to escalate, and creates a major threat to the state and security across the borders. The Sri Lankan conflict remains as a no war, no peace situation. Any resumption of war in Sri Lanka will have horrendous consequences. Bangladesh, it seems, is witnessing a collapse of governance, and whether this will give rise to Islamic fundamentalism is still to be seen.

Human Security in Sri Lanka

Eleven September did have an important effect on the ongoing negotiations between the Government of Sri Lanka and the LTTE. The LTTE, in this instance, may have been compelled to rethink their strategic objectives and discipline their behaviour according to the new standards imposed by the international community.

Sri Lanka is an interesting and compelling case to study as to what causes terrorism as a political phenomenon. There has been considerable writing, debates and conferences on this vexed question. It may be interesting to look at some of the factors, which led to the Tamil, and Sinhalese insurrections, which have dominated the country's politics since the 1970s. These insurrections have been launched by Sinhalese youth, as represented by the JVP in 1971 and 1989, and by the Tamil militant movement since 1975. In both these cases, extreme violence was used extensively to promote political objectives. Both these insurgencies should become a laboratory for those who wish to study terrorism and insurgencies of the future. Many of the ingredients of modern ethno-political mobilization and organization are present here.

The most significant explanation for the rise of Tamil militancy is the failure of nation building. The political elite who inherited the state administration and government since independence in 1948 undertook a policy of exclusion. The Tamil population was excluded from sharing political power and patronage in the country. The evolution of a Sinhala hegemonic state, and the inability of the political elite to design a power-sharing system with its minorities was—and still is—a fundamental question which has not been resolved. Further, the system of discrimination in language, education, and access to resources compounded the feelings of alienation and marginalization felt by the Tamil minority. Therefore, the denial of identity; and the denial of language acted as a powerful mobilizing force for the Tamil insurgency.

In Sri Lanka, the Sinhalese youth launched two major insurrections in the country; in 1971 and 1989. In both cases, the ranks of the insurgency were recruited from underemployed graduates and south from the rural sector. A Youth Commission established to inquire into the youth insurgency concluded that alienation of young people, lack of opportunity and employment, and a class system dominated by the English-speaking elite were some of the major causes of the insurgency Here again, the revolution of expectations created by a consumerist culture, a severe sense of relative deprivation leading to humiliation became the motive force for the insurrection, Even after two insurgencies launched by the JVP, governments have not been able to address the root causes.

If we examine state responses to the insurgencies in Sri Lanka, we can also draw some very important lessons. All governments in Sri Lanka not only failed to meet Tamil aspirations, this failure to accommodate the moderate Tamil elite led to a situation where a younger generation, impatient with non-violence and the parliamentary road decided to take arms against the state to fight for a separate state. What is interesting is to evaluate state responses to the initial phase of Tamil insurgency The government of the day decided that the best way to suppress the Tamil insurgency was to resort to military means. Again, lack of experience and a simplistic military mindset assumed that deploying the armed forces in the Tamil areas, mass arrests, harassment, forced evacuations of populations and pogroms would contain the insurgency. In fact, it did precisely the opposite. The pogroms initiated by the government in July 1983 against Tamils living in Colombo not only legitimized the insurgency amongst many Tamils, they helped to recruit large numbers of Tamil youth into the ranks of the militant movement. The lesson that can be learnt from this experience is the failure of the State to provide security to all its peoples. There was no selective use of force, deployed primarily against the combatants, but there was indiscriminate violence against civilians living in the north and east of the country.

Another critical aspect that we need to examine is the security infrastructure available to contain the Tamil insurgency. There was a distinct and marked failure in the intelligence gathering system of the state, This lack of capacity to collect information, and also to analyse the information for policy makers led to a situation of a self-fulfilling prophecy. Intelligence agencies gave the politicians what they wanted to know. State intelligence continuously downplayed the strength of the insurgent forces, their combat strength, and their popular base amongst the people. This failure of intelligence meant that policy makers went into military adventures at great cost to life and equipment, In the case of Sri Lanka, it led to some spectacular military debacles.

It is also interesting to analyse the response of the Tamil insurgency to the state security apparatus. In a way the Tamil militant movement may have actually provoked the state to retaliate against its acts of terror indiscriminately. If so, the state fell into the trap. Indiscriminate violence by the state helped to bring large numbers of new recruits to the insurgent movement, and helped to legitimize their political goals internationally.

Another factor which helped the cause of the LTTE was the cross border support and sustenance provided by the Indian government. In the early days of the Tamil insurgency the Indian government provided training and financial support to the Tamil militant movement, and found in the end that it could not control the very movement that it had nourished in its own soil, The LTTE eventually turned against the Indian Peace Keeping Force, which was humiliated by the LTTE through a sustained military and propaganda campaign against it. India, which had played an important role as the mediator in the conflict, profoundly misjudged the nature of the insurgency and failed to build the trust necessary to mediate a negotiated solution.

A very significant reason for the expansion and base for the in surgency was the support of the diaspora, which the Tamil insurgency received. On the one hand, the civil war continued to create more and more refugees both external and as Internally Displaced Persons (IDPs). Refugees who fled abroad found employment in the various capitals of the West, such as Toronto,

Washington, London, Paris, Rome, Sydney Oslo, etc. The numbers that live in the diaspora range between 500,000 and 700,000. These refugees who eventfully found gainful employment became a significant tax base for the insurgent movement. The LTTE were able to build an extensive network within the diaspora, where the taxes collected helped to finance the movement. The ever expanding refuges camps of the internally displaced became an important recruitment base for the LITE.

An interesting aspect of the rise of the LTTE is their relationship with international criminal networks, In the early stages of the insurgency; India provided training, arms, and financial support for the Tamil insurgency. As a result of the rupture in the relations between India and the LTTE, the LTTE had to find new resources to continue the war. This meant intensive extortion and taxation of their own population, pillage, plunder, and systematic procurement of arms from the Sri Lankan state. The LTTE built up an extensive network of commercial networks, with over 12 cargo ships, over 60 offices worldwide, and extensive relations with other political and criminal networks. The extent of their relationship with criminal networks is still not clear.

The means adopted by the LTTE to fight the war were multifaceted. One of the most lethal weapons they developed was the "suicide bomber". The suicide squad, it is alleged, became the most popular division for the new recruits. The suicide bomber was selected to become a martyr in the cause of a noble goal. Suicide bombers were the elite corps of the LTTE movement. They enjoyed a personal relationship with their leader, and their families were given pride of place in the annals of the martyrs. Each year, Martyrs' Day is celebrated, the graves are decorated with the photograph of the martyr, and their families given a pension and land.

A fundamental flaw in the counter-insurgency strategy of the state was to ignore human security for all the people in the north cast. An overt and narrow definition of state security became the all-compelling motive force behind the so-called war against terror. The Prevention of Terrorism Act became an indiscriminate weapon in the hands of the security forces. A policy of protecting citizen's rights, the right to life, dignity, and freedom became of secondary importance.

The current peace talks between the Government of Sri Lanka and the LTTE are intended to finally end the protracted civil war in the country. An important bet to note here is that the LTTE are not a defeated army. Neither is the Sri Lankan Army. It is too early in the days to know the final outcome of the talks, Both parties have agreed to federal solution. The existence of an armed movement in the south of India will have security implications for Sri Lanka's neighbours. A well armed entity with a standing army and links with international networks is bound to be seen by India as a source of potential destabilization for the entire region. Whether the international community led by the US and Britain is able to leverage the LTTE to give up their position for a separate state, respect the rights of minorities and the peoples living in the north and the east is still to be seen. But the talks in Oslo, where the LTTE are given equal status whilst being a banned party may open new vistas in international diplomacy. It will also provoke serious concern in countries which are experiencing ethno-political contlict in their own countries, for it sets a new paradigm in the negotiation of internal conflicts.

Changing Nature of Global Security

Over the last two decades, many organizations have maintained that global security must be broadened from the traditional focus on the security of states to include the security of peoples and the planet. As the face of global society has changed, so has the nature of global security. Among the various concepts of security frequently used are common security collective security and comprehensive security. The independent commission on Disarmament and Security Issues chaired by the late Olaf Palme first spelled out [the meaning of] common security The concept articulated by that commission recognizes that lasting security would not be achieved until it could be shared by all, and that it could only be achieved through cooperation, based on the principles of equity, justice, and reciprocity. Recently a new concept that of human security has received attention. This is a people-centred approach that is concerned not so much with weapons as with basic human dignity" As explained in the *Human Development Report*, 1994 (UNDP), human security includes safety from chronic threats such as hunger, disease, and repression, as well as protection from sudden and harmful disruption in the patterns of daily life. In this regard, terrorism then, is the cost of lack of a security regime.

The concept of the security of people recongnizes that global security extends beyond the protection of borders, the ruling elite, and exclusive state interests to include the protections of people. The Commission on Global Governance in its report suggests that:

> *The security of people must be regarded as a goal as important as the security of states. Ultimately, the two objectives arc not in conflict; statues cannot be secure for long unless their citizens are secure. Too often in the past however, preserving the security of the state has been used as an excuse for policies that undermined the security of the people.*

Some of these concerns coincide with demands made by the UN and other think tanks regarding rethinking the global security system. The Brandt Commission, the Palme Commission, the Commission on Global Governance, and the Commission for the Prevention of Deadly Confl icts have, over the years called for a paradigm shift in international relations based on an emphasis on human security and a cooperative system between states and citizens. The US was not particularly enamoured with the recommendation of these think tanks and ignored them. It was only after 11 September that they recognized the need for a common security strategy. How ever, the security threat is perceived in narrow terms, which is to *combat* terrorism rather than to *prevent* terrorism. The resources, therefore which have gone for combating terrorism far exceed the expenditure for preventing terrorism. Further, the coalition is based on a narrow framework, and is likely to evaporate once and if the US has secured its limited objectives.

The new threats to global security require a global cooperative framework to monitor, manage, and establish new standards governing interstate relations. No single country will he able to achieve this; multilateral cooperation is necessary This framework is obviously needed, but must transcend narrow definitions which only call for combating terrorism. It must expand the base of its concerns to establish a truly global security system. A comprehensive security strategy requires a framework where states are obliged not only to focus on State security but also on human security. It must focus on the twin pillars of security, viz. freedom from want, and freedom from fear.

Regional Frameworks

The original impetus to develop a framework for security in Europe was taken by NGOs which met regularly in Helsinki. One organization which seeks to combine this twin approach is the organization for Security and Cooperation in Europe (OSCE), which is the largest regional security organization in the world, with 55 participating states from Europe, Central Asia, and North America. It is active in early warning, conflict prevention, crisis management and post-conflict rehabilitation. The OSCE approach to security is comprehensive and cooperative: comprehensive in dealing with a wide range of security-related issues including arms control, preventive diplomacy, confidence and security building measures, human rights, democratization, election monitoring and economic and environmental security; cooperative in the sense that OSCE participating states have equal status, and decisions arc based on consensus. Whether these values and institutional commitments can be transferred to other regional is open to question. However, early warning, conflict prevention, and all the other elements, which go to make for human security, is a precondition for a stable security environment. The OSCE, however, failed to prevent the violent upheavals in the Balkans, Georgia, and Chechnya.

An important institution which has been developed by the OSCE is the Office of the High Commissioner on National Minorities, which was established in 1992. It seeks the early resolution of ethnic tensions that might endanger peace, stability, or friendly relations between OSCE participating states. Operating independently of all parties involved, the high commissioner is empowered to conduct on-site missions and engage in preventive diplomacy at the earliest stage of tension. The Office of the High Commissioner on National Minorities has become a vital component in preventive diplomacy. The quiet and discreet role of the commissioner, the capacity to open space for dialogue between ethnic communities, the problem solving approaches that he utilizes have all helped to contain and mitigate conflict. How this institution can be developed within other regional forums is open for discussion.

SAARC and a Cooperative Framework

Regional institutions will play an important role in developing a cooperative security framework. The best such example elaborated in this chapter is of OSCE. It is a model in effective cooperation between the countries of Europe. There is, however, no likelihood that SAARC will ever approximate this model in the near future. There has been considerable resistance to this idea, particularly by India.

These factors mean that reaching consensus on common security requires a series of measures to maintain tranquillity and stability in the region. The first is the peaceful resolution of the conflict between Pakistan and India. Second, it requires a protocol that cross border support for insurgent movements will not be practised. Third, it requires a commitment to human security preventive diplomacy and peace building as strategic priorities for the region, and policies enunciated for such a cooperative framework.

Towards a Regional Framework for Preventive Diplomacy and Conflict Resolution

Whilst every effort needs to be given to strengthen regional in situations such as SAARC, it is obvious that we cannot leave the job of protecting and developing a wider form of security to inter state institutions alone. The fact that SAARC has not been able to convene its annual meetings demonstrates how India, as a big power, can veto the organization's effective performance. States are naturally concerned with the management of conflicts, whilst what is required is the transformation of power relations, participation, and power sharing within the existing state system.

Role of Civil Society

Citizens are no longer bystanders with regards to human rights, peace, and security South Asian civil society is composed of a multitude of sectors, composed of women's movements, environ mental movements, human rights and peace, trade unions, professional organizations, universities, and a host of other institutions. What is required is to enhance their capacity for intervention in reshaping human security?

Civil society over the years, has many substantial gains in making states accountable. The human rights movement has increased its ability to monitor and hold accountable states that violate human rights law. Today non-state armed actors come under the purview of these organizations, and we increasingly find that non state actors have to respond to reports and evaluations made on them. The movernellt towards building the International Criminal Court, and holding states and individuals accountable to crimes against humanity is another example.

Political Economy of Internal Conflicts

An intuitive assessment of the situations in South Asia is the lack of data with regards to the political economy of internal conflict. There are still no institutions that are devoted to the study of civil wars. Internal conflicts are still seen as a problem of state security, and are based on the premises of the realist paradigm. Conflict research is largely based on how to ensure state security. Most of the institutions established to study and research internal conflicts are run by retired military personnel with a strong realist bias. There are still no databases which identify potential conflicts and actors in conflict situations, and databases which store information with regards to peace accords reached between parties and the lessons learnt from past negotiations. There arc indeed no comparative studies on internal conflicts within the region. Even in Sri Lanka, which has been well-researched in terms of its civil war, there is still no institution which has retained a record of past negotiations and lessons that can be learnt from them. There arc very little data on the relationship of criminal networks to civil wars, or an identification of such networks and how they operate. Studies on those who gain from internal conflicts are almost non-existent.

Urban centres in South Asia are in most cases multi-ethnic societies, where coexistence between different ethnic and religious identities is commonplace. However, cities are the most vulnerable to ethnic cleansing and pogroms. Studies need to be generated to comparative experiences of so-called riots and pogroms, and how municipalities and provincial governments dealt with them. Such a comparative data bank will be useful in the prevention and timely intervention for prevention.

The indiscriminate use of violence by the security forces and police is a critical variable in conflict escalation. More research and comparative studies arc required on the use of force in internal armed conflicts. More comparative studies arc required on the relationship between the use of state violence and non-state violence. Further, the state, which is responsible for security, needs to understand that if force is necessary, on how to use force effectively and not involve civilians. It is argued here in this paper that the indiscriminate use of violence by the security forces was the principal cause for the escalations of the conflict in Sri Lanka. Training of law enforcement agencies in conflicts resolution, prevention, and mitigation is a prerequisite for ensuring that humanitarian law and human rights law are respects in armed conflicts.

Towards a Comprehensive Strategy for Peace Building

Each country will have to reflect and initiate programmes for a comprehensive peace building strategy. Such a comprehensive strategy is necessary if countries are to ensure that peace and tranquillity prevail for economic and social growth. The lessons learnt from past mistakes indicate that it is cost-effective to invest in preventive measures and ensure human security for all. A comprehensive peace building strategy is multifaceted and requires civil-society engagement at several levels. What follows are a few suggestions on what can be done.

Early Warning Systems

A very important tool in the prevention of conflicts is the establishment of early warning systems. South Asia requires such an early warning system. Early warning of conflict has become a tool in the mitigation and prevention of conflict. The UN, the Organization of African Unity and the European Union have now developed elaborate early warning systems and formulated a variety of response mechanisms for conflict mitigation and prevention. It is now being realized that conflicts can be prevented by timely action. Studies have also revealed that early warning systems, together with preventive capacity building, can help to mitigate conflict.

Early warning can be defined as an information system which can provide timely information to decision makers on impending conflicts, humanitarian disasters, and the mass exodus of peoples. By early warning of conflict, we mean essentially political conflict. Timely intervention can be at any point in the conflict spectrum, viz. conflict formation phase, conflict escalation phase, conflict stagnation phase, negotiations phase, and the transformation phase.

An effective early warning system is essentially an information system with a well-developed database, which can predict, forecast, and extrapolate on future conflict scenarios. After 11 September, many sophisticated models for forecasting are now being developed in the US. It is important to note that early warning is not merely an information system. Early warning information relies heavily on information brokers, experts, and analysts who can help to provide qualitative information. Significant indicators have been developed which are help us in identifying conflict dynamics. Scholars have identified triggers and accelerators which can help us understand what catalyses a particular conflict dynamic.

The model in Fig.19.1 provides a birds-eye view of how such a citizen-based early warning system could look like. Currently, this model is being applied in Sri Lanka, The model specifics a variety of tools which can be applied for information handling. It provides for field monitors who can regularly update and provide information. Such a centre will also initiate rapid response mechanisms through a network of citizen-based organizations.

Early Warning Systems: Comparative Experience

Since the 1950s, repeated efforts have been made to develop early warning systems that could provide decision makers and other key stakeholders with timely information on impending conflicts and humanitarian disasters. Early warning as a term covers a range of distinct activities, from conflict analysis and monitoring, to data analysis, risk assessment, and advocacy. Approaches to early warning range from the predominantly qualitative (the International Crisis Group, or ICG) to largely quantitative (the Country Indicators for Foreign Policy or CIFP programme at Carleton University Canada), FAST, a programme of the Swiss Peace Foundation, relies on a mix of qualitative (field monitoring, fact finding, and expert analysis) and quantitative (event analysis) data, ICG, CIFP and FAST are implemented by one organization. Other efforts at early warning, such as the Forum for Early Warning and Early Response (FEWER), have focused on building networks to share information, expertise, and analysis.

In general, early warning systems have sought to achieve three main objectives: (1) identify the root causes of conflict; (2) predict the outbreak of conflict (ICG, FAST, FEWER); and (3) mitigate or prevent conflict (ICG, FEWER) follow contrasting strategies. ICG relies primarily on widespread coverage of its recommendations in the media and high profile advocacy with key decision and policy makers, while FEWER focuses on bringing potiential actors together to develop their own responses, sharing in analysis of the situation; developing institutional activity and capacity profiles; and mobilizing experts to support efforts to address key problems. Two key lessons from FEWER experience are: (1) it is more effective to provide analysis than to make specific recommendations that rarely fit within the mandates, structures, or procedures of organizations with the capacity to respond, and (2) it is difficult to combine an analytical function, which requires writing about the impact of various factors (and actors) on the potential for conflict, and an early response function that directly engages in mitigating or preventing conflict. A more effective strategy for FEWER, though it is less direct, has been to bring concerned organizations together and facilitate their efforts to formulate their own responses. This has the added advantage of ensuring greater local ownership over both the analysis and responses.

The archetypal early waiting system should include the following seven components: (1) data collection, (2) data analysis, (3) assessments of the conflict potential, (4) action/response formulation, (5) transmission of responses to key stakeholders, (6) implementation of early responses, and (7) assessment of response effectiveness for feedback into the response formulation process. Given the inherently political nature of efforts to mitigate conflict, early warning systems should also ensure that appropriate steps are taken to minimize any political or security risks. These include: (1) an explicit set of values that address a broadly humanitarian concern, peace building and saving people's lives; (2) reliance on open sources of information (which is particularly critical as perceptions of intelligence gathering can put field monitors at risk; (3) complete transparency, particularly as efforts to coordinate action will be compromised by perceptions of secrecy or exclusivity; (4) a consistent stance as expert advisers, not political analysis, with careful attention to ensuring that all statements are defensible based on available data and analysis and the organization's stated values; and (5) adequate contingency planning to address any security concerns.

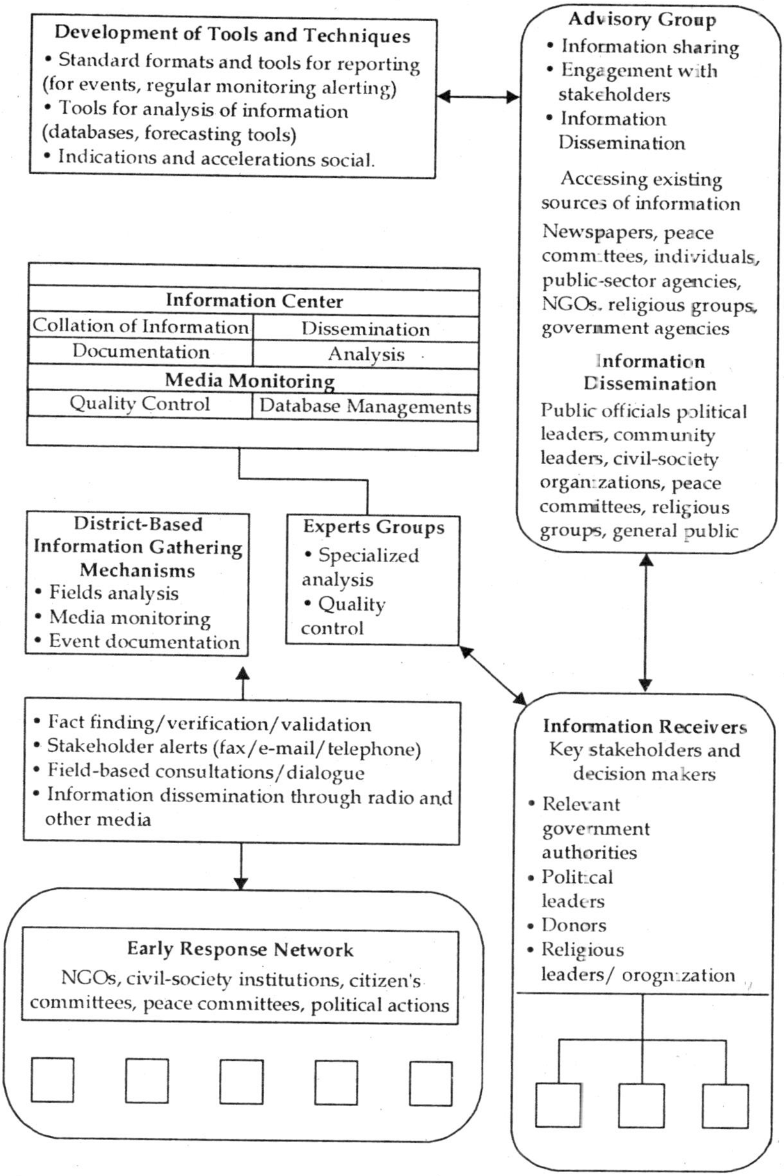

Fig. 19.1: Model for a Citizen-Based Early Warning System

Early warning systems serve as tools for timely action. These means that timely response mechanisms need to be developed which involve citizen networks. What therefore, is being argued here is for a citizen-based early warning and preventive capacity.

During the last few decades, the international community has been able to develop a variety of instruments for the prevention and mitigation of conflicts. Many of these instruments have been deployed in many conflict situations, and evaluations done on the efficacy of these instruments. There is no perfect system. In many cases, early warning systems have failed. If a party is intent on unleashing a pogrom against a hapless community very little can be done. It is also, however, evident that extensive preparations are made before the perpetrators decide to act and unleash violence.

Facilitating Early Response and Preventive Actions

Early response is defined as multiple actions taken to mitigate conflict. As noted above, the purpose of an early warning system is to provide information for timely action: information by itself is of little value, for an early warning system to be effective, the information and analysis generated must be a tool for preventive action at any point along the conflict scale. Rapid response systems and preventive actions are tools which are deployed to mitigate conflict.

Once the potential for an escalation of conflict and violence has been identified, different actions can be taken, generally along parallel tracks. These may include:

1. issuing an alert to all stakeholders;
2. activating an e-mail network to assure wider and more timely dissemination;
3. follow-up telephone calls to key actors and decision makers;
4. deployment of a fact finding mission;
5. activation of other early response mechanisms;
6. ensuring that concerned government agencies are informed;
7. assisting local people's committees in convening meetings;
8. utilizing radio and the mass media to disseminate information locally about the situation;
9. informing political leaders and soliciting their support solicited for preventive action; and

10. preparing a report evaluating results to learn from mistakes.

Such an early response system requires a network of organizations and individuals who can take early action. Members of such an Early Response Network ERN; hold network meetings to share information and analysis and support the formulation and coordination of early responses to potential conflict situations; provide training and other capacity building interventions to network members; and monitor performance. Morė specific activities to be supported will include the following:

1. **Implementation of fact finding missions:** Fact finding missions, early on in the process, can assist in formulating a quick field analysis of a conflict. It is critical that such missions be deployed quickly, and that they be governed by established rules of procedure (of which a member of examples exist). Fact finding missions can help activate network members on the ground, and draw the attention of decision makers and local actors to a potential conflict scenario.
2. **Assist in the organization and training of early response teams:** Early response teams may consist of representatives from local inter-religious organizations, peace committees, and other institutions which has a credible presence in the region. Ongoing training programmes involving hands-on activities and simulations will be conducted to improve their efficency and effectiveness.
3. **Support the development of mechanisms for consultation:** Consultative mechanisms to facilitate the active participation of civil-society organizations in sharing information and developing a common understanding of an emerging conflict scenario need to be quickly put in place. These consultations, local authorities, business organizations, the police and low enforcement agencies, and other local agencies or groups. Political parties may also be included in such consultations.
4. **Conduct workshops or bring parties together in other relevant forums:** Workshops involving key stakeholders and relevant parties can quickly elaborate action plans to mitigate a conflict. Other tools that have been developed to support dialogue among parties to the conflict include mediation, facilitated negotiation, visits by special envoys, human rights monitoring mission, and peace commissions.

5. **Train law enforcement agencies in conflict prevention and mitigation:** Law enforcement officers, in a period of transition, need to be trained in peace building. Although this is necessary, this is not an activity that will be implemented directly by or under PCHS. Rather, the PCHS will complement initiatives already being taken by the berghof foundation for Conflict Studies in collaboration with the security establishment.
6. **Use of local radio and other media:** Timely and will-conceived broadcasts over local radio can help explain and pacify an escalating situation. These can be complemented by published materials in various forms.
7. **Formation of peace committees representing political parties and civil society:** It is essential that proper mapping be done on the capacity of local civil-society organizations, and that effective civil society organizations be supported in developing their capacity to act as catalysts for preventive action in conflict situations.
8. **Support for reciprocal acts reconciliation:** Reciprocal acts of reconciliation can be very useful in reducing tensions and mitigating or preventing conflict. Comparative experience provides a number of well-tested models for designing joint problem-solving interventions to promote reconciliation.

Developing a Regional Capacity to Resolve and Transform Conflicts

Government do not normally involve civil-society institutions in conflict resolution exercises. Track I initiatives are normally initiated by governments where negotiations are done at the high table. Here, protagonists are engaged in positional bargaining methods based on the leverage that each side can utilize. Track I initiatives, on the other hand, are initiatives by civil society to influence the parties to a conflict. Third parties which are influential and which have a strong stake in the outcome of the negotiations process. Often, the protagonists are ill-prepared for serious negotiation, and this lack of preparation serves to protract the can assist both parties to narrow the gap. Capacity building her means the following:

1. **Documentation:** The preparation of essential documentation is a preparation of essential documentation is a pertaining to the conflict, maps, records of previous negations, minutes and newspaper cutting, knowledge of the mistakes make can be very useful for both parties.
2. **Training in conflict resolution and negotiation skills:** Today, there are numerous approaches and methods used for negotiation. They can range from problem solving methods to formats which ensure that both parties seek win-win solutions. Track II initiatives can and should complement Track I diplomacy. Alternative disputed resolution skills require extensive skills in design and framing of conflict dynamics. Such designs require mapping of the conflict parameters, identifying stakeholders, identifying grievances, and providing platforms for dialogue.

Informal Track II efforts can be a vital component in creating space for unofficial dialogue with the parties to a conflict. There are a number of methodologies which are available in the literature. Typically, it could mean that those who are influential and close to the parties and who enjoy their confidence can meet in a safe place where they can begin to unravel the fears, concerns, and issues of the two parties. Methods are employed through visioning exercises, or problem solving techniques for the parties to express their concerns in a safe haven. This exercise can help the parties to understand the fears and concerns, and actually provide channels for communication to the parties. If properly designed, these efforts can be invaluable, and complement the work of a Track I process.

Track III efforts are a vital component in any conflict process design, for it is here that communities need to be engaged in multi-stakeholder dialogue, reconciliation exercises, and building trust and coexistence amongst communities. Often in war-torn societies, the scars o war remain deep within the psyche of communities and traumas and stereotypes of the conflict are difficult to heal. It is here that citizen initiatives to engage in reconciliation and healing and promote forms of coexistence can be a vital component of peace building. What is necessary is to ensure complementarily between the three levels.

Fig. 19.2, drawn from the work of Jean Paul Lederach, explains the three levels and its interrelationships. Level I is a highly visible process, and it usually depends on the top leadership of the country and the leadership of a guerrilla movement. These negotiations usually end up with a cease-fire agreement. Level 2 refers to middle-range leaders who are in a position to influence the course and direction of the negotiations process. They normally engage in different problem solving approaches which can help the parties to examine the assumptions and goals of their negotiations strategy. Middle-range leaders can play a vital role in ensuring communications betweens Levels 3 and 1. Level 3 is of local leaders who experience the trauma and the pain of the conflict. They are community-based organizations which interact with the people. Their work in reconciliation, healing, and promoting coexistence can be a vital component in the process. The figure draws attention to the need for a comprehensive peace building programme which can be sustained at all levels.

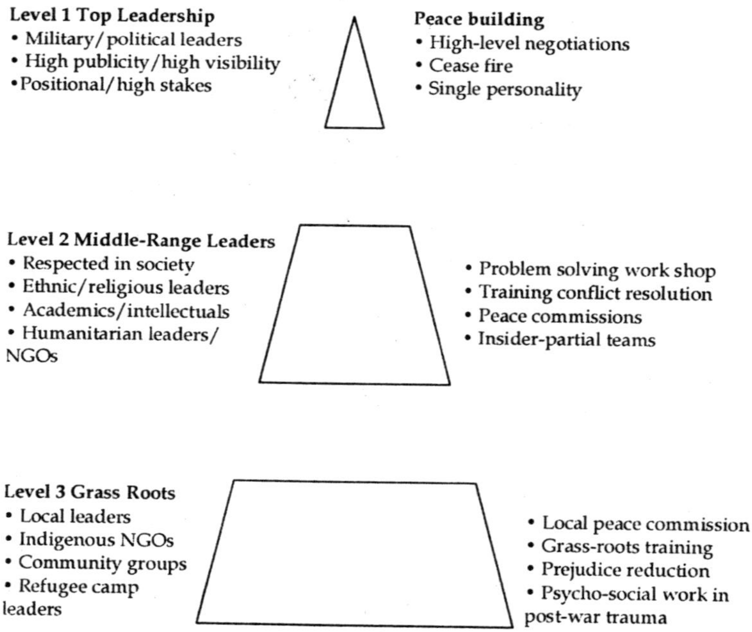

Fig. 19.2. Levels of Interrelationship Between State and Guerrilla Leadership

Summary

The chapter has attempted to highlight the new security threats facing our common future. It emphasizes the need for designing programmes for human security, particularly for vulnerable groups in society. It has argued that early warning and preventive diplomacy centred on human security will rovide the basis for a new social order. The paper has argued that civil society needs to be involved and engaged in the prevention and resolution of conflicts in a volatile region such as South Asia.

20

WORKING ON TERRORISM

The most salient feature that has emerged from the discussion is that terrorism is a ubiquitous phenomenon in the region, and ail countries in South Asia are victims of one or more of the four forms of terrorism identified. These are as a part of the Al Qaeda network arising out of religious fundamentalism; brought about by structural factors like extreme and widely prevalent poverty, glaring inequality and prolonged and gross forms of injustice; and as a result of the general collapse of law and order. Terrorism in each country is influenced by what takes place in the neighbouring countries, and it is not a coincidence that intense terrorism is concentrated in the bordering areas in the region, or the neighborhood of the region.

Outside powers have a definite influence on terrorism in the region. South Asia is in the vortex of the global campaign of outside powers against terrorism. Involvement of other countries in the recent past has spawned terrorism and profoundly influenced interstate relations in South Asia.

There were discussions on the definition of terrorism; its causes and impact; measures for countering and preventing terrorism; on solutions; and on forms of possible cooperation in the future.

Definition

There is no agreed definition of terrorism internationally and that is the main reason why it is not possible to have an international convention on terrorism. However, what is clear is that all forms of violence are not terrorism. Several countries in this region have resorted to violence for different purposes, as in their independence movements, which was not necessarily terrorism. There is a clear shift of emphasis on the importance to be attached to a definition after the 11 September incident. It is now agreed that action to combat terrorism cannot be postponed until agreed definition is arrived at international and should proceed on the basis of a working definition. There is a broad agreement on some elements as a hypothesis which has been agreed upon internationally and gained acceptability.

1. When the violence is resorted to for a premeditated purpose.
2. When it is directed against innocent people or noncombatants.
3. The terms "combatant" and "non-combatant" are controversial. The concept of a "combatant" cannot be extended too widely as it will then be meaningless. For example, it cannot be extended to the families of combatants, or to a whole religious community or nationality Persons targetted for giving signals cannot be classified as combatants.
4. Terrorism should be recognized by the means adopted and the victims of terrorism, not by the goals of the terrorists.
5. "Unlawful" is another term that is frequently used when describing terrorism, and has been brought in to keep the state outside the scope of terrorism. There was a unanimous view at the discussion that this was not acceptable. Legal, political violence, or structural violence by the state against its own people means as much terrorism as violence by non-state actors. This cannot be acceptable in the South Asian context. Democracy has safeguards against structural violence, although it may be practiced imperfectly. But in a totalitarian regime, that safeguard is not generally available. This is the generalization that can be made within the South Asia experiences.

Reasons of Terrorism

1. It is the general consensus that there is no cause or- terrorism that could be applied uniformally to all the countries in the region. The causes are country specific.

2. Without going into all possible causes, some critical variables can be identified.
   (a) Persistence of extreme poverty and accompanying deprivations such as unemployment, low levels of literacy and limited access to health services.
   (b) Non-functioning or malfunctioning of democracy.
   (c) Years of misgovernmce which have made violence the only means of bringing about a change.
   (d) Brutal suppression of human rights over an extended period of time.
   (e) Alienation of whole cultural or ethnic groups brought about by threats to life by frequent communal violence, destruction of means of livelihood, historical humiliation, and continuing de facto discrimination in jobs and opportunities.
   (f) Another important factor is the narrowing of the mind brought about by fundamentalist indoctrination.
3. Social and Political Injustice: In the context of Nepal in particular, there is extreme poverty and illiteracy, and there is the phenomenon of rural-centred terrorism as a result.
4. Globalization: Rise of terrorism in South Asia is associated with some of the adverse effects of globalization. Globalization causes economic dislocations leading to the creation of pockets of unemployment, particularly in the informal, small, and medium-scale industrial sectors. The ensuring frustration, particularly when it is concentrated in particular ethnic, religious or linguistic groups, often fuels the fire of terrorism. In Sri Lanka, privatization and liberalization of imports particularly affected the emerging entrepreneurs among the Sinhalese. This proved to be a major factor contributing to the JVP's descent to the path of terrorism.

   The marginalization of large sections of population brought about by the retrenchment of social development activities under the structural adjustment programmes implemented by South Asian countries and designed to facilitate the process of globalization, has been another contributory factor.

   Globalization is associated with the weakening of the State, the rising salience of realistic as opposed to idealistic paradigms, and the consequent decline of social values. These have adversely affected the functioning of democracy and brought about misgovernance-phenomena closely linked to the rise of terrorism in South Asia.

5. External Factors: Use of non -state actors by external powers in pursuit of their political or strategic goals have played a crucial role in spawning terrorism. This has had a negative effect on democracy in the entire region and strengthened autocratic regimes. Foreign support has also contributed to the heightening of the salience of national security concerns, aggressive nationalism and militarism in the region.

Impact on Interstate Relations

It was agreed that terrorism has brought about a deterioration in bilateral relations between cow1tries in the region. If terrorism was a common problem in all the countries, they could have united in adversity but, unfortunately the same source of terrorism is perceived differently by different countries. There are bilateral problems inherited from the past, which are aggravated due to the differing attitude of the countries towards the same source of terrorism.

Impact of Terrorism

Different types of terrorism have different impacts. The poor suffer most in terrorism perpetrated as a consequence or the breakdown in law and order and collapse of governance. The elite have a nexus with the terrorists in such a situation. But there are also instances of direct attacks being made on the elite, particularly on state actors. The elite also suffer in terrorist violence the main purpose of which is to send out messages. For the bigger the catch, the stronger is the message, hence the greater the chance of its reaching the destination. No attempt has so far been made to draw up a sociological profile of terrorists in South Asia. However, one can safely assume that the poor are the foot soldiers of terrorism mounted as a rebellion against injustice and deprivation.

Cost of Terrorism

Terrorism has adversely affected development and imposed heavy economic costs on most of the South Asian countries.

There were many presentations which attempted to calculate the cost of terrorism. The problems in doing so are:

1. double counting; and
2. isolating terrorism from other factors.

In spite of these difficulties, it is vital to calculate the cost to understand the phenomenon. Such calculations should be the basis of advocacy for combating terrorism and for eliminating the root causes. Costs are both direct and indirect. There is no uniform methodology that can be prescribed for calculation, but guidelines can be established. The calculations in terms of impact on macroeconomic variables such as GNP, foreign exchange position, export growth, FDI flows, fiscal deficit, etc. are more complicated than calculations of the impact of terrorism on particular sectors, commodities, and units of industry.

Combating Terrorism

There is an international consensus that combating terrorism cannot be postponed until a commonly agreed definition is arrived at or until the root causes are eliminated. Progress should be simultaneous.

There is a problem of collateral damage in campaigns for combating terrorism. Given the technology of modern warfare and the interconnectedness among countries and economies, collateral damages are on a much larger scale today than before. Article 50 of the UN Charter provides for resorting to the Security Council in case of collateral damage, but when the charter was drafted, it was not imagined that collateral damage is inherent in the very structure of the economy and society today. In any punitive action to be taken other than in the charter, minimizing collateral damage and putting in place an arrangement for providing compensation against them should be regarded as crucial.

The consensus was that the task of reducing polarization in all countries and professionalization of law and order should be undertaken at the same time.

Areas to be Focused on by RCCS

1. The extent of terrorism spawned by misgovernance and collapse of governance. In several aspects, misgovernance is

endemic in this region. It was explicit in the Bangladesh presentation, and although there was no presentation on India, terrorism is rampant and attributed to outside factors, but there is much "home-grown terrorism" in India which should not be ignored.

2. Calculating the cost of terrorism should continue with improved methodology. It is difficult to prescribe a uniform methodology, but certain guidelines can be laid down.
3. A study of the mainstreaming of indigenous terrorist movements within democratic processes, because it will be a major activity and challenge in the near future, e.g. mainstreaming the LTTE, religious fundame:1tJlist groups in Pakistan, Maoists in Nepal, militants in North-East India, and the remnants of the extreme leftists in Bangladesh.
4. Definition of terrorism in the context of South Asia. This will differ from the definition given by the major powers.
5. Redefining the relationship between the state and non-state actors of violence in the context of changes that have taken place in the recent past.
6. A study on terrorism in border areas and its linkages with domestic terrorist movements in the neighbouring country. A study is required of the role of the state actor in this scenario. There was a suggestion to attempt the social profile of the terrorist movements. The poor are the foot soldiers of some forms of terrorism.
7. A study of the impact of terrorism on the domestic political structure and the nature of the polity.
8. The rise of militarism, chauvinism and lurch to the extreme right; the deleterious effect on democracy; the compelling need for a regime change.
9. Economics of Terrorism: The financial ramifications, sources and methods of financing, its economic networking. Such a study should go beyond the region; draw from work already done in the US, UK, and the UN.
10. Implications of counter-terrorist measures in the context of South Asia. Its effectiveness in our polarized society; and the vested interest it can create which can be a liability.

The Way Forward

The approach should be different in different instances, as no uniform way can be suggested.

The Bangladesh situation is interesting, as they are relatively in a better position so far as the impact of terrorism is concerned. Be cause of social and cultural homogeneity, there is a large margin of safety with regard to all four sources of terrorism, and the challenge to Bangladesh is to ensure that this margin is not eroded.

Nepal's task is to reconstruct the democratic and constitutional order; thoroughly reconsider the basic parameters on which democracy was founded; how disaffected communities can be brought into the mainstream and included in the democratic process.

The maintenance of a pluralistic society is an effective means of containing terrorism. There should be a conscious effort to provide security to different minority groups.

Each country has a stake in maintaining a pluralistic society in other countries, because what happens to pluralism in one country has an effect on others, and nothing should be done in one country which will adversely affect pluralism in another.

Terrorist threats from other regional countries should not be exaggerated. In the contemporary situation, this deflects attention from domestic terrorism and makes it difficult to elicit the cooperation of other countries for fighting terrorism.

All South Asian countries should ensure that there is no "failed state" in the region, because such a situation is ideal for the resurgence of terrorism. There is a role that countries have to play with responsibility in absorbing the economic shocks of other countries which could result in moving towards the status of a "failed state". Countries should invest in the economic futures of each other.

Maintenance of good relations is an important antidote to terrorism. Normal political and economic relationships among the countries of the region should be maintained at all costs. It may not be possible to have very close relationships or integration of the economies, but there is no reason for normal political and economic relationships to be disrupted. Although there is no agreed framework for one country to rise to the occasion and prevent a situation in another country. Which can lead to the resurgence of terrorism and other problems, countries can at least support each other in such situation. If there is a state drifting towards failure and there are strained relationship, no assistance can be given because even a positive overture could be misunderstood.

Building Stakes in Each Other's Stability and Prosperity

1. By undertaking major projects which can withstand vicissitudes of political relations. Any project that is not impacted by political bilateral relations will enhance development.
2. Sharing a common vision even though it may not be based on realistic paradigms. A public movement for South Asian cooperation can be built around such a Vision.

   Ingredients of the vision:

   (a) the goal of the economic community—it should be politically accepted and left to the second track to take it forward;

   (b) the goals of the Social Charter, which could also be accepted politically but left to the civil society movement to get it implemented at the ground level.
3. Transparency: The way South Asian countries deal with domestic terrorism or that affecting their neighbouring countries is often shrouded in secrecy This creates problems all around. There is, therefore, a need for greater transparency in the manner individual South Asian countries deal with terrorism. This can be facilitated by debates in parliaments, taking people into confidence, and more constructive and objective reporting by the media.
4. The Media: The media are used by the terrorists effectively; those who combat terrorism should also use the media to its fullest extent, A discussion could be organized on the role of the media for combating terrorism.
5. Cipil Society: The role of civil society in a variety of ways-in the democratization process, in empowerment, confidence building, in carrying forward the vision mentioned above- can be powerful in building pressure for ensuring greater transparency in the way governments deal with terrorism and for maintaining good relations with neighbours.

6. Cultural Rediswvery: The South Asian society has historically been characterized by cultural diversity and religious perspectives rooted in tolerance and humanism. Conscious nurturing of these values and distinctive cultural features can go a long way towards making the region inhospitable for terrorism based on extremisms of different varieties.

21

Fight Against Terrorism

Today Terrorists take advantage of greater openness and the explosion of information and weapon technology. The new technology of terror and their increasing availability, along with the increasing mobility of terrorists, raise chilling prospects of vulnerability to chemical, biological and other kinds of attacks. This is the threat to all human kind. Likewise, other nations also agree to the extent of damage the terrorists can mete out and that fighting terrorism is beyond the capacity and means of a single nation. Thus fighting terrorism needs careful, concerted and well thought out multilateral strategy. Yet, no concrete plan or strategy have been evolved by the nations, so far. This paper attempts to analyse the inherent weaknesses and the obstacles that mar the united efforts by various nations and a single strategy.

Defination and Meaning of Terrorism

"In its wider sense, terrorism is the tactic of using an act or threat of violence against individuals or groups to change the outcome of some process of politics." Grant Wardlow defines terrorism as the "use of violence by an individual or a group, whether acting for or in opposition to established authority, and such action is designed to create extreme anxiety or fear indicating effects in a target group than the immediate victims with the purpose of coercing that group into acceding to political demands of perpetrators". The International Encyclopedia of Social Sciences defined terrorism as "Terrorism is a term used to describe the method or the theory behind the method whereby an organized group or a party seeks to achieve its avowed aims chiefly through the systematic use of violence. 'Terrorist acts are directed against persons who, as individuals, agents or representatives of authorities, interfère with the consummation of the objectives of such a group. The terrorist threatens death or destruction as part of his program of action and if he is caught his behaviour during trial is generally directed primarily not towards winning his freedom but towards spreading a knowledge of his doctrines. Terrorism as a method is always characterized by the fact that it seeks to arouse not only the reigning government or nation in control but also the mass of the people to realization that constituted authority is no longer safely entrenched and unchallenged. The publicity value of the terrorist act is a cardinal point in the strategy of terrorism. Terrorism in its proper sense implies open defiance of law and is the means whereby an opposition aims to demoralize a governmental authority. to undermine its power and to initiate a revolution or counter revolution. The moral and political justification of the terrorism of a revolutionary or counter-revolutionary party proceeds from its consideration of existing government as an usurper of the people's power."

There have been many more attempts to define the term yet no acceptable definition of terrorism is adopted by various nations. It's a challenge to bring out an all comprehensive an agreed upon definition of the term terrorism. Different people and states have different views on the definition of terrorism. In fact, this is the biggest hurdle in the way of taking any multilateral united action against terrorism.

The work of defining the term can be undertaken by international body like United Nations but no attempt has been done so far. The Security Council Resolution adopted after the 11th September attack on WTC, unanimously made financing of the terrorism a criminal activity, but omitted the larger issue of defining terrorism. Though UN Resolution of August 1998 implicitly defines terrorism as violence for ideological reasons covering political, philosophical, ideological, racial, ethnic, religious or any other nature, the use of the term remains place and country specific. Words like terrorism or hostility are used by western media when incident takes place in western countries. For other countries, words like extremism and militancy or even rebels are being used. Thus terrorism means different things to different countries. Several countries and Human Rights groups want that the term should also include violence by security forces against innocent people. Many Arab countries have argued that the foreign occupation of another country is also terrorism. So Foreign Occupation of another country should also be included in the term terrorism. Anti-Nuclear activist argue that the term should also be applied to countries with nuclear arsenal. Writers like Caleb Carr have extended the definition of terrorism to encompass conventional warfare, dubbing all attacks on non-combatant even during war as act of terrorism.

Fighting Terrorism and Human Rights

Fighting terrorism needs bold strategy and use of force. But in doing so at the time of crisis, danger of adopting measures that may impinge upon the protection of human rights is always present. This invites wide criticism, loosening of support for the cause and pressure on the Government dealing with the terrorism. Indian efforts at eradicating terrorism in Punjab and now in Jammu and Kashmir are always undermined by the Human Rights Groups and States for violating the human rights. US treatment to Taliban and action in Afghanistan have also raised widespread concern. Use of force and bombing have killed thousands of innocent civilians and made a million refugee. US was pressurised to stop bombing during Ramadan period and also for providing humanitarian aid to innocent civilians. Likewise human rights groups have been voicing for detainees of the war.

Human Rights Organisations like Amnesty International urged United States Government that all its actions in relation to those in its custody in Afghanistan and Guantanamo Bay comply with International Law and Standards. US President Bush was criticized for erring in deciding that the Geneva convention do not cover Al-Qaeda detainees and for categorically ruling out prisoners of war status for Ediban detainees without convening a competent tribunal as the Geneva Convention requires, Human Rights Watch Group demanded that the Geneva Convention should apply to both the Taliban and Al-Qaeda detainees being held by US forces at Guantanamo and in Afghanistan, even if ultimately the Al-Qaeda fighters would not be accorded POW status.

Kenneth Roth, Executive Director of Human Rights Watch sent an open letter to members of the General Assembly and urged to assure that the refugees and asylum seekers do not become another casualty of the attacks perpetuated by the US and reaffirmed that the provisions of the 1951 refugee conventions continued to be applied to refugees worldwide that the right to seek asylum is fully protected. When the United Nations General Assembly's Sixth Committee was discussing the draft comprehension convention on International Terrorism, Human Rights Watch expressed concern that the comprehensive convention text uphold long-lasting and universally recognized international human rights standards. Human Rights Watch showed concern that certain provisions of the draft comprehensive convention could be interpreted in such a way as to undermine and conflict with fundamental principles of international humanitarian law and human rights law. Human Rights Watch pointed out such provisions appearing in UN Convention aimed at curbing specific terrorist activities, in particular the international convention for the suppression of terrorist bombings, adopted on 15th December 1997; the International Convention for the suppression of the financing of the terrorism, adopted on 5 December 1999. The Group expressed the belief that the current draft which is intended to be a more comprehensive instrument requires a special effort to achieve thorough human right protection and guarantees. Therefore, it is a difficult task for states to fight terrorists while protecting human Rights.

Terrorism and State Support/State Terrorism

A large part of modern terrorism is supported by Governments. This is done through money, diplomatic facilities, passports, sanctuaries, training camps, weapons, explosives and justifying ideologies. The same terrorists who arc called criminals by the Government whose nationals they attack arc hailed as freedom fighters' or 'fighters for national liberation' by the Governments who support them. Several Arab states particularly Libya and Syria appeared to have maintained training camps not only for Palestinians and other Arab Nationalists but also for various European terrorists whom they regard as allies. Similar cooperation has occurred among various European terrorist movements and Arab Groups in regard to underground international arms trading and transport often with the connivance of same government. The Governments supporting terrorists activities do so within a context of deniability trying to, conceal the involvement of their personnel and the traces of their actions. These so-called sponsors of terrorism distance themselves from the operations they have supported and act of violence. Although totalitarian States can employ terror inside the State easily and are susceptible of supporting it internationally, the sponsors and patrons are also duly elected Governments and Officials .The terrorist groups arc puppet organizations for these governments and officials promoting nation's interests or ideology overseas. State sponsors of terrorism fight proxy war using terror as weapon. This tendency is on rise as State sponsored terrorism can achieve strategic ends where the use of conventional arms forces is not practical or effective. The high cost of modern warfare and concern about non-conventional escalation as well as the danger of defeat and the unwillingness to appear as the aggressor have turned terrorism into an efficient, convenient and generally discrete weapon for attaining state interest in the international realm. United States has identified seven such countries, active in number of embassy bombings in at least 12 countries. These are Iran, Cuba, Iraq, Libya, North Korea, Sudan and Syria. India has requested United States to declare Pakistan a terrorist state. Indian Government has come up with evidences of Pakistan support to terrorist group involving in mass killing of innocent people and attack on democratic structures.

Military *vs.* Non-Military Means of Combating Terrorism

The popular notion include that the swift and harsh retaliation is the best policy for countering terrorism, many, however, advocate non-military or politico-economic reforms as more effective means of combating terrorism. Deutsch wrote terrorism can become a self-perpetuating system which requires a significant social group in extreme discontent because many of its members feel politically, economically or socially oppressed. They also feel bitterly frustrated in the attainment of some cherished religious, national or ethnic ambition. J.F. Ribeiro opines that the only real answer to terrorism is not military counter measures alone but the willing of people's hearts and minds. He made it clear that the people of India think erroneously that only repressive measures succeeded in ridding Punjab of terrorism.

While expressing their support for the US fight against terrorism, many countries including China and Russia called for a switch from military action in Afghanistan to political efforts. Russian foreign Minister Igor Ivanov opined that the problem of Afghanistan could never be overcome by military means. Arab allies offered only fragile support to US action. Malaysian Prime Minister Mahathir Mohammad said that he remained opposed to the US military strikes and believed that the problem of terrorism would not disappear until the Palestinian problem was resolved. Indonesian foreign Minister Hassan Wirajuda, whose country contains large Muslim population, expressed his preference for a collective and wider response to terrorism headed by the United Nations rather than what he called unilateral action by the US and its coalition. I I States, specially United States, try eradication of terrorism by employing use of force, without being sure that it is possible to do so only through military means or needs a wider approach.

Unilateral vs. Multilateral Action against Terrorism

Since terrorism is not confined to any one jurisdiction, it mandates a global response. Repercussions are felt everywhere and at times counter-terrorism requires the ability of more than one state to combat terrorism. Kofi Annan said on 8 October 2001, 'To defeat terrorism, we need a sustained effort and a broad strategy to unite all nations and address all aspects of the scourge we face. The cause must be pursued by all the States of the World, working together and using many different means including political, legal, diplomatic and financial means."

United Nations seems to be most uniquely placed organisation which can provide legal and moral framework for collective international action against terrorism. League of Nations discussed organized terror for the first time in 1937. Since then, international bodies like UN have been discussing the matter time and again. 12 major multinational conventions and protocols on terrorism have been adopted in United Nations ranging from flight safety to the possession of nuclear material. But limitations arise as these conventions have not been ratified by majority of the UN members.

UN playing a stronger role is no doubt a best option strengthening international laws on terrorism and the means to enforce them. The majority opinion in various surveys conducted in western countries support the United Nations Security Council being able to require UN member to all UN sponsored police force to enter countries and conduct investigations, to freeze the assets of suspected terrorist groups, to provide intelligence on them, to arrest them, and if the member country refuses to do so, to send an international military force to capture suspected terrorists. A strong majority favours using international judicial bodies for trying terrorists. International Criminal Court (ICC) can deal with terrorists under its jurisdiction. However, the action against terrorism turns out to be unilateral rather than multilateral affair again and again. United States, sometime with the help of NATO countries or sometime 'with handful of its allies finds itself capable of fighting or waging war against terrorism.

Terrorism, Ideology and Religion

Using an ideology for terrorist purpose is as old as modern terrorism itself. A terrorist cannot survive without a stated cause. Thus terrorist leaders camouflage themselves as righteous forces against some form of oppression or the other. Noel O'Sullivan said that political terrorism occurs when a group, whether holding Government Office or outside Government, resorts to pursue a set of ideological objectives by methods which not only subvert or ignore the requirements of domestic and international law, but which rely for their success primarily upon the threat or use of violence. This definition is applicable not only to Islamic Groups like Al-Qaeda, Hamas and the Hizb-ul-Mujahideen, but also to secular outfits like the IRA, ETA, the Basque Nationalist Group in Spain and the Palestinian Al-Fatah. In a sense, terrorism is the creation of ideological politics. Ideology of freedom that can turn into a violent exercise like a French Revolution, the Communist Revolution etc. It is the basic purpose of terrorist to project its business as a freedom struggle. Like revolutions, terrorist movements identify themselves to an outgroup which is deemed to be responsible for everything wrong with the existing social order. This is the belief of the people like Bin laden. For Bin-laden, support lies in arguing his case as a movement for Islamic resurgence and against western arrogance. Like Muammar Gaddafi's support for terrorism against the West was packaged in his Marxism tinged idea of a first world-third world rift which he tried to narrow down.

US intelligence experts claim that a trend towards and shift away from terrorism motivated by political ideology and towards a dominant religious terrorism is being witnessed. In the 80's, terrorism was politically inspired but in 1990's, it became increasingly religious terrorism in the form of militant Islamic Shiite fundamentalism. However, contrary to the depiction in the Western media and intelligence, religious terrorism is not limited to Islamic Groups in the Middle East. The US domestic threat can also come from Christian Identity Movement or events likc Aum Shinrikyo Sari Gas attack on Tokyo's subway can be repeated anywhere in the world. Terrorism is terrorism and it is faulty to view it only from the religious point of view. It divides the world community on the religious lines and weakens the support to fight against terrorism.

State to State Approach/National Interests

Various States are seen to be adopting different approaches to the same problem. Example of India and United States can be cited. India has been fighting the menace of terrorism since long. United States even after attacks of 11th September and 13th December did not view the problem from the same perspective. National interest and national concerns is the prism and sole deciding factor. Colin Powell had threatened large scale and long-term retaliation against terrorism whether it was legally correct or not and President Bush had made it clear that "he makes no distinction between terrorist and states that harbour them. Those who harbour terrorist will share their fate. He said every nation has to decide if it is with US or with terrorists, the evil ones whose inhuman acts separate them from Society of homo sapiens. In this global war against terrorism, there can be no middle ground, no moral relativism, no policy equivocation, no excuses". These words left no one in any doubt about US intention of fighting terrorism. So Indians saw an opportunity of getting rid of terrorism. Since 11th September attack on WTC, United States and India shared threat perception from terrorists. It hastened bilateral diplomatic exchanges between the two countries. They worked together in the UN to pass UNSCR 1373 and to promote the India sponsored 'comprehensive convention against international terrorism'. These efforts laid to the arrest of hundreds of individuals around the world with possible ties to Al-Qaeda and other terrorist network. With US and India moving in unison to strangle the financial asset of terrorist, more than 112 nations have issued blocking orders and frozen assets used to finance terrorism. US Government designated Jaish-e-Mohammad and Lashkar-e-Tayyiba as foreign terrorist organizations. US-India intelligence cooperation is devoted to identifying terrorists, preventing their atrocities and bringing them to justice. They have also set up a joint working group on counter-terrorism. Despite all these developments, India and US seem to be adhering to different approaches. India wanted stern action against the terrorist groups active in India. US National Security Advisor Condoleezza Rice was asked in an interview if US has given India any assurance to turn its attention to terrorism in India after targeting Osama Bin Laden and the Taliban. Rice categorically made it clear that it is not a matter of Phase II. "We have told the Indian Government that we intend to fight terrorism wherever we see it. That includes in India, that includes in the US." However, the nature of terrorist attack and the countries involved are making a difference. For India, Pakistan is the country, which harbours terrorists and needs to be declared. a terrorist state, US takes a different line directed by its own interests and continues to view Pakistan as important ally in its fight against terrorism. India wants Pakistan to be punished for its involvement, US wants to reward Pakistan for being front-line state in the fight against terrorism . It makes Indian problem unattended even after the global war against terrorism and compels Indian leaders to proclaim that India will fight its problem of terrorism on its own. United States is more concerned about tension between nuclear India and Pakistan rather than terrorism in Kashmir which is still viewed as more a problem emanating from peoples' right of self-determination and posing no threat to US security.

US WAR ON TERRORISM IN AFGHANISTAN

Introduction

The terrorist attacks of September 11, 2001 on World Trade Centre and Pentagon and subsequent American war on terrorism in Afghanistan have increased the concerns of human rights advocates. Both these events have shaken the faith of common masses in the established law and order and the security network of their respective states. Indeed, no one can deny the gravity of the threat and magnitude of the destruction caused by the terrorists in America, yet the air raids and military operations undertaken by the United States against Afghanistan became controversial. In this paper, an attempt has been made to examine the nature of the US response to the terrorist attacks.

The end of Cold War in 1989 has given place to a 'new world order' dominated by the United States after the disintegration of erstwhile Soviet Union in 1991, the USA emerged as the sole superpower. The conduct of Gulf War and its role in Middle East and other major crises have given it the title of 'global policeman'. Despite economic development by countries like China and Japan and regional economic collaborations like the one achieved by European Union, no one could challenge the hegemony of the United States. To create a new 'space shield' for the US and its allies, President Bush has announced his plan to spend billions of dollars on national missile defence system (NMDS). abrogating the ABM treaty But the terrorist attacks on World Trade Centre and Pentagon on September 11, 2001, killing more than 3000 men and women, despite all the military, economic and technological prowess at its command, made the United States very vulnerable. Non-state actors demonstrated their ability to render the sole superpower eminently precarious and proved the futility of the most impregnable security network.

Terrorist attacks were denounced by the United States. These were represented as an epitome of endangerment to the very basis of global order and contemporary International Law—Reacting swiftly to these attacks, President Bush declared them as 'acts of war against America'. In retaliation, he pronounced US 'War on terrorism', a battle of 'good against evil' and emphasised the need to evolve a 'global coalition' to meet the challenge. It was for the first time in the post-Soviet period that the US unilateralism appeared to have been tampered. Osama Bin Laden, a Saudi billionaire and his All-Qaeda, having a network in more than 60 countries, had been identified as the main suspect. Since the Taliban government in Afghanistan had given him shelter, the punitive action was announced against Afghanistan, President Bush vowed to hunt down planners of terrorist attacks and the US Congress authorised him the use of force to strike at the terrorist. Numerous countries ranging from Great Britain and Germany to Turkey and Australia announced their support to the US War on terrorism, India, being a victim of terrorism herself for more than two decades, denounced the terrorist attacks and offered its operational assistance to the United States, Pakistan too assured support to the international coalition against terror. Though it was a tough decision for General Musharraf to join US hands in defeating and destroying the same very forces-the Taliban-who were once created, equipped and funded by his own country. The Central Asian states, who were also facing terrorism from across the borders, declared their support to the US campaign against terrorism in Afghanistan. France and China, while supported the international effort, disapproved the American approach. Foreign Minister of France, Hubert Vedrine termed Washington's approach to the War on terrorism as 'simplistic'. He stated "the US was reducing everything to War on terrorism. You have to tackle the root causes, the situations, poverty and injustice". China was also critical of American approach and it conceded that the US policies attract terror.

The questions that need serious thinking and debate are: were the attacks acts of a few individuals frustrated and alienated and having a sense of grievance and injustice or a reflection of long planning and policy of some group/s or state/s? Were the attacks challenge to the economic and military policies and national prowess of the United States or a challenge to its core values, culture and civilisation as propounded by Hutington. Answers to these questions lack unanimity and international consensus and represent conflicting perceptions of the states of their national interests. The response of the US administration to terrorist attacks has been shaped in accordance to the conception of its national interests, national prestige and international power and position. What is important, from our prospective is the nature and dimension of the US response and its long-term consequences, because, rather than tackling the problem, violence and force beget more violence.

The most formidable superpower in its retribution attacked the most hapless, poor, miserable and defenceless people of Afghanistan. The US led forces dropped cluster bombs and missiles, killing large number of civilians, including woman and innocent children, against the provisions of Geneva Convention. There were relentless air attacks on Afghanistan in which even the UN building in Kabul, a hospital in Herat, Red Cross warehouses in Kabul and other residential areas were hit by US planes. Though US Defence

Secretary, Donald Rumsfeld asserted that war was not targeting civilians, there are reports that about 2000 persons were killed in October 2001 in the US bombings. The death of a number of NGO workers associated with de-mining operations and the UN humanitarian aid and assistance operations was confirmed by the UN spokeswoman, Staphine Bunker. She expressed her fear that civilian casualties would seriously affect humanitarian efforts at the juncture when the Afghan people need them most. While making an appeal for protection of civilians, she observed: "people need to distinguish between combatants and those innocent civilians who do not bear arms".

There were large-scale protests against US attacks on Afghanistan even in European countries like Italy, France and Germany etc. Russia and China, both called for rapid transition from military operation to the political solution. The UN Secretary-General, Kofi Annan appealed to the US that the "human rights laws must be observed during military action". Earlier addressing the general assembly of 189 nations, he said that no effort should be spared to bring the perpetrators of the attacks to justice but pleaded for 'rule of law', national and international. He called the nations to use the United Nations for a 'long-term struggle against terrorism'. He observed:

> *Let us uphold our own principles and standards, so that we can make a difference unmistakable for all the world to see, between those who resort to terrorism and those who fight against it.*

United States' strikes against Afghanistan started with the declared purpose to catch hold of Osama Bin Laden, Mullah Omar, the Taliban leader 'dead or alive' and to destroy the network of Al Qaeda. But with all the use of force, America failed to achieve either of its declared war objectives. Most of the high-profile operations of the US and the British forces in Afghanistan proved futile. Rather thousands of Afghan civilians were killed by off target bombs. The bombing of Afghan cities added to the problems of refugees, who had already suffered for more than two decades and became victims of superpowers politics in their own land.

Widespread poverty among the masses in Afghanistan, like other least developed countries, is a major cause of denial of human rights to the people. But the situation got worse in tl1is regard in the last two decades because of the power struggle, first between exogenous and later indigenous forces in Afghanistan.

In the 'great game' between the two superpowers (1979-89), thousands of Afghans were done to death and there were reports of human rights abuses by both sides. The reports confirmed that about one million Afghans had been killed and four to five million people left their country and became refugees in the neighbouring countries. During the internecine war that followed the Soviet withdrawal from Afghanistan, the human rights situation got deteriorated further as each group tried to capture and consolidate its power by killing the' majority of the resistance' and its opponents. There was no central control and command to provide protection to the innocent people. The behaviour of Taliban government in prosecuting, torturing, rape and murdering of even innocent children and woman was indeed an insult to the civilised world.

When the 'operation enduring freedom' was launched by United States, it was expected that its anti-terror campaign would be more sensitive to the rights and liberties of the people and would respect the principles of International Law and Geneva Convention. While addressing a gathering of anti-war protesters and referring to fears about civilian casualties Prime Minister Tony Blair stated:

> *Every precaution would be taken to avoid civilian losses with strikes targeted only against the Taliban's military apparatus and Osama bin Laden's Al Qaeda's network of terror.*

However, the senseless bombings of cities civilian residential areas, and mountainous tribal regions and caves of Afghanistan to 'smog Bin Laden' had killed and maimed thousands of innocent civilians. Bombing of Herat hospital and destruction of ICRC's food depots were unrelated to the necessity of 'self-defence'. Nothing can justify indiscriminate use of military force. Irony of humanitarian concern was that the food packets dropped along with cluster bombs had either might have perished or had gone 'astray' rather than reaching the targeted impoverished population.

In the 'war against terrorism', human rights law, including those concerning the treatment of war prisoners, non-combatants and humanitarian access have been ignored by the Bush administration. In its anxiety to tackle terrorism, civil liberties have been curtailed. The idea of indefinite detention of non-citizens 'suspected' of having ties with terrorists is illegal and unconstitutional. Many of them were detained on visa violations. But instead of being deported, they continued to be held without trial and charges being framed against them. Their trial before a special military commission as opposed to civilian courts is a repressive weapon threatening civilian liberties and democratic rights. It is unfortunate that those people who have not been charged with crime have been treated like criminals. Detaining non-citizens without any evidence, intimidation, harassment, physical abuses and even killing on account of the looks alone, have certainly changed the situation and undermined the due process of law. Ken Hurwitz, a senior associate of the lawyers committee for human rights observed:

> *By casting aside humanitarian law, the United States risks squandering its credibility and moral authority in the struggle for the rule of law worldwide.*

There is a growing feeling in the human rights advocates that despite the current challenges and grave threats posed by the networks of terrorists, human rights of all, particularly of the lowest and weakest of persons should be upheld. In the US war on Afghanistan, neither Osama bin laden and Mullah Omar and other leaders of Al Qaeda and 'Taliban were found nor the war has diminished America's fear of terrorist attacks. The United States' declaration that it reserves the right to extend its war of 'self defence' to Iraq, Iran, North Korea, Syria and Libya etc. would only lead to more recriminations and in no way would help to increase security for the Americans.

Justice American/European style with a sense of 'self-righteous ness' is going to prove dangerous and counter-productive. In a recent article, Robert Cooper, a British diplomat, has justified the right of' post-modern states' to intervene in the 'modern' and 'premodern' states, whenever intervention is deemed necessary. In the new doctrine of liberal imperialism, he said:

> *When dealing with more old-fashioned kinds of states outside the post-modern continent of Europe, we need to revert to rougher methods of an earlier era-force. Pre-emptive attack, deception, whatever is necessary to deal with those who still live in the 19th century world of every state for itself.*

So, in the new kind of 'voluntary imperialism', use of force 'outside the continent of Europe' (of course America too), has been legitimised and Machiavelli's statecraft has replaced the moral considerations. Rule of law and probably even the rights are only for the 'post-modern' states and their citizens. Bush Administration is developing a new strategic doctrine that supports 'pre-emptive' attacks and defensive intervention against terrorists and hostile states or groups that had been labelled as 'axis of evil'. In a way, the United States and its supporters have been justifying their own imperialist policies, which Noam Chomsky called 'terrorism of the powerful'.

However, discretionary or excessive use of violence is not going to help to win a war against terrorism because terrorists do not belong/represent anyone' state. The strategy of pre-emptive attacks is going to prove counter-productive and it would spread more hatred against the United States. An ill-defined open-ended war with unlimited force, even for a just cause, is going to under mine International Law and the UN Charter. Moreover, it would not reduce the threat of terrorism or increase the security of its citizens. Global terrorism, in all its manifestations, therefore, can be fought with international co-operation through the UN. Rule of law, uniform standard, consistency and respect for human rights of all without discrimination of race religion, colour, language region and state can help to fight terrorism in a better way.

22

Human Violence Search for Peace

Voilence has produced an endless chronology of human sufferening. Throughout history, society has witnessed a seemingly endless array of wars, assessinations, murdersm, rapes, acts of terrorism and form of domestic voilence. On a national scale, there is a growing awareness that agression is a problem of epidemic proportions.

Problems of violence in Kashmir, Punjab, Assam, Andhra, U.P. and Bihar are very alarming. Shooting, looting, bomb blasts abduction are everyday affair. the whole country has stated feeling apprehensive, scared and insecure. you cannot feel secure on road, rail, air and even in your own home.

However, and important implication of the frustration aggression hypothesis is that aggression can be managed and reduced without the expression of aggression but through modifying the frustration stimuli, is now widely accepted. Anger at someone who fails to keep an appointment may be largely or completely reduced should one discover that person was kept away form the appointment because of some emergency. In the same vein, most of us would agree that to the extent hostility towards an 'enemy' arises from miscom-munication and unrealetic fears that hostility can be reduced by fastering a more realistic perception of the enemy.

With reference to the groups fighting in Kashmir, Punjab, Assam, Andhra etc. we must try to understand them and their realist perception and their ungrounded fears and hostility by having a open communication. We may not agree with this proposal as many of us will say that it has failed. But it is not all. We are to look into many more important factors contributing to violence in the group.

If these groups are like a crowd we say according to the Bandura that people can be dramatically transformed, when they are members of the crowd. The transformation, he thought, are pathological; people take on the characteristics of primitive beings. He wrote that crowd display imputivencss, irritability, in capacity of reason the absence of judgement and of critical spirit, the exaggeration of sentiments.

People in groups tend to conform to group opinion. Some of the experiments earned out clearly show that fear of becoming an out-caste is a strong pressure for conformity. In other words one reason for conforming is that non-conforming behaviour is often costly to non-con former. If we observe the violent groups of our country, it seems to be true. There is no other group so dominating with whom they may tend to conform because they feel insecure. Therefore, we should try to manage that non-conformer remain safe and secure in order to not becoming the number of under sirable group.

Experiments and field study as well as every-day experience show that intrusium into what an individual has staked out or marked as his personal territory are likely to evoke defensive response on this part. Observation of larger groups like gangs, tribs, state and nation also confirm the tendenev i react with aggression to invasion of what groups regards as its territory. In case of our country we very well know that there was a tune when we were Indian only and fought our independent war with we feeling and oncess but now we feel that we are more a Punjabi, Kashmiri, Assami, Bihari, Rajasthani etc. than an Indian. This feeling and attitude can be changed by different psychological methods and a national feeling can be developed.

It is also explained by an other concept known as delegitimization. It is the process of categorising groups intoextermely negative social category and excluding them form acceptability. During conflict when in groups percieves the negative goals of an out group as farm reaching and evil, feeling of threats become intensivied and delegitimiation may be used to explain the conflict. Than to prevent danger the ingroup may harm the threatening group and justify the harm by delegitimization, which in turn increases perceived threat and intensifies harmful behaviour toward other group. Even mild conflict can escalate, become violent and lead to dclegitimization as an explanation and later as justification. The most common means of delegitimization which are not mutually exclusive are dehumanization, trait characterization, and use of political levels etc. Until and unless this delegitimization based on the above means is not abolished or changed it will be difficult to bring groups together.

Training has a powerful effect on aggression, both in magnifying the motivation toward it and in repressing fighting. It has been described in greater detail by Dollared and Miller. Weapons effect which indicates that expose to aggressive stimuli (Guns) results in increased aggression, has also been experimentally proved Both the causes of increased aggression training and weapons effect are playing a very important role. So far the aggression and violence is concerned in our country. We may take all care to culture these causes, to have peace in the nation.

Laboratory experiments conducted under controlled conditions have shown constantly that the observation of violence by others both live and in mass media displays, facilitates aggression in the observer. This has been explained by various investigators a; evidence of modeling and in vitation of aggression, disinhibition of aggression impluscs by the modeled behaviour, elicitation of aggression action that have become conditioned to modeled behaviour during the past time and an increase in arousal produced by the observation of aggression which activates dominant responses including aggressive one.

We know that certain models and their behaviour is being followed by others in disturbed parts of the country. We need to put up a better model with healthy and rewarding behaviour in public press electronic media which may be modeled by others.

Others attention also work as a reinforcement. It has an accusal effect on us and it experienced as rewarding. Being ignored is generally non rewarding, depressing or at terms even disturbing. It is also noted that a person who has not been the object of attention for some time deprived of attention would he more responsive than those who have had considerable attention. We in Indian set up are paying all possible attention. All newspapers, radio and T.V. news bulletins are full of such acts committed by the members of those groups. It should be immediately taken notice of and such news should be sensored for mass media.

A very important question can be raised about the moral of the members of those group. Why they do not feel quilty what keeps their morale up? It is very well explained by Bandra when viewed from divergent prospective violent acts are different things for different people. The one groups terrorist activity is another groups liberation movement fought by heroic freedom fighters. This is why moral appeals agonies violence usually fall on deaf ears.

Terrorism and counter terrariums invoke moral principles to justify human atrocities. This poses more troublesome problem for democratic societies than for totalirian ones. Totalirian regimes have fever constraints against institutional power to control media coverage of terrorist events, to restrict individual rights, to scarifies society face the moral dilemma of how to justify counter measures that take some toll on innocent lives in the process of curbing terrorist atrocities without violating the fundamental principles and standards of civilized conduct. Therefore, for the purpose of the solution for the problems the use of violent counter measures is justified on utilitarian grounds. In terms of the benefits to humanity and social orders that curbing terrorist attack will bring.

The adult behave much more aggressively when act of assaulting of person is given a samitized levels. Use of language in different metaphore can change the nature of culpable activities as a murderer called martyers by his heroic job.

Congative restructuring of behaviour through moral justification and palliative characterization of moral self saction. This is because moral restruturing not only eliminates self deterrents but engages self approval in the service of distructive exploits. What was once morally condemnable become a source of self evaluation. After distructive means become invested with high moral purpose, functionaries work hard to become proficient of them and pride in their distructive accomplishments.

Displacement of diffusion of responsibility is another factor which does not allow people is develop quilt or to feel immoral. No one is responsible personally. Operation of displacement or responsibility can very well be seen in the activities in which hostages are taken with the warning to officials of targeted regimes that if they take retaliatory action they will be held accountable for lives of the hostage. In this way justify all their distructive activities. To function more humanely society must establish effective social safe guard against the misuse of institutionalized justificatory power for expletives and distructive purpose.

One more factor responsible for the creation of conflict and aggression is that people in democratice country tends to think of a society, as being grouped into various caste and classes, and they tend to consider themselves as belonging tone or other of them. It is seen that political tie-up with caste, class and status, is very behaviour of the public and the public voting for a particular party expects and pressurized them to do something for that particular class. This class and caste alignment must be discouraged and modified for better integrated society and nation. After discussing some of the factors above. I invite all the psycholigist, sociologist and other mental health professionals to work on this line and find out some psychological and behavioural measures and suggest the public. Press electronic mass media ad the Government how can be help this country for curbing the violence and creating the peace in the society as a Psychologist.

Direction of the negotiations process. They normally engage in different problem solving approaches which can help the parties to examine the assumptions and goals of their negotiations strategy. Middle-range leaders can play a vital role in ensuring communications betweens Levels 3 and 1. Level 3 is of local leaders who experience the trauma and the pain of the conflict. They are community-based organizations which interact with the people. Their work in reconciliation, healing, and promoting coexistence can be a vital component in the process. The figure draws attention to the need for a comprehensive peace building programme which can be sustained at all levels.

Summary

The has attempted to highlight the new security threats facing our common future. It emphasizes the need for designing programmes for human security, particularly for vulnerable groups in society. It has argued that early warning and preventive diplomacy centred on human security will rovide the basis for a new social order. The paper has argued that civil society needs to be involved and engaged in the prevention and resolution of conflicts in a volatile region such as South Asia.

BIBLIOGRAPHY

Ahmad, Imtiaz, "Secular State and Communal Society," in Communalism: The Razor's Edge,-Ed., Ashish Rajaadhyaksha, Ranka, Bombay, 1983, pp. 15-28.

Alexander, Yonah, "Terrorism, Media and the Police," Journal of International Affairs, Vol. 32, No. l, Spring/Summer 1978, pp. 101-113.

Bassiouni, Chelif M., "Problems in Media Coverage of Non-State Sponsored Terror-Violence Incidents," in Perspectives on Terrorism, op. cit., pp, 179-80.

Bassiouni, cp. cit., pp. 196-197.

Bell, Bowyer J., Transnational Terror, AEI-Hoover Policy Study 17, September 1975, p 89, Stanford, California.

Bo"., Mani Lal, North Eastern htdla, Concept Pab.ishin;, New D:Ild, 1979.

Chaure, Hill Politics in North East India, Orient Longman, Bombay, 1973. 24. Anand, V.K., Insurgency and Counter-Insurgency, Deep & Deep Publications, New Delhi, 1981.

Cooper, op. cit., p, 144.

Cooper., H.H.A., "Terrorism and the Media" in Terrorism: Interdisciplinary Perspectives, Alexander, Yonah and Finger, S.M. (Eds.), New York, John Day Press, 1977, p. 143.

Crelinsten, R.D., "Power and Meaning: Terrorism as a Struggle Over Access to the Communication Struggle" in Contemporary Research on Terrorism, op. cit., pp 419-450.

Deutsch, Karl W., "External Involvement in Internal War," in Eckstein, Harry (Ed.), International and Transnational Terrorism, New York, Free Press, 1964, p. 100.

Easton, David, Political System, Alfred A Knopf, New York, 1960, pp. 83-101.

Encounter, Volume 44, June 1975, pp. 9-13 and 15-16.

Freedman, L.Z. and Alexander, Y., Perspectives on Terrorism, Scholarly Resources Inc., Wilmington, 1985.

Hacker, Frederick J., "Dialectic Inter-relationships of Personal and Political Factors in Terrorism," in Perspectives of Terrorism, op. cit., pp. 19-21.

Hussain, Ak11al, Strategic Issues in Pakistan's Economic Policy, Lahore: Progressive Publishers, 1986.

Hussain, Akmal, et al., Overcoming the Crisis: Poverty, Growth and Governance, UNDP, National Human Development Report (forthcoming).

Hyams, Edward, Terrorists and Terrorism, London, J.M. Dent, 1975, p. 11.

Jenkins, Brian, "International Terrorism: A Balance Sheet", Survival, Vol. 17, No. 4, July-August 1975, p. 158.

Jenkins, Brian, International Terrorism : A New Mode of Conflict, California Arms Control and Foreign Policy Seminar, December 1975, p. 4.

Jillani, 5., et ai., Labour Migmtioll, Research Report No. 126, Islamabad: Pakistan Institute of Development Economics.

Khan, Zia-ul- Hasan, "The Rise of Secrarianism in Pakistan, Causes and Implications", research paper (mimeo), Lahore: Pakistan Administrative Staff College, 1995.

Mack, Andrew, Counter Insurgency in the Third World, International Studies, 1. October 1975, pp. 226-53.

Mankekar, D.R., A Revolution of Rising Frustrations, Vikas, Delhi, 1975. 9. Yonah, A. Carlton and Silkinson, Terrorism: Theory and Practice, Westview Press, Boulder, 1979.

Mao Tse Tung, Gurrilla Warfare, Cassel & Co., London, 1969.

Marighella, Carlos, Minimanual of the Urban Guerilla, Havana, Tricontinental, n.d., p. 103.

Mohanty, Manoranjan, Revolutionary Violence, Sterling Publishers, New Delhi, 1977.

Morning News (The Daily), 20 January 1980.

Murty, T.S., Assam in Dilrcult Years, Himalayan Books, New Delhi, 1983. 28. Gaur, Ted, A Causal Model of Civil Strife, American Political Science Review, Vol. 62, 1968, pp. 1104-28.

Myrdal, G., Asian Drama , Vintage Books, Random House, New York, 1972, pp. 20-59.

Nath, Shaileshwar, Terrorism in India, National Publishing House, Delhi, 1980.

Noman, Omar, The Political Economy of Pakistan, London: Routledge Kegan and Paul, 1988.

Parkinson, Roiecr, Encyclopedia of Modern War, Routledge and Kagan Paul, London, 1977.

Proeramme of the Executive Committee of Naroduye Volga, Para II, Section, 1879.

Rapoport, D.C. and Yonah, A., eds., The Morality of Terrorism, Pergamorl Press, Oxford, 1982.

Ryan, Claude, "The French-Canadian Dilemma," Foreign Affairs, 43, April 1965, p. 45.

Sabine, G.W. "The State" in international Encyclopedia of Social Sciences, The Macmillan Co., N.Y., 1968, p. 328.

Schmid & Graff, Violence as Communication, Sage Publications, London, 1982.

Shakir, Moin, Politics of Minorities, Ajanta, Delhi, 1980.

Sineh. S.N., The Dilemmar of Indian Policy, Print House, Lucknow, 1984,

Sineli, Satindcr, Khalistan-An Aeadendc Analysis, Amar Prakashan, New Delhi, 1982.

Syed, Najam Hussain, Recurrent Patterns in Punjabi Poetry, 2nd edn, Lahore: Punjab Adabi Markaz, 1986.

Terroristic Activity : International Terrorism. Hearings before the subcommittee to investigate the Administration of the Security Act and Other Internal Security Laws of the Commission of the Judiciary, US Senate, Washington, D.C., US Government Printing Press, 1979.

Thompson, R., War in Peace, Orbis Publishing, London, 1981.

Tuchman, Barbara, The Proud Tower, New York, Bantam Books, 1972, p. 118.

Tugwell, M., "Terrorism and Propaganda: Problem and Response," in Wilkinson, Paul and Stewart, A.M. (Eds.), Contemporary Research on Terrorism, Aberdeen, Aberdeen University Press, 1987, p. 409.

Wardlaw, Grant, Political Terrorism: Theory, Tactics and Counter, measures, Cambridge, Cambridge University Press, 1982, p. 16.

Wilkinson, Paul, op. cit., p, 176. 19. Tugwell, M., op. cit., pp. 413-414.

Wilkinson, Paul, Terrorism and the Liberal State, (2nd edition), Macmillan Education Ltd., 1986, Hongkong, p. 51.

Wilkinson, Paul, Terrorism and The Liberal State, Macmillan Press, London, 1974.

Wilkinson, Paul. Political Terrorism, Macmillan Press, London, 1974.

Wolfang, Marvin, Criminal Violence, Sage Publications, London, 1982.

Yonah, A., International Terrorism, Preager Publishers, N.Y., 1976.

INDEX

11 September, 9

A

Adolescence, 52
Adult Hood, 52
Adventuresome, 48
Aggressive, 48
Al Qaeda, 5, 7
All Tripura Tiger Force, 205
  Party Conference, 258
Annual Development Programme, 216
Anti-Conservative, 74
Appeasement, 187
Arya Dharma, 77
ASEAN, 8
ASEM, 8
Asia Europe Meeting, 8
Authoritarian, 73
Azad Kashmir, 133

B

Bad Customs, 98
  News, 21
Balancing Loops, 21
Being Ignorant, 57
  Tough, 57
Belief System, 42
Bhagwat-Geeta, 174
Bhikkhus, 266
Bhishma Pitamah, 174
Bible Belt, 72
Bilateral Relations, 111
Booming, 200
Bottom Line, 19
Bourgeoisie Capitalism, 43
Brahmin, 173
Buddha Jayanthi, 291
Buddhist Revivalism, 70, 263
  Temporalities, 80
  Theosophical Society, 275

C

Camper School, 157
Castes Conflict, 173
Chandler Report, 6
Child-Marriage, 88
Chittagong Hill Tracts, 203
Civilizations, 59

COAS, 220
Coercive Tactics, 56
Cold War, 338
Colonialistic, 83
Combatant, 365
Communist Party, 244
Conflict, 19
Conservative, 73
Constitutional Restlessness, 242
Counter Terrorism Committee, 6
Countering Terrorism, 5
Counter-Terrorism Committee, 69
Country Indicators For Foreign Policy, 365
Crimes, 158
Crisis, 52
Crusade, 106
Cultural Sub-Nationalism, 167

D

Democracies, 21
Development, 19
  Failure, 25
Dharma Shastras, 95
Dictatorships, 21
Direct Economic Losses, 12
Distributive Justice, 57
Disuniting, 187
Donations, 124
Dramatic, 120

E

Early Warning Systems, 354
Education Occupation, 39
Election Commission, 222
Electronic Church, 72
Emancipation, 88
Enduring Freedom, 5
EPRLF, 244
Equipment, 13
Ernest Sandeen, 71
Eros, 244
Ethnic Community, 180
European Union, 7
External Security, 4
Extremely Extroverted, 45

F

Female Emancipation, 90
  Improvement, 89
Fewer, 356
Fighting Terrorism, 375
Financial Systems, 10
Fissiparous Tendencies, 85
Foreign Intelligence
  Surveillance Act, 34
Freedom Fighters, 104
  Movement, 112
  Struggle,108
  Fighter, 31
Frustration-Aggression Theory, 48

G

Gautam Sutra, 173
General Assembly Debate, 60
Generic, 18
George Marsden, 71
Global Challenge, 5
  Environment, 10
  War Against Terrorism, 105, 107

Golden Age, 132
    Triangle, 124
Grandiose Self, 50
Great Game, 385
    Parasol, 84
    Umbrella, 84
Guerrilla Warfare, 119
Guiding And Controlling Spirit, 230

H

Heathen, 83
Hellish Life, 95
Hindu Degeneracy, 78
    Rashtra, 135
    Revivalism, 70
Homo Fighters, 160
Human Violence, 388

I

Idealised Parental Ago, 50
Indicators Of States And Risk, 16
Infancy, 52
Infrastructure, 40
Institute of Policy Studies, 251
Insurance Losses, 13
Insurgency, 152
Internal Security, 4, 247
Internally Displaced Persons, 347
International Criminal Court, 349
    Terrorism, 34
    Trade, 10
Inter-Services Intelligence, 108
Intimidation, 152
IPKF, 115
Irreplaceable Role, 64
Islamic Fundamentalism, 213
    Order, 213

K

Kamtapur Liberation Organisation, 116
Kashmir Question, 169
Katiagats, 96
Khalistan, 131
Kofi Annan, 7
Kshatriya, 173

L

La Condition Humaine, 36
Lanka Tamil State Party, 244
League of Terror, 158
Legal Framework Order, 223
Les Justes, 36
Liberal, 73
Liberation Tigers of Tamil Eelam, 12
Life Stage, 52
Load-Bearing Pillars, 230
Lost Human Productive Value, 13
LTTE, 12, 105, 115

M

Madrasas, 214
Mahajana Eksath Peramuna, 295
Majority, 87
Manusmriti, 173
Mar Thoma, 80
Marital Status, 38
Mature Age, 52
Methods, 138

Military Costs, 12
  Hardware, 33
Mind-Set, 48
Minorities, 87
MMA, 107
Modern Terrorism, 337
Moh Mahi, 97
Mohajirs, 126
Muslim Revivalism, 70
  Youth Movement, 236
Muttahida Majlis-E-Aman, 107
Mythological Instruction, 194

N

Narcissistic, 44
  Rage Theory, 50
National Liberation Front of Tripura, 205
National Missile Defence System, 382
  Security Council, 224
Native Indians, 77
Negative/Confused Identity Theory, 51
Neurotically Hostile, 45
Newly Industrialized Countries, 202
Non-Combatant, 104, 365
  Theistic, 75
Nuclear Terror, 158

O

Objectives Resolution, 228
One-Party States, 21
OSCE, 351
Outside Powers, 12

P

Pakistan National Alliance, 231
  Occupied Kashmir, 108
Pap-Yoni, 174
Pathans, 126
Patriot, 31
Peace Building, 16
Perceptual Prominence, 57
Perfect Market, 21
Play Stage, 52
PLOTE, 244
Policy Imperative, 260
Political Assassinations, 161
  Bhikkhus, 282
  Community, 180
  Nationalism, 167
  Philosophy, 39
  Reform Package, 258
  Terrorism, 30
Politicians, 26
Polygamy, 88
Poor Communication, 56
Post-11 September, 342
Post-9/11, 106
Practitioners, 26
Premeditated, 104
Preventing Deadly Conflict, 15
  Terrorism, 5
  of Terrorism Act, 184
Problematic Behaviour, 17
Prophetic, 75
Purans, 173
Pure Land, 84
Purush, 173
  Sukta, 173

R

Radical, 73
  Reconversion, 75
  In-Reverse, 74
Ram Rajya, 188
Rashtriya Swayamsevak Sangh, 77
Reactionary, 74
Reconversion, 75
Reinforcing Loops, 21
Revolution, 152
Rigveda, 173
Rim Land Insurgencies, 164
Romantic Messianism, 152
Rural Urban Origin, 38

S

SAARC, 9, 117
Sacrificial Animal, 56
  Victims, 43
Sada Talla, 96
Sanatana Dharma, 77
Sangh Parivar, 114
Sangha, 266
Sanyasis, 175
Scheduled Caste, 182
  Tribe, 182
School Stage, 52
Self-Fulfilling, 49
  Interest, 14
  Perception, 43
September 11 Events, 105
Shiromam Gurdwara Prabandhak Committee, 85
Shudra, 176
Sikh Revivalism, 70
Smoking, 26
Smritis, 173
Software, 13
Soul Searching, 65
South Asia, 103
Spurious Justification, 196
Sri Lanka Freedom Party, 243
  Muslim Congress, 244
State Terrorism, 33
Stockholm Syndrome, 55
Strategy, 138
Stress-Seeking, 44
Structural Prevention, 16
Structures, 13
Successful Development, 25
Superior Bargaining Power, 57
Suspicion, 56
Sutta Pitaka, 263
System Dynamics Model, 18

T

Tactics, 138
Taliban, 7
Tamil Congress, 244
  Eelam, 245
  New Tigers, 246
  United Liberation Front, 244
Targets, 138, 155
TELO, 244
Tent Meeting, 72
Terrorism, 11, 103, 115, 364
Terrorist and Disruptive Activities Act, 184
  Condition, 47
  Personality, 48
Thalikettu, 98

Theistic, 75
Thirandukuli, 98
Three-Language Formula, 182
Transaction Costs, 13
Typology, 48

U

United Liberation Front of
    Assam, 205
    National Party, 243
    Nations, 6
Urgent Steps, 59

V

Vaishya, 173
Varnavyavastha, 178
Vibuti Sangama, 77
Violence Begets Violence, 68
Visvamitra, 175

W

War Against Terrorism, 219
War on Terrorism, 219
Winebibbers and Porkeaters, 86
Wipe Out Terrorism, 247
World Trade Center, 106
World-Conqueror, 85

X

Xeno Fighters, 160

Y

Yagyavalkya Smriti, 173
Ymcas, 275
Young Adult, 52